Holger Südkamp

Tom Stoppard's Biographical Drama

Martin Middeke (Ed.)

CDE Studies

Band 17

CDE Contemporary Drama in English

Holger Südkamp

Tom Stoppard's Biographical Drama

wvt Wissenschaftlicher Verlag Trier

D 61
Südkamp, Holger: Tom Stoppard's Biographical Drama
Holger Südkamp. -
Trier: WVT Wissenschaftlicher Verlag Trier, 2008
        (CDE Studies; Bd. 17)
        ISBN 978-3-86821-043-9

Cover Photo: Richard Mildenhall/ArenaPAL

Cover Design: Brigitta Disseldorf

© WVT Wissenschaftlicher Verlag Trier, 2008
ISBN 978-3-86821-043-9

Alle Rechte vorbehalten
Nachdruck oder Vervielfältigung nur mit
ausdrücklicher Genehmigung des Verlags

WVT Wissenschaftlicher Verlag Trier
Bergstraße 27, 54295 Trier
Postfach 4005, 54230 Trier
Tel.: (0651) 41503, Fax: 41504
Internet: http://www.wvttrier.de
E-Mail: wvt@wvttrier.de

Acknowledgements

During the writing of this doctoral dissertation, I incurred a number of debts I gladly acknowledge. I thank Prof. Dr. Therese Fischer-Seidel for arousing my interest in the topic and for supervising my doctoral thesis. The *German Research Foundation* provided me with a scholarship and a liberal grant towards the printing of this book for which I am very grateful. I also thank Prof. Dr. Johannes Laudage and Prof. Dr. Wilhelm G. Busse for accepting me as a stipendiary at the research training group *Europäische Geschichtsdarstellungen* at Düsseldorf from 2004 to 2006, its many postgraduates for the interesting exchanges about various topics on various occasions and Prof. Dr. Martin Middeke for allowing me to publish my study in this series.

Furthermore, I owe debt to Dr. Michael Heinze for proofreading my text. The same is true for Dr. Florian Kläger and Dr. Ursula Hennigfeld, the former for also proofreading the first draft and both for their inspiring interest in the topic and their invaluable advice. Finally, the support of my family and friends have been vital to me. I thank my parents especially, and gratefully dedicate this book to them.

All history becomes subjective;
in other words, there is properly no history; only biography.

(Ralph Waldo Emerson, "History", in: *Essays: First Series*, 1841)

Life's but a walking shadow, a poor player,
That struts and frets his hour upon the stage,
And then is heard no more. It is a tale
Told by an idiot, full of sound and fury,
Signifying nothing.

(William Shakespeare, *The Tragedy of Macbeth*, V.v.24-28)

[I]t's better to be quotable than honest.

(Tom Stoppard, *The Guardian*, 21 March 1973)

CONTENTS

I.	INTRODUCTION	1
II.	BIOGRAPHY	11
1.	The problems of a definition	12
2.	The development of English biography	15
a.	Moralistic functions of antique biography	15
b.	English biography in the eighteenth century: Johnson and Boswell	17
c.	Romantic and Victorian biography	20
d.	New Biography: Freud, Strachey and Woolf	23
e.	From modern to postmodern biography	32
3.	Biography today: An assessing overview	45
a.	Functions of biography	45
b.	Forms of biography	48
4.	Points of contention in biography	54
III.	BIOGRAPHY IN DRAMA	63
1.	Historical drama: Definition and types	63
2.	Biographical drama: Definition and types	68
3.	New Biography and biographical drama	74
4.	The literary biography play	76
5.	Some common literary concepts in biographical drama	79
a.	'Pre-judices' and stereotypes	79
b.	Intertextuality and intermediality	82
c.	Parody	83

IV.	*Rosencrantz and Guildenstern are Dead*: The Blurred Boundary between Myth and Biography	85
1.	The biographical mode of the play	86
a.	The *Hamlet* myth as a reference matrix for the deconstruction of stereotypes	86
b.	Debunking the anti-heroes	90
c.	Biographical reconstruction of Ros's and Guil's dark areas with *Hamlet* as a 'primary source'	94
2.	The relationship between dramatic fact and biographical fiction	96
3.	Reasoning from novel to play: The topic of biography in *Lord Malquist and Mr Moon*	107
4.	Recapitulation: *Truth is only that which is taken to be true*	113
V.	*Travesties*: Biography as '*Memoir Play*'	115
1.	*Travesties* as a historical and biographical drama	116
a.	The fictionalisation of fact	121
b.	Memory going Wilde: *Travesties* as a metahistorical and metabiographical drama	122
2.	Carr debunking the heroes: Joyce, Lenin and Tzara through the biographer's eyes	125
3.	Representations and contradictions of history, art and politics in the four main characters	132
4.	Recapitulation: *My memoirs, is it, then?*	140
VI.	*Arcadia*: Accenting the Epistemological Process of Biography	143
1.	Ideological landscapes	144

a.	Landscape gardening: The change from Classicism to Romanticism	144
b.	Apposing universes: 'Classical' Newtonian physics and 'Romantic' chaos theory	148
2.	The twofold structure: Semantic doublings and varying characteristic repetitions	155
3.	'Byrongraphical' constructions	159
4.	Chaotic structure and design	167
5.	Recapitulation: *It's wanting to know that makes us matter*	170
VII.	*INDIAN INK*: THE RELATIONSHIP BETWEEN BIOGRAPHICAL FACTS AND ART	173
1.	The post/colonial debate	175
a.	Flora Crewe and Nirad Das	176
b.	Mrs Eleanor Swan and Anish Das	180
c.	Eldon Pike and Dilip	182
2.	The construction of biographical identity	186
3.	Researching biographical truth	188
4.	The relation of art to life	194
5.	Recapitulation: *The truth will never be known*	199
VIII.	*THE INVENTION OF LOVE*: THE SUBORDINATION OF BIOGRAPHICAL FACTS TO ARTISTIC TRUTH	201
1.	The dichotomous structure: Metadramatic and metabiographical disclosure	203
2.	Oxford lecturers and London journalists: Vice *vs.* virtue	208

3.	AEH and Housman: Identity formation in a divided self	214
4.	AEH and Wilde: The Apollonian and Dionysian	221
5.	The difference between biographical facts and artistic truth	227
6.	Recapitulation: *Biography is the mesh through which our real life escapes*	231
IX.	THE COAST OF UTOPIA: THE 'CAUSAL-REALISTIC' PRESENTATION OF BIOGRAPHY	235
1.	The macroscopic level: *The Coast of Utopia* as a conventional and realistic biography play	236
a.	The Aristotelian plot of the trilogy	237
b.	Language as a means of realism	242
c.	Intermediality and intertextuality as non-disturbing elements	243
2.	The microscopic level: *Voyage*, *Shipwreck* and *Salvage* as innovative biography plays	246
a.	*Voyage*: The reversal of the Aristotelian cause-and-effect chain	246
b.	Idealism *vs.* realism: Schelling, Kant, Fichte and Hegel	250
c.	Illusion *vs.* truth: Deconstructing Chekhov through Chekhov	267
d.	*Shipwreck*: *Reprise* and *continuation* – The swirl of history	273
e.	*Salvage*: Reflecting on the macrostructure – The Aristotelian plot	277
f.	*The Coast of Utopia*: The apposition of characters – Bakunin, Herzen, Belinsky and Turgenev	280

g.	*Voyage*, *Shipwreck* and *Salvage*: Mediating the ambiguity of language through language, and identity formation through language	299
h.	*Salvage* and *Shipwreck*: Intertextuality and intermediality as metafictional and metabiographical means – *Fathers and Sons* and *Le Déjeuner sur l'herbe*	308
3.	The dialectics of *The Coast of Utopia*	313
4.	Recapitulation: *History itself is the main character of the drama and also its author*	317
X.	CONCLUSION	329
	WORKS CITED	339

I. Introduction

Tom Stoppard once told a reporter he wanted his own biography "to be as inaccurate as possible", denying the request of his biographer "Ira somebody or other" to "read the typescript to correct any factual errors" (Stoppard in Spencer 1999). And after receiving his copy of the first ever complete biographical account of himself, he apparently acted with surprise, exclaiming: "How is it so big?" (Stoppard in Nadel 2004: 537). At the same time Stoppard usually begins his preparation for a new play by devouring life-writings of its historical subjects, incorporating passages of them often *verbatim* into his plays, and this to such an extent that some critics like Charles Rowan Beye describe Stoppard's theatre as "[n]either theater of ideas nor theater of the absurd, but the theater of facts" (Beye 2002). Stoppard, it seems, has an ambivalent attitude towards the genre of biography, on the one hand questioning its truth and its relation to an actual life, while on the other hand relying on the factual information it yields for his work. As Jeremy Treglown writes in his review of *The Invention of Love*:

> It's one of the paradoxes of Stoppard's work that while it often satirizes academics and biographers, no British dramatist since Shaw has been so concerned to teach, or to use theatre as a medium for biography – or rather biographies, since Stoppard is above all a cultural historian. (Treglown 1997)

Historical personalities – famous, infamous and not so famous at all – such as James Joyce, Lenin, Tristan Tzara, Lech Walesa, Lord Byron, A.E. Housman, Oscar Wilde, William Shakespeare, Alexander Herzen and Ivan Turgenev, to name only a few, have been the main characters of some of Stoppard's screen- and stage plays. Add to this a metahistorical and metabiographical constituent and the continuous discussion of different historical concepts. Considering solely this sheer multitude of historical material and the grade of reflection present in Stoppard's work, I share Mark Berninger's astonishment about the fact that, despite the plenitude of publications on Stoppard, those regarding him as a historical dramatist are few and far between (cf. Berninger 2006: 18).[1] In the present study I will go even further by claiming that with his focus on the individual in history[2] and by broaching the question of the (im)possibility of its reconstruction, Stoppard is not only a *historical*, but chiefly a *biographical* dramatist.

So far, there is no book-length study of Stoppard's work primarily concerned with his presentation of biography – and this in spite of the fact that the major topics of scholarly analyses of his texts, as Anja Müller-Muth and Doris Mader summarise in their respective surveys, are the presentation of the *conditio humana*, man's confrontation with reality, the question of epistemology, the uncertainty of the perception of reality, the individual's effort to meaningfully structure a world perceived as unstable (cf. Müller-Muth 2001: 1-20, especially 7) or the question of reality *per se* (cf. Mader 2003: 59 and Mader 2000: 28-41). All these factors, however, are also of central concern in and to life-writing, which has as its centre a human being. As James Walter explains, "[i]ndeterminancy [...] has long been recognized as the characteristic feature of modern biography, and the fact that biographical truth can never finally be settled, that biography is always tendentious, has inflected every other methodological strategy" (Walter 2002: 322). Biography, its conventions and contradictions, then, appears to be almost a "natural" genre for Stoppard to reflect his utmost concerns in his drama. Thus, it is even more important that the following study will try to bridge the gap between abstract scholarly questions of epistemology and Stoppard's actual engagement with the biographical in his plays, be it historical, metabiographical or metadramatic as regards the genre of the biographical drama. Furthermore, by considering all of his 'biography plays' in order of their publication, it will point out, for the first time,

---

[1] Berninger names Broich 1993 and Klein 1998 as exceptions. This has to be complemented by Innes 2006 and 2006a.

[2] As John Bull points out in his essay about the playwright's politics: "Stoppard's suspicion of logical constructs [such as concepts of history] is predicated on a belief in the supremacy of the individual and the particular over the determined and the enforced; his fascination with them comes from his firm sense that there must be order for the aspirations of the individual to flourish" (Bull 2001: 136; cf. also Bull 2003: 70f., where he stresses the point in the context of *Arcadia*).

the development of Stoppard's engagement with and presentation of biography in his drama.

Stoppard has treated biographees created from imagination, from other works of fiction and authentic historical personalities. He has extended his presentation of the biographical subject, merging ideas and methods in his presentation of biographical (re)construction to reflect on the relationship between fact and fiction and to question the alleged claim of historiography and biography to objectivity and truth. In the television film *Squaring the Circle* (1984), for example, Stoppard gives an account of the rise and fall of *Solidarność* in the Poland of 1980/81. The historical and biographical accounts are commented on by witnesses and a narrator who states that "[e]verything is true except the words and the pictures" (Stoppard 1984: 27). Certain scenes are repeated from a different perspective, again undermining the objectivity of so-called factual historiography and of the medium of television. Many of Stoppard's screenplays such as to *The Empire of the Sun* (1987), after the novel of the same title by J.G. Ballard, *Shakespeare in Love* (1998, with Marc Norman),[3] *Vatel* (2000, with Jeanne Labrune), *Enigma* (2001), based on the novel of the same title by Robert Harris, or the unproduced *Galileo* (1969/70)[4] deal with historical and biographical topics as well. However, these are rather adaptations than original screenplays and the problem with them is, as stated exemplarily in Stoppard's introduction to *Squaring the Circle* (cf. 9ff.), that in their process of creation the author naturally has to give in to the ideas and wishes of the directors and producers, his employers. Stoppard himself much earlier described film as "a kind of three-ring circus, and the director's the elephant act and the writer's a sort of clown who comes on afterward and clears up the mess" and that "with a film a writer hasn't even got … [a] casting vote" (Stop-

---

[3] On *Shakespeare in Love*, cf. Puschmann-Nalenz 2001; on the treatment of the historical figure Shakespeare in the film, cf. Fedderson/Richardson 2001; on the film's metanarrative elements, cf. Womack/Davis 2004.

[4] On *Galileo*, cf. Fleming 2001: 66-81 and Nadel 2004: 216f. Although Stoppard apparently reshaped *Galileo* into a stage play in 1971/72, it nevertheless stayed unproduced. The full text of his screenplay was first published in *Areté: The Arts Triquarterly* (11, Spr/Sum 2003) and an adaptation first put on stage by the Collapsible Theatre Company at the Edinburgh Fringe on August 4, 2004.

pard in Guralnick 2001: 78). Hence, the artistic outcome of Stoppard's work for film is compromised, and an analysis would have to consider additional aspects such as production details and different screenplay versions. A book-length study dealing with the presentation of history and biography in Stoppard's work for film – especially as regards his own adaptation of *Rosencrantz and Guildenstern are Dead* (1990)[5] – because of its many difficulties still remains to be written.[6] For the very same reasons, this study concentrates exclusively on Stoppard's biographical feature-length stage plays. At the same time, it considers Stoppard as a biographical stage dramatist and, thus, is limited *per definitionem* to this genre. Therefore, the textual corpus of my study consists of what I refer to as Stoppard's 'biography plays', namely *Rosencrantz and Guildenstern are Dead* (1966/67), *Travesties* (1974), *Arcadia* (1993), *Indian Ink* (1995), *The Invention of Love* (1997) and *Voyage, Shipwreck, Salvage: The Coast of Utopia part I-III* (2002). Each chapter will be dedicated to a single play in chronological order so that the biographical theme of every play can be discussed individually, while at the same time placing it in the context of the artistic and thematic development of Stoppard's biographical drama.

Rosencrantz and Guildenstern are Dead, Stoppard's play about Hamlet's "[excellent] good friends" (Shakespeare 1974: 1155), is probably the most unusual of all the plays to be considered in this study as its protagonists are not representatives of authentic historical personalities. Nevertheless, the respective chapter will establish the play as Stoppard's first biography play, a mode which so far only Werner Huber has commented on briefly (cf. Huber 1999: 459). To do so, the focus will be laid on the question to what extent the hypotext of Shakespeare's *Hamlet*

---

[5] On the film *Rosencrantz and Guildenstern are Dead* in comparison to the play, cf. Abbotson 1998; on the cinematic incorporation and interjection of the play into the film, cf. Hotchkiss 2000; on the film's relationship to *Hamlet*, cf. Courson 1999 and Sheidley 1994; on the use of light and motion in the film, cf. Wheeler 1991.

[6] The lack of studies of his screenplays is partly due to the fact that Stoppard seems to view his work for film as a break from coming up with an idea for an original play. On Stoppard's screenplays, cf. Nadel 2001, which unsurprisingly addresses the topic from the point of view of Stoppard's life, and Hodgson (ed.) 2001: 168-173.

and its mythopoeic quality become a reference matrix for the deconstruction of stereotypes about *Hamlet* and tragedy *per se*. It is especially the concept of the hero – or rather anti-hero – as well as the tragic conventions of heroism which are debunked in the play as is a common feature in biographical drama. In *Rosencrantz and Guildenstern are Dead* Stoppard proceeds in a way similar to biographical reconstruction: he artistically and imaginatively (re)constructs the 'dark areas' of the lives of his biographees, i.e. the unknown and undocumented episodes in the lives of Rosencrantz and Guildenstern, by using *Hamlet* as a 'primary source'. And the main point of interest in the play is the relationship between life facts and fictional myths, one of the central concerns of life-writing and of Stoppard's biographical drama.

Compared to *Rosencrantz and Guildenstern are Dead*, *Travesties*, at least as regards the cast of historical personalities, seems without question to be a biographical drama. The main characters of the play are versions of authentic historical figures, well-known and unknown. Joyce, Lenin and Tzara come together in Zurich during World War I in the memory of the historical nonentity Henry Carr to the hypotext of Wilde's *The Importance of Being Earnest*. While the play has prompted many explicitly scholarly reactions with respect to its treatment of history,[7] so far most have only briefly touched on the topic of biography in it and this only indirectly in the context of historiography.[8] Nevertheless, while *Travesties* is a metahistorical drama, it is more precisely a metabiography play as the biographical (re)construction is undertaken solely from the retrospective perspective of Old Carr by applying narrative discourses and juxtaposing different concepts of history.

The only historical character in *Arcadia* is Lord Byron, who dominates the play by means of his constant stage absence. At the same time, he has the function of the (meta)biographical butterfly of the so-called butterfly effect. His 'Romantic' character affects most of the events in both time frames. Via a time shuttle and by applying modern mathematics and physics as well as landscape gardening as metaphors for the para-

---

[7] Cf., for example, Geraths 1979, Billman 1980, Wolf 1986, Broich 1993, Klein 1998, Er 2005, Berninger 2006: 262-280 and Innes 2006: 227f. and 236.

[8] Exceptions which focus on the topic of biography in *Travesties* are Fischer-Seidel 1996 and Kramer 2000: 60 and 67f.

digm shift from Classicism to Romanticism, Stoppard questions the possibility of biographical reconstruction. Alongside *Rosencrantz and Guildenstern are Dead* and *Travesties*, *Arcadia* is probably the play which has inspired the greatest amount of scholarly commentary, most of which more or less identifies its problem field of biographical reconstruction.[9] However, in order to arrive at a complete picture of this topic, the multifarious matters present in the play have to be related to the aspect of what I will call 'Byrongraphical' constructions in *Arcadia*.

Indian Ink, based on Stoppard's radio play *In the Native State* (1991), depicts a life episode of the fictitious poetess Flora Crewe in an equally fictitious Indian native state called Jummapur in 1930 and, in a second time frame a generation later, the effort of an academic biographer struggling to enlighten the dark area concerning this episode in her life. While in *Rosencrantz and Guildenstern are Dead* the offstage moments of *Hamlet*'s "real" fictional characters Rosencrantz and Guildenstern are (re)constructed on stage, a purely fictitious character becomes the biographical subject in *Indian Ink*, giving the term 'fictional biography' an entirely new meaning. Events such as Mahatma Gandhi's Salt March and personalities such as Amedeo Modigliani constitute the historical background to the play. Scholarly attention to this play is almost the diametrical opposite to *Arcadia*. This is probably due to the fact that it is seen as a "fairly minor play in the Stoppard intellectual canon" (Innes 2004: 183). Publications focus rather on the relationship between radio and stage play,[10] the question of postcolonialism[11] and cultural relations in the play.[12] Nonetheless, it is rather the question of the construction and formation of the identity of the biographical subject as well as the relationship between art and life facts which is of central concern in *Indian Ink*.

---

[9] Cf., for example, Kramer 1997, Scolnicov 2004, Niederhoff 2001/02 and 2003/04, Müller-Muth 2002/03 and Berninger 2006: 223-241; exceptions which explicitly deal with the topic of biography in *Arcadia* are Huber/Middeke 1996, Huber 1999 and Müller-Muth 2001: *passim*, which gives the most detailed interpretation of the play.

[10] Cf. Kaplan 1998 and Lee 2001.

[11] Cf., for example, Burton 2001 and Berninger 2001.

[12] Cf., for example, Russel 2004 and Innes 2004.

Introduction

In *The Invention of Love*, the biography of A.E. Housman is presented in the context of the aesthetic movement in Oxford towards the end of the nineteenth century and of Wilde's court trial for 'gross indecency' in 1895. The biographical dark area Stoppard addresses this time is the question why the brilliant student Housman failed his final exams. Classical literature and their scholarship become a metaphor for the (im)possibility of biographical reconstruction, and the dichotomous nature of the historical Housman becomes a structuring device for the play which culminates in the fictitious encounter between Housman and Wilde. As regards scholarly commentary, *The Invention of Love* is considered more in the context of Wilde[13] or the topic of love[14] than in the context of life-writing, although "[i]n spite of its postmodern structure, the play is the most purely biographical of any written by Stoppard" (Palmer 1998: 54). Hence, the main points of interest are rather the metadramatic and metabiographical elements of the play and the dichotomous structure with respect to the construction and formation of identity in biography. And the main dichotomy *The Invention of Love* picks out as a central theme is the dichotomy between facts and truth.

With the chronologically last plays to be considered in this study, it can be remarked that Stoppard produced works even more purely biographical than *The Invention of Love*, effectively reneging on his own statement that after *The Invention of Love* "he will think twice before doing another biographically based play" (Fleming 2001: 302n8). With the trilogy *The Coast of Utopia* and its sequential plays *Voyage*, *Shipwreck* and *Salvage*, Stoppard presents a 'group biography play' in which he reflects on the idea that life is less the assertion of a single will than the product of innumerable and shifting relationships. The trilogy, which Stoppard also views as three self-contained plays, has as its biographical subject the lives of the nineteenth-century Russian intelligentsia, among them Alexander Herzen, Michael Bakunin, Vissarion Belinsky and Ivan Turgenev. The protagonists and their families become mixed up in the European revolutions of 1848/49, and the question arises whether man is at the mercy of historical forces or whether his-

---

[13] Cf., for example, Müller-Muth 2002, Hesse 2002 and Krämer 2000.

[14] Cf., for example, Seeber 1999, Zeifman 2001 and Mader 2003.

tory is in turn shaped by certain personalities. With his manifold cast of historical characters, Stoppard again juxtaposes different historical concepts derived from varying understandings of man in German Idealism. Nonetheless, the main focus of discussion of this ambitious work of art is on the relationship between the macrostructure of the trilogy and the microstructures of the three individual plays. Regarding this relationship is necessary in order to arrive at a holistic understanding of the presentation of biography in *The Coast of Utopia*.

In order to arrive at an understanding of biography in Stoppard's drama, however, it is necessary first to consider the genre of life-writing in itself. The definition of biography and its inherent aporia that the genre must reconcile objective truth with artistic authorial autonomy already hints at a basic concern in Stoppard's biographical drama, which, in a nutshell, is the relationship between fact and fiction. To understand how this aporia became a constituting factor of life-writing, a short survey of the development of the genre of English biography from Samuel Johnson and James Boswell to the present must be given. It is especially its (post)modern representation, its functions, forms and points of contention which will serve as a theoretical framework for the assessment of biography in English drama in general and in Stoppard's work in particular. Stoppard, of course, is not the only contemporary English playwright to engage in the topic of biography, although he is one of the most sophisticated and complex biographical dramatists. The chapter dealing with biography in drama will show that biography plays are the most common form of putting history on stage. As Richard H. Palmer points out, "[h]istory, particularly in the theatre – with its circumscribed time frame, staging limitations, and emphasis on the actor – still appears most frequently in the guise of biography" (Palmer 1998: 13).[15]

---

[15] Another genre where this is true is film. One only has to consider the Academy Award nominees and winners for best picture over the last ten years to find plenty of examples such as *Letters from Iwo Jima* (2006), *The Queen* (2006), *Good Night, and Good Luck* (2005), *Munich* (2005), *Capote* (2005), *Ray* (2004), *Finding Neverland* (2004), *The Aviator* (2004), *Seabiscuit* (2003), *The Pianist* (2002), *Gangs of New York* (2002), *The Hours* (2002), *A Beautiful Mind* (2001), *Erin Brockovich* (2000), *Gladiator* (2000), *The Insider* (1999), *Saving Private Ryan* (1998), *Elizabeth* (1998), *Titanic* (1997), *Shine* (1996), *The English Patient* (1996) and, of course, *Shakespeare in Love* (1998).

In addition, Sherrill Grace writes that over the past thirty years, at least in Anglophone countries, there has been an increase in plays dealing with the topic of auto/biography. Major playwrights have written life stories that depict historical personalities or explore the question of identity within a wider socio-historical context (cf. Grace 2006: 15). Hence, as a second theoretical framework for Stoppard's biographical drama, it is also necessary to consider the genre of the *history play*, and especially its subgenre, the *biography play*, in order to elaborate a definition and types and to show in how far it has inflected the methodological strategies of life-writing and how it converts them on stage. Only then can Stoppard's biographical drama be considered in terms of the presentation of biography by drawing on the theoretical framework of biography and its manifestation in drama.

Finally, as it is both a blessing and a curse with studies about a contemporary artist, this study, too, cannot claim completeness with regard to the material it is trying to cover. In 2006, a new play by Stoppard was first staged at the Royal Court Theatre in London and then transferred to the Duke of York's Theatre. This play, *Rock 'n' Roll*, as could be expected, also revolves around historical personalities such as Syd Barret, the psychedelic Czech band *The Plastic People of the Universe* and Václav Havel. It also deals with historical events such as the Prague Spring of 1968, the genesis of Charter 77 and the Velvet Revolution of 1989. Nevertheless, *Rock 'n' Roll* will only be discussed briefly in the conclusion of this study in form of an outlook which at the same time will function as a confirmation of the main hypothesis. Writing an additional detailed chapter about this latest play would have only made sense because it continues Stoppard's engagement with the topic of biography and history after *The Coast of Utopia*. But, as the young Housman explains in *The Invention of Love* to his older *alter ego*: "we're already all of us so late!" (*TIoL* 98). Perhaps there is also someone with her or his 'Stoppard' coming out next year and who knows how many of my conjectures with regard to the topic of biography s/he will anticipate? Postponed is not abandoned.

II. Biography

The concept of life-writing has long surpassed the mere idea of simply "writing about someone's life" and since its origins in classical antiquity, it has undergone vast changes in form and function, which makes it sometimes hard to regard Plutarch's *Parallel Lives* with the same "biographical gaze" as, for example, Richard Holmes's *Dr. Johnson and Mr Savage* (1993) or David Nye's so-called anti-biography of Thomas Edison *The Invented Self* (1982). Such a special form as biography, which has man at its particular centre, is bound to undergo transformations as the understanding of its subject changes depending on currents of natural science, philosophy, cultural politics and sociology such as (anti-)humanism and the (biological and psychological) concept of man. Therefore, it is necessary to first consider some of the definitions of biography which reflect the various stages the biographical genre has undergone. An outline of its development has to be undertaken, though it is not necessary in this context to trace its full history from ancient Egypt to the postmodern present.[16] Rather, the main focus will be laid on modern English biography, which was more or less initiated by Samuel Johnson, improved by William Mason and perfected by James Boswell. The genre suffered a set-back in the Victorian age, which in retrospect actually gave the modern biography its *raison d'être*. The most prominent representatives of this 'New Biography' were Lytton Strachey and Virginia Woolf. Finally, in the second part of the twentieth century, biography has had to face the critical concepts of postmodernism and poststructuralism. The notion of biography as presented in Stoppard's biographical drama is based on the genre as it developed from Johnson onwards. Hence, the methodological reconsiderations which stem from these biographies and their criticisms form the basis of interpretation of his work.

---

[16] For a complete historical overview of the biographical genre, cf. Hoberman 2001, Parke 2002: xxi-xxviii (Chronology) and 1-34 and Hamilton 2007.

1. The problems of a definition

In her "General Survey" in the *Encyclopedia of Life Writing*, Ruth Hoberman states that, "[b]ecause it borrows from and overlaps with other genres, biography [...] is a notoriously difficult form to define". She continues by attributing the following characteristics to the genre: it is "nonfictional and narrative, with the passage of time playing an important part in its structure", it "resembles fiction in its effort to evoke its subject's inner life as well as in its literary 'realism'", "its scope is limited by its subject's birth, death, and actions" and "its distinction from fiction rests on an extratextual relationship of trust between author and reader" (Hoberman 2001: 109). In another encyclopaedia, in the eleventh edition of the *Encyclopaedia Britannica* in 1910, Edmund Gosse,[17] himself biographer and one of the first representatives of the break between Victorian biography and New Biography (cf. II.2.d), also defines and gives a broad historical overview of biography from ancient Greece to the end of the nineteenth century, which is still very useful today. According to this entry, biography is

> that form of history which is applied, not to races or masses of men, but to an individual. [... B]iography is not the record of "life" in general, but of the life of a single person. The idea of the distinction between this and history is a modern thing; we speak of "antique biography", but it is doubtful whether any writer of antiquity [...] clearly perceived its possible existence as an independent branch of literature. [...]
>
> The true conception of biography, therefore, as the faithful portrait of a soul in its adventures through life, is very modern. [...] In considering what biography in its pure sense, ought to be, we must insist on what it is not. It is not a philosophical treatise nor a polemical pamphlet. It is not, even, a portion of the human contemporary chronicle. Broad views are entirely out of place in biography [...]. Biography is a study sharply defined by two definite events, birth and death. It fills its canvas with one figure, and other personages, however great in themselves, must always be subsidiary to the central hero. [...] It was very difficult to persuade the literary world that, whatever biography is, it is not an opportunity for panegyric or invective, and the lack of this perception destroys our faith in most of the records of personal life in ancient and medieval times.
>
> (Gosse 1910: 952f.)

---

[17] On Gosse, cf. Nadel 1984: 46ff.

Gosse implies that biography is a branch of literature and a form of history, presenting a truthful and impartial portrait of an individual from birth to death. In his entry, he concentrates more on distinguishing ancient biography from biography as it was understood from the seventeenth century onwards. The difference lies in being "truthful and impartial", i.e. in the confidence in giving an objective account of someone's life and not the functionalised exposure of an individual's moral or a-moral behaviour in order to set an example or a deterrent, respectively, for the reader and for society. However, as we will see in the next, more contemporary but nevertheless "traditional" or "conventional" definition, truth and objectivity seem to be impossible to reconcile with biography *per se*.

According to the definition of the *Oxford English Dictionary*, biography describes "the history of the lives of individual men, as a branch of literature" (*OED*, s.v. "biography, *n.*" 1). In a defence of biography, Peter Alexander summarizes the three major points of this definition: history, the individual and literature. With regard to content and form, these three points form the frame of any definition: 1) biography has to be historical, i.e. "it must be governed by a desire to tell the truth and nothing but the truth, insofar as it can be ascertained"; 2) it concerns individuals, i.e. it excludes any forms of collective history; 3) as a branch of literature, "it should be judged as art: the biographer should constantly be making aesthetic judgements about the presentation of material" (Alexander 1996: 78). This core definition has to be revised by two items. Firstly, biographical practice shows that biographies also focus on groups, as the examples of Norman and Jeanne MacKenzie's *The Fabians* (1977) or Leon Edel's *Bloomsbury: A House of Lions* (1979) demonstrate. These 'group biographies' concentrate on the unique characteristics of the respective group as well as on the role of the individual in her or his group in connection with the other individuals which constitute the faction. In this case, 'group' would probably then best be described – following the first definition of the term in the *OED* which actually concerns the fine arts – as an assemblage of (two or more) subjects forming in combination either a comprehensive idea or a distinctive segment of an idea (cf. *OED*, s.v. "group, *n.*" 1). Secondly, the notion of being historical signifies more than just being truthful. According to the *OED*, 'history' also implies a "written narrative constituting a continuous methodical record, in order of time, of important or public events, esp. those connected with a particular country, people, individual, etc." (*OED*, s.v. "history, *n*." 2). According to this, the definition of biography of the *OED* could be revised to the following: 1) biography has to be committed to history, i.e., it needs to tell the truth insofar as it can be ascertained, and it is a written narrative which is ordered chronologically and/or by the importance of events; 2) it concerns individuals or groups in which individuals play a decisive role; 3) as a branch of literature, it is an art form and the biographer has to realize points one and two through aesthetic judgements.

However, there seems to be a contradiction implicit in this last issue: the discrepancy between truthful history, written narrative and art:

> True biography is interdisciplinary, poised always between the poles of history and literature. It strives to be precise, rational, scientific; and at the same time intuitive and imaginative. The continual need to reconcile these two irreconcilable elements constitutes the greatest practical problem of writing biography, and it is inherent in the form itself. [...] This strict insistence on objective truth tends to the exclusion of life-writing in which the motivation of the author is anything but a dedication to arriving at an objective record of a human life.
>
> (Alexander 1996: 78)

Persistence in objectivity seems to be the major characteristic of "true" or rather conventional biography, but at the same time it is irreconcilable with any creative autonomy of the author. The incompatibility of fact and fiction is already inherent in the conventional understanding of biography itself and constitutes the aporia of the genre. To overcome either fact or fiction would be a Pyrrhic victory as "true" biography paradoxically must consist of both elements. Biography's aporetic character has only been fully realized with the arrival of the 'linguistic turn' and the discussion about the possibility of the reconstruction of the past through language.

In his essay about truth and falsehood in biography, Bernhard Fetz writes that all the animadversion on biography as a mere substitute for knowledge of 'the other' or for self-knowledge, as an illusion with ideological side-effects and as a catalogue of stereotypes of the individual and fateful – stereotypes which have long ceased to be individual and fateful – has made the theory of biography reach a point where it mistrusts both the written transfer and the act of writing (cf. Fetz 2006: 7f.). James Walter also views indeterminacy as the distinctive feature of late modern biography. In his essay on biographical methodology in the twentieth century he explains the preoccupation with biographical truth which can never really be ascertained. The dispute about the tendentiousness of biography has influenced any modern methodological approach:

> Most methodological essays have been preoccupied with one or more of the following elements. First, acknowledging the problem of 'other minds' entails accepting that biography works by analogy and inference rather than empiricism alone, and that methods of persuasive argument are as important as research. Second, that the meaning of facts is not self-evident, and that discrimination in what is discussed is as important as the comprehensive garnering of knowledge, puts a premium on analysis. Third, the admission of the centrality of interpretation brings in its wake open resort to various bodies of theory as providing tools for interpretation. (Walter 2002: 322f.)

By surveying the methodology of biography, Walter gives an overview of the questions which preoccupy today's biographers and their critics. To understand how these questions have come into being, it may be helpful to consider the developments which have led to contemporary biography.

2. The development of English biography

a. Moralistic functions of antique biography

The usual approach to the determination of the origin of biography is through the compounds of the term, the two Greek words *bios* (βίος), usually translated as '(a) life' or 'lifetime', and *graphein* (γράφειν), meaning representation by means of lines, hence 'drawing', 'writing' or 'the art of writing'. However, as Sergei Averintsev in his essay on the antique and medieval roots of biography and hagiography shows, Greek had another word for life, namely *zoe* (ζωή). While *zoe* referred to "vital energy, either natural and physical or – in Christian authors – spiritual and divine, that is, the quality of being alive", *bios* rather meant "mode of life, manner of living, often what we name 'conduct' or 'behaviour'". By reference to a Byzantine lexical work dating to the twelfth century but representing earlier sources, Averintsev demonstrates that *bios* was also defined as *eidos zoes*, meaning "way [literally shape] of life" though in different cases, *bios* was also used in the modern sense, i.e. "story of a life" (Averintsev 2002: 20). The understanding of *bios* as "way of life" has implications for the inner form of the oldest biographical and hagiographical literature:

> For us the 'life' of a person is first of all a process, a flux, a chronological succession of events, and consequently a biography must be a narrative, a *chronicle of the subject's life*. But if the *bios* is to be considered primarily as *eidos*, a form, a pattern, a mode, then description seems to be more appropriate a procedure than narrative. And we rather frequently find facts that fit exactly this descriptive paradigm. (20)

Greek and Roman biographers used a different narrative method than the conventional chronological one because they followed a different aim than contemporary biographers – a point already mentioned in Gosse's entry in the *Encyclopaedia Britannica*. Biography in classical antiquity was regarded "by its most intelligent and ambitious practitioners as a sort of psychologico-ethical essay, analysing each public or private deed, word, or gesture as a display of this or that virtuous or vicious trait of character (which meant subordinating narrative to description)" (24). This general premise was the basic principle of the Greek and Roman biographical genre and it was embellished with "particular episodic narratives", which had the function to exemplify the pronouncements: "Because of this auxiliary function, such narratives are frequently presented not in chronological but in logical order, not *per tempora* but *per species*" (25). The biographers treated their subjects – which sometimes were of merely sensational interest but, nevertheless, were pictured as examples – as "potential objects of implicit comparison" and used the genre as an illustration of "general moral principles" (26f.).

Medieval hagiography, not unlike ancient biography, was concerned with depicting the lives of saints as examples for those who had access to the texts. Therefore, it is not necessary to consider it in this context in any detail. It was not until the late Renaissance that biography in

Western Europe digressed from the *de-viris-illustribus* model and concentrated on lives of, for example, contemporary poets. They were praised in human as well as in artistic terms, because, as Martin McLaughlin plausibly explains, the purpose of print culture was to sell their work and not to put off potential customers (cf. McLaughlin 2002: 56). For the purpose at hand, it is not necessary to dwell on English biographies written before the seventeenth century, and even those first few examples of manifestations of a change in the biographical genre shall only be discussed briefly.

b. English biography in the eighteenth century: Johnson and Boswell

According to Gosse, the general practice of biography began in England with William Roper's *The Life of Sir Thomas More* (c1570) and George Cavendish's *The Life and Death of Cardinal Wolsey* (c1557), which both remained in manuscript until the seventeenth century.[18] The pioneer of "deliberate English biography" was Izaak Walton, who, between 1640 and 1678, published a whole series of life-writings, which were later reprinted under the title *Walton's Lives*. And in 1668, Thomas Sprat, by omitting anecdotes and picturesque detail, with his *Life of Cowly* reintroduced "moral effect and a solemn vagueness" as biographical aims (Gosse 1910: 953).

According to Gosse, after Sprat English biography lacked any characteristics of sincere portraiture for more than half a century; it became artificial and rhetorical. Although William Oldys was the first to openly oppose this fashion in his preface to the *Biographia Britannica* (1747), it was not until Johnson's *An Account of the Life of Mr Richard Savage* (1744) and his *Prefaces Biographical and Critical to the Works of the English Poets* (1779-1781, better known as *Lives of the English Poets*), Mason's *Life and Letters of Gray* (1774) and even more importantly Boswell's *The Life of Samuel Johnson LL.D.* (1791) that biography made an innovative and self-reforming comeback. Mason introduced the prac-

---

[18] On Roper's *The Life of Sir Thomas More*, cf. Robson 1998; on Cavendish's *The Life and Death of Cardinal Wolsey*, cf. Crewe 1988.

tice of using private correspondence to illustrate and develop the narrative about the biographee and Boswell followed and improved his model (cf. 953f.). The convictions of these 'men of letters' can also be found in their critical work about biography and their own private correspondence, which give insight into views on the biographical genre at the time.

Johnson favours biographies over all other forms of literature, as he openly proclaims in his famous article in *The Rambler*. For him "no species of writing seems more worthy of cultivation than biography, since none can be more delightful or more useful, none can more certainly enchain the heart by irresistible interest, or more widely diffuse instruction to every diversity of condition" (Johnson 1962: 40f.) In contrast to general historical narratives, the advantage of biography for him lies in its application to private life. The job of the biographer is "to pass slightly over those performances and incidents, which produce vulgar greatness, to lead the thoughts into domestic privacies, and display the minute details of daily life, where exterior appendages are cast aside, and men excel each other only by prudence and by virtue". He criticises those life-writers who "rarely afford any other account than might be collected from public papers, but imagine themselves writing a life when they exhibit a chronological series of actions or preferments" (42). According to Johnson, the reason for plain, useless, unpleasant and unintelligent biography derives from the problem of distance to the subject's life. On the one hand, this distance may be of time:

> If a life be delayed till interest and envy are at an end, we may hope for impartiality, but must expect little intelligence; for the incidents which give excellence to biography are of a volatile and evanescent kind, such as soon escape the memory, and are rarely transmitted by tradition. (43)

On the other hand, the distance may also be of sympathy with the subject, as Johnson formulates in his 1759 article in the *Idler*, when he balances biography against autobiographical writing:

> He that writes the life of another is either his friend or his enemy, and wishes either to exalt his praise or aggravate his infamy: many temptations to falsehood will occur in the disguise of passions, too specious to fear much resistance. Love or virtue will animate panegyric, and hatred of wickedness embitter censure. The zeal of gratitude, the ardour of patriotism, fondness for an opinion, or fidelity to

> a party, may easily overpower the vigilance of a mind habitually well disposed, and prevail over unassisted and unfriended veracity. (Johnson 1962a: 45)

Several years later, Boswell considered different problems of biographical writing. In a journal entry of 19 October 1775, he describes the impossibility

> to preserve in words the peculiar features of mind which distinguish individuals as certainly as the features of different countenances. [...] Perhaps language may be improved to such a degree as to picture the varieties of mind minutely. In the meantime we must be content to enjoy the recollection of characters in our own breast. (Boswell 1962: 50)

What Boswell could not know was that in the "postmodern future", language was not to be improved but to be questioned and considered an inadequate instrument for presenting an individual's past. In one of the many "Hypochondriack" essays, Boswell mentions the trouble and necessity of selection in recording someone's life in a journal. In this essay, he opines that "a man should not live more than he can record", and he remarks that he has "regretted that there is no invention for getting an immediate and exact transcript of the mind, like that instrument by which a copy of a letter is at once taken off" (Boswell 1973: 259). This passage shows his preoccupation with the (im)possibilities of comprehending and putting on paper all the experiences of a life, whether it be his own or a different subject's like Johnson's.

Regarding Boswell's *Life of Johnson*, which was published only eight years later, these doubts all seemed to have disappeared. He explains with absolute self-confidence his approach to, and understanding of, biography, which is worth quoting at some length:

> Wherever narrative is necessary to explain, connect, and supply, I furnish it to the best of my abilities; but in the chronological series of Johnson's life, which I trace as distinctly as I can, year by year, I produce, wherever it is in my power, his own minutes, letters or conversation [...]; whereas there is here an accumulation of intelligence from various points, by which his character is more fully understood and illustrated.
> Indeed I cannot conceive a more perfect mode of writing any man's life, than not only relating all the most important events of it in their order, but interweaving what he privately wrote, and said, and thought; by which mankind are enabled as it were to see him live, and to "live o'er each scene" with him, as he actually advanced through the several stages of his life. [...]

> And he will be seen as he really was; for I profess to write, not his panegyrick, which must be all praise, but his Life; which, great and good as he was, must not be supposed to be entirely perfect. To be as he was, is indeed subject of panegyrick enough to any man in this state of being; but in every picture there should be shade as well as light, and when I delineate him without reserve, I do what he himself recommended, both by his precept and his example. (Boswell 1952: 2)

In his introductory remarks, Boswell summarizes those biographical concepts which were to set the standard for generations of biographers to come. He argues for thoroughly researched chronology – sometimes being "obliged to run half over London, in order to fix a date correctly" (xi) –, uses the biographee's own sources like letters and even handwritten recordings of his conversations as the basis of his work and connects them when necessary with a narrative; his aim is an impartial account which strives for a "complete" depiction of the other person and not a panegyric.

Through the work of Johnson, Mason and especially of Boswell, biography re-entered English literature as a painstakingly researched subgenre of historical writing with a claim to aesthetic value. And although impartiality is always a matter of dispute in any biography, with the help of correspondence of all sorts as "proofs" for their arguments, their biographies distanced themselves from an openly biased panegyric style of writing. They had the ambition to arrive at an understanding of the person behind the mere "factual" subject as represented through public records and public appearances. This was the first time in English biographical writing that such an approach formed the basis for serious biography. The time of Johnson, Mason and Boswell is considered by many scholars as the originary point of literary biography, i.e. artists' biographies, especially of an author. The Boswell model has also been considered the conventional type of biography against which any derivations have had to be measured since.

c. Romantic and Victorian biography

The general history of literary biography sees the genre "as coming into being alongside the emergence of modern subjectivity during the Romantic period" (Pite 2003: 173). This modern subjectivity is usually referred to as 'the depth model of the self'. According to Ralph Pite, Romanticism engendered a tradition of heroic biography. Biography, during the Romantic period, "is committed to self-determination and the exposition of an autonomous individuality – an autonomy which is either glorious or self-contradictory or both" (175). The "'great man' tradition" apparently derives from "Romantic conceptions of the deep, autonomous self" and all kinds of biography invest in life-stories as a further consequence of the depth model (176).

In an 1832 review of Croker's edition of Boswell's *Life of Johnson*, Thomas Carlyle, later the author of the key text of the 'great man' tradition, *On Heroes and Hero Worship and the Heroic in History* (1841), formulated the purpose of biography, which corresponds to the prototypical model of the self. For him, biography enables the reader to gaze *into* the biographee as well as perceive the world through the biographee's eyes. Life-writing depicts the uniqueness of each biographee as well as their likeness to everybody else:

> Of these millions of living men, each individual is a mirror to us; a mirror both scientific and poetic; or, if you will, both natural and magical; – from which one would so gladly draw aside the gauze veil; and peering therein, discern the image of his own natural face, and the supernatural secrets that prophetically lie under the same! (Carlyle 1962: 79)

Furthermore, "in all Art too [...] Biography is almost the one thing needful" and "History [...] is the essence of innumerable Biographies" (79f.). Thus, biography for Carlyle "does not reveal the variety of people so much as the uniqueness of each individual (which is the source also of their identity with an undifferentiated humanity)" (Pite 2003: 180).

However, in his essay on 'unRomantic' biography, Pite shows that during the early nineteenth century, biography was determined by an interaction of the taxonomic and organic-historic epistemes, i.e. defining individuals through classification and their histories. He describes the biography of the time as follows:

> The form remained a study of exemplary persons, whose description was justified by their exemplariness more than their uniqueness and who were exemplary less as individual persons than as types – types usually linked to the visible social identity offered by professions. (179)

As examples, Pite names William Wordsworth's *The River Duddon: A Series of Sonnets* (1820), which includes the "Memoir of the Rev. Robert Walker", and Samuel Taylor Coleridge's *The Friend* (1818), which ends with the "Sketches of the Life of Sir Alexander Ball". Both present their biographees as paragons of their trade, meditating in their texts between taxonomic and organic-historical perspectives (cf. 182). Pite points out, then, that "for the Romantics, the shift towards a depth model of the self was not absolute. Carlyle's example and his later importance may indicate that this model was retrospectively imposed on Romantic writings by the Victorians" (180).

James Field Stanfield's *An Essay on the Study and Composition of Biography*, the first full-scale monograph on biography, illustrated as early as 1813 the considerations of the genre which were to become commonplace in life-writings of the Victorian period:

> The two great ends of biography are – to obtain a deeper insight into the principles of the human mind, and to offer examples to practical observation and improvement. For the one, accurate fidelity is necessary; and for the other, moral illustration. Were we a generation of philosophers or profound thinkers, perhaps the accuracy of minute narration would be only wanting; but when we consider, that as, from the entertaining and interesting nature of personal history, it finds its way to the closets and bosoms of the young and unthinking, – in such possible circumstances, to send vice abroad in the specious colours it so generally assumes, without exposing its deformity and loathsomeness, would be seduction and not warning – would be to deteriorate and not to improve and instruct.
> (Stanfield 1962: 66f.)

In his study, Stanfield insists on meticulous research, knowledge of the nature of man, insight into the subject's character, practical application of the biography to the reader's life, impartial justice, decency, selection and historical truth. He opposes abundance, redundancy, mere chronology, panegyric and satire in biography. And it is especially his emphasis on accuracy and exemplariness for improvement that we predominantly find in Victorian biography. Towards the end of the nineteenth century it became customary to write biography in the years (sometimes only months) following the death of an individual who had in some way attracted public attention (cf. Gosse 1910: 954). Owing to this, the biographical style coined by Johnson, Mason and Boswell became once again vapid and eulogistic during the Victorian period. The biographies of that era consisted mainly of large two-volume issues, and the Victorian contemporaries chiefly avoided any possible negative representation of the biographee (cf. Shaffer 2002: 132).

d. New Biography: Freud, Strachey and Woolf

With the beginning of the twentieth century, the attitude towards the form changed. A new biographical theory and practice emerged transnationally and synchronically among writers who had little, if any, contact, namely Lytton Strachey, André Maurois, Emil Ludwig, A.J.A. Symons and Gamaliel Bradford (cf. Marcus 2002: 194f.). Although their similarities may have been overstated by some critics, they were evident. The tenets and characteristics of their so-called New Biography included, or were held to include

> a new equality between biographer and subject, by contrast with the hero-worship and hagiography of Victorian eulogistic biography; brevity, selection, and an attention to form and unity traditionally associated with fiction rather than history; the discovery of central motifs in a life and of a 'key' to personality, so that single aspects of the self or details of the life and person came to stand for or to explain the whole; and a focus on character rather than events. (196)

However, the break between Victorian biography and New Biography may not have been as vehement as biographers of the twentieth century wanted to make their readers and themselves believe, as the praxis of the editors of the *Dictionary of National Biography*, Leslie Stephen and Sidney Lee, at the end of the nineteenth century shows. This monumental undertaking of a biographical dictionary included, besides the mere accumulation of facts, concision and candour, analysis and synthesis, as Laura Marcus remarks, although the number of individuals alone who were to fill the dictionary makes such a biographical approach to the depiction of someone's life probably natural.[19] Therefore, the "representation of a total break between Victorian and modern biography may thus say as much, or more, about the moderns' need to demarcate themselves

---

[19] On National Biographies and related topics, cf. McCalman/Parvey/Cook (eds.) 1996.

sharply from their immediate predecessors as about the differences themselves" (196).

The most influential figure for psychology and for biography at the beginning of the twentieth century was Sigmund Freud, the founder of psychoanalysis. As his work and impact are too immense to be adequately presented here, I only want to look briefly at one of his biographies, or rather pathographies or psychobiographies.[20] In *Leonardo da Vinci and a Memory of his Childhood* (*Eine Kindheitserinnerung des Leonardo da Vinci*, 1910), Freud bases his psychobiographical account on a single childhood memory, the only one which (to Freud's knowledge) was handed down in written form by da Vinci himself. In the course of the text, he points out the homosexuality of the artist and scientist and how it was caused by his relationship with his mother, her consequent excessive love and the non-presence of a father. The study itself has been vehemently criticised for its reliance on "a dazzlingly unsubstantiated interpretation of a (mistranslated) early memory Leonardo may have had" so that, "[a]s an illustration of the pitfalls of the biographical enterprise, its potential for locating chimerical beliefs in spurious sources, Freud's Leonardo book remains unsurpassed" (Churchwell 2006). Nevertheless, it is Freud's understanding of biography and his technique of psychoanalysis as it was used from then on by many biographers which are most interesting in the present context.

The first taboo Freud broke with was the consideration of the sexuality of the biographee. In contrast to the general reservation towards explicit detail of anything sexual or intimate relating to the subject in Victorian biography, Freud had a different conviction: "If a biographical study is really intended to arrive at an understanding of its hero's mental life it must not – as happens in the majority of biographies as a result of discretion or prudishness – silently pass over its subject's sexual activity or sexual individuality" (Freud 1989: 16).[21] Freud's theories on sexuality

---

[20] On Freud, biography and psychobiography, cf., for example, Bowie 2002, Marcus 1998 and Elms 1994.

[21] "Wenn ein biographischer Versuch wirklich zum Verständnis des Seelenlebens seines Helden durchdringen will, darf er nicht, wie dies in den meisten Biographien aus Diskretion oder aus Prüderie geschieht, die sexuelle Betätigung, die geschlechtliche Eigenart des Untersuchten mit Stillschweigen übergehen" (Freud 1995: 37f.).

such as repressed sexual desires in the unconscious and infantile sexuality caused widespread opposition in general. His adversaries were "Victorian moralists", the bourgeoisie. They stood for moral attitudes that might be subsumed under the rubric of the 'philistine'. Their fundamentally materialistic ideals opposed anything which disturbed the traditional norms of society (cf. Silva 1990: 46). It was also the biographical manner of those moralists which New Biography rejected.

Freud scrutinises pathography in his text on Leonardo and expresses the reasons for the distaste it engenders in many readers:

> We can discover them [the motives for the opposition of pathography] if we bear in mind that biographers are fixated on their heroes in quite a special way. In many cases they have chosen their hero as the subject of their studies because – for reasons of their personal emotional life – they have felt a special affection for him from the very first. They then devote their energies to a task of idealization, aimed at enrolling the great man among the class of their infantile models – at reviving in him, perhaps, the child's idea of his father. To gratify this wish they obliterate the individual features of their subject's physiognomy; they smooth over the traces of his life's struggles with internal and external resistances, and they tolerate in him no vestige of human weakness or imperfection. They thus present us with what is in fact a cold, strange, ideal figure, instead of a human being to whom we might feel ourselves distantly related. That they should do this is regrettable, for they thereby sacrifice truth to an illusion, and for the sake of their infantile phantasies abandon the opportunity of penetrating the most fascinating secrets of human nature.[22]   (Freud 1989: 91f.)

---

[22] "Man findet sie [die Motive des Widerstrebens gegenüber Pathographie] auf, wenn man in Erwägung zieht, daß Biographen in ganz eigentümlicher Weise an ihren Helden fixiert sind. Sie haben ihn häufig zum Objekt ihrer Studien gewählt, weil sie ihm aus Gründen ihres persönlichen Gefühlslebens von vornherein eine besondere Affektion entgegenbrachten. Sie geben sich dann einer Idealisierungsarbeit hin, die bestrebt ist, den großen Mann in die Reihe ihrer infantilen Vorbilder einzutragen, etwa die kindliche Vorstellung des Vaters in ihm neu zu beleben. Sie löschen diesem Wunsche zuliebe die individuellen Züge in seiner Physiognomie aus, glätten die Spuren seines Lebenskampfes mit inneren und äußeren Widerständen, dulden an ihm keinen Rest von menschlicher Schwäche oder Unvollkommenheit und geben uns dann wirklich eine kalte, fremde Idealgestalt anstatt des Menschen, dem wir uns entfernt verwandt fühlen könnten. Es ist zu bedauern, daß sie dies tun, denn sie opfern damit die Wahrheit einer Illusion und verzichten zugunsten ihrer infantilen Phantasien auf die Gelegenheit, in die reizvollsten Geheimnisse der menschlichen Natur einzudringen" (Freud 1995: 99). The picture Freud describes here reminds one of

Freud's antipathy towards the biographies of the nineteenth century and their panegyric style is evident from this remark, although he, too, has "succumbed to the attraction of this great and mysterious man, in whose nature one seems to detect powerful instinctual passions which can nevertheless only express themselves in so remarkably subdued a manner" (97).[23]

At the end of his study, Freud outlines the contribution of psychoanalysis and its possibilities for biography:

> The material at the disposal of a psycho-analytic enquiry consists of the data of a person's life history: on the one hand the chance circumstances of events and background influences, and, on the other hand, the subject's reported reactions. Supported by its knowledge of psychical mechanisms it then endeavours to establish a dynamic basis for his nature on the strength of his reactions, and to disclose the original motive forces of his mind, as well as their later transformations and developments. If this is successful the behaviour of a personality in the course of his life is explained in terms of the combined operation of constitution and fate, of internal forces and external powers. Where such an undertaking does not provide any certain results – and this is perhaps so in Leonardo's case – the blame rests not with the uncertainty and fragmentary nature of the material relating to him which tradition makes available. It is therefore only the author who is to be held responsible for the failure, by having forced psycho-analysis to pronounce an expert opinion on the basis of such insufficient material.[24] (97)

Woolf's "The Art of Biography" where she writes that "the majority of Victorian biographies are like the wax figures now preserved in Westminster Abbey, that were carried in funeral processions through the street – effigies that have only a smooth superficial likeness to the body in the coffin" (Woolf 1981: 120f.). Woolf of course was familiar with Freud's work because Strachey's brother James, himself a psychoanalyst, was the general editor of its only authorised translation and he arranged in 1924 that the Hogarth Press, founded by Woolf and her husband Leonard in 1917, undertook the publication of all of Freud's papers. On Freud's influence on Woolf's work and the Bloomsbury Group, cf. the chapter "Virginia Woolf the Critic" in Silva 1990: 170ff.

[23] "Ich bin wie andere der Anziehung unterlegen, die von diesem großen und rätselhaften Manne [da Vinci] ausgeht, in dessen Wesen man mächtige triebhafte Leidenschaften zu verspüren glaubt, die sich doch nur so merkwürdig gedämpft äußern können" (Freud 1995: 103).

[24] "Der psychoanalytischen Untersuchung stehen als Material die Daten der Lebensgeschichte zur Verfügung, einerseits die Zufälligkeiten der Begebenheiten und Milieueinflüsse, anderseits die berichteten Reaktionen des Individuums. Gestützt

However, Freud also admits to some limitation of psychoanalysis with regard to the secret of artistic genius:

> We are obliged to look for the source of the tendency to repression and the capacity for sublimation in the organic foundations of character on which the mental structure is only afterwards erected. Since artistic talent and capacity are intimately connected with sublimation we must admit that the nature of the artistic function is also inaccessible to us along psycho-analytic lines.[25]　　(98f.)

Freud's articulation of the unconscious motivational drives, especially those imprinted in childhood, his sexual theories and their meaning for the interpretation of the biographee shaped the understanding of biography in the twentieth century and also created the biographical subgenre of psychobiography. Catherine N. Parke summarises this influence as follows:

> So profoundly did the founder of psychoanalysis influence twentieth-century notions of who we are, how we develop, our degree of self-awareness, and the need for psychoanalytic insight to become conscious of these processes that, after Freud, no responsible biographer can justify knowing nothing about psychoanalytic interpretive methods, though like any other interpretive or investigative methods, its assets and liabilities, insights and blindnesses, even its very presence, must be consciously examined.　　(Parke 2002: 26)

---

auf ihre Kenntnis der psychischen Mechanismen sucht sie nun das Wesen des Individuums aus seinen Reaktionen dynamisch zu ergründen, seine ursprünglichen seelischen Triebkräfte aufzudecken sowie deren spätere Umwandlungen und Entwicklungen. Gelingt dies, so ist das Lebensverhalten der Persönlichkeit durch das Zusammenwirken von Konstitution und Schicksal, inneren Kräften und äußeren Mächten aufgeklärt. Wenn ein solches Unternehmen, wie vielleicht im Falle Leonardos, keine gesicherten Resultate ergibt, so liegt die Schuld nicht an der fehlerhaften oder unzulänglichen Methodik der Psychoanalyse, sondern an der Unsicherheit und Lückenhaftigkeit des Materials, welches die Überlieferung für diese Person beistellt. Für das Mißglücken ist also nur der Autor verantwortlich zu machen, der die Psychoanalyse genötigt hat, auf so unzureichendes Material hin ein Gutachten abzugeben" (Freud 1995: 103f.).

[25] "Verdrängungsneigung sowie Sublimierungsfähigkeit sind wir genötigt auf die organischen Grundlagen des Charakters zurückzuführen, über welche erst sich das seelische Gebäude erhebt. Da die künstlerische Begabung und Leistungsfähigkeit mit der Sublimierung innig zusammenhängt, müssen wir zugestehen, daß auch das Wesen der künstlerischen Leistung uns psychoanalytisch unzugänglich ist" (Freud 1995: 105).

One biographer who was influenced by Freud's work and whom Edel calls "the father of 'psychobiography'" (Edel 1984: 143) was the historian Lytton Strachey, "the great debunker" (France 2002: 83). Besides numerous biographical essays, he wrote three major biographies: *Eminent Victorians* (1918), *Queen Victoria* (1921) and *Elizabeth and Essex: A Tragic History* (1928), which all became chief exemplars of New Biography in England. In them, he iconoclastically broke with the habit of putting the subject of biography on a pedestal and introduced irony and satire into the genre which, according to his preface to *Eminent Victorians*, seemed "to have fallen on evil times in England" (Strachey 2002: 4). In this preface, he also summarises his biographical approach:

> It is not by the direct method of a scrupulous narration that the explorer of the past can hope to depict that singular epoch. If he is wise, he will adopt a subtler strategy. He will attack his subject in unexpected places: he will fall upon the flank, or the rear; he will shoot a sudden, revealing searchlight into obscure recesses, hitherto undivined. He will row out over that great ocean of material, and lower down into it, here and there, a little bucket, which will bring up to the light of day some characteristic specimen, from those far depths, to be examined with a careful curiosity. (3)

Strachey's guiding biographical principles are a "haphazard" selection of subjects "by simple motives of convenience and of art", illustration rather than explanation, brevity "which excludes everything that is redundant and nothing that is significant" and "to lay bare the facts of the case, [...] dispassionately, impartially, and without ulterior intentions". For him, the importance of his subjects is not only historical but also biographical: "Human beings are too important to be treated as mere symptoms of the past. They have a value which is independent of any temporal processes – which is eternal, and must be felt for its own sake" (3f.).

On the publication of *Eminent Victorians* in May 1918, five months before the Armistice of World War I, it was accounted a revolution in biography and a representation of a total cut between old and new. The main reason for this was Strachey's debunking of the Victorian heroes through satire. Moreover, Marcus states that it was recognized as the first text of post-war England, "opening up to ridicule the workings of power and the blind submission to God and Country which had led to the mass slaughter of World War I" (Marcus 2002: 197).

Another prominent figure at that time who represents an additional spectrum of New Biography and who was associated with Strachey through the Bloomsbury Group was Virginia Woolf. She critically examined the generic change in her non-fictional essays and experimented with it in her semi-fictional semi-auto/biographies *Orlando* (1928) and *Flush* (1933). Her involvement with the genre must have begun much earlier, though, as it was her father, Leslie Stephen, who was the first editor of the monumental *Dictionary of National Biography*.

In her essay "The New Biography" (1927), Woolf dwells on a dilemma inherent in biography, which coined the oppositional terms *granite* and *rainbow* for the contrast between fact and fiction:

> On the one hand there is truth; on the other there is personality. And if we think of truth as something of granite-like solidity and of personality as something of rainbow-like intangibility and reflect that the aim of biography is to weld these two into one seamless whole, we shall admit that the problem is a stiff one and that we need not wonder if biographers have for the most part failed to solve it. (Woolf 1958: 149)

She sees "a virtue in truth". It "stimulates the mind, which is endowed with a curious susceptibility in this direction as no fiction, however artful or highly coloured, can stimulate it". However, if a biography "stuffed with truth" seems "dull" and "unreadable", the biographer "failed to choose those truths which transmit personality. For in order that the light of personality may shine through, facts must be manipulated; some must be brightened; others shaded; yet, in the process, they must never lose their integrity" (149f.). According to Woolf, personality entered into biography with Boswell. Until then the genre had maintained that life consisted of actions or works. In Victorian biography, although truth of fact was scrupulously observed, personality was again distorted. However, biography, like fiction and poetry, was transformed with the advent of the twentieth century:

> The first and most visible sign of it was in the difference in size. In the first twenty years of the new century biographies must have lost half their weight. [...] But the diminution of size was only the outward token of an inward change. The point of view had completely altered. [... T]he author's relation to his sub-

ject is different. He is no longer the serious and sympathetic companion, toiling even slavishly in the footsteps of his hero. Whether friend or enemy, admiring or critical, he is an equal. In any case, he preserves his freedom and his right to independent judgement. Moreover, he does not think himself constrained to follow every step of the way. Raised upon a little eminence which his independence has made for him, he sees his subject spread about him. He chooses; he synthesizes; in short, he has ceased to be the chronicler; he has become an artist. (151f.)

To these artists – Woolf refers in her essay in particular to Harold Nicolson as the author of the New Biography *Some People* (1927) – the "man himself is the supreme object of their curiosity". The biographer is able to understand him through little hints "in the tone of a voice, the turn of a head, some little phrase or anecdote picked up in passing" (153), thus describing the subject in a much more condensed and effective way than his/her Victorian predecessors in their multivolume biographies. The author, however,

> is as much the subject of his own irony and observation as they [his biographees] are. He lies in wait for his own absurdities as artfully as for theirs. Indeed, by the end of the book we realize that the figure which has been most completely and most subtly displayed is that of the author. […] And though the figure thus revealed is not noble or impressive or shown in a very heroic attitude, it is for these very reasons extremely like a real human being. It is thus, he would seem to say, in the mirrors of our friends, that we chiefly live. (153f.)

Woolf sees this reflection of the biographer through his biography as a "freedom from pose, from sentimentality, from illusion" and as a victory which proves "that one can use many of the devices of fiction in dealing with real life. He [Nicolson] has shown that a little fiction mixed with fact can be made to transmit personality very effectively". As great as this victory may be, Woolf holds it to be perilous as well because, although "the truth of real life and the truth of fiction" are genuine, they are opposed to each other: "Let it be fact, one feels, or let it be fiction; the imagination will not serve under two masters simultaneously" (154). Nonetheless, although these truths are irreconcilable, the biographer needs to combine them for "it would seem that the life which is increasingly real to us is the fictitious life". Therefore, "the biographer's imagination is always being stimulated to use the novelist's art of arrangement, suggestion, dramatic effect to expound the private life", but he will lose both truths "if he carries the use of fiction too far", if he ignores or inappropriately draws on the truth. Then, "he has neither the freedom of fiction nor the substance of fact" (155).

In "The Art of Biography" (1939), Woolf further ponders the idea of biography as an art and elaborates on her earlier considerations of fact and fiction. For her, "the art of biography is the most restricted of all the arts". While, for example, the novelist is free, the biographer is tied. Biography and fiction differ in the very substance they are made of: "One is made with the help of friends, of facts; the other is created without any restrictions save those that the artist, for reasons that seem good to him, chooses to obey" (Woolf 1981: 120). By comparing Strachey's *Queen Victoria*, "a triumphant success", with his *Elizabeth and Essex*, "a failure" (122), she comes to the conclusion that biography

> imposes conditions, and those conditions are that it must be based upon fact. And by fact in biography we mean facts that can be verified by other people besides the artist. If he invents facts as an artist invents them – facts that no one else can verify – and tries to combine them with facts of the other sort, they destroy each other. (123)

Being bound to this kind of fact is "a necessary element in biography" and also a "necessary limitation". In fiction, the facts are only verified by the artist; it is in the truth of his own vision that their authenticity lies:

> The world created by that vision is rarer, intenser, and more wholly of a piece than the world that is largely made of authentic information supplied by other people. And because of this difference the two kinds of fact will not mix; if they touch they destroy each other. No one, the conclusion seems to be, can make the best of both worlds; you must choose, and you must abide by your choice. (124)

However, such a "failure" opens up new possibilities in Woolf's view, as well. While bound to facts, the biographer is also entitled to use all available facts. But these facts are "subject to changes of opinion" and those opinions change with the times. New interpretations of those facts emerge while old ones are discarded:

> Thus the biographer must go ahead of the rest of us, like the miner's canary, testing the atmosphere, detecting falsity, unreality, and the presence of obsolete conventions. His sense of truth must be alive and on tiptoe. Then again, since we live in an age when a thousand cameras are pointed, by newspapers, letters, and

> diaries, at every character from every angle, he must be prepared to admit contradictory versions of the same face. Biography will enlarge its scope by hanging up looking glasses at odd corners. And yet from all this diversity it will bring out, not a riot of confusion, but a richer unity. (124f.)

Woolf comes to the conclusion that the biographer is "a craftsman, not an artist; and his work is not a work of art, but something betwixt and between", because fiction will survive the facts biography is built upon. Nonetheless, by telling and selecting the true facts and thus by giving shape to the whole so that the reader recognizes the outline of the subject, the biographer makes use of this high degree of tension contained in reality, which cannot be achieved by poets and novelists, and he can give the reader "the creative fact; the fertile fact; the fact that suggests and engenders" (125f.).

Freud, Strachey and Woolf can be regarded as the three central figures for the emergence of New Biography. Not only did they experiment actively with life-writings, but they also discussed the genre and its limitations and possibilities in critical essays. It is their theories and writings which have had a profound influence on the biographies of the twentieth century and which continue to be considered and developed by biographers and biographical theorists such as Leon Edel or James Clifford.[26]

e. From modern to postmodern biography

In the decades following the emergence of New Biography, the understanding of the biographical subject, especially in literary biography, came under attack from certain historical, literary and cultural theories, which divided biographers and scholars of biography alike into different camps. Most of these critical concepts came from structuralist and poststructuralist theory, which led to a postmodern understanding of biography.[27] Moreover, postmodern biographical writing has never super-

---

[26] Cf. Edel 1984 and Clifford 1970.

[27] There seems to be a great uncertainty in literary criticism about the terms 'poststructuralism' and 'postmodernism' as they are sometimes used congruently to describe a theory of literature and sometimes to describe different aspects of a the-

seded its modern antecedent: rather it has become a version of biography in which authors experiment with and try more or less desperately to reform the genre. As much as biographers search for new ways of interpreting and depicting their subject, there are always authors who object to any new form of the conventional, chronological, unified presentation of the biographee. It is this debate which still dominates today's generic discussion on biography.

Dominating English literary criticism from the 1940s and until the late 1960s, New Criticism

> opposed the prevailing interest of scholars, critics, and teachers of that era in the biographies of authors, in the social context of literature, and in literary history by insisting that the proper concern of literary criticism is not with the external circumstances or effects or historical position of a work, but with a detailed consideration of the work itself as an independent entity. (Abrams 2005: 188)

Naturally, this form of criticism does not rely on any form of biographical writing to contain necessary information for the interpretation of the texts of the biographee. Any form of consideration of an author outside her or his text was seen as a totally different and in some way dangerous approach to the text. Thus literary biographies became irrelevant as additional information on the creation of an author's works. This becomes apparent in the essay "The Intentional Fallacy", one of the key texts of New Criticism. Here, W.K. Wimsatt and Monroe C. Beardsley distinguish between "criticism of poetry" and "author psychology". If the latter is historical, it becomes literary biography, "a legitimate and attractive study in itself, one approach [...] to personality, the poem being only a parallel approach". While Wimsatt and Beardsley respect biographical studies in their own right, they see a "danger of confusing personal and poetic studies; and there is the fault of writing the personal as if it were poetic". Biographical evidence is too uncertain for critical inquiries: "while it may be evidence of what the author intended, it may also be evidence of the meaning of his words and the dramatic

---

ory of culture (cf., for example, Hutcheon 1987: 3ff.). As it is more important in this context to make clear how certain theories influenced the understanding and practice of biography, it is not so important whether they are called poststructuralist, postmodernist, postmodernist-poststructuralist or something else along these lines.

character of his utterance. On the other hand, it may not be all this" (Wimsatt/Beardsley 1967: 10f.).

Structuralist criticism, which was part of the movement of French structuralism in the 1950s, took the ideas of New Criticism even further. Roland Barthes, "the father of literary structuralism", followed Claude Lévi-Strauss's structuralist analysis in cultural anthropology and endorsed "semiology, the science of signs, developing a theory of literary interpretation from a theory of language" (Stannard 1998: 4). In his influential essay "The Death of the Author" ("La mort de l'auteur", 1968), Barthes criticises the supremacy of the author and at the same time the self-understanding of writers of literary biographies:

> The *author* still reigns in histories of literature, biographies of writers, interviews, magazines, as in the very consciousness of men of letters anxious to unite their person and their work through diaries and memoirs. The image of literature to be found in ordinary culture is tyrannically centred on the author, his person, his life, his tastes, his passions [...]. The *explanation* of a work is always sought in the man or woman who produced it, as if it were always in the end, through the more or less transparent allegory of the fiction, the voice of a single person, the *author* 'confiding' in us.[28]   (Barthes 1995: 126)

According to Barthes, the absence of an author would change the modern text. Whereas the author, if believed in, "is always conceived of as the past of his own book", as somebody who "exists before it, thinks, suffers, lives for it". Contrary to this author, "the modern scriptor is born simultaneously with the text, is in no way equipped with a being preceding or exceeding the writing, is not the subject with the book as predicate" (127). For Barthes, the text is an intertextual conglomerate, "a multi-dimensional space in which a variety of writings, none of them original, blend and clash. The text is a tissue of quotations drawn from

---

[28] "*L'auteur* règne encore dans les manuels d'histoire littéraire, les biographies d'écrivains, les interviews des magazines, et dans la conscience même des littérateurs, soucieux de joindre, grâce à leur journal intime, leur personne et leur œuvre; l'image de la littérature que l'on peut trouver dans la culture courante est tyranniquement centrée sur l'auteur, sa personne, son histoire, ses goûts, ses passions; [...] l'*explication* de l' œuvre est toujours cherchée du côte de celui qui l'a produite, comme si, à travers l'allégorie plus ou moins transparente de la fiction, c'était toujours finalement la voix d'une seule et même personne, l'*auteur*, qui livrait sa 'confidence'" (Barthes 2002: 41).

the innumerable centres of culture" (128).[29] In his essay, Barthes vehemently disapproves of any form of contemporary literary criticism, even New Criticism, and also of biographies when he writes:

> Once the Author is removed, the claim to decipher a text becomes quite futile. To give a text an Author is to impose a limit on that text, to furnish it with a final signified, to close the writing. Such a conception suits criticism very well, the latter then allotting itself the important task of discovering the Author (or its hypostases: society, history psyché, liberty) beneath the work: when the Author has been found, the text is 'explained' – victory to the critic. Hence there is no surprise in the fact that, historically, the reign of the Author has also been that of the Critic, nor again in the fact that criticism (be it new) is today undermined along with the author.[30] (128f.)

And this is exactly why for Barthes the author has to die. He opposes any form of literary criticism that looks for a final answer to the meaning of an author's work through a reflection of his or her life. Structuralist criticism therefore rejects biographies (especially literary ones) and the practice of interpreting an author's work through life facts. According to Barthes, this is impossible because

> writing ceaselessly posits meaning ceaselessly to evaporate it, carrying out a systematic exemption of meaning. In precisely this way literature (it would be better from now on to say *writing*), by refusing to assign a 'secret', an ultimate meaning, to the text (and to the world as text), liberates what may be called an

---

[29] "L'Auteur, lorsqu'on y croit, est toujours conçu comme le passé de son propre livre: [...] qu'il existe avant lui, pense, souffre, vit pour lui [...]. Tout au contraire, le scripteur moderne naît en même temps que son texte; il n'est d'aucune façon pourvu d'un être qui précéderait ou excéderait son écriture, il n'est en rien le sujet dont son livre serait le prédicat [...]. [... Un texte est] un espace à dimensions multiples, où se marient et se contestent des écritures variées, dont aucune n'est originelle: le texte est un tissu de citations, issues de mille foyers de la culture" (Barthes 2002: 43).

[30] "L'Auteur une fois éloigné, la prétention de 'déchiffrer' un texte devient tout à fait inutile. Donner un Auteur à un texte, c'est imposer à ce texte un cran d'arrêt, c'est le pourvoir d'un signifié dernier, c'est fermer l'écriture. Cette conception convient très bien à la critique, qui veut alors se donner pour tâche importante de découvrir l'Auteur (ou se hypostases: la société, l'histoire, la psyché, la liberté) sous l'œuvre: l'Auteur trouvé, le texte est 'expliqué', le critique a vaincu; il n'y a donc rien d'étonnant à ce que, historiquement, le règne d l'Auteur ait été aussi celui du Critique, mais aussi à ce que la critique (fût-elle nouvelle) soit aujourd'hui ébranlée en même temps que l'Auteur" (Barthes 2002: 44).

> anti-theological activity, an activity that is truly revolutionary since to refuse to fix meaning is, in the end, to refuse God and his hypostases – reason, science, law.[31] (129)

Instead of focusing on the author, Barthes proclaims that it is the reader who has to be at the centre of attention. Hence, "the birth of the reader must be at the cost of the death of the Author" (130).[32]

While Barthes is preoccupied with the disappearance of the author, Michel Foucault asks what an author is and concentrates on "the empty space left by the author's disappearance" (Foucault 1995: 233).[33] For him,

> the name of the author remains at the contours of texts – separating one from the other, defining their form, and characterizing their mode of existence. It points to the existence of certain groups of discourse and refers to the status of this discourse within a society and culture. The author's name is not a function of a man's civil status, nor is it fictional; it is situated in the breach, among the discontinuities, which gives rise to new groups of discourse and their singular mode of existence. [… T]he function of an author is to characterize the existence, circulation, and operation of certain discourses within a society.[34] (235)

---

[31] "[L]'écriture pose sans cesse du sens mais c'est toujours pur l'évaporer: elle procède à une exemption systématique du sens. Par là même, la littérature (il vaudrait mieux dire désormais l'*écriture*), en refusant d'assigner au texte (et au monde comme texte) un 'secret', c'est-à-dire un sens ultime, libère une activité que l'on pourrait appeler contre-théologique, proprement révolutionnaire, car refuser d'arrêter le sens, c'est finalement refuser Dieu et ses hypostases, la raison, la science, la loi" (Barthes 2002: 44).

[32] "[L]a naissance du lecteur doit se payer de la mort de l'Auteur" (Barthes 2002: 45).

[33] "[L]'espace ainsi laissé vide par la disparition de l'auteur" (Foucault 1994: 798).

[34] "[Le nom d'auteur] court, en quelque sorte, à la limite des textes, qu'il les découpe, qu'il en suit les arêtes, qu'il en manifeste le mode d'être ou, du moins, qu'il le caractérise. Il manifeste l'événement d'un certain ensemble de discours, et il se réfère au statut de ce discours à l'intérieur d'une société et à l'intérieur d'une culture. Le nom d'auteur n'est pas situé dans l'état civil des hommes, il n'est pas non plus situé dans la fiction de l'œuvre, il est situé dans la rupture qui instaure un certain groupe de discours et son mode d'être singulier. […] La fonction auteur est donc caractéristique du mode d'existence, de circulation et de fonctionnement de certains discours à l'intérieur d'une société" (Foucault 1994: 798).

Foucault names four main characteristics of the 'author-function':

> the 'author-function' is tied to the legal and institutional systems that circumscribe, determine, and articulate the realm of discourse; it does not operate in a uniform manner in all discourses, at all times, and in any given culture; it is not defined by the spontaneous attribution of a text to its creator, but through a series of precise and complex procedures; it does not refer, purely and simply, to an actual individual insofar as it simultaneously gives rise to a variety of egos and to a series of subjective positions that individuals of any class may come to occupy.[35] (239f.)

The last two characteristics are important in the context of biography. Modern literary criticism, according to Foucault, considers an author's (socio)biography to explain why certain events exist and change within a text. When those modifications are explained through an author's "evolution, maturation, or outside influence", s/he constitutes "a principle of unity in writing". The reasons for any contradictions in a series of text are always put down to its author, who is more or less manifested "equally well, and with similar validity" in his entire work. Though Foucault identifies those principles as inadequate to modern critics, "they, nevertheless, define the critical modalities now used to display the function of the author" (238).[36]

Nonetheless, the 'author-function' is more complex because the signs in the text referring to the author do not only stand for a real historical figure, but also for "a 'second-self' whose similarity to the author is never fixed and undergoes considerable alteration within the course of

---

[35] "[L]a fonction-auteur est liée au système juridique et institutionnel qui enserre, détermine, articule l'univers des discours; elle ne s'exerce pas uniformément et de la même façon sur tous les discours, à toutes les époques et dans toutes les formes de civilisation; elle n'est pas définie par l'attribution spontanée d'un discours à son producteur, mais par une série d'opérations spécifiques et complexes; elle ne renvoie pas purement et simplement à un individu réel, elle peut donner lieu simultanément à plusieurs ego, à plusieurs positions-sujets que des classes différentes d'individus peuvent venir occuper" (Foucault 1994: 803f.).

[36] "L'auteur, c'est également le principe d'une certaine unité d'écriture – toutes les différences devant être réduites au moins par les principes de l'évolution, de la maturation ou de l'influence. [… Il] se manifeste aussi bien, et avec la même valeur, dans des œuvres […]. [… Cette critères définissent les] modalités selon lesquelles la critique moderne fait jouer la fonction auteur" (Foucault 1994: 802).

a single book". Nor is the author identical with the actual writer or the narrator; "the 'author-function' arises out of their scission – in the division and distance of the two", and Foucault makes clear that this phenomenon does not only apply to the novel or to poetry, but to all discourses which support this 'author-function' (239).[37] This poses a problem to the literary biographer who views the author as the one unique historical figure s/he is writing the biography about, but instead finds a "variety of egos" and a "series of subjective positions" (240).[38] A narration of a unique, unified individual would be impossible then, as the author "is undoubtedly only one of the possible specifications of the subject and, considering past historical transformations, it appears that the form, the complexity, and even the existence of this function are far from immutable" (245).[39] In the last consequence, this would make the question of who is actually speaking obsolete.

While (post)structuralism, as Seán Burke states, concentrates on salvaging "language from the oblivion to which Western metaphysics had consigned it, but failed to pose the question of writing", the French philosopher Jacques Derrida was mainly concerned with uncovering the repression by the "metaphysics of presence" of "the written sign and modelled language according to metaphors of self-presence and vocalisation". To facilitate this, he deconstructed the text, i.e. he applied the method of remaining conscientiously true to the letter of the text. The outcome was a perpetually inward analysis "within which the relationship of these texts to the general history of metaphysics was constantly implied, but never stated in any systematic fashion" (Burke 1992: 116). In *Of Grammatology* (*De la grammatologie*), Derrida approaches the

---

[37] "[U]n alter ego dont la distance à l'écrivain peut être plus ou moins grande et varier au cours même de l'œuvre. [… L]a fonction-auteur s'effectue dans la scission même – dans ce partage et cette distance" (Foucault 1994: 803).

[38] "[E]lle ne renvoie pas purement et simplement à un individu réel, elle peut donner lieu simultanément à plusieurs ego, à plusieurs positions-sujets que des classes différentes d'individus peuvent venir occuper" (Foucault 1994: 804).

[39] "L'auteur […] n'est sans doute qu'une des spécifications possibles de la fonction-sujet. Spécification possible, ou nécessaire? À voir les modifications historiques qui ont eu lieu, il ne paraît pas indispensable, loin de là, que la fonction-auteur demeure constante dans sa forme, dans sa complexité, et même dans son existence" (Foucault 1994: 811).

author problem in a philosophical context which goes far beyond literary-critical issues and is too complex to discuss here.⁴⁰ Therefore, I will concentrate on those issues of his author criticism which concern the biographical genre.

In a chapter named "The Exorbitant: Question of Method", Derrida famously states that our reading

> cannot legitimately transgress the text towards something other than it, towards a referent (a reality that is metaphysical, historical, psycho-biographical, etc.) or towards a signified outside the text whose content could take place, could have taken place [...] outside of writing in general. [...] *There is nothing outside of the text* [...].⁴¹ (Derrida 1995: 118)

According to Derrida, this may be because the life of the author or of any character in her or his text is of no prime interest to the reader or because the only access he or she has to their alleged "real" existence is through the text. However, for Derrida, there are more radical reasons. To him, what one calls "real" existence is not real because

> there has never been anything but writing; there have never been anything but supplements, substitutive significations which could only come forth in a chain of differential references, the 'real' supervening, and being added only while taking on meaning from a trace and from an invocation of the supplement, etc. And thus to infinity, for we have read, *in the text*, that the absolute present [... has] always already escaped, [has] never existed; that what opens meaning and language is writing as the disappearance of natural presence.⁴² (119)

---

⁴⁰ On Derrida's deconstruction of metaphysics, cf. Burke 1992: 117f.

⁴¹ "[La lecture] ne peut légitimement transgresser le texte vers autre chose que lui, vers un référent (réalité métaphysique, historique, psycho-biographique, etc.) ou vers un signifié hors texte dont le contenu pourrait avoir lieu, aurait pu avoir lieu [...] hors de l'écriture en général. [...] *Il n'y a pas de hors-texte*" (Derrida 1967: 227).

⁴² "[I]l n'y a jamais eu que de l'écriture; il n'y a jamais eu que des suppléments, des significations substitutives qui n'ont pu surgir que dans une chaîne de renvois différentiels, le 'réel' ne survenant, ne s'ajoutant qu'en prenant sens à partir d'une trace et d'un appel de supplément, etc. Et ainsi à l'infini car nous avons lu, *dans le texte*, que le présent absolu [...] se sont toujours déjà dérobés, n'ont jamais existé; que ce qui ouvre le sens et le langage, c'est cette écriture comme disparition de la présence naturelle" (Derrida 1967: 228).

Derrida, therefore, rejects any reading for manifestations of the "real life" of an author in his or her text:

> The reading of the literary 'symptom' is most banal, most academic, most naive. And once one has thus blinded oneself to the very tissues of the 'symptom', to its proper texture, one cheerfully exceeds it towards a psychobiographical signified whose link with the literary signifier then becomes perfectly extrinsic and contingent.[43] (119)

Similar to Barthes, Derrida criticises the misleading notion of connecting passages of an author's text to her or his biography and thus those literary biographers who do not realize the "textualness" of their subject and for whom art always imitates life. He finds it impossible "to separate, through interpretation or commentary, the signified from the signifier, and thus to destroy writing by the writing that is yet reading" as every person writing "is inscribed in a determined textual system". Any text which is written includes "the project of effacing itself in the face of the signified content which it transports and in general teaches" (119f.).[44]

However, Derrida opposes authorial intention not in the sense the New Criticism or Barthes's "The Death of the Author" does. On the contrary, if those intentions are to be deconstructed, they must be present and recognizable in our reading. Only then can authorial intentions be separated from that which escapes or upsets their prescriptions. Deconstructivism follows the line of authorial intention until it encounters opposition in the text. From then on, the opposition can be used against the author to demonstrate that her or his text differs from itself,

---

[43] "La lecture du 'symptôme' littéraire est la plus banale, la plus scolaire, la plus naïve. Et une fois que l'on s'est ainsi rendu aveugle au tissu même du 'symptôme', à sa texture propre, on l'excède allègrement vers un signifié psycho-biographique dont le lien avec le signifiant littéraire devient alors parfaitement extrinsèque et contingent" (Derrida 1967: 228f.).

[44] "S'il nous paraît impossible au principe de séparer, par interprétation ou commentaire, le signifié du signifiant, et de détruire ainsi l'écriture par l'écriture qu'est encore la lecture [... parce que] l'écrivant est inscrit dans un système textuel déterminé. [...Tout les textes comporte] le projet de s'effacer devant le contenu signifié qu'il transporte et en général enseigne" (Derrida 1967: 229).

from what s/he wished to say, which instead is rather inscribed within or engulfed by the larger signifying structure:

> We should begin by taking rigorous account of this *being held within* [prise] or this *surprise*: the writer writes *in* a language and *in* a logic whose proper system, laws, and life his discourse by definition cannot dominate absolutely. He uses them only by letting himself, after a fashion and up to a point, be governed by the system. And the reading must always aim at a certain relationship, unperceived by the writer, between what he commands and what he does not command of the patterns of the language that he uses. This relationship is not a certain quantitative distribution of shadow and light, of weakness or of force, but a signifying structure that critical reading should *produce*.[45] (117f.)

The production of a signifying structure, however, does not mean the reproduction of "the conscious, voluntary, intentional relationship that the writer institutes in his exchanges with the history to which he belongs thanks to the element of language" (118).[46]

Deconstructivism is not an "assassination attempt" on the author, but rather opposes him or her through the author's own text. According to Burke, thus, the deconstructivist critic "accepts the author, but on condition that the critic can produce the text as a broader signifying structure within which the author's determining will is inscribed as one factor amongst others" (Burke 1992: 143). This implies the priority of the critic over the author and also deconstructs the traditional understanding of biography: that the biographer can, with the help of writings of any sort by the biographee, depict the one true "real" historical personality of the subject.

---

[45] "Nous devons commencer par tenir un compte rigoureux de cette *prise* ou de cette *surprise*: l'écrivain écrit *dans* une langue et *dans* une logique dont, par définition, son discours ne peut dominer absolument le système, les lois et la vie propres. Il ne s'en sert qu'en se laissant d'une certaine manière et jusqu'à un certain point gouverner par le système. Et la lecture doit toujours viser un certain rapport, inaperçu de l'écrivain, entre ce qu'il commande et ce qu'il ne commande pas des schémas de la langue dont il fait usage. Ce rapport n'est pas une certaine répartition quantitative d'ombre et de lumière, de faiblesse ou de force, mais une structure signifiante que la lecture critique doit *produire*" (Derrida 1967: 226f.).

[46] "[L]e rapport conscient, volontaire, intentionnel, que l'écrivain institue dans ses échanges avec l'histoire à laquelle il appartient grâce à l'élément de la langue" (Derrida 1967: 227).

Another mode of literary as well as cultural and historical criticism is New Historicism in which, since the 1980s, its proponents have "combat[ed] empty formalism [of New Criticism, structuralism and deconstructivism] by pulling historical considerations to the center stage of literary analysis" (Veeser 1989: xi). New historicists do not deal with a text "in isolation from its historical context", but they "attend primarily to the historical and cultural conditions of its production, its meaning, its effects, and also of its later critical interpretations and evaluations" (Abrams 2005: 190). This form of literary criticism has gone hand in hand with a trend in the study of history which has questioned the supreme position of facts in the scholarship of history. Historians such as Hayden White view history as presented in historiography as a fictional construction: "one's philosophy of history is a function as much of the way one construes one's own special object of scholarly interest as it is of one's knowledge of 'history' itself" (White 1989: 302). Hence, key assumptions of New Historicism are

> 1. that every expressive act is embedded in a network of material practices;
> 2. that every act of unmasking, critique, and opposition uses the tools it condemns and risks falling prey to the practice it exposes;
> 3. that literary and non-literary "texts" circulate inseparably;
> 4. that no discourse, imaginative or archival, gives access to unchanging truths nor expresses inalterable human nature;
> 5. finally [...] that a critical method and a language adequate to describe culture under capitalism participate in the economy they describe. (Veeser 1989: xi)

New historicists adopt anthropological approaches to understand human behaviour, they reject linear chronology of cultural developments and are convinced that details of cultural practices usually seen as insignificant expose the inherent incongruous forces of a culture. Individuals are not conceived as clearly defined entities, "but, in reference to Marx's critique of capitalist society, historically constituted subjects, an ensemble of social forces" (Volkmann 1996: 332).

The most opposing criticism of New Historicism with regard to life-writing concerns these individuals, the subjects of biography. For new historicists, the "humanistic concept of an essential human nature" – as shared by author, characters in her or his work and readers – and the view that it is an independent author with "a unified, unique, and enduring personal identity" who creates any kind of literary work are "ideological illusions" generated by "capitalist culture". Although some new historicists credit authors with a certain amount of freedom and initiative, they do not do so to explain an author's literary creation and distinctive talent, but "in order to keep open the theoretical possibility that an individual author can intervene so as to inaugurate radical changes in the social power structure of which that individual's own 'subjectivity' and function are themselves a product" (Abrams 2005: 193).[47]

While postmodern criticism towards the author figure may primarily have involved literary biography, it has been the so-called 'crisis of the modern subject' in the twentieth century which has affected the entire genre of biography. In his seminal study on subject theory, Peter A. Zima explains which subject postmodernism denies:

> Es ist das individuelle und transzendentale Subjekt der idealistischen Philosophen (Descartes', Kants, Fichtes und Hegels), das sich als *cogito* oder Geist die Wirklichkeit ganz oder teilweise unterwirft; das als reines, stets zu sich selbst zurückkehrendes Denken die Natur beherrscht. Es ist das *subiectum* als Zugrundeliegendes, als anthropozentrisches Ebenbild des göttlichen Subjekts, das die Weltschöpfung im rationalistischen oder dialektischen System von neuem inszeniert; es ist die säkularisierte Gottheit.[48] (Zima 2000: 86)

To come to terms with this subject in the form of a conventional biographical narration, however, would be almost impossible if it has dissolved into fragments due to the postmodern condition. Zima summarises the postmodernist argument which has influenced the idea of the subject in the second half of the twentieth century:

---

[47] On how Derrida's dissolving author, New Criticism and New Historicism can even "help" the biographer, cf. Honan 1995: 190f., 191-194 and 196ff. respectively; on the importance of biography as "the arena of dispute" in opposition to postmodern criticism, cf. Fish 1991: 12ff.

[48] "It is the individual and transcendental subject of the Idealistic philosophers (Descartes, Kant, Fichte and Hegel) which completely or partly conquers reality as *cogito* or intellect; which commands nature as thought which is pure and constantly reverting to itself. It is the *subiectum* as the foundation, as the anthropocentric counterpart of the divine subject, which re-enacts Creation in the rationalistic or dialectic system; it is the secularised divinity" (my translation).

> Die Grundthese der nachmodernen Denker [...] lautet, daß das individuelle Subjekt fremdbestimmt ist, weil es sich an das Andere des Unbewußten, der Sprache oder der Natur verliert. Bei Lyotard verliert es sich an der Natur als Erhabenes [...], welches das Fassungsvermögen des Verstandes und der Einbildungskraft übersteigt. Bei Derrida [...] verliert es sich an die Naturseite der Sprache als Zusammenwirken sinnfreier Signifikanten, die eine Subversion subjektiver Sinngebungen bewirken.[49] (206)

On the one hand, Jean-François Lyotard questions subjectivity as an aesthetic category and outlines an aestheticism which destroys the subject. On the other hand, Derrida's linguistic theory with its concepts of *différance* (endless shift of meaning) and *itérabilité* (repetition subverting meaning) denies a stable, identifiable meaning. In this context, the identity of the individual who is subject to *différance* and *itérabilité* becomes an illusion. The permanent shift in meaning makes it impossible to define and identify the subject (cf. 205ff. and 211). Biographies which try to do so must fail; they only describe a biographic illusion, at least according to the postmodernists.[50]

New Criticism, French structuralism, deconstructivism, poststructuralism, New Historicism, subject criticism – all these modes of criticism decentre the author or rather the human subject in one way or another. Hence, biography, the genre which has at its centre this very human subject, which revolves around its interpretation and whose narra-

---

[49] "The basic assumption of postmodern thought amounts to the thesis that the individual subject is determined from the outside because it loses itself to the other of the unconscious, of language, or of nature. For Lyotard, it loses itself to nature as the sublime which transcends comprehension with the mind and the imagination. For Derrida, it loses itself to the natural aspect of language as the concurrence of meaningless signifiers producing a subversion of subjective interpretations" (my translation).

[50] Jürgen Schlaeger questions the cultural – not the philosophical – myth of "the unified subject and closure in general", as well as "the relationship between reality and experience on the one hand and fiction on the other" and "the belief that the sense of the self [...] is inextricably linked to narrativity" (Schlaeger 2006: 428). For him, all these myths enjoy "some kind of universal acceptance in all debates about biography" (427). While Schlaeger's ideas are worth mentioning, in the context of this study, however, it is more important how biographers conceive of their biographical subject, how they aim at representing it, and how this affected life-writing in the second half of the twentieth century.

tion is dependent on its understanding, must – overtly or covertly – consider and integrate those changes of perception and this new way of thinking, or it must ignore and oppose them. Whatever the choice of the biographer may be, generic variations are the resulting consequence, which may compete with one another for the reader's favour.

3. Biography today: An assessing overview

After considering the cultural and literary criticisms sketched above, which have affected the biographical genre in one way or another in the second half of the twentieth century, it is necessary to regard the position of life-writing today. Has it changed into a postmodern genre, taking into account and integrating poststructuralist and postmodern theories? Has it retreated into its "traditional shell", hiding as an anachronism from contemporary literary theory? Or has it taken a new direction into a post-postmodern reality? One way towards an answer would be to look at the proposed diverse functions of contemporary biographical methodology, the various forms it can assume and the contradictory elements of the genre.

a. Functions of biography

At a conference organised by the Texas Committee for the Humanities in the early 1980s, the participants stressed the humanistic aspect of biography. In the edited proceedings, James Frank Veninga enumerates the possible insights of biography. To him, it is "a prism of history and also of the human personality" and it imparts "knowledge of how people have given shape to their lives, knowledge of other ages and cultures, knowledge of the conditions of freedom and fate" (Veninga 1983: 68). In a response to a different lecture at the same conference, Ronald Steel points out two additional facets of the genre: "First, biography reveals how we deal with the world. It is the chronicle of events, of our actions. Second, it is a reflection of the prevalent belief system of the society in which we live. That is to say, a biography is phrased in terms of what society values" (Steel 1983: 26). For Steel, biography and the cultural value system go hand in hand:

> Biography may be an agent of humanism, but it also reflects a culture's values. We respond to the kind of biography – to the account of a person's conflict with life – that confirms the values we hold. And those values are, of course, transmitted to us through our culture. Our culture teaches us that the human being matters. It teaches us that a person should be in harmony with the system of values prescribed by his culture. (27)

However, Phyllis Rose also sees the negative consequences of this connection between life-writing and the cultural value system when she writes that

> [i]n starkly political terms, biography is a tool by which the dominant society reinforces its values. It has ignored women; it ignores the poor and working class; it ignores the unprivileged; it ignores noncelebrities. Such formulation is useful only up to a point, because in fact biography ignores almost everyone. As a genre, it is much more elitist than the novel, which has always taken middle-class and middling characters as subjects. (Rose 1985: 68)

The constitution of cultural identity through biography is a different functional aspect. In reviewing Australian biography, Walter shows that "the rupture and reconstruction integral to the social identity of a settler society impacts on the individual identities (and the stories told about individuals) within it" (Walter 1996: 22). Before an individual can answer the question of her or his identity, it must know her or his collective identity. Therefore, to fill a cultural space and to achieve this identity, life stories are told, "but stories at first also preoccupied with the collective cultural project" (23). Following a similar idea, Marita Sturken situates life-writing between history, i.e. "narratives that have been sanctioned in some way, that often tell a self-conscious story of the nation", and cultural memory, i.e. "the stories that are told outside official historical discourse, where individual memories are shared, often with political intent, to act as counter-memories to history" (Sturken 1996: 31). She ascribes to certain biographies the ability to construct a national image:

> Within national discourse the stakes of biography are high; the meaning of certain life stories helps to shape the ways in which the nation and its history are defined. Yet, there is a way in which biography as a form can be seen to exist in

the porous boundary between cultural memory and history, emerging in the tension between the history and counter-memory. Biographies and autobiographies mark the moment when personal stories are imbued with cultural meaning. (31)

Leaving aside the context of cultural identity and focusing on a more individualistic aspect, Ina Schabert remarks that, since New Biography, the understanding of the biographee's personality has been seen as the main function of life-writing. According to this view, biography is expected to "trace the inner workings of the mind" and to "discover the self as unique unifying principle, to comprehend the individual as 'the source, not the sum of his acts'" (Schabert 1990: 49). By summarising certain conceptual guiding questions for the biographer, Parke approaches these functions from a more practical point of view:

> Translated into question, such matters do, however, motivate biographical research and subsequently challenge biographers to dramatize their findings in written form: How and why did a particular person do what she did, think what she thought, imagine what she imagined? How did the person's private and public lives relate to and influence one another? How did childhood affect the adult life? To what degree is the subject conscious of various shaping forces? How did cultural and historical events and context affect that life? How may these elements, organized as pattern by the biographical narrative, serve, in turn, to account for and explain a particular life and the forms it took? What makes one life more worth writing about than another? How and why does a biographer choose a particular biographical subject? How does a biographer reconstruct imaginatively the subject's inner life on the basis of available external evidence and how and why has imaginative reconstruction come to be understood as the principal aim of modern biography – at least in Western societies? (Parke 2002: xiv)

Parke here lists those characteristics which we are already familiar with from the *OED*'s definition of biography. Her questions deal with the individual subject, historical shaping forces and the literary presentation of the material, in short, with the essence of biography.

Paula Backscheider mainly takes on the biographer's perspective and gives very personal reasons for life-writing. For her, the primary purpose of the genre is "to give a vivid picture of an interesting person whose life matters. [...] For some people, the work *is* the life, but others of us believe that the work is part of a larger canvas, that rich, nuanced portraits reveal quite varied degrees to which the work was the life" (Backscheider 2002: xviii). She lists "intellectual or personal passion"

(31), "'affinity' for their subjects" (33), identification with the subject and the belief "that the subject is misunderstood or unjustly neglected" (34) as possible motives for writing a biography. However, Backscheider also perceives the perils of those personal reasons when she points out that

> [i]t is not uncommon for people to remark on the similarities between a biographer and the subject and to believe that the biographer at some level recognized the affinity and was influenced by it. Whether these similarities [...] existed before the biography was written, were written into the biography and, therefore, imposed on the subject, or were adopted by the biographer from long and intense exposure to the subject's habits, mannerisms, and speech patterns will always be a tangled question. (35)

The more personal the reasons to write a biography, the more the biographer writes her- or himself into the text and those "tangled questions" may estrange the reading process, something Johnson already observed in the eighteenth century.

The functions of biography are multifarious. It can be seen as the opportunity to gather knowledge about the life of other people in different ages and cultures and under different conditions than our own; as the reflection or reinforcement of the (dominant) cultural values under which the biography was written, as a tool for constructing collective identities and national images; as a way of understanding the biographee's or the biographer's personality alike; and as a literary challenge of how to put all these diverse functions into a narrative and imaginative (re)construction despite all the contradictions which go hand in hand with such an undertaking. What follows function is, then, usually form, and therefore I will have to consider some common biographical subgenres which have developed in the course of the twentieth century.

b.   Forms of biography

Different intended functions imply different focuses and, thus, in the twentieth century, biographical subgenres developed which are based on different interpretative models or are based on different biographical angles of approaches. According to Schabert, it is because of "the sceptical attitude concerning [biography's] epistemological status" that biographical alternatives came into being: "The search for a new way of life-writing that would avoid uncontrolled subjectivity has led into several, different directions" (Schabert 1990: 52). Most commonly those directions are summarised under the terms psychobiography, socio- or ethnobiography, imaginative biography, fictional (meta)biography and group biography.

The term 'psychobiography' has already been mentioned above in the discussion of its founding father Freud and of New Biography. For Schabert, psychobiography "aims at objectivity by trying to reconstruct the inner life of a person on scientific principles". As Freud's *Leonardo da Vinci and a Memory of his Childhood* and other prominent examples show, psychobiographies can base their "detailed description of intrapsychic conflicts, both on the conscious and the subconscious levels", on "a minimum of documentary evidence". Nonetheless, this "scarcity of proper material" appears to be the central problem with this subgenre. With only a slim basis of evidence, it is more probable that it runs the risk of misinterpretation or false conjecture. This "disproportion between the scant evidence and the far-reaching conclusions drawn from it" makes psychobiographies appear haphazard (54f.). However, this is not the only criticism towards psychoanalytical assessment in biography:

> The main objections refer to limitations of psychoanalysis as such: psychobiography reduces the person to his innerpsychic conflicts; it ignores the possible historical and cultural differences concerning the structure of the psyche; it tends to conceive of human life in terms of psychopathology; it is not interested in the comprehension of particular individuals but in the confirmation of general laws, laws pertaining to a developmental pattern with heavy emphasis on childhood experience. (56)

And as much as psychobiographers have tried to avoid these errors by, for example, taking into account social psychology and abandoning the clinical point of view, this has mainly served to undermine the claims for objectiveness in their method (cf. 56).

Socio- or ethnobiography, which stresses the outer perspective of a life, is diametrically opposed to the concept of psychobiography. Clifford, the founder of this biographical subgenre, does not distinguish sharply between ethnology and sociology. For him, both terms describe "the complex ways in which cultural patterns shape individual behavior and experience". He tries to distinguish between synchronic and diachronic aspects in biography, i.e. "portraying a person 'in his time', as distinguished from attempts to trace the trajectory of an identity 'over' or 'through' time" (Clifford 1978: 42). Interestingly enough, Clifford views ethnobiography as an answer to the (post)structuralists' questioning of the unified subject which biography usually tries to establish. Biography presupposes a pattern which Clifford calls "the myth of personal coherence" and it strives to make the reader believe in the existence of a self, presenting it as an integral whole (44). Ethnobiography, however, abandons this view of identity and portrays the biographee "as a compromise of influences, negotiated once and for all" (50). The ethnobiographical subject "is a sequence of culturally patterned relationships, a forever incomplete complex of occasions to which a name has been affixed, a permeable body composed and decomposed through continual relations of participation and opposition" (53f.).

A third variant of contemporary biography is usually considered in the context of what Walter calls "new romanticism" (Walter 2002: 332) and to which Schabert refers to as "imaginative biography" (Schabert 1990: 57). Backscheider calls their authors the "British professionals", implying a certain commerciality (Backscheider 2002: 182). In imaginative biography, "factual truth and imaginative vision, science and art" are treated on equal terms (Schabert 1990: 57). It is based upon the conviction that there is truth in the "well-informed, disciplined imagination", aiming "at the comprehension of a historical individual by means of a creative process leading from meticulous research to imaginative insight" (60). While going beyond the limits of conventional biography "in mingling fact and authorial licence, between [...] fact and fiction", imaginative biography is based upon "obsessive, boundless research" and their authors "struggle to make their subjects live and connect to our time":

> This painstaking accretion of fact and of quotations leads in their work to a step few biographers take. They create a voice that is the blend of their own writing style and the quotations, the 'familiar voice' they have come to recognize. Often called ventriloquists, impersonators, or mimics, they quote, paraphrase, and im-

itate, often without acknowledgement. By borrowing the style and syntax of their subjects, they release the 'inner man' and his characteristic public and private personae. (Backscheider 2002: 184)

Examples of imaginative biographies are mainly to be found among literary biographies with an emphasis on authors. This may result from the preferences of biographers who view themselves as writers rather than as mere biographers. They

> consider themselves entitled, if not obliged, to profit from the whole range of literary techniques that have been developed for the purpose of representing the reality of human life. [...] Faced with the far-reaching developments in human knowledge that have occurred in our time, the biographers resort to the innovatory modes of fiction in order to give a more truthful account of a life. (Schabert 1990: 58f.)

Imaginative biographers experiment with "voice and with the degree of the biographer's presence [... and they are] not afraid to reveal some biases and opinions" (Backscheider 2002: 190), paying a lot of attention "to sexual and emotional life, especially as that emotional life is related to the subject's sexuality" (190).[51]

The next biographical subgenre we ought to consider is what Schabert calls 'fictional biography' and which is situated somewhere between factual biography and the biographical novel. For Schabert, fictional biography is "engaged in the comprehension of real historical individuals by means of the sophisticated instruments of knowing and articulating knowledge that contemporary fiction offers" (Schabert 1990: 4). Its authors are convinced that

> through a methodical process of acquiring and gradually internalizing all the information available about a historical person, one may arrive at a recognition of the unique reality of the person. The interpersonal knowledge takes shape as a vision of the other's life and can be communicated as a literary representation of the life. (31)

---

[51] Focusing on anything remotely scandalous in the life of a subject, as Backscheider describes it, is something which has a long history in life-writing. The historical complexity of the term scandal itself indicates "that scandal works rather well as a conceptual instrument for framing and foregrounding connections within and around an individual life that might otherwise remain invisible" (Buckridge 1998: 314).

Nonetheless, fictional biography "does not assimilate individual reality to novelistic habits but rather subverts those habits in order to come as close as possible to the individual reality". In this biographical subgenre, "narrative conventions are rejected as generalizations that work against the purpose of giving expression to real, unique personhood" (32). The narrative undertakes to accommodate complex and discrepant views of the biographee. Fictional biographies "tend to be multilayered and multiperspectival texts", trying to consider "their subjects' varying conceptions of themselves, their memory images, their anticipated selves and ideal selves and the selves they dream of", representing social roles from the subject's and from an outsider's perspective as well (35). In Schabert's opinion, it succeeds where the biographical novel and the factual biography fail:

> By virtue of the creative imagination, fictional biographers transform the documentary evidence concerning a person into a vision of an alien personal world. Respect for the documentary evidence referring to the other person distinguishes them from novelists proper, whereas they share with the latter the confidence in the imagination as a truthful principle for the selection, organization and interpretation of the materials. On the other hand, the respect for the evidence is something that fictional biography has in common with "straight" biography. Yet when it comes to the shaping of the materials into a life story, fictional and factual biographies proceed in different ways. Factual biographers subordinate the imagination to scholarly conventions of creating meaning and coherence. They borrow their formative principles from historiography and psychology. Their methods impose considerable restrictions on the act of comprehending the other as a full person, of participating in the inner life of a biographee. Fictional biography makes up for these limitations characteristic of factual biography. (48)

Ansgar Nünning has called for a broader definition because, in his view, Schabert neglects those fictional biographies which shift their focus from the depiction of the biographee's life to the problems of the biographer's reconstruction attempts (cf. Nünning 2000: 24). His request has only recently been answered by Julijana Nadj in her study of fictional metabiographies (cf. Nadj 2006). She describes this genre as

> novels that focus on the conventions and poetics of traditional biography and thus foreground the problems of a narrative re-presentation of an individual's (past) life. Similar to historiographic metafiction, metabiographical novels raise

questions about epistemological knowledge, the existence and problematic status of a clear-cut fact-fiction boundary, and the possibilities and impossibilities of re-presentation. The special feature of metabiographies, however, is that they link the epistemological scepticism of postmodernism to a foregrounding of another genre's poetics. (Nadj 2006a: 411)

For Nadj, "fictional metabiographies centre on questions of identity within the context of a postmodern crisis of stable subject, author and identity concepts" (411f.). They disclose the claim of non-fictional biography to be able to constitute an objective account of a biographee's identity as a narrative illusion. The difference between fictional biographies and fictional metabiographies lies in the fact that while the former are "concerned with understanding another person's life, using the means of fictional literature", the latter "are marked by the literary staging and the explicit discussion of biographical genre conventions and concerned with the process and problems of biographical understanding". Furthermore, while the former's definition "is limited to texts dealing with 'real historical individuals'", the latter's concept "does not include a distinction between historical and fictive biographees, since metabiographical genre critique is based on structural features and can be applied equally well to texts with real or fictional biographees" (413).

Another form of biography which can be presented in combination with any of the above mentioned forms and therefore concludes this section on the forms of biography is group biography. Margot Peters defines it

> as the interweaving of a number of lives by one writer to show how they interact with each other. These lives may be linked in common by any number of forces: a family, a place, an organization, a movement, a cultural affinity, a point in time. But implicit in group biography will be the notion that the individual is less than the whole, that the sum is greater than any of its parts. (Peters 1981: 41)

Group biography has some similarity to sociobiography, but while the latter deals with *culturally* patterned relationships of the individual, group biography "sees that the course of human events depends less on individualism than upon the endless ramifications of human interaction, much of which is beyond control or even consciousness" (44). As group biography is a form of life-writing that all the other forms can implement, it exhibits no common form, although its presentation is dominated by chronology. Usually, this chronology will be accompanied by the announcement of the theme of place, "a theme supported by place-name chapter heads" (46). Owing to the complexity of its subjects, the major difficulties for group biography are focus, proportion and arrangement. Patterns such as a rapid back-and-forth movement, the *vita-brevis-ars-longa* theme or the recurring theme of place, are some of the solutions offered in group biography (cf. 49ff.).

Biography can take on many diverse forms. The most representative ones in terms of scientific and literary methodology are psychobiography, sociobiography, imaginative biography and fictional (meta)biography, sometimes paired with group biography. However, they are not always as easy to distinguish as it might seem from the characteristics outlined above. Every biographer incorporates to a greater or lesser extent elements associated with psycho- and sociobiography in her or his work. And, as it is widely acknowledged by now that authors of any sort of text rely on fictional techniques, the only difference is whether they do so overtly as in (meta)fictional or imaginative biography, or covertly, as in so-called academic factual biography. The use of narrative elements makes for bones of contention in life-writing, which have already been mentioned in the context of the aporetic character of biography and on which the focus will now be placed.

4. Points of contention in biography

Besides methodological influences on biography, like psychoanalytical and sociological models, cultural myths and adult development theory, fictional novelistic forms have always had a strong impact on the genre as well.[52] Elinor S. Shaffer makes this explicit when she writes that the genre of the novel was at the beginning still too new and too controversial to be a vehicle for a seriously historical and moralistic examination of a person and, thus, not fit to become a model for biography just then. It was not until the German *Bildungsroman*, e.g. Johann Wolfgang von

---

[52] On the relationship between biography and the novel, cf. Rollyson 2001.

Goethe's *Wilhelm Meister's Apprenticeship* (*Wilhelm Meisters Lehrjahre*, 1795/96), that this fictional novelistic form became a model for some of the most artfully constructed life-writings at that time such as, for example, for Elizabeth Gaskell's *Life of Charlotte Brontë* (1855):

> It is plain enough that Victorian contemporaries were more concerned about the representation of living persons in a negative light, while modern critics wish the biographer to be even more daring in her revelations. In this case, however, the biography partakes so powerfully of fictional truth that both sets of complaints seem to pale in significance. In this sense the *Bildungsroman* stands as an 'ideal' form which could resolve the clash between unvarnished fact and edification. The power to shape and transform the facts through an imaginative portrayal [...] was in the course of the nineteenth century accorded, not without struggle, to the new dominant form, the novel, in particular the *Bildungsroman*, and its near relation, the biography. (Shaffer 2002: 132f.)

However, when the novel "left behind the close partnership with truth and experience which it forged in the eighteenth century" and since it "does no longer claim legitimacy through its closeness to experience and truth" (Schlaeger 1995: 66f.), when "in our 'postmodern' age, the collapse of the realist novel has left a gap in the market" (Stannard 1996: 33), it was and in most cases still is biography which for readers has taken over the function of the realistic novel. Nonetheless, Schabert shows that not every form of biography fills this gap or fulfils this function: "Whereas in the realistic novel aspects of social identity predominate in the representation of persons, the authors of [...] fictional biographies [... are preoccupied] with the mystery of existential identity" (Schabert 1990: 37). They have been influenced by the novel of consciousness, whose authors "have preceded the fictional biographers in the revolt against the realistic novel, anticipating their reservations against it as too narrow and too shallow a medium for expressing the truth of the human soul" (36). The influence of the novel, especially the *Bildungsroman* and the novel of consciousness, and the suggestion that life-writing may have taken the place of the realistic novel explain why biography is comprised so much of fictional narrative elements. Inevitably, when a genre that claims to be a precise factual historic enterprise incorporates fictional artistic and novelistic elements, certain points of contention emerge.

One of the most disputed questions in biography is the question of arrangement. How is the subject's life to be told, with what purpose and, thus, in what order? The most common solution is the depiction of life as a chronological succession, because life is usually understood as a progress from life to death. Whereas the novel from its beginnings "has rebelled against chronology", as Rose writes, "biography has tended to begin placidly and obediently at the start of the subject's life, to proceed in an orderly and annual fashion, and to conclude with his death" (Rose 1985: 70). Rose describes the "archetypical biographical plot" which is associated with "conventional chronology":

> the subject is born, has a childhood full of latent talent; in early adulthood, the subject has troubles, but they are overcome; his talent, like a bulb pushing its stalk up through the ground, inevitably expresses itself. And, like a flower, his talent after a while withers, and the writer dies. Too many literary biographies still have as their guiding metaphor the organic image of the writer as a kind of plant, whose genius has a seed-time, an inevitable flowering, and a blowzy stage of decay. This image, and its correlative assumption that the child is the father of the man, dates back at least as far as Wordsworth. And it has been reinforced by Freudian psychology, which we must also hold responsible for the tedious way that most biographies begin with the least interesting part of a writer's life and seem, in some crucial ways, never to move beyond it. (70)

As we have seen this was quite different in classical antiquity, when the presentation *per species* was more common than the one *per tempora*. The modern Western concept of chronology in biography developed in the opposite direction to this. Averintsev makes our "cultural conditions", the importance of our *curriculum vitae* in every day life, responsible for our inclination towards this form of narration. Because the life of nearly every single person in our world is "more or less abundantly delineated in documents available in archives, etc.", our understanding of biography has been conditioned into expecting "a chronicle of the subject's life" (Averintsev 2002: 21f.).

Mark Kinkead-Weekes enumerates reasons for a strictly chronological approach in biography. According to him, "[m]isconceptions show up, puzzles can be clarified, unexpected connections appear, simply through careful attention to the exact sequence and context of events". His main argument for the chronological method, however, is "to resist the urge, so powerful in biographers, to structure a life too early and too simply into some overall pattern and explanation" (Kinkead-Weekes 2002: 237f.). With this method, emphasis is put "on the experience of the biographee rather than the commentary of the biographer". On the downside, however, while the chronological method "does tend to delay verdicts until there has been sufficient exploration of process and development", every gain "will increase the length, slow the pace, and involve a degree of repetition when the eventual bearing of previous developments becomes clearer" (251).

Edel, on the other hand, would leave the choice to the biographer. In the final principle of his four *principia biographica*, he addresses the question of the form and structure of life-writing. He comes to the conclusion that

> [e]very life takes its own form and a biographer must find the ideal and unique literary form that will express it. In structure a biography need no longer be strictly chronological, like a calendar or datebook. Lives are rarely lived in that way. An individual repeats patterns learned in childhood, and usually moves forward and backward through memory. Proust is perhaps a better guide to modern biography than Boswell. (Edel 1981: 10)

It becomes quite clear that Edel favours the psychoanalytical approach to life-writing and while he does not deny that a life may have an order of some kind, he states that there is not *one* single order which can be applied to every life, and that it must be the biographer's task to choose the correct mode of presentation, which is again dictated more or less by the life of the biographee. Backscheider sees it in a similar way, although her emphasis is not on the question of arrangement as such, but rather on the "emotional power" with which the biographical evidence is presented:

> It is in the patterns that the evidence forms that the most important truths are usually found. The difference between a list or a chronology is this flesh and blood, this emotional power, that actually arranges facts and clothes them in meaning. [...] T]he evidence must be presented in ways that make this arrangement seem to have arisen almost irresistibly from it. Sometimes the biographer must be flexible about life patterns, for the power of an experience and especially of memory's work upon it can rearrange the order of events. Something the subject knows or is experiencing in another domain of life can utterly transform the experience and the order in which even individual bits of information are told. (Backscheider 2002: 88)

To her (as to Edel), it is not so much about opting for a particular order, but rather the application of psychological theories that seems to be central as "biographers benefit from the broad field of psychology in concrete ways. At the least, knowledge of psychology's findings function somewhat analogously to historical knowledge". Thus, the arrangement of the biographical material more or less depends on psychological analysis. Nonetheless, Backscheider also realizes that biographers "have strong conceptions of personality and aspects of personality" and they have to "project other models and other categories for their subjects' lives. […] They may go back to their original model, but they will have chosen it rather than fallen comfortably into it" (122).

For Miranda Seymour, an order in life is understood as something artificial, a mere creation: she writes that "[l]ife in the raw is often shapeless; the biographers must create their persuasive narrative by inserting a connecting thread. Subjectivity inevitably comes into play in this manufactured coherence" (Seymour 2002: 264). Alexander's view is similar when he calls it a misrepresentation to give life any kind of order:

> The imposition of order on life is untruthful and a distortion. The imposition of order always requires the biographer to suppress facts or accentuate them, to downplay or omit. This tension between the artistic and historical functions of biography is one of the challenges of writing biography; and a biography is liable to be judged successful or unsuccessful to the extent it succeeds in overcoming this problem. (Alexander 1996: 80)

On the one hand, biographical order, especially in terms of chronology, is thought to be vital for the correct interpretation of facts and necessary to arrive at an understanding of the biographee. It is s/he who, through her or his life with its biographical evidence, allegedly dictates the order to biography. The imposition of any order on life, on the other hand, is seen as an artificial creation caused by subjective decisions on behalf of the biographer. Those decisions can make the biography a failure or a success in the eyes of the reader.

This brings us to two further subjective decisions with regard to narrative elements in biography which are a constant matter of dispute: point of view and voice. Rose sees as the typical point of view "that of the disciple or worshipper – the biographer, in short, who has a great deal invested in establishing his or her subject's stature". However, when the biographer adopts the point of view of the "detractor or deflator, [...] the subject must be special to merit taking down a peg or two". This is also a narrative element borrowed from fiction because "point of view, as any fiction writer knows, can shift from scene to scene, and should, depending on what the author wants to convey" (Rose 1985: 72).

For Backscheider, "the perspective supplies continuous commentary and the voice is a nearly inseparably integrated blend of narration and interpretation" (Backscheider 2002: 5). She understands voice to be "the contract the biographer has established with the reader. More than a bridge, it is the primary signal of the writer's relationship to readers and to content" (10). This relationship with regard to content can, according to Catherine Peters, go to such an extent that

> the biographer seeks to annihilate the distance between self and his subject by taking on the subject's own voice. Identification is no longer seen as a danger, or at least a necessary but temporary stage in the biographer's relationship with his or her subject. Now it is deliberately cultivated to an extent where the two voices are merged. (Peters 1995: 45)

Peters calls this "the ventriloquist biography", a style which, as mentioned above, is usually associated with imaginative biography. But she indicates the importance of Richard Holmes's warning that "all real biographical evidence is 'third-party' evidence; evidence that is witnessed ... the biographer ... is continually being excluded from, or thrown out of, the fictional rapport he has established with his subject". She thus feels that "biographical ventriloquism belongs in fiction, where the novelist is not on oath" (45f.).

The questions of arrangement, point of view and voice are the main aspects of a discussion which has preoccupied biography since at least Woolf. The overall question it boils down to is whether biography is defined by fact or by fiction, whether it is history or rather literature, whether it is an art or a craft. Edel concentrates on the idea of biography as an art. He calls the composition of biography "a noble and adventurous art, as noble as the making of painted portraits, poems, statues". However, whereas a poet uses icons, metaphors etc. and a novelist forms characters out of her or his passions and experiences of human life, the biographer "begins with certain limiting little facts" (Edel 1981: 2). This is to say that her or his obligation to facts limits his creativity, at least, according to Edel, at the beginning. But what happens after the beginning? Why may the biographer set her- or himself free during the course of their work? Edel finds reasons for this liberation in the life of the subject of the biography. For him a "historian of human lives" may not succumb to the many voices of the biographee; biography need not painstakingly record every hour of the day, every day of the year, every year of the life. Instead, it must bridge the gaps which Woolf called "'moments of being.' And what survives can have its own measured eloquence" (1). Does this mean that the biographer simply omits the "useless bits", concentrates on the episodes of someone's life which are interesting and which fit her or his scheme and embroiders this with expressiveness? This seems to be as far away from truthfulness, impartiality and objectivity as the ancient and medieval biographies Gosse and his contemporaries had lost faith in. But for Edel "biography [...] is a record in words of something that is as mercurial and as flowing, as compact of temperament and spirit, as the entire human being" (2). This belief in biography as the possible reconstruction of a human being with all its facets, fragmentations, contexts etc. would explain why biography is obliged to fact, but in obliging needs to rely on the elements of fiction.

Isobel Grundy describes this dilemma between the construction of narratives and life's fragmentariness:

> Biographers have to find the story in the muddle. We work in tension between on one hand the fragmentariness both of lived experience and of one person's knowledge of another, and on the other hand the impulses of writer, subject, and readers to construct narratives, to find meaning, to make sense of other people's lives as we try to make sense of our own. None can escape the constant friction between the narrative drive to coherence and the moments-of-being drift to fragmentation. Even if in principle we accept the idea of multiple selves, as narrators we are impelled to flatten and simplify. As narrators, that is, *and* as readers. Indeed, readers of a life want to feel they have 'got to know' the subject of that life; a biographer who strives to resist oversimplification may be experienced as vague or woolly. (Grundy 1998: 111)

Seymour agrees and names the profound consequence this implies for life-writing:

> We, in our emotional human state, can establish and develop and retain different interpretations of people familiar to us. It is part of the biographer's difficult challenge to examine these untethered interpretations and create from them a portrait which will be identifiable from every angle. A biography cannot present a life in the inchoate, multi-faceted form which is its familiar and daily form. A biography is, in this respect, a work of illusion, a cheat. (Seymour 2002: 255)

When biography turns out to be a lie, why is it, then, that it is practised and read more than ever before? What is the key to its success despite its many inherent contradictions? William Epstein comments on these questions:

> [B]iography is a vital contemporary "arena of dispute" in which important issues can be, indeed, cannot avoid being, contested. This is so because [...] the narratives of biography and biographical criticism are "life-texts", powerful and influential discourses precisely and strategically situated at the intersections of objectivity and subjectivity, body and mind, self and other, the natural and the cultural, fact and fiction, as well as many other conceptual dyads with which Western civilization has traditionally theorized both the practices and the representations of everyday life. (Epstein 1991: 2)

Jürgen Schlaeger, on the other hand, evaluates the success of the biographical genre with regard to the many postmodern theories which actually oppose it. To him,

> [c]ompared with the images of our culture which postmodernism projects, biography is [...] fundamentally reactionary, conservative, perpetually accommodating new models of man, new theories of the inner self, into a personality-oriented popular mainstream, thus always helping to defuse the subversive potential of postmodern lifestyles and strategies for self-fashioning. (Schlaeger 2006: 426)

According to him, on the one hand, biography resists postmodernist scepticism and gives comfort and orientation in a fragmented reality:

> In biography, one could say, an individualistic tradition reasserts itself. Where postmodernist theory detected aggravating symptoms of disintegration, biography tries to provide a cure or compensation. [...] Now, with the pressing need for a reassertion of individualism, it seems to have come into its own. Life as lived and experienced is complex, is a mixture of fact and fiction, of *Sein* and *Bewusstsein* – and biography, this bastard genre, is, as Richard Holmes put it [...], "wonderfully suited to represent these complexities". It tells and shows them.
> (426)

This cure and compensation, however, are seen by Schlaeger only as part of the story of biography since the 1950s. Life-writing has, on the other hand, also become a favoured genre of postmodern minds because

> its character as neither historiography nor literature in the narrower sense, as a hybrid form uncomfortably hovering between fact and fiction, seems to have become more than any other type of text a perfect platform for representing the contemporary condition, a form that seems to accommodate particularly well all its needs for the erasure of boundaries, the dispersal of identities and for heightened self-reflexivity. (427)

It seems to be once again the dichotomous nature of life-writing, what we have called the biographical aporia, which is the reason why biography satisfies both the traditional-minded and postmodern minds at the same time.

By considering the diverse disparities of contemporary biography, it can be seen that, like their subjects, biographers have neither been immune to the literary and cultural criticism of the second half of the twentieth century, nor have they totally given in to it. While some exemplars stay faithful to the genre's roots in terms of the attitude towards and the treatment of historical facts, the biographical method of presentation and the use of narrative techniques, innovative forms of the genre have, at the same time, created subgenres which undermine, contradict or substantiate the conventional biographical idea by integrating or toying with new theories. Therefore, it is possible to deduce from the many diverse forms and understandings of biography how many different roles the subject has and plays in society. The biographical genre is anachronistic while simultaneously being *avant-garde*, depending on each particular author and her or his view of the subject and its possible historical representation, making it doubly "subjective". This would underline Woolf's statement that through biography, the reader learns at least as much about the biographer as about the subject of the biography in question.

III. Biography in Drama

What does the theory of biography imply for Stoppard's drama? To answer this question, we need to relate the genre of biography to the genre of drama – not any drama but historical drama and, thus, its subgenre, which I want to call 'biographical drama'. Its respective conception for the stage will be referred to as 'biography play' and it may also be read, *pars pro toto*, for biographical drama. It will be made clear later on why this study uses these terms to describe the manifestation of biography in drama. But before this is possible it is necessary to explore briefly certain characteristics of historical drama. Only then is a discussion of its subgenre, biographical drama, and its diverse characteristics possible. These characteristics in turn show elements which we have already encountered in New Biography by Woolf, Strachey and Freud, such as the contrast of fact and fiction, the debunking of heroes as well as the psychological approach to the characters.

1. Historical drama: Definition and types

In his study on British and Irish historical drama since 1970, Mark Berninger states that most studies about it start by pointing out the difficulty of a generic definition (cf. Berninger 2006: 23). Usually, they all face the same problem: if historical drama is defined too broadly, the definition defeats its purpose. It then would be almost impossible not to consider a play a history play in one way or the other as, for example, any play becomes historical after a certain amount of years. If it is defined too narrowly, the critic is in danger of applying her or his ideological definition of what is understood by history and thereby will often neglect those plays which stress exactly this doctrinal utilisation on a metahistorical level. It is not the purpose of this study to recapitulate at length the generic historical development of the history play and the different angles of interpretation of the genre, since other studies have already done so in a very thorough way.[53] I will only consider the genre as much as is necessary to establish a basis for its subgenre, the biographical drama. Therefore, as a working basis, I would like to adopt Berninger's definition of the historical drama as it neatly avoids the dilemma mentioned above. He does so by first giving a broad definition of the genre and then by narrowing it down, differentiating between different types of the history play.

According to Berninger, historical drama is drama which refashions history and, thus, deals with the subject of history in one of many possible ways (cf. 47). By dealing with the subject of history he means dealing with the historical past (actions, subjects and objects) and their dramatic representations, as well as dealing with history and its creation process in total. It also includes the dramatic staging of historical interpretations (e.g. that of the audience) and the opposition of those interpretations. Berninger leaves the term history vague because this allows for the existence of diverse historical concepts:

> The understanding of what is to be considered as history is not fixed but rather subject to change and discussion. From this follows that a history play needs to

---

[53] Cf., for example, Broich 1987, which considers the European history play; Goetsch 1973, which, besides the history play, concentrates on English social drama, absurd drama, religious drama, comedy and tragedy, and which does not count religious plays with a historical topic and biography plays as history plays; Hammerschmidt 1972, which addresses the topic of the history play by considering the influence of the historians Sir Herbert Butterfield and R.G. Collingwood in the fifties and sixties on the history play; Harben 1988, which sees historical factuality as the bridge connecting playwright and recipients; Krieger 1996 and 1998, for which history plays need to have a historical topic; Palmer 1998, which looks at the history play from the new historicist's point of view, differentiating between psycho-, oppositional, Marxist, social, local, feminine, deconstructivist and postmodern history; Peacock 1991, which concentrates on the political perspective of the history play and makes historical factuality a requirement; Schnabl 1982, which deals with the socialist history play; and Tetzeli von Rosador 1976, which focuses on the concepts of history represented in the plays – in connection with the historical topic, its manner of presentation and the recipients – as the main characteristic of the history play. The list could easily be continued, but all studies more or less apply certain attributes to the genre and, thus, are too restrictive to apply to Stoppard's plays. For the latest overview of the generic development of the history play and a discussion on its problematic definition, cf. Berninger 2006: 23-47.

> be considered in the context of the understanding of history upon which it is based. (Berninger 2002: 37f.)

Hand in hand with Berninger's wide definition, then, goes a typological differentiation. He first distinguishes between the traditional (cf. 39) or the conventional and the innovative (cf. Berninger 2006: 49ff.) history play. The traditional/conventional play takes the part of the genre-model from which "the degree of difference" of the innovative play can be measured.

Berninger identifies the traditional/conventional history play with the following features:

> Interest in the central (mostly male) figures of history, concentration on political and military events (on what has been called 'Haupt- und Staatsaktion' in German), Eurocentrism, use of stage realism (in the paradoxical form of 'historical realism'), chronological presentation of events, adherence to documented history but with the addition of fictional elements (which do not undermine the plays' claim of historical authenticity), and a subscription to the dominant view of history and the prevailing interpretation of the historical events presented. Connected elements include: 'tushery', the use of archaic speech, 'costume drama', hero-worship, and a tragic plot. (Berninger 2002: 39)

The play which can mainly be identified with the traditional/conventional history play is the realistic history play because

> it contains a mixture of documented material and fictional elements which do not contradict historiographical knowledge and the dominant interpretation of the events. Formal features of the realistic history play also coincide with the 'traditional history play' (chronological presentation, stage realism, etc.). (39f.)

The realistic history play follows the principle of verisimilitude, and thus is based on scientific concepts such as causality, rationality, empiricism and linear chronology, as well as the consideration of psychological or sociological motivational forces. The latter two concepts transfer the natural scientific idea of causality to individual or group behaviour, which is then explained through the individual past or the sociological background of the subject (cf. Berninger 2006: 55ff.). In the context of drama, this entails that realistic drama, especially under the influence of Freudian psychoanalysis, has concentrated on experiences in the nucleus of the family, on untreated traumatic events, experiences of frustration and other factors which influence and explain the psychological conditions of existence. However, the psychoanalytic method has not only influenced content, but also form (cf. Goetsch 1992: 92f.). In this context, Berninger mentions the importance of language as an indicator for the psychological and sociological background of the characters in drama (cf. Berninger 2006: 57). Goetsch also writes that the main tendency of realistic drama is the individualisation of language and its plausible adaptation to the characters, their origins, milieus and particular situations (cf. Goetsch 1992: 11). Other characteristics of the realistic history play include the construction of meaning by the foregrounding and/or marginalisation of certain elements following patterns similar to the 'whig-interpretation of history' (cf. Hammerschmidt 1972: 8) or the *grand récits* – the grand or metanarratives which dominated historiography at least until the mid-twentieth century – and the differentiation between the great, mostly male, movers as the subjects and the faceless mass of the population as the object of the historical process and of the play (cf. Berninger 2006: 58f.).

However, all these elements of the traditional/conventional/realistic history play lead to a paradox inherent in the form. In the broader sense, this paradox consists of the mingling of the formal requirements of realism, the splendour of costume drama, the commitment to historiography, the over-acting and interpretation of certain characters and events according to the rigid ideas of dominant images of the past, as well as of the generally established patterns of dramaturgy (cf. 69f.). In addition to these formal difficulties, the realistic history play has encountered the doubts of the postmodern age about what Linda Hutcheon summarises as "origins and ends, unity, and totalization, logic and reason, consciousness and human nature, progress and fate, representation and truth, not to mention the notions of causality and temporal homogeneity, linearity, and continuity" (Hutcheon 1987: 87). Therefore, according to Berninger, the position of the conventional history play has been re-evaluated through innovative means which so far have gone from the extensive use of documentary and source material to the use of fiction as the principle of truth in the history play (cf. Berninger 2006: 72 and Hammerschmidt 1972: 14). The innovative history play can only be identified with its traditional/conventional generic predecessor through its reference to history, which, however, has become (self-)reflexive by now. The contemporary history play, especially of the nineties (cf. Berninger 2002: 56), substitutes the intertextual reference to its traditional generic form with a reference to the contemporary discourse about history in all its possible forms (cf. Broich 1987: 157). Moreover, innovation has not only taken place with regard to the content, but also to the form. In this context, Ulrich Broich mentions the digression of the contemporary European history play away from the Aristotelian concept of tragedy and a tendency towards alienation, epic style and a rejection of mimesis – even with those playwrights who have not adopted the means of Bertolt Brecht's epic drama (cf. 162).

To bring this innovative change to a point, or rather four points, Berninger differentiates between four innovative variations of history plays: 1) the documentary history play, in which realistic and revisionist tendencies mix; 2) the revisionist history play; 3) the metahistorical play or reflexive history play; and 4) the posthistorical play (cf. Berninger 2006: 78 and Berninger 2002: 39f.). The transitions between the different types are, of course, fluent and represent tendencies, possibly even in a single history play.

The documentary history play relies extensively on documentary material and avoids fictional elements as far as possible: "Thus, the documentary history play often reaches a high mimetic level and places historical authenticity as its first priority" (Berninger 2002: 39).[54] The revisionist history play, as the name indicates, revises formal elements or content of the realistic history play and presents a historical alternative, usually for the reason of "inconsistencies and misrepresentation in the dominant version of history" (40).[55] The metahistorical play or reflexive

---

[54] As possible examples for the documentary history play, Berninger names Peter Cheeseman's *The Knotty: A Musical Documentary* (1970) and Stephen MacDonald's *Not About Heroes* (1982). In their respective introductions, Cheeseman argues that, in documentary drama, the material used on stage must be primary source material (cf. Berninger 2006: 89) and MacDonald accordingly ensures that his information is entirely drawn from published sources (cf. 91).

[55] Amongst others, Berninger names as examples for socialistic revisionist history plays David Hare's *Fanshen* (1975) and Edward Bond's *The Woman* (1978), for feminist revisionist history plays Caryl Chruchill's *Vinegar Tom* (1976) and Sarah Daniels's *The Gut Girls* (1988), for postcolonial revisionist history plays Aileen Ritchie's *The Juju Girl* (1999) and Nick Stafford's *Luminosity* (2001) and for homo-

history play usually discusses different views and concepts of history or reflects upon the mechanisms of historical construction. For this reason, "it very often contains two time levels (past and present), between which the process of history-making can be debated. Metadramatic, metascientific and intertextual elements quite naturally combine with the metahistorical" (40).[56] In the posthistorical play, the emphasis rests on "fictionalised history", challenging the allegedly clear distinction between history and myth: "History is understood as similar to fiction, fiction as historically relevant" (40). Berninger names symbolism, non-mimetic language, non-realistic settings, undefined or unfixed character identities, non-linear chronology, anachronisms and dramatic before temporal logic – i.e. everything which breaks the conventions of stage realism – as various possible forms of a non-mimetic drama (cf. 40). This form of the history play reflects on all those forms of doubt attributed to the postmodern age.[57]

So far, we have established the difference between conventional/traditional/realistic and innovative history plays. The latter we have then again divided into the revisionist, the documentary history play and the metahistorical and posthistorical play. In the following, the main focus will be on the biographical drama by applying the criteria of the history play to its subgenre.

2. Biographical drama: Definition and types

What distinguishes the history play as characterised above from biographical drama when biography is usually considered a form of histori-

---

sexual revisionist history plays Hugh Whitemore's *Breaking the Code* (1986) and Mark Ravenhill's *Mother Clap's Molly House* (2001; cf. Berninger 2006: 79ff.).

[56] As examples for the reflexive history play, Berninger discusses, amongst others, David Edgar's *Pentecost* (1994; cf. Berninger 2006: 192-211) and Brain Friel's *Making History* (1988; cf. 171-192), whose metahistorical character is already anticipated in its title.

[57] As examples for the posthistorical play, Berninger discusses Howard Barker's *The Bite of the Night* (1988; cf. Berninger 2006: 360-372) and Frank McGuinness's *Mutabilitie* (1997; cf. 372-387).

ography? As biography is one of many forms to engage with history from a certain angle, biographical drama is one option to engage with history in dramatic form. While a history play, however, does not necessarily have to stress the biographical, but can, for example, engage with the topic of history on a more general or metahistorical level, every biography play is a history play as the biographical mode always implies a (self-reflexive) retrospective confrontation with the past of a biographee and its reconstruction.

In her seminal study of feminist biographical drama, Stephanie Kramer sees the difference between historical and biographical drama in that the former aims to illustrate representative human beings of one epoch and of exemplary and universal behaviour. The latter, however, is limited to individual life sketches, the disclosure of socio-cultural integration and the relativity of the presentation of one's life as well as of understanding an *alter ego* (cf. Kramer 2000: 56). Like Kramer, Werner Huber and Martin Middeke consider it one of the main characteristics of the biography play as compared to the history play that it redirects attention "to the individual life-story" (Huber/Middeke 1996: 134f.). Nevertheless, they continue by stating that the history and biography play share

> the condition of 'greatness' (fame, notoriety), which the biographical subject must fulfil (great writer, great artist), since greatness implies a certain amount of guaranteed presuppositions shared by audience and author alike. It is only from this common ground that the voyeuristic dimension can be opened up – in the sense of showing the respective artist-figure in a 'new' or 'different' light. (135)

It is difficult to define such a "condition of 'greatness'" because, although a biography may have as its subject an unknown historical person or a person who has not so far stood in the centre of the grand narratives of historiography, as soon as a biography or a biography play is written about this person, her or his "greatness" is established through the act of becoming the biographical subject. Thus it is not so much the "greatness" of a subject, but its part in the general educational canon and familiarity with the work of the person – and the epoch (cf. Kramer 2000: 57) – which imply a "presupposition shared by audience and author alike". Secondly, especially in Stoppard's plays (e.g. *The Coast of Utopia* about the Russian intelligentsia or *Indian Ink* about a fictitious biographee), we now and again encounter unfamiliar subjects or subjects which are not part of the educational canon of a regular London theatre audience. Therefore it is rather 'pre-judices' and stereotypes which form a common ground for audience and author. I will return to the use of 'pre-judices' and stereotypes in biographical drama later (cf. III.5.a).

The term "greatness" used by Huber and Middeke in the context of the historical and biographical drama is similar to Palmer's "traditional shaker and mover plays" (Palmer 1998: 23), describing the traditional biographical concept as referred to in historical drama. Thus, when Kramer and Huber and Middeke speak of historical drama, they mean what we have established to be the conventional/traditional/realistic history play. Moreover, what Kramer calls 'fictional biography in drama' (cf. Kramer 2000: 56) or Huber and Middeke call "bio-drama" (Huber/Middeke 1996: 134) actually summarises *all* types of biography plays, conventional as well as innovative. Therefore, what Kramer and Huber and Middeke compare is the conventional history play with the conventional *and* the innovative biography play – which is not possible, as the innovative forms only exist in opposition to the conventional one.

Kramer remarks that so far, there has not been a common name for this subgenre of the history play. She lists the terms *biographical plays*, *bio-drama* and *biofictions* as possible examples (cf. Kramer 2000: 58) and then adopts Schabert's concept of fictional biography (cf. II.3.b) for her study. In this case, the term 'fictional' implies that, in contrast to scientific biography, the depiction of a life can be modified at will, and that access to the biographee occurs by means of imagination and the fictional means of design. She then adapts this concept to the genre of drama (cf. 59). Although Kramer may be right to apply the term 'fictional' to certain types of biography plays, it does not work for all. Some biography plays, just like conventional/traditional/realistic history plays, see their didactic function in the painstaking reconstruction of their subject's life with the help of sources in order to arrive at a "complete" depiction of the biographee's life. Kramer, however, defines fictional biographies as plays which present, focus on, stage or theoretically reflected upon past lives or life sketches from another historical era by the medium and depictive manner of drama and which feature a tension between at least two time levels (cf. 61).

If we keep in mind Berninger's approach to the historical drama by differentiating between the conventional/traditional and innovative types of the history play, this would also work for biography in drama. This means that on the one hand we have a conventional/traditional/realistic biography play which is congruent with the conventional/traditional/realistic history play but with the emphasis on the individual's life story. On the other hand, we have biography plays which challenge this conventional depiction of a subject's biography and which subdivide into different types. Thus, while accepting Kramer's definition of the presentation of biography in drama, for a general, non-differentiating description of this dramatic subgenre I would simply like to use the terms *biography play* or *biographical drama*.

The conventional/traditional biography play shows characteristics of the *well-made play*. It follows the Aristotelian unity of plot and his concept of the plot with incentive moment, climax and resolution. Additionally, it keeps to the unities of time and space and includes language as a means of the plausible presentation of characters (excluding monologue and chorus), the individualisation of the characters, an intensive plot and the logical succession of scenes following the principle of causality (cf. 69f.). Like the realistic history play, the realistic biography play is mainly identified with conventional/traditional biographical drama. In it, historical referentiality is sometimes combined with fictitious elements, especially as regards the plot or some of the characters. These fictitious elements, however, do not undermine authenticity. Concerning the biographee, this type of drama usually concentrates on the 'dark areas', i.e. the non-documented episodes in the life of a subject. Therefore, the presented story adds to, rather than revises, a biography. In these plays intertextuality and intermediality are not a means of disrupting mimesis, but, for example in the case of the literary biography play, situate the artist in her or his cultural era. The mood is usually non-comic and other forms of the disruption of the biographical illusion are not common (cf. 115f.).[58]

If we accept this form of the conventional/traditional and realistic biography play, we cannot apply the term 'fictional' to it as Kramer

---

[58] As an example for the realistic biography play, Kramer names Alan Bennett's *The Madness of George III* (1991; cf. Kramer 2000: 116).

does, as the conventional/traditional/realistic biography play stresses historical referentiality, and the presented life of the subjects cannot be altered arbitrarily. Fictional biography in drama would rather apply to innovative forms of biography plays, which, as Kramer rightly states, interpret and depict the biographical subject through fictional means.

Kramer distinguishes between three types of fictional biography in drama:[59] 1) the documentary biography play; 2) the revisionist biography play (differentiating between a dominant revision as regards content and a revision as regards content and form); and 3) the metabiography play (differentiating between dominantly implicit and explicit metabiographies; cf. 62). Again following Berninger as well as considering the main forms of biography, especially Schabert's remarks about fictional biography, it would also make sense to speak of 4) the postbiography play. As with the history play, the transitions between the innovative biography plays are fluent.

The documentary biography play presents the events in accordance with historical source material. An eventful, scenic arrangement as well as a dominant reference to the past are typical characteristics of this type of play. The temporal presentation is in chronological order, the plot is teleological and logical in terms of causality, the presented places are used to create the atmosphere of a certain era and the majority of the characters in the play are historically authentic and presented in a realistic manner. This concerns especially the language on stage, which is suited to the respective historical era and tries to avoid anachronisms. Disruption of mimesis through, for example, parodistic and metadramatic elements or intermediality are not elements of this type of drama (cf. 114). As in the documentary history play, realistic and revisionist elements mix in documentary biographical drama.[60]

---

[59] To typologically classify a drama, Kramer suggests nine categories: pattern of selection and reference to reality, dramatic forms of presentation, intertextuality and intermediality, metadrama, representation of time, representation of space, representation of characters and their characterisation, language and finally the potential of its function and its effect (cf. Kramer 2000: 62).

[60] Kramer names Robert Bolt's *Vivat! Vivat Regina!* (1970) as an example for the documentary biography play which, however, also bears resemblance to the realistic biography play and must be regarded as a marginal case (cf. Kramer 2000: 115).

In revisionist biographical drama, the privileges of fiction are applied to the selection processes of the playwright. The selected sources are used primarily to revise, foreground or stress certain parts of biographical knowledge. Thus, the emphasis is put on change as the difference between past and present is accentuated. However, as much as the reference to the present is foregrounded, the dominant reference is still to the past as the action takes place in it. Playwrights often approach the characterisation of historical personalities by debunking their heroes and by iconoclastically pushing them from a pedestal. A formal revision usually concerns the temporal presentation, the form of presentation – especially in dissociation to the *well-made play* – and the use of intertextuality and metadramatic element. (cf. 118ff.).[61]

The metabiography play emphasises the presence of the past in the present and usually consists of two time levels with a dominant reference towards the present. It is not so much the scenic presentation of historical events, but the self-reflexive retrospective preoccupation with the past or the biography of a historical personality, the possibilities of understanding an *alter ego* and the difficulties which emerge from it, which are the central issues in metabiographical drama. It reflects upon subjectivity, incoherence, the construction processes of historiography, biography, identity and questions the concepts of reality and authenticity. The use of anachronisms and the dissolution of logical and physical laws are quite common in this type of drama (cf. 125).[62]

Similar to Berninger's posthistorical drama, a 'postbiographical drama' ought also to be possible. Using Berninger's definition of the posthistorical drama and Schabert's definition of the fictional biography, I want to briefly outline the postbiographical drama as a possible type of biographical drama.

As in the posthistorical play, the emphasis lies on the relation of history to fiction and *vice versa*, and as the fictional biography tries to

---

[61] As an example for the revisionist biography play, Kramer names, amongst others, Claire Tomalin's *The Winter Wife* (1991; cf. Kramer 2000: 167-173) and John Arden's and Margaretta D'Arcy's *The Hero Rises Up* (1968; cf. 120ff.).

[62] Kramer, amongst others, lists Terry Eagleton's *Saint Oscar* (1989; cf. Kramer 2000: 127ff.) and Liz Lochhead's *Mary Queen of Scots Got Her Head Chopped Off* (1987; cf. 130) as possible examples for the metabiography play.

comprehend authentic historical individuals by the methods available from contemporary fiction, postbiography plays emphasise the fictionality of biography, the blurred transition from myth to biography and should present a possible insight into the historical characters on stage. The postbiographical play should not show one single, however fictional, interpretation of a character, but should present the many different, even discrepant views on a person. Multiperspectivity and multilayeredness should be central to postbiography in drama, fulfilling the conditions of the biographee's varying conceptions of her- or himself: how s/he pictured her-/himself in the past, what s/he anticipates and expects of her-/himself and what s/he longs or dreams to represent, taking into account the private and the social role of the subject as well as the role attributed to the biographee from an outside position, which, for example, in the case of the drama could be the audience. It would do so by using symbolism, non-mimetic language, non-realistic settings, undefined or unfixed character identities, non-linear chronology, anachronisms and dramatic before temporal logic. Postbiographical drama would self-reflexively take into account the theories of New Criticism, French structuralism, deconstructivism, poststructuralism, subject criticism and New Historicism as regards the decentred and fragmented subject (cf. II.2.e).[63]

3. New Biography and biographical drama

If we recall New Biography, certain elements of it can be found in biographical drama. Similar to the way New Biography was a dissociation from 'Victorian biography', certain types of biographical drama represent a generic development whose innovative character can only be understood in contrast to a traditional, conventional and realistic form. New Biography could only be new by opposing an old, i.e. Victorian

---

[63] It appears that the postbiography play has no literary basis for its existence, but examining examples from the genre of biography and the history play, the considerations have a theoretical basis which cannot be denied. Furthermore, it will be shown that certain plays by Stoppard, namely *Rosencrantz and Guildenstern are Dead* and *The Invention of Love*, feature postbiographical elements.

tradition. Similarly, fictional biography in drama can only be a revision, a meta- or postbiographical type, when before there existed a form which represented biographical concepts that it was necessary to revise, to reflect upon or to leave behind.

Let us briefly recall the characteristics of New Biography. As we have seen above, New Biography was innovative in terms of iconoclasm and brevity. It used fictional forms and devices and focused on character and central motifs in a life and their psychoanalytical significance for the interpretation of the subject. Freud made psychology the basis for any biographical undertaking, including the subject's sexuality. He emphasised personality and individuality in contrast to a panegyric and iconic treatment of the biographee. Strachey introduced the method of satirically debunking the hero in contrast to Victorian hagiographic biography. He relied on haphazard selection processes instead of trying to give a complete picture of his subject and saw the human being as an individual, timeless person, and not as a symptom of the past. Woolf declared the biographer an artistic craftsman, who utilises the devices of fiction in combination with a factual basis and who needs to balance the proportions of fact and fiction so that they will not destroy each other.

The innovative biography play has adopted the idea of debunking its heroes, though this is not to say that it did so in conscious recourse to Strachey. Like New Biography, it often elucidates the fictional elements of historiography and biography, for example through intertextuality and intermediality (cf. Huber/Middeke 1996: 134). The biographical drama usually does not depict the whole life of the biographee, but presents historical and personal key events or focuses on dark areas. These events are then used to give a picture of the individual subject rather than of the represented epoch, as biographical drama usually concentrates on the psychological and personal motifs of the biographee.[64] Undoubtedly, authors of biography plays are artists who utilise the devices of biography and historico-biographical facts and combine them with fictional dramatic elements to either – overtly and/or covertly, depending on the didactic function of the play – keep the proportions of fact and fiction in balance or to deconstruct the former by means of the

---

[64] In his typological approach, Palmer even calls one type of biographical drama "psychohistory" (Palmer 1998: 40).

latter. If the latter is the case, the factual elements take on a different function than the one they have in conventional biography:

> Life-writing for the playwright obviously takes place within the formal conventions of drama, thereby allowing only "a pictorial statement". Beyond that the biographical facts are primarily used as signs, symbols, or metonymies representing a reality beyond themselves. The hard biographical facts of the life at issue, therefore, "operate as the constituent parts of an aesthetic structure". This function transcends the mere provision of factual information. This aesthetic structure, whatever shape it may possess in each case, is primarily a self-reflexive or "self-referential unit", and the biographical data delineate first of all a specific inner reality rather than satisfying the demands of so-called objective historical research. (135f.)

For Andreas Höfele, the similarities between New Biography and contemporary biographical drama go even further. He sees New Biography "to contain first hints of a literary use of historico-biographical material not in opposition to, but in accord with the disintegrative powers eroding the traditional ideas of history and personality". History and biography were utilised by authors such as Strachey and Woolf "as quarries for an aesthetics of play". Their aim was not "the restoration of an irretrievably lost single truth, but a very self-conscious act of composing variations on the theme of epistemological uncertainty" (Höfele 1990: 82). This would also conform to the emergence of biographical subgenres such as psycho-, socio-, imaginative and fictional (meta)biography, which in themselves present different perspectives to engage with the biographical subject, but, considered in the context of the conventional factual biography, represent in their variety a form of criticism towards the notion of the unique, unified subject and the grand narratives.

4. The literary biography play

Most biography plays have as their protagonists artist figures, usually authors. They "constitute a poetological and self-reflexive *conditio sine qua non* in that they focus our attention on what it means to be an artist and on the attendant circumstances in the creation of art" (Middeke

1999: 3). Such a trend towards literary biography has already been noted in the context of Johnson, Mason and Boswell as well as for the biographical subgenre of imaginative biography. As we have seen above, literary biography was well suited for notions of subjectivity during Romanticism. Therefore it is not surprising that most of the fictional biographies in drama focus on Romantic artist figures, as Middeke notes:

> Turning back to the Romantics as the historical foil of contemporary biofictions is a far from arbitrary gesture. [...] T]he Romantics were probably the first artist-figures in the modern understanding of the word. Similar to what Hegel conceived of in *The Phenomenology of Spirit* [...] as the "inner revolution", the Romantic artists fashioned themselves after the ideal of a non-conformist, independent consciousness that strives to arrive at absolute freedom and, thereby, became icons of the artist. (6)

Middeke subsumes Romantic notions such as "the power of the artistic imagination, the return to nature, the emphasis on wonder, strangeness, and beauty, as well as the Faustian yearning for the infinite" under the term "subjectivity":

> Romantic subjectivity relates to the various manifestations of individuality and especially to the historicization of human existence. Romantic thought envisaged a potentially changing universe as a continuum of past, present, and future, and Romanticism set this view of an organically changing world against the traditionally rigid concepts of neoclassicism. That is why the Romantic era constitutes the starting point of a mode of historical thought that is based upon dynamic instead of static categories, and in which relativistic conceptions of truth replaced absolute and timeless ones. (7)

Middeke names those aspects of Romanticism which can also be found in postmodern thinking, which are emphasised in metabiographical and postbiographical drama, and which play an important role as regards form and content in Stoppard's plays, as we shall see later on. However, Middeke also names a difference between postmodern biographical drama and Romanticism, which lies in the latter's attempt "to bridge the gap between subject and object" (8). According to him, postmodern aesthetic means include

> a departure from coherence, the insight that all knowledge of the "other" is necessarily characterized by difference and affected by perspective and that former teleological, linear forms of representation stressing the hermeneutic

> determinacy of historical truth have been replaced by autoreflexive, allusive, collage-like, achronological discontinuities. (19)

These means are reflected through prevailing stylistic features like "palimpsest, the paradox involved in repetition, travesty, parody, and pastiche" and they run contrary to Romantic ideas of "originality, framing the metaphorical contexts of the past with contemporary issues, questions and interests, and thus necessarily highlighting the difference between past and present, subject and object" (19).

The contemporary biography play foregrounds history not as an end in itself, but in order to provide a perspective on the present, which focuses on contemporary issues. It questions the past and is most interested in the epistemological difficulties which emerge with the undertaking of understanding man, but, at the same time, "it entails the appeal not to surrender the search for such knowledge to the idea of an encompassing relativity and arbitrariness" (19). Middeke here stresses an important point. He states that as much as contemporary playwrights deconstruct their historical subjects and objects, historical reconstruction and engagement with historical personalities are still considered of central importance even for an expression of the view that true, i.e. absolute, knowledge is impossible to achieve. This marks the difference between factual truth and poetic truth, between granite and rainbow. Therefore

> the fact that contemporary biofictions ultimately consider poetic truth more valuable than factual accounts is an echo of the Romantic view of the imagination. [...] In the poetological discourses of both Romanticism and contemporary biofictions stress is laid on the commensurability of history and fiction, which takes care of the possibility that a fictional statement on a particular life may invariably look as committed to real life as an historical account. (20)

Parallel to the focus on the relationship between present and past and the historico-biographical artist-figure, Schaff also points to a self-reflexive component in literary biographical drama, as the playwright engages with the function of art and the artist and their role in society (cf. Schaff 1992: 11). In her view, *Künstlerdrama* – literary biographical drama, following the biographical subgenre of the literary biography – is a subgenre of the history play, but it is more usefully considered as a mode of biographical drama with regard to content, with its emphasis on the aspects of art and artists.

5. Some common literary concepts in biographical drama

As I mentioned above in the context of presuppositions in biography plays on the side of the recipients, I would now like to consider some literary concepts which are common in biographical drama, but, because of their inflationary use in literary criticism, need to be defined if they are to be used effectively in discussing Stoppard's biographical drama. The terms I want to consider here are 'pre-judice' and stereotype, intertextuality and intermediality and parody.

a. 'Pre-judices' and stereotypes

In her essay on biography in drama, Therese Fischer-Seidel justly points out the importance of intertextual devices for many dramatists, especially the device of quotation. She identifies the stereotype "as basic pre-knowledge or pre-text and thus as essential precondition for the adequate response to these plays". Pre-knowledge, in her view, comes close to the term 'prejudice': with reference to Hans-Georg Gadamer's *Truth and Method* (*Wahrheit und Methode*, 1960), she explains it "as an ineluctable condition for understanding and the basis for the modification of our 'horizon of expectation'" (Fischer-Seidel 1996: 198). This requires some additional clarification because Gadamer's use of the term 'prejudice' is too broad, as Andreas Dorschel convincingly shows in his *Rethinking Prejudice*. What Gadamer calls 'prejudice' ought rather to be termed 'expectation', as the following outline will show.

According to Dorschel, a prejudice somehow is and, at the same time, is not a judgement. While "a judgement presupposes that someone has considered and weighed the alternatives between which one might waver in a given case", a prejudice "takes something as decided without ever making clear to itself the reasons for the alternatives". Dorschel agrees with Gadamer's view that the base from which a reader approaches a text must always be part of her- or himself as it cannot stem from the yet undetermined text. Nonetheless, he shows that it does not logically follow that this base should be prejudice and not simply expectation. The phenomenon of dismissing one's anticipation as soon as one makes a different experience shows that expectation and prejudice are not the same when prejudice is understood as "something which is upheld precisely against counter-evidence because it reinterprets that evidence in a way suitable to fit the original prejudice". The necessary preconception of an "intellectual endeavour" has to be distinguished with regard to whether or not it is held dogmatically, i.e., as a prejudice (Dorschel 2000: 57ff.). Therefore, Dorschel concludes:

> Gadamer's account of the rôle of prejudice in understanding is either false or, alternatively, coincides with [...] the function of expectations. It is false if prejudice connotes an attitude that is upheld even when there is textual evidence to the contrary. For sometimes exegetes change their view of a text's meaning in the process of understanding and interpretation; Gadamer himself wishes to allow for this possibility [cf. Gadamer 1975: 366]. If this possibility is taken seriously, prejudice simply means the stance that one adopts towards something when approaching it in order to understand. In this case the point worth making is this: Contrary to that *façon de parler*, it is an illusion that 'the facts speak for themselves'. We can avoid a misleading expression of this point by referring to expectations rather than to prejudices. (59)

For the present study of biography plays, this would imply that the recipient's pre-knowledge, which the drama relies on for its realization, ought rather be termed 'expectation'. It cannot be prejudice when one purpose of the author's work is, as for example in a metabiography play, the deconstruction of biography and the reflection on the construction processes of history because prejudices cannot be deconstructed. Deconstructing prejudice, i.e. showing that the conceptual distinctions on which prejudice relies fail on account of the inconsistent and paradoxical use made of these very concepts, would mean that the recipients actually become aware of their prejudices. However, this is impossible because on the one hand, one can only discover a prejudice after losing it and, on the other hand, as soon as a prejudice is recognized as a prejudice, it ceases to be one as this process requires judgement – the kind of achievement by contrast with which prejudice, in one respect, is defined (cf. 63f.).

In his study about structures of prejudice in modern British drama, Werner Oberholzner expresses a similar view when he writes that in Gadamer's hermeneutics, prejudices are not identical with rigid social prejudices but are rather to be understood as 'pre-judgements' (*Vorausurteile*) or predispositions (cf. Oberholzner 1989: 20). However, as a basis for an author-recipient communication in Modernism, 'prejudice' would again imply more activity on the part of the recipients than would 'expectations'. While 'expectation' always implies a somewhat passive activity – the *OED* defines it as "the action or state of waiting for or awaiting (something)" (*OED*, s.v. "expectation" 1) – the concept of pre-knowledge or pre-judice presupposes a more active involvement on the part of the recipient. The recipient's knowledge, which has been garnered before the dramatic event, needs to be actively applied to the ideas of the dramatist because the communication between author and recipient works both ways.

As an intermediary term between 'prejudice' and 'pre-judice', Fischer-Seidel's concept of 'stereotype' is useful. However, it needs to be distinguished from 'prejudice'. A very brief excursion into sociology and psychology can explain why. Wolfgang Stroebe and Chester A. Insko define 'stereotype' as *"a set of beliefs about the personal attributes of a group of people"* (Stroebe/Insko 1989: 5). With regard to the difference between 'stereotype' and 'prejudice', they come to the conclusion that

> [t]he distinction between stereotype and prejudice parallels the distinction commonly made between beliefs or opinions and attitudes. Stereotypes are beliefs or opinions about the attributes of a social group or its members, whereas prejudice is usually conceptualized as a negative intergroup attitude […]. An attitude is a tendency to evaluate an entity (attitude object) with some degree of favor or disfavor. *A prejudice is an attitude toward members of some outgroup and in which the evaluative tendencies are predominantly negative* […]. (8)

While "attitude" can again imply an unreflected, sort of dogmatic stance, "belief or opinion" is reached through a process of weighing alternatives, similar to a judgement as described by Dorschel.

The word 'stereotype' actually derives from a printing technique developed in 1789. It describes in a figurative sense "[s]omething continued or constantly repeated without change" (*OED*, s.v. "stereotype, *n.* and *a.*" 3. *fig.* a). The first time that the term was used in a sociological context was in Walter Lippman's book *Public Opinion* (1922) in which he famously refers to stereotypes as 'pictures in our heads' (cf. Lippman 1998: 3ff.). Similarly, in the cultural domain, Ruth Amossy views stereotypes as the equivalent of standardised objects. For her, they are prefabricated pictures in the heads and texts which always resemble each other. Contrary to real objects, however, stereotypes are not concrete, their contents and forms are not clear or without ambiguity. Depending on the context and the decipherment, they are being dissolved and reassembled constantly, but not in an identical manner or "without change" as the *OED* claims. The stereotype is reconstructed from a pattern out of the recipients' collective cultural memory. It is a programmed reading of the reality or the text (cf. Amossy 2002: 222). In the field of literature, Amossy adapts the definition of the stereotype as suggested by Herschberg-Pierrot, explaining stereotype as a thematic structure which integrates one or more predicates. For example – and anticipating Joyce's character in *Travesties* –, the topic of *the Irish* is attributed with the predicates *money scrounging*, *jovial* and *shrewd*. Thereby, the stereotype is dismantled into its fundamental elements and becomes a textual construction (cf. 233). This shows that stereotypes function as the basis of an author-recipient communication; it is they and not prejudices which can be deconstructed during the course of reception of a play.

b. Intertextuality and intermediality

As we have seen above, intertextuality is a common metafictional device of biographical drama. With its help, the recipients are actively engaged in constructing meaning during the reception instead of receiving a prefabricated one. Intertextuality in biography plays can be used as a way to illustrate the 'constructedness' of the presented topic and to point out the connection between past and present and the ambiguity of art. Since the 1990s, the term 'intertextuality' has been increasingly replaced by the term 'intermediality', which has often been misinterpreted as being a derivative of its "textual" predecessor. Nevertheless, the debate about intertextuality has always gone hand in hand with different concepts of the term 'text'. In her seminal study of intermediality, Irina O. Rajewsky summarises the two most radically opposed positions. One follows Julia Kristeva's perception of a radical metaphorisation of the terms 'text' and 'intertextuality', the other calls for a narrower concept of both terms, concentrating on the intentional references between texts and their functions inside the text (cf. Rajewsky 2002: 48ff.). I agree with Rajewsky's plea for a narrower understanding of the terms 'text' and 'intertextuality' and for a concept of 'intermediality' which takes these restricted models into account. 'Text' then stands for a written record of verbal sounds and is not to be confused with the hyperonym 'media product'. 'Intertextuality' implies the reference of one text, the hyper- or posttext, to another or certain other particular texts, the hypo- or pretext(s) (cf. 60). 'Intermediality' in general can then be seen as a hyperonym, including all those phenomena which cross the boundaries of media, i.e. all phenomena which, as the prefix 'inter' indicates, are located *between* different media. According to this definition, it is a logical consequence to differentiate '*inter*mediality' from '*intra*mediality'. 'Intramediality' refers to all those phenomena which do not leave the boundaries of their particular medium, i.e. which, as indicated by the prefix 'intra', are located *inside* a medium. Thus, the hyperonym 'intramediality' includes the subsumable concept of 'intertextuality' (cf. 12).

c.   Parody

A term closely related to the concept of 'intertextuality' is parody. Simon Dentith calls it "one of the many forms of intertextual allusion out of which texts are produced" (Dentith 2000: 6). While there are many different and imprecise definitions of the term, for this study I will adapt the concept of parody as presented by Margaret A. Rose and Robert Phiddian.

Rose defines parody as *"the comic refunctioning of preformed linguistic or artistic material"*. The term 'refunctioning' refers to "the new set of functions given to parodied material in the parody and may also entail some criticism of the parodied work"; 'preformed material' describes "the way in which the materials targetted [sic] in a parody have been previously formed into a work or statement of some kind by another". In pointing out the possible metafictional elements of parody, Rose's definition is quite helpful for the study of Stoppard's plays (such as *Travesties*). When, in metafictional parody, familiar literary structures are deliberately "foregrounded", the parodied work "may also serve to bring into the 'foreground' of the parody work aspects of the writing of literature and of its reception in general" (Rose 1995: 52).

Phiddian extends Rose's argument by applying the notions of Barthes's 'death of the author' and Derrida's concept of 'erasure' to question the fundamentals of writing through parody. Phiddian explains, with Barthes's help, that because the perception of parody "is a process of 'entering into mutual relations of dialogue, parody, contestation' with a miscellany of texts and their traces", there exists "no single and unified origin of sense or meaning, and no single role designated for the reader" (Phiddian 1995: 7). He then describes the perception of parody with Derrida's notion of erasure, which "covers the difference between something which has never been thought (or written) and that which has been cancelled" (13). For Phiddian, "the chief value of perceiving parody as a sort of erasure lies in the sense the idea captures of simultaneously recalling and displacing the pre-texts" (14). Both Rose's understanding and Phiddian's extended conception of parody are very useful with regard to the question of fact and fiction in biographical writing as presented in Stoppard's work. Parody, then, can be seen as one of many methods in biographical drama to deconstruct and to question the function of biography in particular and of historiography in general. This can be seen, for example, in *Rosencrantz and Guildenstern are Dead*, Stoppard's first major play and also his first engagement with the biographical in drama.

IV. *Rosencrantz and Guildenstern are Dead*: The Blurred Boundary between Myth and Biography

Surely *Rosencrantz and Guildenstern are Dead* seems to be the odd one out in a study of Stoppard's biography plays. However, this is only apparently so. So far, only Werner Huber has remarked on the treatment of the topic of biography in Stoppard's drama from his first days as a playwright and novelist:

> From the very beginning he has been preoccupied with the recreation of fictional lives and the question of chaos versus the grand design in history and biography. Stoppard's first major play *Rosencrantz and Guildenstern Are Dead* (1966) took up the life-stories, however fragmented, of these minor characters from *Hamlet* and exposed their disorientation, their querying the sense or senselessness – as the case may be – of their biographical destinies. (Huber 1999: 459)

As Huber's essay treats only Stoppard's biography plays of the nineties, i.e. *Arcadia*, *Indian Ink* and *The Invention of Love*, regrettably this is all he can afford to say about the biographical aspects of *Rosencrantz and Guildenstern are Dead*. Therefore, it is necessary to bolster Huber's claims, in terms of theme and of presentation. The play is actually one of Stoppard's most complex and diversified biography plays to date. It takes the mythopoeic quality of *Hamlet* and its myth as a reference matrix for the deconstruction of the audience's stereotypes about Shakespeare's play, its characters and tragedy in general. Moreover, it features "classic" elements of the biography play, such as the debunking of the heroes and the reconstruction of the biographee's dark areas. The central question in *Rosencrantz and Guildenstern are Dead* is whether life progresses through the individual's free will, whether it is determined by supernatural causes or by a succession of accidents. By depicting Ros and Guil as anti-heroes, Stoppard presents the end of a world view that saw history as a drama directed by great men, a position similar to Lord Malquist's in Stoppard's sole novel *Lord Malquist and*

Mr Moon (1966). Hence, it will also be helpful to consider the novel, which was written more or less simultaneously with *Rosencrantz and Guildenstern are Dead*, in order to strengthen the hypothesis of Stoppard's preoccupation with the topic of biography at that time.

1. The biographical mode of the play

a. The *Hamlet* myth as a reference matrix for the deconstruction of stereotypes

It might seem absurd to attribute to *Rosencrantz and Guildenstern are Dead* characteristics of biographical drama because the characters of the play have no historical models. Instead, they derive from another fiction, *viz.*, Shakespeare's *Hamlet*. This curious fact, however, is at the same time what makes *Rosencrantz and Guildenstern are Dead* a biography play. While Stoppard himself supposes *Hamlet* to be "the most famous play in any language, it is part of a sort of common mythology" (Stoppard in Page 1986: 14f.), at the same time it represents the prototype of Elizabethan tragedy – even for non-scholars who have never read the drama or seen the play.[65] Robert Gordon remarks:

---

[65] David Lodge describes the myth-like status of *Hamlet* for the self-image of English literary criticism in *Changing Places* (1975). In the novel, Assistant Professor Howard Ringbaum "wins" a game called 'Humiliation' ("a game you won by humiliating *yourself*. The essence of the matter is that each person names a book which he hasn't read but assumes the others have read") by fielding *Hamlet*. This leads to him flunking his review three days later "because the English Department dared not give tenure to a man who publicly admitted to not having read *Hamlet*" (Lodge 1993: 116f.). More support for the notion of *Hamlet* being part of common mythology can be found in popular culture. In the episode "Tales from the Public Domain" (season 13 episode 14, DABF08, original airdate: 17 March 2002) of the immensely successful cartoon sitcom *The Simpsons*, the characters re-enact a shortened version of Shakespeare's play. In this re-enactment, Homer's colleagues Carl and Lenny become Rosencarl and Guildenlenny. The title of the episode, which also features two other popular myths (Homer's *Odyssey* and the legend of Joan of Arc) already hints at *Hamlet* being part of a cultural public domain. Michael Gruteser *et al.* argue that *The Simpsons* operate on the basis of public knowledge, or rather that the series makes knowledge public (cf. Gruteser/Klein/Rauscher 2002:

> Whether or not one has read *Hamlet* – and the vast majority of people probably know something about the play without ever having read it – Shakespeare's tragedy has an archetypal significance, evoking a theatrical style of rhetorical bombast which in turn suggests vivid if generalised notions about the dilemma of a sensitive individual confronted by a corrupt society. (Gordon 1991: 9)

What Gordon describes here is the "mythopoeic" quality of the play. This refers to the phenomenon that a play such as *Hamlet* tends "to create or recreate certain narratives which human beings take to be crucial to their understanding of their world" (Coupe 1997: 4). William E. Gruber even attests a mythic status to the play and assumes that any audience holds the belief that *Hamlet* captures "the mystery of human destiny" (Gruber 1988: 23). *Hamlet*, then, does not only achieve myth-like status in terms of the genre of drama or of literature in general, but also as a play which is read as an allusion to the deeper meaning of life.

The main characters of *Hamlet* Claudius, Polonius, Gertrude, Ophelia and, of course, Hamlet are probably more familiar to a western theatre audience than some of the historical characters which Stoppard has used in his later plays, such as Tristan Tzara in *Travesties* or Alexander Herzen in *The Coast of Utopia*. Jim Hunter even goes so far as to claim that "Shakespeare's characters turn out to be far better known worldwide than almost any figures from history, politics or even legend" (Hunter 2005: 25f.). In *Rosencrantz and Guildenstern are Dead*, then, Stoppard refers to the mythopoeic hypotext of *Hamlet* and integrates its characters into his play because "[t]he sense of disbelief is suspended to a different degree, certainly a more intense degree, when a new frame of reference has to operate for characters that previously existed in another work" (Chetta 1992: 127). However, by integrating the characters of *Hamlet*, Stoppard does not adopt Shakespeare's character focus. Rather, he takes two minor characters from the margins of (dramatic) history and makes them his main characters, i.e., with regard to the level of familiarity of his protagonists, he exchanges periphery and centre.

---

12). Stoppard himself has evidently become part of this public domain: in the *Simpsons* episode "Girls Just Want to Have Sums" (s17e19, F78065 SI-1712, original airdate: 30 April 2006), he is credited as the author of the book for "Stab-A-Lot: The Itchy and Scratchy Musical".

Jill L. Levenson contends that "Stoppard seemed to view *Hamlet* [...] as a familiar text whose interpretation he could share with his audience" (Levenson 2001: 160). This familiarity with Shakespeare's play and characters goes to such lengths that "any production of *Hamlet* has 'always already begun' before the spectators get to the theatre" (Sales 1988: 17). For *Rosencrantz and Guildenstern are Dead*, *Hamlet* functions as a reference for the audience's pre-knowledge and at the same time as a presupposition for Stoppard to deconstruct the recipients' stereotypes of Shakespeare's tragedy. Furthermore, Peter N. Chetta states that already the ancient Greeks used characters from older works in creating new ones, and that the mythology from which their characters were taken "was part of the consciousness of the entire literate society".[66] In his play, "Stoppard differs from these [classic Greek playwrights] in that he does not reinterpret old myths but rather presents previously created characters in an entirely new context" (Chetta 1992: 127f.). He exchanges alien ancient Greek mythology for familiar *dramatis personae* from a work of the English national bard. Nevertheless, because of this familiarity, Stoppard expects his audience to be more interested in the presentation of the *Hamlet* subject-matter than the subject-matter itself. Just like the classic Greek playwrights, Stoppard anticipates his audience

---

[66] This has already been pointed out by Friedrich Dürrenmatt in his essay "Theater Problems" ("Theaterprobleme", 1954): "Now, Greek tragedy had the advantage of not having to invent a backstory, because it already had one: the spectators knew the myths that were enacted on the stage, and the fact that these myths were public, a given, a part of religion, made possible the audacious and unequaled feats of the Greek tragedians: their abbreviations, their directness, their stichomythia, and their choruses, and therefore also Aristotle's unities. The audience knew what the play was about, its curiosity was not focused on the story so much as on its treatment" (Dürrenmatt 2006: 139f.). – "Die griechische Tragödie nun lebte von der Möglichkeit, die Vorgeschichte nicht erfinden zu müssen, sondern zu besitzen: die Zuschauer kannten die Mythen, von denen das Theater handelte, und weil diese Mythen allgemein waren, etwas Vorhandenes, etwas Religiöses, wurden auch die nie wieder erreichten Kühnheiten der griechischen Tragiker möglich, ihre Abkürzungen, ihre Gradlinigkeit, ihre Stichomythien und ihre Chöre und somit auch die Einheit des Aristoteles. Das Publikum wußte, worum es ging, war nicht so sehr auf den Stoff neugierig als auf die Behandlung des Stoffes" (Dürrenmatt 1980: 35f.). As an example for such a dramatic backstory, Dürrenmatt names the story of the murder of Hamlet's father (cf. Dürrenmatt 2006: 139).

to hold stereotypes about *Hamlet*, its plot and characters, which will be reactivated during their reception of his play (cf. Huston 1988: 57). In this case, then, the intertextual reference to an entire work of fiction has become a substitute for classical mythology in Stoppard's play, even more so as *Hamlet* has a myth-like status in the western literary canon itself. According to J. Dennis Huston, Stoppard's agenda is twofold. Firstly, he juxtaposes *Hamlet* with his own play to show that classic dramatic conventions such as tragic plot, character and language have been reduced to trivial and confused inaction in contemporary theatre. Secondly, and more importantly in our context of biographical drama, by deconstructing the audience's stereotypes about Shakespeare's classic, i.e. by revisioning, reinterpreting and recontextualising the characters and the *verbatim* passages from *Hamlet*, "he loosens the audience's hold on the foundations of their perceptions, skewing their perspective" (Huston 1988: 57). This notion is also central in biographical drama. Fischer-Seidel has shown that myth is a basis of communication between playwright and recipients in contemporary English and American drama. As regards the signification of the term 'myth', both the English and the American culturally specific traditions have in common the topic of history, on an impersonal as well as a personal level (cf. Fischer-Seidel 1986: 21). Furthermore, Fischer-Seidel points out that life-writings have become a substitute for classical mythology in terms of a common knowledge shared by playwright, actor and audience – something which is reflected in the immense popularity of biographies in general as well as on stage (cf. Fischer-Seidel 1996: 198f.). As Huber acknowledges for Stoppard's later biography plays in comparison to *Rosencrantz and Guildenstern are Dead*,

> [d]ifferent biographies constitute the pre-texts or intertexts in Stoppard's latest plays in much the same way as *Hamlet* serves as a foil for *Rosencrantz and Guildenstern Are Dead*. It appears that Stoppard – against all the odds laid on him by postmodernism and the fashionable spurning of *grands récits* – is recouping some of the Aristotelian associations of *mythos* ('action') as a dramatic essential through his extensive use of biographical fantasies and myths.
>
> (Huber 1999: 464f.)

Thus, intertextual – and probably intermedial – references, in addition to biographical knowledge, fill the communicative gap between playwright, actor and audience, functioning as pre-knowledge (as formerly attributed to classical mythology). This shows that the idea behind *Rosencrantz and Guildenstern are Dead* is identical to the intention of a biography play: *Hamlet* becomes the audience's "common knowledge" – both as a dramatic and mythopoeic hypotext and as the "biographical" information about the characters of the play. Additionally, Stoppard's *modus operandi* in *Rosencrantz and Guildenstern are Dead* also exhibits characteristics of the biography play, such as 'debunking the heroes' and focusing on the biographee's dark areas.

b. Debunking the anti-heroes

Rosencrantz and Guildenstern are underparts in *Hamlet* to such an extent that some productions cut their roles entirely.[67] Stoppard, however, reverses this procedure by making "Ros" and "Guil" his protagonists and actually giving them additional lines,[68] although he also cuts some of their dialogue from the hypotext.[69] At first glance, this belated call to fame appears to run counter to the idea of 'debunking the hero' in biographical drama. Nonetheless, in order to debunk a hero, s/he first has to be established, which is already accomplished by the title, "reminding an audience that these two minor characters in Shakespeare have become major characters in another play" (Gordon 1991: 19). However, once Ros and Guil are established as the protagonists, it is not so much they who are debunked as characters, but the idea of them being actual heroes in a dramatic sense. Rather, they become representatives of postmodern anti-heroism:

---

[67] Stoppard does so himself in his *The Fifteen Minute Hamlet* (1972). The one-act play was first performed as *The (Fifteen Minute) Dogg's Troupe Hamlet* on 24th August 1976, exactly ten years after the first performance of *Rosencrantz and Guildenstern are Dead* at the Edinburgh Festival Fringe on 24th August 1966.

[68] On Stoppard's plot inventions, cf. Gordon 1991: 18.

[69] These omitted lines are III.ii.51 and 296-372, and iii.1-27 (all references to *Hamlet* in the form of 'Act.scene.line' correspond to Shakespeare 1974). On the question why Stoppard cut the interrogation scene between Hamlet and Ros and Guil in particular, cf. Brassel 1987: 43f.

> Far from trying to rescue Rosencrantz and Guildenstern from obscurity, Stoppard's play aims to puncture the tragic pretensions of the play from which it poaches and, indeed, the whole tradition of tragedy with its trappings of fate, nobility, pity and terror. If Hamlet is the very imprint of the modern hero, tormented by the vagaries of subjectivity, Stoppard's Rosencrantz and Guildenstern may be models for a postmodern heroism, which is, of course, no heroism at all.
> (Buse 2001: 51)

This anti-heroism manifests itself in various ways. Ros and Guil only receive a brief characterisation in the stage directions. The former's *"character note"* is simply that *"he is nice enough to feel a little embarrassed at taking so much money off his friend"*. The latter, on the other hand, *"is not worried about the money, but he is worried by the implications; aware but not going to panic about it – his character note"* (*RaGaD* 7). He has no desires (cf. 11) and both have no recollections of the past except that they were sent for by a messenger with a royal summons (cf. 11, 13 and 28). Ros also recalls that there once was a time when he used to remember his own name, a time when "[t]here were answers everywhere you *looked*" (28). Now, however, even their names are doubtful. Neither Ros (cf. 16 and 31f.) nor the other *Hamlet* characters (cf. 25f. and 37ff.) know for certain which of the two is Rosencrantz and which is Guildenstern. Ros is also at first unable to comprehend the role play Guil suggests to "[g]lean what afflicts" Hamlet (33). The anti-heroes fail to establish an identity through the simplest means possible, which is their names. They also fail to literally 'know themselves' – and therefore their tragic fate – in the form of their tragedian *Doppelgänger* (cf. 60). They lack Aristotelian *anagnorisis*, i.e. "a change from ignorance to knowledge", and thus fail to bring about the *peripeteia*, "a change from one state of affairs to its opposite" (Aristotle 1977: 46). They do not know where they come from (cf. *RaGaD* 41f.) nor where to go to (cf. 14 and 63f.). They are unable to establish their position in space and time with the aid of the sun, and because they are also unable to trigger any action, they rather count on somebody coming in (cf. 42): "We have no control. None at all" (51). Nor do they have any knowledge of their own, as they only know what they are told, which might not even be true (cf. 48): "Words, words. They are all we have to go on" (30). As much as *Rosencrantz and Guildenstern are Dead* needs *Hamlet*, Ros and

Guil need Hamlet, because "[n]othing will be resolved without him.... […] We need Hamlet for our release!" (87, dialogue omitted). Even at the end of their play they do not know "[w]hat was it all about? When did it begin? […] There must have been a moment, at the beginning, where we could have said – no. But somehow we missed it" (91, dialogue omitted). The consequence to their anti-heroism, which consists of indecision, passivity and utter ignorance, is a non-heroic, non-tragic "[n]ot-being" (78) as it is also formulated by Oscar Wilde in *De Profundis* (1905):

> Towards the close [of *Hamlet*] it is suggested that, caught in a cunning springe set for another, they [Rosencrantz and Guildenstern] have met, or may meet with a violent and sudden death. But a tragic ending of this kind, though touched by Hamlet's humour with something of the surprise and justice of comedy, is really not for such as they. They never die. (Wilde 1976: 950)

This non-death comes to Ros and Guil in Stoppard's play in the form of "the absence of presence, nothing more… the endless time of never coming back" (*RaGaD* 90f.): "Well, we'll know better next time. Now you see me, now you – (*And disappears*)" (91). Stoppard endows Ros and Guil with Wildean immortality by making them the protagonists of their own play. In it, however, they are anti-heroes because, as Karl S. Guthke writes,

> their "fate" is not the exalted one that afflicts the heroes of high tragedy. On the contrary, their grotesque irrelevance condemns them to remain ludicrous figures, even and particularly in their sudden and fatal calamity. Their subjective tragedy is thus transformed into a metaphysical farce; the disaster overtaking their miserable little lives is transformed into "sports" for the gods or for that "fate" that they are so quick to invoke. (Guthke 1976: 124)

This metaphysical farce, the merging of tragedy and comedy, "finds itself unable […] to use the heroes and non-heroes which the traditional dramatic genres thrived on" (136). Hence, heroism in itself is presented as a dramatic cliché, and Ros and Guil become the anti-heroes of *Rosencrantz and Guildenstern are Dead*.[70]

However, it is not only Ros and Guil, but also Shakespeare's hero Hamlet who is debunked in Stoppard's play. His famous soliloquy is re-

---

[70] On Stoppard's heroes, cf. Bigsby 1976: 9.

duced to a mere sentence in the stage directions: "HAMLET *enters upstage, and pauses, weighing up the pros and cons of making his quietus*" (*RaGaD* 53). In the third act, Hamlet is discovered behind "*a gaudy striped umbrella* [...] – *one of those huge six-foot diameter jobs*" (72) and when he spits from the "boat" into the audience, he is hit in return by his own sputum (cf. 84), giving the Elizabethan spitting row a new self-reflexive dimension. The audience witnesses how Hamlet, during the night, thievishly replaces the king's letter (which orders his execution) with a new version which cites Ros and Guil as the ones to be beheaded (cf. 80). His greatest action in this final act is his "heroic" jump into one of the three man-sized casks on deck in order to escape the pirate's raid (cf. 86). Hamlet's death is also non-heroic and non-tragic in so far as we do not witness it. At the end of *Rosencrantz and Guildenstern are Dead*, the audience is confronted with "*the tableau of court and corpses which is the last scene of* Hamlet" (92). When Hamlet jumps into the barrel and disappears from the stage, he is dead as far as Ros and Guil are concerned, and *vice versa* (cf. 87). Hamlet's death is the same as Ros's and Guil's, namely "the absence of presence, nothing more... the endless time of never coming back".

The whole concept of the hero, which, according to Guthke, came into being with tragedy (cf. Guthke 1979: 119), is debunked in *Rosencrantz and Guildenstern are Dead*, both with regards to the main characters and to the tragic conventions of heroism. In a manner reminiscent of Stracheyan New Biography, the marginal figures of dramatic history, Ros and Guil, are put on a pedestal as "protagonists", only to have the rug pulled from underneath this pedestal. Ros and Guil become what is the title of a chapter in Stoppard's *Lord Malquist and Mr Moon*, 'spectators as heroes', i.e. anti-heroes. Contrary to Guil's outcry that they might lose their momentum (cf. *RaGaD* 82), it is obvious that they never had one. Near the end of the play, they stop questioning and doubting, and they simply perform (cf. 78) what is expected from them in the hypotext, even if this means facing their own nonentity.

c. Biographical reconstruction of Ros's and Guil's dark areas with *Hamlet* as a 'primary source'

Rosencrantz and Guildenstern are Dead is unique in that it incorporates *verbatim* passages from *Hamlet* into its plot.[71] Tim Brassel puts this in the context of metadrama when he writes:

> All three acts of *Rosencrantz and Guildenstern are Dead* alternate between the characters' 'on-stage' and 'off-stage' selves. The 'on-stage' sections are provided by incorporating pertinent passages of *Hamlet* directly into the play; the much longer 'off-stage' sections show Rosencrantz and Guildenstern left to their own devices, generally trying to make sense of the 'on-stage' episodes and of their own relationship to them.   (Brassel 1987: 39)

Brassel differentiates between 'onstage' sections, i.e. the passages when Ros and Guil mime Shakespeare's characters, and 'offstage' sections, i.e. when they are Stoppard's own. Or as the Player remarks: "every exit [...] is] an entrance somewhere else" (*RaGaD* 20). What is described here as 'offstage' sections is actually Stoppard's version of what Ros and Guil do before they arrive at Elsinore, before their entrances or after their exits in *Hamlet*.[72] Hence, from a biographical point of view, the *Hamlet* lines can be seen as a 'primary source' from which the biographer reconstructs the dark areas of his subjects, Ros and Guil. Or, as Guil unhappily describes this biographical reconstruction process: "We act on

---

[71] These lines are *Hamlet* II.i.74-81 and 84-97 (as a pantomime); II.ii.1-49, 202-208, 213-218, 220-226, 366-383, 389-393 and 534-548; III.i.10-31, 88-91, 146-149 and 162-169; ii.135-136 (stage directions), 154, 265, 268 and 270; IV.i.32-39; ii.1-30; iii.11-15; iv.9-14 and 29-31; V.ii.367-386.

[72] It is interesting to see in this context that in Stoppard's play Ros and Guil start onstage (cf. *RaGaD* 7), that Elsinore actually comes to them via a light change altering *"exterior mood into interior"* (24) and that they do not have any exits throughout the entire play. Only the other *Hamlet* characters enter and exit the stage, except for the end of Act II when Ros *"moves towards exit"* followed by Guil. Nonetheless, there is no implicit Shakespearean *Exeunt Ros and Guil* – Stoppard's initial idea for the title of his play – but simply *"[t]hey go"*, literally following Hamlet's wish that they *"[g]o [...] a little before"* (69), until the act comes to an end with a blackout. On entrance and exit in *Rosencrantz and Guildenstern are Dead* and their implications for literature, cf. Gustafsson 1970.

scraps of information... sifting half-remembered directions that we can hardly separate from instinct" (74).

The entire plot of the 'offstage' sections contains direct references to *Hamlet*. It explicates the meeting between Ros and Guil and the tragedians on their way to Elsinore at which Rosencrantz hints in Shakespeare's play: "We coted them [the players] on the way, and hither are they coming to offer you service" (*Hamlet* II.ii.317-318), integrating commentary-like information such as the explanation for the "aery of children" (II.ii.339): "Juvenile companies, they are the fashion" (*RaGaD* 17). When Ros and Guil have their first direct encounter with the world of Shakespeare's play, when they watch Hamlet pursue Ophelia, the recipients witness, word for word – onstage in a pantomime or in the stage directions (cf. 24f.) – Ophelia's description of her encounter with Hamlet to her father Polonius (cf. *Hamlet* II.i.74-97). The tragedian's dumbshow (cf. *RaGaD* 55f.) is also partly a quotation of the stage directions from *Hamlet* (cf. *Hamlet* III.ii.135-136), summarising important parts of the plot such as "'The Closet Scene', Shakespeare Act III, Scene iv" (*RaGaD* 59) or the King's reaction to "The Murder of Gonzago", the play-within-the-play-within-the-play (cf. 62), and foreshadowing the ending of *Rosencrantz and Guildenstern are Dead* and *Hamlet* (cf. 59f.) as well. Finally, the third act of Stoppard's play is loosely based on Hamlet's retelling of the events on the ship to Horatio (cf. *Hamlet* IV.vi.13-30 and V.ii.4-62). Thus, while Ros's and Guil's lines and reactions are Stoppard's innovative creation, they all refer directly to *Hamlet*. Therefore, the plot of *Rosencrantz and Guildenstern are Dead* is plausible as regards the structure of Shakespeare's tragedy. The fiction *Hamlet* becomes a factual 'primary source' of reference for the recipients. It is this "factual" reference which actually renders the self-contained fiction of *Rosencrantz and Guildenstern are Dead* possible. However, similar to the symbol of the Ouroboros, of the snake that bites its own tail, this fiction, in turn, is the initial point for Stoppard's deconstruction of tragedy, verisimilitude and biography, i.e. of the very things that entails its existence.

2. The relationship between dramatic fact and biographical fiction

So far I have argued that *Rosencrantz and Guildenstern are Dead* can be seen as a biographical drama because it turns a myth-like fiction into an authentic reference matrix. Furthermore, Stoppard proceeds in the same way as in other biography plays when he debunks the concept of the hero and reconstructs the dark areas of his biographees by relying loosely on primary sources. However, Stoppard, just like the Player, is at least "[o]perating on two levels" (*RaGaD* 47). By foregrounding the fictional elements of biographical narration, playing with the relationship between fact and fiction, and, in this context, using the "biographical facts" as self-referential means for drama, Stoppard does not argue in favour of the possibility of life-writing in an objective sense, but rather questions the concept of objective truth.

As stated by Gosse (cf. II.1), conventional biography consists of two indispensable *cæsurae* in the life of the biographee: birth and death. In between these poles, the progress is usually narrated in chronological fashion. This is also realised by Guil when he states: "The only beginning is birth and the only end is death – if you can't count on that, what can you count on?" (28). Neither Ros and Guil nor the recipients can rely on this, because the two characters simply start on: "*Two* ELIZABETHANS *passing the time in a place without any visible character*" (7). This they do by flipping coins, which continually come up heads. After a seventy-seven consecutive run of heads, Guil is moved to philosophise about faith, i.e. faith in the law of probability: "A weaker man might be moved to re-examine his faith, if in nothing else at least in the law of probability". However, in Guil's further explanations, the coins suddenly turn into monkeys:

> The law of averages, if I have got this right, means that if six monkeys were thrown up in the air for long enough they would land on their tails about as often as they would land on their –
> ROS: Heads. (*He picks up the coin.*) (8)

Guil confuses coin tossing here with what is usually referred to as the 'infinite monkey theorem'. The modern version of this theorem was probably first formulated by the French mathematician Émile Borel in his essay "Statistical Mechanics and Irreversibility" ("La Mécanique Statistique et l'Irréversibilité", 1913)[73] and introduced into the English speaking world by the Cambridge Professor of Astronomy Arthur Stanley Eddington in his Gifford Lectures in 1927.[74] Many versions of this theorem abound, differing in the number of monkeys or the time at hand, but in principle they all say that if a small number of monkeys were to randomly hit keys on a typewriter for an indefinite amount of time, they would almost certainly eventually type Shakespeare's *Hamlet* or even his collected works.[75] By referring to the 'infinite monkey

---

[73] "Concevons qu'on ait dressé un million de singes à frapper au hasard sur les touches d'une machine à écrire et que, sous la surveillance de contremaîtres illettrés, ces singes dactylographes travaillent avec ardeur dix heures par jour avec un million de machines à écrire de types variés. Les contremaîtres illettrés rassembleraient les feuilles noircies et les relieraient en volumes. Et au bout d'un an, ces volumes se trouveraient renfermer la copie exacte des livres de toute nature et de toutes langues conservés dans les plus riches bibliothèques du monde. Telle est la probabilité pour qu'il se produise pendant un instant très court, dans un espace de quelque étendue, un écart notable de ce que la mécanique statistique considère comme la phénomène le plus probable. Supposer que cet écart ainsi produit subsistera pendant quelques secondes revient à admettre que, pendant plusieurs années, notre armée de singes dactylographes, travaillant toujours dans les mêmes conditions, fournira chaque jour la copie exacte de tous les imprimés, livres et journeuax, qui paraîtront la semaine suivante sur toute la surface du globe. Il est plus simple de dire que ces éscarts improbables sont purement impossibles" (Borel 1972: 1702). The title of the essay in Borel's collected works is misprinted as "La Mécanique Statique et l'Irréversibilité" (cf. 1697).

[74] "If I let my fingers wander idly over the keys of a typewriter it *might* happen that my screed made an intelligible sentence. If an army of monkeys were strumming on typewriters they *might* write all the books in the British Museum. The chance of their doing so is decidedly more favourable than the chance of the molecules returning to one half of the vessel" (Eddington 1929: 72). With this last sentence, Eddington refers to the second law of thermodynamics and the according chapter is aptly named "The Running-Down of the Universe". This is also one main topic of *Arcadia* (cf. VI.1.b), where the 'infinite monkey theorem' is again picked up in the context of Thomasina's advanced preoccupation with fractal geometry, this time placing the monkey at a piano (cf. *Arcadia* 47).

[75] Cf., for example, Douglas Adams's *The Hitch Hiker's Guide to the Galaxy*, when Ford and Arthur are picked up by the *Heart of Gold*, a ship powered by the

theorem', Stoppard alludes to a central concern in his play, which is the contradistinction of free will, authorial self-reflexivity, determinism and chance:

> GUIL: It [the coin tossing] must be indicative of something, besides the redistribution of wealth. (*He muses.*) List of possible explanations. One: I'm willing it. Inside where nothing shows, I am the essence of a man spinning doubleheaded coins, and betting against himself in private atonement for an unremembered past. (*He spins a coin at* ROS.)
> ROS: Heads.
> GUIL: Two: time has stopped dead, and the single experience of one coin being spun once has been repeated ninety times.... (*He flips a coin, looks at it, tosses it to* ROS.) On the whole, doubtful. Three: divine intervention, that is to say, a good turn from above concerning him, cf. children of Israel, or retribution from above concerning me, cf. Lot's wife. Four: a spectacular vindication of the principle that each individual coin spun individually (*he spins one*) is as likely to come down heads as tails and therefore should cause no surprise each individual time it does. (*It does. He tosses it to* ROS.) (10f.)

Guil is weighing up possible explanations for the consecutive run of heads which are 1) free will as in willing to have it happen; 2) metadramatic self-reflexivity or authorial intervention as in the neutralisation of the unity of time by stopping it dead; 3) supernatural causes as in divine intervention; and 4) chance as in the even probability for heads and tails. In a similar vein, Brian Richardson suggests four possible forms of causation in fiction: naturalistic, metaliterary, supernatural and chance. He states that "some of the most intriguing and compelling interpretive tensions arise whenever incompatible causal systems are made to collide. This may occur within fiction, as when different characters offer competing explanations of the same events" (Richardson 1997: 38) or, as in the above-quoted lines, when this is done by a single character. The tension Guil becomes aware of lies in the alleged unity of what he calls nature:

Infinite Improbability Drive: "'Ford!' he said, 'there's an infinite number of monkeys outside who want to talk to us about this script for *Hamlet* they've worked out" (Adams 1996: 68); or David Ives's play *Words, Words, Words* about three lab monkeys named Milton, Swift and Kafka *"pecking away at three typewriters"* (Ives 1995: 21), expected to come up with Shakespeare's play. The title is of course already a direct reference to *Hamlet* (cf. II.ii.192).

> The equanimity of your average tosser of coins depends upon a law, or rather a tendency, or let us say a probability, or at any rate a mathematically calculable chance, which ensures that he will not upset himself by losing too much nor upset his opponent by winning too often. This made for a kind of harmony and a kind of confidence. It related the fortuitous and the ordained into a reassuring union which we recognized as nature. The sun came up about as often as it went down, in the long run, and a coin showed heads about as often as it showed tails. Then a messenger arrived. We had been sent for. Nothing else happened. Ninety-two coins spun consecutively have come down heads ninety-two consecutive times... and for the last three minutes on the wind of a windless day I have heard the sound of drums and flute.... (*RaGaD* 12)

The impossible run of heads makes the recipients aware that Ros and Guil are not in a naturalistic or mimetic surrounding.[76] It is made clear that they are in the artificial world of the theatre because the harmony or unity of what the characters and recipients take as the imitation of nature is disturbed by the unnatural series of heads. Only when order is temporarily restored, i.e. when Ros discovers that the coin is finally tails, Ros and Guil are transported "into a world of intrigue and illusion" (16) which is the world of *Hamlet* (cf. 24): "*Rosencrantz* is about to be flipped over to *Hamlet*" (Sales 1988: 26). Dramatic self-reflexivity gives way to the mythopoeic matrix of Elizabethan theatre conventions.

Ros and Guil notice that somehow their world does not work according to the laws of nature or to the conventions of naturalistic art. However, they are unable to realise that indeed they are inhabiting an artificial world and that they, too, are only dramatic characters in two play worlds. They cannot comprehend this as their very existence depends on the dramatic system and thus they are unable to leave it to examine themselves from an outside perspective:

> But since Rosencrantz and Guildenstern are not aware of the fact that their world is a play world, in turn dependent upon yet another play world, they are constantly baffled and confused about the failure of all their assumptions about such matters as the numerical odds of heads and tails turning up in games of coin flipping or other operations of natural laws. Probability is not only absurdly determined by Stoppard but also determined by Shakespeare.
> (Chetta 1992: 129; cf. Brassel 1987: 49)

---

[76] On the metaphysical implications of the coin tossing with regard to the influence of probability and chance on man's life, cf. Lenoff 1982: 46ff.

Because of this twofold dramatic situation they have no recollection of a personal past except for being summoned by a name- and faceless messenger:

> GUIL (*tensed up by this rambling*): Do you remember the first thing that happened today?
> ROS (*promptly*): I woke up, I suppose. (*Triggered.*) Oh – I've got it now – that man, a foreigner, he woke us up –
> GUIL: A messenger. (*He relaxes, sits.*)
> ROS: That's it – pale sky before dawn, a man standing on his saddle to bang on the shutters – shouts – What's all the row about?! Clear Off! – But then he called our names. You remember that – this man woke us up.
> GUIL: Yes.
> ROS: We were sent for.
> GUIL: Yes.
> ROS: That's why we're here. (*He looks round, seems doubtful, then the explanation.*) Travelling.
> GUIL: Yes.
> ROS (*dramatically*): It was urgent – a matter of extreme urgency, a royal summons, his very words: official business and no questions asked – lights in the stable-yard, saddle up and off headlong and hotfoot across the land, our guides outstripped in breakneck pursuit of our duty! Fearful lest we come too late!!
>
> (*RaGaD* 13)

The messenger is the only naturalistic causal origin for Ros and Guil throughout the entire play. Left by him to their own devices they are lost, lacking both origin and *telos*:

> GUIL: We better get on.
> ROS (*actively*): Right! (*Pause.*) On where?
> GUIL: Forward.
> ROS (*forward to footlights*): Ah. (*Hesitates.*) Which way do we – (*He turns round.*) Which way did we – ?
> GUIL: Practically starting from scratch…. An awakening, a man standing on his saddle to bang on the shutters, our names shouted in a certain dawn, a message, a summons…. A new record for heads and tails. We have not been… picked out… simply to be abandoned… set loose to find our own way…. We are entitled to some direction…. I would have thought. (14)

Unable to find their own way, they expect somebody to explain their purpose in their drama. The messenger threw them in at the deep end apparently without finishing his job. However, this messenger is not only the inner-textual dramatic naturalistic cause for Ros and Guil to be on their way to Elsinore, but also a metaphor for the outer-textual metadramatic existence of an author as creator. Ros's and Guil's first and only recollection is that a "man standing in his saddle in the half-lit half-alive dawn banged on the shutters and called two names. He was just a hat and a cloak levitating in the grey plume of his own breath, but when he called we came. That much is certain – we came" (28). What Guil describes here might be seen as the actual process of character creation by an author figure (cf. De Vos 2007: 107). In the case of the two protagonists, it is the creation of Ros and Guil by an author under a *nom de plume*, as Stoppard playfully hints at with "names" and "plume". The playwright here reminds the recipients of three points: 1) that his birth name is Tomáš Sträussler,[77] making 'Tom Stoppard' his pen name; 2) of the question of authorship of Shakespeare's plays and the *Ur-Hamlet*; and 3) that *Rosencrantz and Guildenstern are Dead* is based on a play by another author. Stoppard's Ros and Guil have received their names and limited identity originally from Shakespeare: "We can't afford anything quite so arbitrary. Nor did we come all this way for a christening. All *that* – preceded us" (28). What Shakespeare did not do, however, was to furnish them with an offstage life. The same is true for an enacted death or a life after *Hamlet*. That is why in *Rosencrantz and Guildenstern are Dead* Ros and Guil do not die but simply disappear at the end of the play. Contrary to a biographical subject with its "natural" *cæsurae* of birth and death, Ros and Guil simply start on and simply end off.

Ros and Guil are not amnesiacs, which would be the good news for them, as Hunter states, but they have no existence prior to, after or outside their performance: "Their growing terror is that in fact they have no life offstage" (Hunter 2005: 53). They do not possess a past or a future, they only have their moment in time:

GUIL: Yes, one must think of the future.
ROS: It's the normal thing.
GUIL: To have one. One is, after all, having it all the time… now… and now… and now…. (*RaGaD* 50)

---

[77] For a brief overview of Stoppard's life, cf. Delaney 2001.

Ros and Guil lack everything which conventionally constitutes an identity in biography, such as a name, a past and a future, or more precisely a unique character, a history and a *telos* in life. Their present state of being is like living in a box, just as Ros describes: "Do you ever think of yourself as actually *dead*, lying in a box with a lid on it?" (50). This "timelessness" of their characters is also the reason why Ros cannot believe in England or cannot imagine them both landing there, as this would presuppose a future: "But my mind remains a blank. No. We're slipping off the map. [...] We drift down time, clutching at straws. But what good's a brick to a drowning man?" (78, dialogue omitted).

The drama *Rosencrantz and Guildenstern are Dead* and thus the alleged reconstruction of Ros's and Guil's "life episodes" in between scenes of *Hamlet* is an artificial construct, as Stoppard makes abundantly clear. Biography is shown to be nothing more than the artistic creation by an author figure saturated with intertextual allusions. Therefore, the play draws not only on Shakespeare's *Hamlet*,[78] but also on Samuel Beckett's *Waiting for Godot* (*En Attendant Godot*, 1953),[79] Luigi Pirandello's *Six Characters in Search of an Author* (*Sei Personaggi in Cerca d'Autore*, 1921) and *Henry IV* (*Enrico IV*, 1921),[80] Wilde's *De Profundis* and T.S. Eliot's poem "The Love Song of J. Alfred Prufrock" (1915),[81] to name only a few.[82] Intertextual allusions become the dominant pattern for the construction of Ros's and Guil's dark areas.

---

[78] Cf., for example, Makowski 1980, which establishes *Rosencrantz and Guildenstern are Dead* as a play not necessarily dependent on *Hamlet*, especially with regard to the fabrication and refraction of fiction.

[79] Cf., for example, Callen 1969, which points out the French influences on *Rosencrantz and Guildenstern are Dead*; Londré 1981, which sees Shakespeare's "complex, richly textured tragedy" and Beckett's "spare, lean, abstract tragicomedy" (34) as the main influences on *Rosencrantz and Guildenstern are Dead*; Sales 1988, which sees Stoppard exchanging theatrical Renaissance stereotypes with modern ones such as the tramp figures Vladimir and Estragon (cf. 140), and which sees *Rosencrantz and Guildenstern are Dead* as a parody of *Waiting for Godot* (cf. 147); and Broich 1993, which also views Didi and Gogo as role models for Ros and Guil (cf. 423f.).

[80] Cf., for example, Tandello 1993, which offers a 'Pirandellian' reading of the structure of *Rosencrantz and Guildenstern are Dead*. Stoppard himself adapted Pirandello's *Henry IV* in 2004.

Like the *mise en abîme* structure of the play *Rosencrantz and Guildenstern are Dead* in the play *Hamlet*, biography is reduced to a fictional recollection of a fictional life, i.e. having no objective historical basis of the reconstruction of a life. *Hamlet*, the "biographical data" behind *Rosencrantz and Guildenstern are Dead*, delineates, then, primarily a specific inner reality, which is metadramatic and metabiographical.

The only character aware of Ros's and Guil's *conditio fictionalis* is the Player. He recognises them "as fellow artists" (16) who are, just as the six tragedians, not real people: "We're *actors* – we're the opposite of people!" (45). The Player is also aware of the common assumption about the mythopoeic quality of *Hamlet* and about drama in general when he states that "we [the tragedians] keep to our usual stuff, more or less, only inside out. We do on stage the things that are supposed to happen off" (20). That is why the Player is "[a]lways in character" (24). Contrary to Ros and Guil, the Player is in full control of himself at all times on the stage: "I can come and go as I please" (47). He knows what end awaits Ros and Guil (cf. 47, 57 and 60) because he knows the artistic conventions and the design behind drama: "There's a design at work in all art – surely you know that? Events must play themselves out to aesthetic, moral and logical conclusion" (57). Nobody in this drama has a choice, no one decides as "[i]t is *written*": "We're tragedians, you see. We follow directions – there is no *choice* involved. The bad end unhappily, the good unluckily. That is what tragedy means" (58). With this variation of a line from Wilde's *The Importance of Being Earnest* (1895) in which Miss Prism states about her never published three-volume novel that "[t]he good ended happily, and the bad unhappily. That is what Fiction means" (Wilde 1976: 341), the Player makes clear that a

---

[81] Cf., for example, Rusinko 1986, which sees Stoppard borrowing the idea of the 'still point' from Eliot (cf. 34f.); Brassel 1987, which sees in Eliot's poem the real origin of *Rosencrantz and Guildenstern are Dead* (cf. 67); and Gordon 1991, which sees Eliot extending Wilde's "notion of the insignificance of Hamlet's college friends" taken up by Stoppard (cf. 12f.).

[82] Cf. furthermore, for example, Brassel 1987, which names also William Schwenk Gilbert's burlesque *Rosencrantz and Guildenstern* (1874) and Franz Kafka (cf. 46 and 67). Boldizsár Fejérvári even goes so far as to claim that Christopher Marlowe's *Edward II* (c1592) interacts with *Rosencrantz and Guildenstern are Dead* (cf. Fejérvári 2003).

tragedy such as *Hamlet* is a fiction constructed to meet certain dramatic principles that are Aristotelian. They are, as regards the end of "men who are necessarily either of good or of bad character" (Aristotle 1977: 33), that the "change in fortune will be, not from misery to prosperity, but the reverse, from prosperity to misery" (48), and, as regards the scope of the plot, that "tragedy is the representation of an action that is complete and whole and of a certain amplitude [...]. Now a whole is that which has a beginning, a middle, and an end" (41). Furthermore, according to Aristotle, tragic poetry is a form "of imitation or representation" (31). Its function is to describe "the kinds of thing that might happen, that is, that could happen because they are, in the circumstances, either probable or necessary"; it is concerned with "universal truths" (43f.). Accordingly, when it comes to drama, Ros wants "a good story, with a beginning, middle and end" and Guil prefers "art to mirror life" (*RaGaD* 58). Both wishes are all the same to the Player as they constitute Aristotelian mimesis and as Guil's is also in accordance with Hamlet's description to the Player about the purpose of playing, i.e. "to hold as 'twere the mirror up to nature" (*Hamlet* III.ii.21-22).[83] This kind of mimesis is of course in itself not authentic in its relation to nature *because* it follows Aristotelian conventions, which are an artificial set of rules themselves. Nevertheless, it is the kind of realism which an audience is conditioned to believe in, as is explained by the Player in the context of staged death:

> GUIL: (*fear, derision*): Actors! The mechanics of cheap melodrama! That isn't *death*! (*More quietly.*) You scream and choke and sink to your knees, but it doesn't bring death home to anyone – it doesn't catch them unawares and start the whisper in their skulls that says – "One day you are going to die." (*He straightens up.*) You die so many times; how can you expect them to believe in your death?
> PLAYER: On the contrary, it's the only kind they do believe. They're conditioned to it. [...] Audiences know what to expect, and that is all that they are prepared to believe in. (61)

---

[83] In "The Decay of Lying" (1889), Wilde has Vivian explain that Shakespeare's "unfortunate aphorism about Art holding the mirror up to Nature, is deliberately said by Hamlet in order to convince the bystanders of his absolute insanity in all art-matters" (Wilde 1976: 981). This insanity is taken up by Guil in *Rosencrantz and Guildenstern are Dead* when he stabs the Player.

Nonetheless, Guil is not convinced. With a dagger at the Player's throat he desperately wants to differentiate between dramatic reality and authentic reality. And because he wishes his existence to be real, he expects death to be real as well, something not even the tragedians could know, as it is a once in a life time experience:

> I'm talking about death – and you've never experienced *that*. And you cannot *act* it. You die a thousand casual deaths – with none of that intensity which squeezes out life... and no blood runs cold anywhere. Because even as you die you know that you will come back in a different hat. But no one gets up after *death* – there is no applause – there is only silence and some second-hand clothes, and that's – *death* –
> (*And he pushes the blade in up to the hilt. The* PLAYER *stands with huge, terrible eyes, clutches at the wound as the blade withdraws: he makes small weeping sounds and falls to his knees, and then right down:*)
> (*While he is dying,* GUIL [... *is*] *nervous, high, almost hysterical* [...]) (89)

However, Guil's own expectations about death are "disappointed" when the Player suddenly seems to cheat it:

> (*The* TRAGEDIANS *watch the* PLAYER *die: they watch with some interest. The* PLAYER *finally lies still. A short moment of silence. Then the* TRAGEDIANS *start to applaud with genuine admiration. The* PLAYER *stands up, brushing himself down.*)
> PLAYER (*modestly*): Oh, come, come, gentlemen – no flattery – it was merely competent–
> (*The* TRAGEDIANS *are still congratulating him. The* PLAYER *approaches* GUIL, *who stands rooted, holding the dagger.*)
> What did you think? (*Pause.*) You see, it *is* the kind they do believe in – it's what is expected.
> (*He holds his hand out for the dagger.* GUIL *slowly puts the point of the dagger on to the* PLAYER's *hand, and pushes... the blade slides back into the handle. The* PLAYER *smiles, reclaims the dagger.*)
> For a moment you thought I'd – cheated. (90)

Stoppard here cleverly deconstructs the audience's stereotypical assumptions about drama in a twofold manner. Firstly, contrary to the audience's expectations, Guil's sudden act of desperate violence comes unexpectedly in a play that resolves the brutality of *Hamlet* such as the slaying of Polonius merely in the play-within-the-play-within-the-play (cf. 59 and 90). The sudden gust of seriousness and brutality "ambushes" the audience's expectations about the farce of *Rosencrantz and*

Guildenstern are Dead in contrast to the tragedy of *Hamlet*, where such an incident would be plausible. And because of this, the recipients accept the "reality" of Player's death within the dramatic framework of the Elizabethan tragedy. They believe, as Ros has told them at the end of the second act, that "anything could happen yet" (69; cf. Pankratz 2005: 99f.). Secondly, then, with the Player's "resurrection", which again reverses the now tragic tone of the play back to the farcical, Stoppard returns to the initial audience expectation, which is death as fake fiction. In this twofold deconstruction of audience's stereotypes he reveals the Elizabethan dramatic style as "theatrical sham" (Holubetz 1982: 428) and proves his point that only that is real which is accepted as such by the spectators. This is similar to Guil's notion about colours and his parable of the unicorn. He explains that reality does not equal truth. Rather, it is a "mystical experience shared by everybody" (*RaGaD* 14) like the colour yellow which, although it is not a primary colour, man perceives as one.[84] Reality is the majority opinion, "mystical encounters" (14) spread thin and become reasonable like seeing a unicorn. The more who see the unicorn, the more it ceases to be true because reason changes it to a "horse with an arrow in its forehead". Truth alters to reality, "the name we give to the common experience" (15). Or as one of

---

[84] In the RGB colour model by Thomas Young (1773-1829) and Hermann von Helmholtz (1821-1894) which to this day is used to explain man's colour vision, yellow is created by mixing the two primary colours red and green (the third "real" colour in this model being blue, hence RGB). Although yellow appears as a primary colour in the eye of the beholder, it is actually created in the brain by an additive colour mixing because the retina does not possess special cones for the yellow wave length, but only for red, green and blue. However, the 'opponent theory of colour vision' by Ewald Hering (1834-1918) takes into consideration that there are four basic colour perceptions despite the lack of one corresponding cone. In this model, the four 'physiological primary colours' are arranged into the two opposing pairs blue and yellow, green and red, complemented by black and white for intensity. Since 1966 neurophysiological research results have confirmed this theory, leading to the now accepted notion that excitation activities through light impulses on the retina work according to the Young-Helmholtz theory, but the processing into colour perceptions occurs according to Hering's theory through neural processes (cf. Welsch/Liebmann 2003: 227f.). As regards Guil's "mystical experience" of the colour yellow, it is also interesting to note that yellow is symbolically seen as both the colour of ignominy and deity (cf. 75).

Wilde's "Phrases and Philosophies for the Use of the Young" (1894) puts it: "A truth ceases to be true when more than one person believes in it" (Wilde 1976: 1205).

Throughout *Rosencrantz and Guildenstern are Dead* it is emphasised that objective truth does not exist, not in life, not in biography and not in drama. There is only subjective truth. Objective truth or reality is merely the majority coming to an agreement. Drama is shown to be not the mirror of nature, but rather the mirror of the construction process of nature. As the Player says,

> [f]or all anyone knows, nothing is [true]. Everything has to be taken on trust; truth is only that which is taken to be true. It's the currency of living. There may be nothing behind it, but it doesn't make any difference so long as it is honoured. One acts on assumptions. (*RaGaD* 48)

In the case of Stoppard's play, mimetic art is nothing more than a contract between the actors and the audience to accept the artificial as reality for the short duration of the performance. It is this assumption that Stoppard deconstructs in *Rosencrantz and Guildenstern are Dead* by relating the fiction *Hamlet* to alleged biographical fact and again to the fiction of his own play. Biography becomes subjective fiction, which only relies on assumptions about truth but lacks any factual basis for the objective reconstruction of a life.

3. Reasoning from novel to play: The topic of biography in *Lord Malquist and Mr Moon*

Stoppard's first and only novel *Lord Malquist and Mr Moon* was published in the same year as the revision of his one-act play *Rosencrantz and Guildenstern Meet King Lear* (1964) was performed at the Edinburgh Festival. According to Stoppard's introduction in the latest edition of his novel, *Lord Malquist and Mr Moon* was written as soon as he had finished *Rosencrantz and Guildenstern are Dead* and while writing the radio serial *A Student's Diary* about an Arab medical student in London for the BBC World Service (cf. *LMaMM* vii). The novel, then, originated at the same stage of creation as did *Rosencrantz and Guilden-*

stern are Dead, on which he also must have worked after the novel's publication if one compares the circular ending of the first edition of the play (cf. Brassel 1987: 270f.) with the linear ending in the editions afterwards. Therefore, it will be useful for the understanding of what preoccupied the author during the time of the creation of *Rosencrantz and Guildenstern are Dead* to consider his novel and its leitmotifs in relation to his play.

Stoppard, who has always thought of himself as an erratic writer "whose plays had much more to disconnect than to connect them", has himself started to notice "the conscious and unconscious recycling" in his work (*LMaMM* viii). He especially draws on the connection between *Lord Malquist and Mr Moon* and *Rosencrantz and Guildenstern are Dead* when he hints at the line *"I clutch at straws, but what good's a brick to a drowning man?"* as used in both works (52 and *RaGaD* 78), and when he states:

> 'We're spectators,' says Rosencrantz to Guildenstern, or the other way round, and the chapter heading [in *Lord Malquist and Mr Moon*] 'Spectator as Hero' would have done well enough as a title for the novel or the play, and even for the author's philosophy of art in those happy days.　　　　　　(*LMaMM* viii)

For these reasons, I will briefly touch on the topic of biography in Stoppard's novel to indicate that life-writing has been a major theme in his work ever since *Rosencrantz and Guildenstern are Dead*.

Biography is an unobtrusive but nevertheless omnipresent topic throughout the entire novel. The relationship between Lord Malquist and Moon is that of Johnson and Boswell. The difference, however, is that Moon is not writing a biography about Lord Malquist because of his extraordinary personality, but rather because Lord Malquist has engaged "the services of Boswell Incorporated", i.e. Moon, on the terms of "two thousand guineas per annum" to record his "pensées and general observations, travels, etc., fully and fairly" (*LMaMM* 78). Boswell Inc. is a company which offers a kind of "life after death" as advertised on Moon's business card:

> BOSWELL INC.
> If you wake up feeling witty, if
> you are ready to impart your wis-
> dom to the world, don't count on

> word of mouth, don't lose the cre-
> dit. Send for Our Man Boswell,
> chronicler of the time, to dog
> your footsteps, record your word.
> Posterity assured. Copyright
> respected. Publication arranged.
> Two transcripts supplied.
> *'I am nearly dead and no one knows
> I was ever alive'* – Anon.
> Ten guineas per day. Weekly terms. (57)

The business card illustrates Moon's understanding of biography. While the original Boswell's explanation for having written a biography about Johnson is that he "has been equalled by few in any age" (Boswell 1952: 1), Boswell Inc. is a purely for-profit organisation that offers its services to anybody who is self-confident enough and well-off, such as Lord Malquist – were it not that his self-confidence amounts to vanity, and that his cheque bounces (cf. *LMaMM* 187). And it is Lord Malquist who points out the difference between Moon and Boswell: "Your illustrious namesake wasn't in it for the money. To be seen in such company was enough" (187). But this is news to Moon, who has not even read Boswell's biography of Johnson (cf. 137).

Also, quite unlike Boswell, who traced Johnson's life as distinctly as possible, year by year, and produced his own minutes, letters and conversations, Moon does not pay much attention to his subject's wit and wisdom and is rather untalented in taking down any minutes of conversations with Lord Malquist in his notebook:

> Moon, snatching at the tail-ends of recollection, trusting the echo in his skull to reproduce a meaning that had not touched him, scribbled with a kindergarten fist against the sway, and caught up – *the comic inaccuracy of his remark* – before the turn into Cockspur Street dragged his pen arabesque across the page. (8)

Sentences by Lord Malquist such as "Against such vast immutability the human struggle takes place on the same scale as the insect movements in the grass" (8) and "I am an island, Mr Moon, and when the bell tolls it tolls for thee" become in Moon's notebook a confusing *"Vast immutability of insects"* and *"send not for whom the bell tolls, etc."* (9). The process of conserving his biographee's utterings is frustrated ultimately when Moon's notebook goes up in flames (cf. 89). The whole sixth chapter, entitled *"Chronicler of the Time"*, constitutes Moon's attempt to recollect the circumstances of the first encounter with Lord Malquist and their first business meeting as biographer and biographee. This recollection, however, is more about appearances and events than about the personality of his subject as Moon's memory constantly fails: "I find it very difficult now to capture the flavour of his conversation, or to recall the actual words he used, or to recollect exactly what he talked about" (98). Moon again muddles up different remarks by Lord Malquist:

> Lord Malquist talked wittily about greatness and dignity – I wish I could reproduce the light touch he had with words. I recall that he mentioned a certain French king – one of the Louis I believe – who said that 'nothing' was the history of the world. [...] Lord Malquist was reminded that Lord Nelson had copied his clothes from those worn by one of his (Lord Malquist's) ancestors, I believe. Lord Malquist also quoted from the poets, 'No man is an island, etc.'
> (100)

All these alleged facts are wrong. At the very beginning of the novel, Lord Malquist stated that "[o]n the day the Bastille fell Louis XVI of France returned home from the hunt and wrote in his private diary, *Rien*" and that "Nothing [...] is the history of the world viewed from a suitable distance" (8). He also told Moon that the boots worn by Wellington at the battle of Waterloo were originally Malquist boots (cf. 9), and he actually altered some lines from John Donne's Meditation XVII from *Devotions Upon Emergent Occasions* (1624) in order to underline his conviction that he is only interested in himself because "[p]eople are not the world, they are merely a recent and transitory product of it. [...] And yet man persists in behaving as though he were the beginning and the end. What a presumption" (188).

Moon's "posterity business" is only "a sideline" (56) because he actually sees himself as a historian. His aim is nothing less than to write a history of the world, just like H.G. Wells's work of the same title which depicts "[h]uman history [... as] one history and human welfare [... as] one whole", seeing history as "the drama of the great necessities for human unity struggling with the narrow purposes and egotisms of mankind" (Wells 1927: 12). For Moon, the reason for his undertaking is to understand his own person as to him everything is causally connected:

> He had not meant to write a history of the world at all, at the beginning, merely to examine his own history and the causes that determined it. The rest of the world intruded itself in a cause-and-effect chain reaction that left him appalled at its endlessness; he experienced a vision of the billion connecting moments that lay behind and led to his simplest action, a vision of himself straightening his tie as the culminating act of a sequence that fled back into pre-history and began with the shift of a glacier. (*LMaMM* 68)

The ultimate purpose of his undertaking is *"to discover whether we live and die by accident or design"* and to do so *"you must be prepared to go back to Babylon; because everything connects back, to the beginning of the history of the world"* (69).[85] Moon's method is to organise history into what Wells calls "the elements of history" (Wells 1927: 6), i.e. into "sequences, and categories… science, wars, law, commerce…" (*LMaMM* 139). When Moon has got everything he

> can put it all down in the form of a big chart, all over a wall, with different races and so on, so you can see where things cross and where they join up, so you can relate all the things to each other, and this great map will be a kind of skeleton to my book – like a diagram of everything that counts, so it might be possible to discover the grand design, find out if there is one, or if it's all random – if there's anything to it. (139)

His grand plan, however, is questioned by the Malquists. Lady Malquist does not understand why Moon is so eager to find out whether it is all random or inevitable, as for her discovering that life goes one way or the other would not make it any more meaningful: "There doesn't have to be a point at all, Bosie. [...] No point at all. You have to provide your own. Enter God. For instance" (140). Nor does Lord Malquist see the

---

[85] A very similar project is undertaken by the character named Bone in Stoppard's play for television *Another Moon Called Earth* (1967). Bone does not so much write a history of the world but dissects it, in order to "lay bare the logic which other men have taken to be an arbitrary sequence of accidents" (Stoppard 1993: 51). He is "discovering the patterns – exposing the fallacy of chance – there are no impulsive acts – nothing random – everything is logical and connects into the grand design", because "[i]f it's all random, then what's the point?" He continues: "I hadn't meant to do a history of the world, only of myself …but the thing keep[s] spreading, making connections back, wider and deeper all the time, the real causes, and suddenly I knew that everything I did was the culminating act of a sequence going back to Babylon…" (59f.). The similarities between the two characters are so evident that the play could also be called *Another Moon Called Bone*.

point of writing a history of the world (cf. 68). His attitude is that of a disinterested dandy. In his letter to Moon, he announces that (the unnamed) Churchill's death stands for the change of "an age that saw history as a drama directed by great men" in the heroic posture "to that of the Stylist, the spectator as hero, the man of inaction who would not dare roll up his sleeves for fear of creasing the cuffs" (79). Accordingly, Lord Malquist tries "to avoid detail" and makes it "a rule to have no past" (84). This makes it all the easier for Moon to alter the facts for his biography – for example by making the letter a conversation that never occurred in order to satisfy his biographee, who would not like it if the journal featured no quotes (cf. 118f.). Details in biography as well as history are technicalities to Lord Malquist, because his understanding of life-writing is more poetic than scientific, as he explains to Moon:

> The secret of biography is to let your imagination flourish in key with your subject's. In this way you will achieve a poetic truth that is the jewel for which facts are merely the setting. Be poetic, dear boy, be poetic, and take your text from d'Aurevilley – *La verité m'ennuie*. (187)

In Stoppard's novel, the historian-turned-biographer succumbs to his struggle with the world, which clouds his objective judgement. Moon writes biography by changing facts. Because he is hired to Boswellize, his notes flatter his biographee and the biography becomes a panegyric, as cautioned against by Johnson. Moon also alters facts unknowingly because his memory fails. He transfers his own convictions on his biographee and refers to works of fiction for his reconstruction attempts. Moon artificially applies categories to history and superimposes history and the life of his biographee with causality, without realising that because he is trying to find a universal meaning in life his connections are subjective and conditional on his ideology. This is opposed by the Malquists. While Lady Malquist sees history – and thus one's life and its written recording – as an accumulation of accidents, Lord Malquist proposes a denial of detail and belittles the role of the individual as the shaker and mover of history. His understanding of biography resembles that of another dandy in a later drama by Stoppard, namely of Wilde in *The Invention of Love*, where he says: "Nothing that actually occurs is of the smallest importance" (*TIoL* 102). But it also bears resemblance to Woolf's notion of biography: d'Aurevilley's quote 'The truth bores me' is similar to Woolf's idea that dull biography is the biographer's failure to manipulate the facts according to the biographee's personality. Lord Malquist's announced change of the times marked by Churchill's death is represented in the shift of the construction of the biographical subject in modern and postmodern biography. At the same time, it also refers to the conceptual change from heroism to anti-heroism, which can be observed in the apposition of the tragedy *Hamlet* with the metaphysical farce *Rosencrantz and Guildenstern are Dead*.

4. Recapitulation: *Truth is only that which is taken to be true*

Rosencrantz and Guildenstern are Dead is Stoppard's first biography play, which was written shortly before and revised after *Lord Malquist and Mr Moon*, his first and only novel, which also has as a central theme the relationship between biographical fact and fiction. The play takes the mythopoeic quality of *Hamlet* and its myth as a reference matrix for the deconstruction of the audience's stereotypes about Shakespeare's play, its characters and tragedy and drama in general. The *modus operandi* in *Rosencrantz and Guildenstern are Dead* is similar to Stoppard's later biography plays. Ros and Guil are characters taken from the margins of dramatic history. As Woolf writes in her essay on New Biography, "the life which is increasingly real to us is the fictitious life; it dwells in the personality rather than in the act". Instead of depicting the biography of "Hamlet, Prince of Denmark", Stoppard focuses on two fictional "John Smith[s], of the Corn Exchange" (Woolf 1958: 155) in *Hamlet*, i.e. Ros and Guil. He gives them Hamlet-like status in his play by exchanging periphery and centre. The hypotext functions as a basis for the dramatic communication between playwright, actors and recipients in the same way references to actual historical personalities and events do in conventional biography plays. In the course of his play, Stoppard deconstructs the classic hero Hamlet, as well as heroism as such, through the depiction of Ros's and Guil's anti-heroism. The *verbatim* passages from *Hamlet* function as 'primary sources' from which Stoppard reconstructs his biographee's dark areas, i.e. what Ros and Guil actually do before they arrive at Elsinore, after having left for England and in general before and after their exits in *Hamlet*. By doing so, Stoppard questions what in conventional biography are constituent factors of its subjects, namely a unique character, a history and a *telos* in life. The central question in *Rosencrantz and Guildenstern are Dead* is whether life progresses through the individual's free will, whether it is determined through supernatural causes or by a succession of accidents. By introducing a metadramatic level, Stoppard shows that whatever may be the case, the representation of a life with artistic devices such as in biography is dependent on authorial design and artistic conventions. *Hamlet*, the "biographical data" behind *Rosencrantz and Guildenstern are Dead*, primarily delineates a specific inner reality, which is both metadramatic and metabiographical. Stoppard demonstrates that art follows certain conventionalised principles, which may be Aristotelian or, ten years later after Beckett's innovative deconstruction of mimetic theatre, may be what in general is still referred to as 'Theatre of the Absurd' and thus has become another artificial predefinition. *Rosencrantz and Guildenstern are Dead* can be considered in parts a postbiography play as it emphasises the blurred boundaries between myth and biography. By switching between Elizabethan and contemporary English, it questions mimetic language in drama. The play has at its centre two undefined or unfixed character identities, incorporates anachronisms with regard to Elizabethan drama and gives preference to dramatic over temporal and naturalistic logic. According to Stoppard, biography cannot be a truthful depiction of the life of a historical person, as objective truth does not exist. Biography turns out to be a narration of a dominant author dependent on intertextual allusions, *Weltanschauung* and artistic conventions.

V. *Travesties*: Biography as *'Memoir Play'*

With *Travesties*, Stoppard follows up on what he began with *Rosencrantz and Guildenstern are Dead*, i.e. the mixture of a pseudo-factual with a fictional level. As regards biographical drama, however, he this time mixes fictional characters derived from Wilde's *The Importance of Being Earnest* with authentic historical ones. The title of the play already suggests that with *Travesties*, Stoppard has not written a conventional biography play, but, among other things,[86] a travesty of the life episodes of James Joyce, Tristan Tzara, Vladimir Ilyich Ulyanov, better known under his *nom de guerre* Lenin, and Henry Carr, mocking "the political, literary, and aesthetic problems of the twentieth-century by attaching both insolent humor and outrageous nonsense to some of its larger-than-life intellectual figures" (Orlich 2004: 373). *Travesties* is similar to *Rosencrantz and Guildenstern are Dead* in that Stoppard reduces historical characters to a human size, this time not relying on mythopoeic fiction, but on authentic biographical data as a reference matrix. The biographical nexus behind the play is the historical fact that Joyce, Tzara and Lenin all spent time in Zurich during World War I. At the beginning of the play, we see Tzara composing a Dadaist poem, Joyce in the midst of writing *Ulysses* (1922) and Lenin writing *Imperialism, the Highest Stage of Capitalism* (1917). Although it is unlikely that these three characters ever met in Zurich, in *Travesties* Stoppard makes them come together and interact. He does so through the memory of the fourth historical character, Henry Carr, a minor British consular official in Zurich. Although, or rather because, he was a historical nonentity, Carr functions as the biographer of the play, as he is the only person who attestably had business with one person of this illustrious group, namely Joyce. Stoppard attests to this fact through a short biographical sketch preceding the play, titled "Henry Wilfred Carr, 1894-1962" (cf. *Travesties* 11ff.).

---

[86] On the various layers of travesties in *Travesties*, cf. Londré 1981: 85.

1. *Travesties* as a historical and biographical drama

In his seminal article about *Travesties* in the context of New Historicism,[87] Werner Wolf reads the play as a historical drama with an emphasis on history because stations of occidental literature, art and intellectual history are connected with essential events of political history such as the recurring references to the First World War and the Russian Revolution (cf. Wolf 1986: 338). Similarly, for Armin Geraths, *Travesties* conforms to the popular notion of historical drama because it relies on standard books about Lenin, Joyce and Dadaism (cf. Geraths 1979: 91). These reference books are enumerated by Stoppard in his *Acknowledgements*. He even goes so far as to state that "[n]early everything spoken by Lenin and [his wife] Nadezhda Krupskaya herein comes from his Collected Writings and from her *Memories of Lenin*". However, it becomes clear that Stoppard does not state his sources like a historian in order to fend off accusations about his fictional presentation of historical events. He rather takes full "responsibility for the use to which this and all other material is put" (*Travesties* 15). Accordingly, his play – exquisitely based on factual knowledge (cf. Geraths 1979: 91) – actually challenges the authenticity of the presented events.

Despite its alleged faithfulness to the facts and the ideological dialogues in the drama, which refute dogmatic positions, *Travesties* is for Geraths not a historical *drama* but a historical *farce*, something which he deems inadequate for a topic such as Stoppard's. The playwright supposedly compromises the seriousness of the addressed problems by ridiculing the historical characters, their actions and speeches through the form of farce (cf. Geraths 1979: 91). Although Geraths quotes Stoppard, who describes the mixture in his plays and also his personality as "[s]eriousness compromised by frivolity" (Hudson/Itzin/Trussler 1974: 13), Geraths thinks this form ruinous for engaging with such a serious topic.[88] And he is not alone in doing so: Alfons Klein, too, is of the

---

[87] On a similar reading of *Travesties*, cf. Er 2005; on Stoppard in the context of White, cf. Innes 2006: 227f. and 236.

[88] As a successful way of presenting history on stage, Geraths names Robert Bolt's *A Man for All Seasons* (1960), *State of Revolution* (1977) and *Vivat! Vivat Regina!* (1970; cf. Geraths 1979: 91f.); all three plays are more or less conventional

opinion that *Travesties* is not a historical drama, since it lacks a specific historical interest. He even goes so far as to claim that references to historical events and figures in *Travesties* only serve as the focal point for a dramatic conception, whose interest lies mainly in the dramatically entertaining realisation of conflicting ideas about art and politics (cf. Klein 1998: 383f.). Berninger is right, in my view, to disagree with Geraths and Klein's readings, and he attributes their judgements to their traditional concept of history. To him, *Travesties* is a parodistical history play, because it parodies its literary hypotexts as well as history and its reconstruction attempts (cf. Berninger 2006: 263f.).

In this matter, it could be helpful to shift the focus onto the presentation of biography in *Travesties*, as this still allows for ample consideration of the historical agenda of the play, but at the same time facilitates a discussion of the inherent thematic conflicts. The discussion shows that *Travesties* is a play which cannot be pigeonholed that easily, and that it is rather a play that is unique in its diversity and ambiguity, something which can be seen as characteristic of the genre of biography and the representation of fact *and* fiction. For John William Cooke, the central focus of the play is not illusion *vs.* reality but the process of the making of meaning, because "in *Travesties* illusion and reality are not opposed" (Cooke 1981: 526). According to Cooke, Stoppard emphasises in his play the similarities between Lenin, Joyce and Tzara, namely that "they are all makers, composing their works from facts out of context, apparent scraps. Whether the products are novels, histories, or dadaist poems, the process is the same" (528). However, while identifying the central theme of the play correctly, Cooke does not go so far as to connect the subjective epistemological processes described in the play to the construction processes of historiography and biography, also denying *Travesties* the status of a history play (cf. 526).

Although Wolf associates *Travesties* with historical drama, at the same time he deems it almost impossible to attribute it to any single dramatic subgenre. Stoppard himself, in an oft-quoted phrase, explains that what he tried to achieve was "to end up by contriving the perfect marriage between the play of ideas and farce or perhaps even high comedy. [...] *Travesties* [... is] in this area of trying to marry the play of ideas to

---

history plays (cf. Berninger 2006: 131-135 and 150 and Kramer 2000: 115).

comedy or farce" (Hudson/Itzin/Trussler 1974: 7f.). Wolf comments on this remark that *Travesties* is a play of ideas as regards the recurrent topic of discussion between the different characters, the relationship between art and politics/revolution; it is a farce as regards the farcical, action-accentuated events which are integrated in these almost expository passages of discussion. Some of these elements are connected with the compositional level of Wilde's *The Importance of Being Earnest*, not only in terms of content but also of structure. Because the plot of *Travesties* is similar to Wilde's play, it can also be seen as a travesty of it (cf. Wolf 1986: 339).

Most of the events presented in *Travesties* derive from Old Carr's memories. At the beginning of the play, he is depicted as a senile, old man, who tries to remember the historical events and to give an account of them. Thus Stoppard's play is a *memory play* – or rather *memoir play* – and takes place in Old Carr's personal and highly subjective memories. This way of presenting the dramatic events gives Stoppard ample opportunity to toy with biographical facts. All reconstruction attempts by Old Carr become a caprice of his recollection (cf. Cahn 1979: 128f.). His soliloquy is an interior monologue, adopting the major narrative style of *Ulysses*. Especially Old Carr's attempts to structure his recollections about the Zurich events is stressed by associative catenations of inconsistent thoughts as regards content and shortened syntax as regards form (cf. Neumeier 1986: 143 and Shultz 1984: 160).

Because Wilde's play and the court hearings with Joyce play such a significant role in Old Carr's memories, constituting his historical 'fifteen minutes of fame', the characters of *Travesties* are also "cast" parallely to *The Importance of Being Earnest* in his memory, mixing fiction and fact. Carr takes the role of Algernon Moncrieff, Tzara that of Jack Worthington, James Augusta Joyce that of Lady Augusta Bracknell and Bennett that of Lane. This corresponds to historical fact insofar as the historical Carr really did play Algernon, the name of the actor playing Jack in the company called the 'English Players' was really Tristan, Joyce's middle name was Augusta,[89] and Bennett was actually Consul in

---

[89] Stoppard realised these historical facts only after he made Joyce play Lady Bracknell and Tristan Tzara Jack Worthington (cf. Hayman 1982: 3). This is a fine example of the Wildean *bon mot* that life imitates art far more than art imitates life.

Zurich (cf. *Travesties* 98). Gwendolen and Cecily have no historical counterparts. The former, Algernon's cousin in *The Importance of Being Earnest*, becomes Carr's younger sister in *Travesties*, and the latter, Jack's ward in Wilde's play, becomes the librarian and Lenin's disciple. Only Lenin and his wife are not integrated into the travesty of *The Importance of Being Earnest* (cf. Neumeier 1986: 138), which some critics have deemed a fault in the play (cf., for example, Bigsby 1976: 27f. and Hayman 1982: 124f.). As Stoppard himself commented in 1976, the Lenins have an extra-ordinary position in his play:

> I felt very strongly – and now believe I was right – that one thing I could not do was to integrate the Lenins into the *Importance* scheme. [...] It would have been disastrous to Prismize and Chasublize the Lenins, and I believe that that section saves *Travesties* because I think one's just about *had* that particular Wilde joke at that point. (Stoppard in Hayman 1982: 10)

The reason for the extra-ordinary position of the Lenins has to be considered from a formal point of view. Stoppard proceeds with the beginning of Act II and the role of the Lenins similarly to Guildenstern stabbing the Player in *Rosencrantz and Guildenstern are Dead*. The parodistic and comic mode in *Travesties* is taken for granted by the recipients after the first act because of the many instances of literary parody, especially of *The Importance of Being Earnest*:

> There are several levels going here, and one of them is that what I personally like is the theatre of audacity. I thought, 'Right. We'll have a rollicking first act, and they'll all come back from their gin-and-tonics thinking "Isn't it fun? What a lot of lovely jokes!" And they'll sit down, and this pretty girl will start talking about the theory of Marxism and the theory of capitalism and the theory of value. And the smiles, because they're not prepared for it, will atrophy.' And that to me was like a joke in itself. (9)

From the second act, the audience expects the continuation of literary parodies, but this expectation is "ambushed" by Cecily's didactic lecture (cf. Berninger 2006: 278f. and Tan 1993: 21) – "a Brechtian newsreel of the historical events providing the backdrop against which the action of the play takes place" (Billman 1980: 48) – just as the comic mode of *Rosencrantz and Guildenstern are Dead* is disturbed by Guildenstern surprisingly stabbing the Player. However, when the recipients have then accepted the new mode of the play because of the length and complex topics of the lecture, Carr *"has come to the library as a 'spy', and his manner betrays this"* (*Travesties* 71). The frivolity of the first act sneaks back in:

> What was supposed to be happening was that we have this rather frivolous nonsense going on, and then the Lenin section comes in and says, 'Life is too important. We can't afford the luxury of this artificial frivolity, this nonsense going on in the arts.' Then he says, 'Right. That's what I've got to say,' and he sits down. Then the play stands up and says, 'You thought *that* was frivolous? You ain't see nothin' yet.' And you go into the Gallagher and Shean routine. That was the architectural thing I was after.   (Stoppard in Hayman 1982: 10)

Just as the Player gets up again, the travesty begins again, taking place around the autobiographical remarks of the Lenins, which appear as contradictions in terms and, thus, partly grotesque (cf. 10).

In 1993, however, *Travesties* was revived by the Royal Shakespeare Company and Stoppard must have changed his mind about certain aspects of the play, especially regarding the Lenins in the second act:[90] they are now integrated into the plot of *The Importance of Being Earnest*, corresponding to Rev. Canon Chasuble, D.D. and Miss Prism (cf. *Travesties* 1993: 53). Another alteration John Fleming points out is that the Lenin section of the 1993 edition fits better into the *memory play* as Old Carr *"enters, interrupting, consulting a tattered book"* (58) when Lenin speaks, "and this device is introduced by having the mise-en-scène mimic one of Lenin's public orations, but the words he speaks are a paraphrase of Algernon and Lady Bracknell" (Fleming 2001: 104f.). Nonetheless, because this study proceeds chronologically, and because the alterations in the 1993 version are not overly consequential with regard to the biographical aspects of *Travesties*, the text which forms the basis of my analysis will be the 1975 one.

---

[90] To Bull, it is the collapse of the Soviet Union which made Stoppard re-evaluate the role of the Lenins in *Travesties*. Therefore, "the debate about the feasibility of a genuine proletarian revolution in Russia in 1917 becomes for Stoppard a diminished theoretical issue to be discussed as part of a wider intellectual game about 'art and politics' – and one that needs to be addressed less ambiguously" (Bull 2001: 141).

a. The fictionalisation of fact

To Richard Ellman, whose Joyce biography Stoppard mentions in the *Acknowledgements* (cf. *Travesties* 15), the period in which the play takes place becomes the first historical misrepresentation:

> We seem to pass rapidly from 1916, when Tzara, according to his friend Hans or Jean Arp [...] gave Dadaism its title, to 1917, when Lenin, train-sealed, went to Petrograd, to 1918 and 1919, when Joyce was business manager of a company called the English Players, and quarrelled with A. Percy Bennet, the British Consul-General in Zürich, and with one of his employees [Henry Carr]. Four years are telescoped into one. (Ellman 1974)

The opening sequence takes place in a public library in Zurich where Joyce, Tzara and Lenin pursue their individual work. All the three periods Ellmann names, i.e. 1916, 1917 and 1918/19, are thrown together from the very beginning at a place which is a symbol for the intertextual allusions of *Travesties* and "where fiction and fact exist side by side" (Londré 1981: 71). The play confronts the proximity between literature and history (cf. Berninger 2006: 277), something which, from the beginning, is exemplified by swapping the "Oxen of the Sun" chapter from Joyce's novel *Ulysses* with a passage from Lenin's non-fictional *Imperialism, the Highest Stage of Capitalism* (cf. Broich 1993: 427).

The penetration of fiction from the compositional level of the travesty of comedy to the compositional level of the biographical drama is another distinctive feature of *Travesties*. This is accomplished by presenting the historical events to which the play refers parallel to the fictional events, which in turn follow another fictional play. History and biography appear saturated by fiction. This is emphasised by the mediation of life episodes through recognisable fictive texts. For Manfred Draudt, Stoppard "deliberately blurs the distinction between illusion and reality" (Draudt 1985: 44), for Kinereth Meyer, he "employs the drama of the intertext to affirm the mutual permeability of art and history" (Meyer 1989: 107), and for Beate Neumeier, history in the play becomes a collection of "scraps", and art and history are put on the same epistemological level, rendering fact and fiction undistinguishable (cf. Neumeier 1986: 158). The practice of intertextuality, which is applied to a great extent in *Travesties*, exchanges the mimetic reconstruction of biography for an amimetic self-reflexivity of one fiction to other fictive hypotexts, blurring the line between fact and fiction (cf. Wolf 1986: 340). This does not only account for the hypotext of *The Importance of Being Earnest*, but also for quotations from Shakespeare (cf. *Travesties* 53f.), which make up an entire dialogue between Tzara and Gwen, Joyce (cf. 18), the use of Limericks (cf. 33ff.), the melody of "Mr Gallagher und Mr Shean" (cf. 89ff.) by Al Shean and Ed Gallagher (1921), snippets from William Wordsworth (cf. 27 and 41) and Alfred Tennyson (cf. 41) and many more (cf. Shultz 1984: 151f. and Berninger 2006: 271). Carr's comment that "my art belongs to Dada 'cos Dada 'e treats me so – well then" (*Travesties* 25) is also an allusion, *viz.*, to the song "My Heart Belongs to Daddy" (1938) by Cole Porter, who is also the composer of *Kiss me Kate* (1948), a play-in-a-musical about the staging of Shakespeare's *The Taming of the Shrew*. The references to the Porter song as well as to the "Mr Gallagher und Mr Shean" routine are anachronistic references, as they were written after the events which Old Carr remembers, hinting at his erratic and prejudiced memory.

b. Memory going Wilde: *Travesties* as a metahistorical and metabiographical drama

An additional fictionalisation of biography is accomplished by introducing Carr as the mediator on the level of the *memory play*. Neil Sammells points out that this idea probably stems directly from the Wildean hypotext, for in *The Importance of Being Earnest*, Miss Prism remarks: "Memory, my dear Cecily, is the diary that we all carry about with us", and Cecily answers, "Yes, but it usually chronicles the things that have never happened, and couldn't possibly have happened" (Wilde 1976: 340). Old Carr's memories prove to be a diary filled with impossibilities, stereotypes and images (cf. Sammells 1986: 381f.).

For Wolf, Old Carr becomes a historian who selects, constructs, structures and criticises history from mnemonic data and proofs (cf., for example, *Travesties* 63f.). Accordingly, *Travesties* advances from a historical to a metahistorical drama because it also broaches the issue of how history is "made". The way Old Carr reconstructs history illustrates the subjectifying factors of historiography and biography (cf. Wolf 1986: 341f.). Rodney Simard views this as a parallel to Joyce when he compares T.S. Eliot's defence of *Ulysses* with *Travesties*:

> T.S. Eliot notes that *Ulysses* was perceived, quite wrongly, in early reviews as Dadaist, and in his defense of the novel, he states that its form "is simply a way of controlling, of ordering, of giving a shape and a significance to the immense panorama of futility and anarchy which is contemporary history," a process that is paralleled in *Travesties*. (Simard 1988: 188f.)

In the same way, *Travesties* can also be seen as a metabiographical drama, as it reflects upon subjectivity, incoherence and the construction processes of historiography and biography. The parody of history, as Berninger notes, emphasises the process of historical construction and the relationship between art and history (cf. Berninger 2006: 271). This relationship is also omnipresent in biographical reconstruction, so the historical parody in *Travesties* is more precisely a biographical parody. With Old Carr's erroneous biographical re-creation the play encompasses what Cooke sees as Stoppard's main point, namely "that art and history are both creative endeavours, the product of 'makers'. Carr's account is, like *The Odyssey*, 'delightful fiction in the form of fact...' – art as history" (Cooke 1981: 531). This epistemological process also involves the audience, as Cooke points out, making *Travesties* "a play which is about what it does" (536 and cf. Neumeier 1986: 158): "in its excess of forms, the play challenges perceivers to become makers themselves, and thereby exalts the efficacy of the imagination while questioning the locus of truth" (Cooke 1981: 537).

Old Carr's biographical reconstructions are of a constructional character because his memory proves to be fragmentary and unreliable: "*most of the play [...] is under the erratic control of Old Carr's memory, which is not notably reliable, and also of his various prejudices and delusions*" (*Travesties* 27). The unreliability of biographical construction is stressed by Old Carr's senility, which partly makes for postmodern manifestations of disintegration in the narration. Among these, Wolf considers the many linguistic deformations such as "comraderaderie" (23) and "etceterarera" (24) and the so called *time slips*. These are the reasons for the fact "*that the story (like a toy train perhaps) occasionally jumps the rails and has to be restarted at the point where it goes wild*" (27).

They disturb the linearity and coherence of time and thus of the narration. History and biography are presented in a fragmented way. Many versions of a historical event are presented and none of these is marked as authentic or true. The historical reliability of these passages seems rather dubious. The deconstruction of historical objectivity is paralleled with the deconstruction of traditional narration (cf. Wolf 1986: 341 and Geraths 1979: 93), which is also true for conventional biographical narration. With the *time slips*, the Marxist philosophy of history, which dogmatically argues for a teleological progress of history, is challenged (cf. Geraths 1979: 93). This dogmatic concept of history is further ridiculed by Carr at the end of the play: "Anyway, according to Marxist theory, the dialectic of history will get you to much the same place with or without *him*. If Lenin did not exist it would be unnecessary to invent him. Or Marx, for that matter" (*Travesties* 83).

Old Carr sketches a biography from facts of his life – his work in the British Consulate in 1917, Joyce's presence there, Lenin's and Tzara's time in Zurich and the clerk's participation in a performance of *The Importance of Being Earnest*, but by merely chronologically stating the historical facts, he is already mistaken. Old Carr is corrected at the end of *Travesties* by his wife, Old Cecily: he only met Joyce in 1918 and he never encountered Lenin personally, Cecily never helped Lenin write his book on imperialism, which was actually written in 1916, another anachronism, and not Carr but Percy Bennett was Consul in Zurich (cf. 97f.). Old Carr's biographical versions are exposed as nonsense, albeit methodical nonsense. Exemplarily, this exposes the biographer's subjectivity, which distorts perception. It is an additional element in *Travesties*, which is responsible for the fictionalisation of history (cf. Wolf 1986: 342).

However, Old Carr's mistakes in relying on his memory as basic data in terms of an 'eye witness report' as "historical source" and hence the historical falsifications, are not the manifestation of an overt tampering with the facts. In fact, his errors show that Old Carr realised the historical relevance of Joyce, Tzara and Lenin only with hindsight and now wants to downplay his original ignorance. This he makes especially clear with regard to Lenin by trying to explain why he did not foresee his political significance and did not stop him from leaving his exile: "And don't forget, *he wasn't Lenin then! I mean who was he?* as it were". In the same breath he also tells the audience of the burden of responsibility laid upon him: "So there I was, the lives of millions of people hanging on which way I'd move, or whether I'd move at all, another man might have cracked" (*Travesties* 81). With this kind of dialectic, Stoppard stages the negation of a possibility of objective historical insight in *Travesties*. As regards the psychological standpoint of his character, Old Carr's vested interests must be explained by his personal convictions.

2. Carr debunking the heroes: Joyce, Lenin and Tzara through the biographer's eyes

From a historical perspective, Carr is a minor and unimportant clerk at the British Consulate and a non-professional actor. His desire for recognition is disproportionate to his self-assigned historical role in his memoirs. Christopher Bigsby describes his role from a Wildean perspective:

> In 'The Critic as Artist', Oscar Wilde remarks of memoirs that they are 'generally written by people who have either entirely lost their memories, or have never done anything worth remembering'. This proves all too accurate a description of Carr's memoirs, which tend to confuse his own fictions with those of *The Importance of Being Earnest* in which he had once scored a minor success. (Bigsby 1976: 25)

By retrospectively aggrandising himself into a historical figure of great importance, Old Carr tries to give himself the role he has always aspired to. That is why he constantly points out his artistic achievement in playing Algernon in *The Importance of Being Earnest*, and misleadingly presents his acquaintances with Joyce and Tzara. Old Carr's opening soliloquy becomes "a mischievously telling parody of the august tone adopted by so many biographers and autobiographers" (Brassel 1987: 138). This is poignantly shown by cliché titles such as "James Joyce As I Knew Him" (*Travesties* 22), "The Ups and Downs of Consular life in Zurich During the Great War: A Sketch", "Halfway to the Finland Station with V.I. Lenin: A Sketch" (23), *"Memories of Dada by a Consular Friend of the Famous in Old Zurich: A Sketch"* (25) or by cliché phrases such as "To those of us who knew him" (22), "To be in his presence was to be aware of a complex personality" (23) and "To those of us who lived through it" (25). This wording is meant to suggest to the recipients that the biographer Old Carr was then aware of the historical importance of his subjects. But, as Wolf makes clear, Old Carr only invents Cecily's and his own acquaintance with Lenin to make his desired historical role in stopping Lenin plausible: "I [...] could have changed the course of history" (64), "in fact I might have stopped the whole Bolshevik thing in its tracks" (81; cf. Wolf 1986: 342). Martin Brunkhorst sees in Old Carr's efforts an attempt at a historical correction from a consciously subjective point of view (cf. Brunkhorst 1980: 233). Nonetheless, although Old Carr emphasises his own role in history, he never goes so far as to claim, for example, to have stopped Lenin and to have changed the course of history. His historical revisions always have a reference point in the possible.

Besides this self-aggrandisement caused by vested interest, the subjectively distorted perception of the past manifests itself in the *"various prejudices and delusions"* (*Travesties* 27) that influence Old Carr's historical view (cf. Wolf 1986: 342). Through them, history pauses in its familiar form, and it becomes clear that the biographical sketches are a fiction. All the characters presented are "two-dimensional dream people", as Stoppard himself says (Stoppard in Hayman 1982: 6), stereotypical comedy characters without any hint of psychological realism (cf. Berninger 2006: 265). The public lie of the biographical stereotypes is complemented by Old Carr's personal ones. With these stereotypes, he can control the world and the characters in it (cf. Sammells 1986: 381). Through his depiction, the recipients can guess at his attitude towards his biographees. He becomes the character "most completely and most subtly displayed" in the play, as Woolf put it of the biographer in general (Woolf 1958: 153f.). This is especially evident in the case of Joyce, against whom Carr lost in court and therefore is unable to maintain "the biographer's traditional objectivity" (Brassel 1987: 141).

Old Carr only briefly hints at the fact that Joyce immortalised and showed him up in *Ulysses*: "Carr of the Consulate! – first name Henry, that much is beyond dispute, I'm mentioned in the books" (*Travesties* 25). In his soliloquy he first explains that he is not resentful of Joyce: "Not one to bear a grudge, however, not after all these years, [...] no hard feelings either side, unpleasant as it is to be dragged through the courts for a few francs" (22). Nevertheless, his attitude towards the Irish author affects his memory and Old Carr's presentation of the historical events gives him the possibility of paying him back.

His attempt to paint an objective picture of Joyce ends in contradictions, because the allegedly non-existent anger prevents any positive depiction until the character of Old Carr betrays his real feelings about Joyce:

> A prudish, prudent man, Joyce, in no way profligate or vulgar, and yet convivial, without being spend-thrift, [...] in short [...] an obsessive litigant and yet an essentially private man [...] – in short a liar and a hypocrite, a tight-fisted, sponging, fornicating drunk not worth the paper, that's that bit done.   (22f.)

This bitterness about the writer also finds an expression in ethnic parodies. In his mind, Joyce becomes an *"Irish nonsense"* (33) and money-sponger, who opens his conversations with a Limerick. The stereotype of the Irish money-sponger is borrowed directly from *Ulysses*. In the novel, Mr Deasy asks Stephen Dedalus in the "Nestor" episode: "Do you know what is the proudest word you will ever hear from an Englishman's mouth? [...] *I paid my way. I never borrowed a shilling in my life*" (Joyce 1998: 30f.; cf. Shultz 1984: 165f.). This statement is travestied in *Travesties*, when Joyce, who wants to repay his debt of £100 to the Civil List by staging *The Importance of Being Earnest*, says: "I am an Irishman. The proudest boast of an Irishman is – I paid back my way..." (*Travesties* 50).

Shultz also points out some other elements of Old Carr's recollections which are allusions to *Ulysses*. On the one hand, there is the travesty of Mr Deasy's sense of duty and his teleological concept of history in the character of Joyce. Joyce lacks a patriotic sense of duty and his "name is in bad odour among the British community in Zurich" (49) because of his neutral and anti-imperialistic attitude (cf. 49f.). On the other hand, there is the incorporation of the personal catechism from the "Nestor" episode in the dialogue between Joyce and Carr (cf. 52) and the impersonal catechism from the "Ithaca" episode in the questioning of Tzara by Joyce (cf. 56ff.). The former gives away Carr's narcissism, showing that what he despises in a character is subconsciously always a part of his own. The latter reflects Old Carr's opinion about

Joyce, that he is egocentric, scrounging, insular and of a litigious nature. With the help of the impersonal catechism, Old Carr mocks the arrogance of artists and their self-acclaimed importance in the world (cf. Shultz 1984: 166ff.). At the same time, the scene between Tzara and Joyce also bears resemblance to the interrogation of Jack by Lady Bracknell in *The Importance of Being Earnest* (cf. Wilde 1976: 332ff.) and thus still remains part of the Wildean frame of *Travesties* (cf. Neumeier 1986: 150).

Although Lenin's role in the 1975 edition of *Travesties* is different from Joyce's or Tzara's with regard to the integration into the travesty of *The Importance of Being Earnest*, there are similarities between the way Old Carr proceeds with him and the way he does so with Joyce. This time, however, he is motivated not by personal disaffection but rather by ignorance. In Old Carr's opening soliloquy, it soon becomes obvious that he cannot really recall anything about Lenin. He even starts by picturing him in the disguise of the blonde Swede (cf. *Travesties* 23) which Lenin planned on using in order to sneak into Russia – a strand of narration picked up in the the second act of his recollections (cf. 79). Although Carr could have known Lenin only as a visitor of the library, he pretends to have possessed insider information about his plans. Retrospectively, Old Carr wants to achieve importance because the course of history made Lenin important. Nonetheless, the fact that Carr never knew Lenin nor realised his political impetus affects the narrative style in his memories at the beginning of Act II. This narrative style is in a harsh contrast to Old Carr's interior monologue in the first act. Most of the Lenin part is based on biographies and Lenin's own documents, while Carr's lines derive mainly from his imagination. Carr's remarks may be more entertaining than Lenin's matter-of-fact style, but they question his assertions of having possessed a serious sense of duty. They define Carr in contrast to Lenin, the latter's main declaration being the necessity to act and the importance of acquittal at any cost (cf. Shultz 1984: 162f. and 173f.).

The topic of the Russian Revolution as well as Lenin's temporary residency in Zurich remind Old Carr of another "revolution", which took place in the same street: Dadaism. He gives a short lecture about the meaning and intentions of this art form, and the same questions about Dadaism are asked again by Joyce in his interrogation of Tzara (cf. *Travesties* 25 and 56ff.). At the end of Act II Old Carr asks himself what he actually did during the First World War, and the conflict between duty and pleasure emerges, which in Old Carr's memories and mind is fought out between Joyce, Lenin and Tzara (cf. Shultz 1984: 164).

Old Carr also treats Tzara like Joyce in his depiction of the historical events. Tzara, too, is first sketched as an ethnic parody; he becomes a "*Rumanian nonsense*" (*Travesties* 32), travestying Jack's first stage appearance in *The Importance of Being Earnest* (cf. Wilde 1976: 322). Tzara's art reflects Carr's lack of artistic talent; his ludicrous art theory is Carr's main point in ridiculing the Dadaist. In the scene in which Tzara cuts up Shakespeare's Sonnet No. 18, followed by Gwen's chance rearrangement of the pieces, both have a conversation in a pastiche of Shakespearean drama (cf. *Travesties* 53f.). This form of imitation trivialises Tzara's conviction that "everything is Chance, including design" (37), by inverting it to state the opposite, i.e. that everything is design, including chance. Tzara's Shakespeare quotes are to show his disdain of the traditional understanding of poetry, while Gwen's contradict his statements. According to Shultz, Stoppard chooses the collage technique of the pastiche – a technique which uses parts of the past in order to point out universal human convictions – in order to transport the playwright's open and Carr's jealous admiration of Joyce's art. Gwen's presence in this scene as Joyce's disciple and thus as his representative, supports this idea (cf. Shultz 1984: 173f.). In the end, Shakespeare's sonnet, cut up and reordered by Tzara, proves to be, contrary to the Dadaist's intention, a modern version of the original poem (cf. Neumeier 1986: 146). This situation is similar to that of his opening poem, which, when read with a French accent, becomes conclusive with regard to content.[91] Tzara's belief that everything is chance is contradicted here as well.

---

[91] Tzara's apparently Dadaistic lines "Eel ate enormous appletzara / key dairy chef's hat he'lllearn oomparah! / Ill raced alas whispers kill later nut east, / noon avuncular ill day Clara!" (*Travesties* 18) then read "*Il est énorme, s'appelle Tzara, / Qui déréchef se hâte. Hilare nonpareil! / Il reste à la Suisse parcequ'il est un artiste. / 'Nous n'avons que l'art,' il déclara!*" (Londré 1981: 72).

Old Carr's biographical account exhibits subjectivity and a constructional character. An additional element which fictionalises his account is his inclination to specific discourses. This is expressed by narrative passages which give the historical events the shape of a biographical narration. Wolf points out that the alleged encounters between Carr and Joyce, Lenin and Tzara are in retrospect instilled with artistic and political meaning, which they did not have at that point in history. Old Carr conducts a realignment of the past: with the help of an intentional focus, he links the past actions of Joyce, Lenin and Tzara teleologically with their historical achievements. This implies at the same time a fictional narrative act. Carr did not realise the significance of their individual actions in the way he wants to convey to the recipients now. The cut and dried language of Old Carr's soliloquies is closely connected with the fictional structuring and sense-making of biography. He characterises Joyce, Lenin and Tzara with almost identical phrases, following the pattern of "[t]o be in his presence was to be aware of an amazing intellect" (*Travesties* 22; cf. 24 and 25). The stencilled conception contingent to narrative discourses makes historical insight and the formulation of truth problematic (cf. Wolf 1986: 343). Another pattern which Old Carr uses is *The Importance of Being Earnest*. The events around Joyce and Tzara unfold according to the play, and large portions of the dialogue in *Travesties* are fashioned after it, too. In Carr's memory, the reconstruction of one's life is pressed into patterns, so that history and biography only come into view as contours of a secondary kind (cf. Geraths 1979: 94).

Certain formal compositional methods are also an essential part of literary patterns which communicate history and deform and fictionalise it. On the one hand, there is what Wolf calls the microtextual arrangement of the discourse according to poetic criteria such as alliteration (cf. Wolf 1986: 345). That a discourse following this aesthetic principle can be falsifying is shown by Carr's remark about the causes of World War I:

CARR: [...] Something about brave little Belgium, wasn't it?
TZARA: Was it? I thought it was Serbia...

> CARR: Brave little Serbia...? No, I don't think so. The newspapers would never have risked calling the British public to arms without a proper regard for succinct alliteration. (*Travesties* 36f.)

On the other hand, there is what Wolf refers to as the macrotextual arrangement of discourse according to certain genres and conventions. This arrangement is responsible for the collage of lyrical, dramatic and narrative forms in *Travesties*. The play becomes lyrical in its sonnets, limericks and songs; dramatic, for example, in Cecily's lecture about Lenin, which resembles an epic didactic play; and narrative in Old Carr's soliloquies with regard to his memoirs. The collage of different styles and genres in combination with the other distinctions of Old Carr's discourse illustrates the fictional character of biography. The deconstruction of historical objectivity corresponds to the deconstruction of the narration of the autonomous subject, which is supposedly capable of an authentic discourse about reality (cf. Wolf 1985: 345).

However, Wolf countervails his own hypothesis that *Travesties* illustrates the fiction of historical epistemology with two points. Firstly, in Stoppard's play there are some passages which, due to their documentary character, are exempt from fictionalisation. Secondly, at the end of *Travesties*, Old Cecily corrects Old Carr's depiction of the events, and the tarnished historical objectivity seems to be established again. With regard to his first point, Wolf refers mainly to the Lenin passages, questioning at the same time whether the objective documentary character of Cecily's lecture makes Lenin's Marxist concept of history really appear objectively true, a point which is confirmed by the *ex post* fictionalisation of the Lenins in the 1993 edition of the play. With regard to the second point, Wolf remarks that Old Cecily corrects only certain historical facts, affecting only the raw material of the chronicle and not the meaningful conjunction of selected events, which actually constitutes historiography. Old Cecily exposes Old Carr's biography as a fiction and destroys the meaning of the narration, but without reconnecting her facts to form a new, true (hi)story (cf. Wolf 1986: 345f.).

3. Representations and contradictions of history, art and politics in the four main characters

In order to understand the biographical depiction of the individual characters, one has to consider the themes of the play. *Travesties* explores whether and how artists can contribute to society. Stoppard himself said that the play asks "whether the words 'revolutionary' and 'artist' are capable of being synonymous, or whether they are mutually exclusive, or something in between" (Hudson/Itzin/Trussler 1974: 11). These three standpoints are represented by three of his protagonists. Joyce stands for being "mutually exclusive", Lenin for "synonymous" and Tzara for "something in between" (cf. Shultz 1984: 118). And because the artist-playwright Stoppard feels "uneasy in trying to work out questions that involve *oneself*, in terms of authentic geniuses" (Hudson/Itzin/Trussler 1974: 16), he places the authentic non-genius Henry Carr as a mediator between the other three characters to function as a prism, and to refract the conflict between art and politics (cf. Shultz 1984: 114).

As the entire first act is permeated by *The Importance of Being Earnest*, it presents a structure which follows the aesthetic concept of *l'art pour l'art*. Serious and earnest topics are excluded, but the occasional collapse of this world is dramatised by disruptions, among other things by Carr's emotional releases (cf. *Travesties* 37 and 40f.) and Tzara's outbursts of fury (cf. 47 and 62). In the second act, then, it is the indirectly insinuated Russian Revolution which finally causes Wilde's world to collapse. Attention switches from a hedonistic world to one of *Realpolitik*, although the focus is still on the role of art in such a world.

Lenin has only one short stage appearance in the first act because his dystopian *Weltanschauung* would interfere with Wilde's world of eloquence. Nonetheless, in the second act the spy thriller around Lenin, as Shultz calls it, fills in for the plot of *The Importance of Being Earnest*, thus emphasising the danger Lenin's ideology constitutes for western civilisation (cf. Shultz 1984: 124f. and Geraths 1979: 99). The integration of the Lenins into the plot of *The Importance of Being Earnest* in the 1993 edition of the play would suggest that after the fall of Communism, Stoppard felt comfortable enough to travesty the historical Lenin as well, but not without still accentuating the ideological threat of his dogmatic system. His later plays *The Coast of Utopia* and *Rock 'n' Roll* show very well that the playwright is still concerned about Communism and Marxist ideology.

In the following sections, I will consider the characters of Joyce, Lenin and Tzara more closely in order to explain what ideology they respectively stand for in Old Carr's biographical account. The character of Joyce sees it as his duty solely to create the kind of art that preserves the past and present as an immortal work of beauty for the future. The character of Lenin, Joyce's polar opposite, deems it his obligation to create a socialist society in which art functions only as medium for socialist realism. In between them stands the character of Tzara, who sees his purpose and finds great pleasure in deconstructing western culture and capitalist society (cf. Shultz 1984: 127).

In *Travesties*, Joyce stands for a cyclical and aesthetic concept of history. For him history is a continuous cycle of destruction and reconstruction. If there is any meaning to history at all, it lies in the way it is passed down through art, which in turn immortalises mankind (cf. Shultz 1984: 129 and Wolf 1986: 347):

> The temples are built and brought down around [... man], continuously and contiguously, from Troy to the fields of Flanders. If there is any meaning in any of it, it is in what survives as art, yes even in the celebration of tyrants, yes even in the celebration of nonentities. (*Travesties* 62)

In his concept of history, even "nonentities" like Carr have their place. In his novel, Joyce searches for parallels between Leopold Bloom in Dublin and Ulysses in Greek antiquity. His aim is not to render this past obsolete, but to reduplicate it with his *Ulysses*:

> It is a theme so overwhelming that I am almost afraid to treat it. And yet I with my Dublin Odyssey will double that immortality, yes by God *there's* a corpse that will dance for some time yet and *leave the world precisely as it finds it* [...]. (62f.)

The world is not to be changed, since for Joyce, history repeats itself. Following *Hamlet* (cf. Shakespeare 1974: 1157 [II.ii.436-437]), he defines himself as a "fine writer who writes caviar / for the general, hence

133

poor –" (*Travesties* 33), i.e. as an artist whose work is luxurious, but not destined to make him rich. The Joyce in *Travesties* is apolitical: "As an artist, naturally I attach no importance to the swings and roundabout of political history" (50), and, as Shultz correctly remarks, words such as "swings" and "roundabout" are also reminders of a cyclical concept of history (cf. Shultz 1984: 129).

Lenin represents historical materialism; his concept of history is linear and progressive. Because of the determination of all historical phenomena through basic economic conditions, according to this dogmatic system historical events are determined causally. Analogically to the teleology of dialectic materialism, history develops in a reasonable, progressive way and necessarily towards socialism (cf. *Travesties* 30). Whereas Joyce wants to preserve the past and connect it with the present, Lenin's aim is to lead the present into a socialist future, if necessary by the use of brute force. Joyce ignores the war as it does not serve art. Lenin is against intervening in World War I because it is a capitalist war. Furthermore, art ought to serve socialism. Nevertheless, even Lenin is moved by bourgeois art such as Gorki, Chekhov and Beethoven, although he feels reluctant about it as it softens his revolutionary mind:

> I don't know of anything greater than the Appassionata. Amazing, superhuman music. It always makes me feel, perhaps naïvely, it makes me feel proud of the miracles that human beings can perform. But I can't listen to music often. It affects my nerves, makes me want to say nice stupid things and pat the heads of those people who while living in this vile hell can create such beauty. Nowadays we can't pat heads or we'll get our hands bitten off. We've got to *hit* heads, hit them without mercy, though ideally we're against doing violence to people... Hm, one's duty is infernally hard...   (89)

For Shultz, Lenin thus carries out an internal conflict between his duty to free the proletariat and the aesthetic indulgence which paralyses him mentally (cf. Shultz 1984: 130ff.).

Tzara shares Lenin's antipathy to bourgeois society, albeit for different reasons. Where Lenin does not succeed in despising bourgeois art at large because "[h]e is a reactionary in art" (*Travesties* 83), it is Tzara's purpose to demolish it in its entirety. As regards politics, he also wishes to overcome capitalism, but his artistic and political pursuit is not dedicated to Communism, but rather to regressive primitivism. His ideal conception is of an archaic past long gone; the present is for Tzara the degeneration of a golden age (cf. Shultz 1984: 135).

Tzara's concept of history is the total deconstruction of historical meaning. According to his Dadaistic-nihilistic notion, teleologically concentrated causality is no longer applicable: "causality, is no longer fashionable owing to the war" (*Travesties* 36). History, like his art, appears as purely coincidental: "To a Dadaist history comes out of a hat too" (83). Culture, reason and tradition have, according to Tzara, destroyed the spontaneous creative intelligence of the artist. Art has been corrupted by material interests and it lacks true, free and original creativity. The only artists able to enrich society are "vandals and desecrators, simple-minded demolition men" (62). Tzara does not pursue *l'art pour l'art*, he rather favours art as a basis for composing moral and intellectual statements: "Artists and intellectuals will be the conscience of the revolution" (83).

Politics, in particular World War I, is an omen for Tzara that the material corruption as well as the corruption of rational intelligence have reached their apex. Capitalism twists and contorts language and music, and it is the artist's duty to protest against this. This is what Tzara attempts with his anti-art of Dadaism: "That's what we [Dadaists] have against this [... present society]. There's a place for us in it" (84). A revolution could render bourgeois society obsolete and have natural art prosper again in a new Eden. Therefore, Tzara views himself as an ally of left-wing politics: "[Lenin] is moved by a vision of a society of free and equal men. And he will listen" (83). But Tzara's idea is of a natural and primitive understanding of art, not of socialist realism. The Tzara of *Travesties* is neither a socialist revolutionary nor a traditional artist, but "something in between" (cf. Shultz 1984: 135ff.).

Torn between approval and aversion, Carr represents the bourgeois position in *Travesties*. Aesthetically, he agrees with Joyce, but he rejects the Irishman's political apathy; ethically, he rejects Lenin's political ideology, and Tzara's anti-art and anti-politics disturb him deeply. While Carr rejects the Marxist concept of history, he nevertheless argues for causality, teleology and thus historical meaning. In his opinion, history progresses as the realisation of bourgeois ideals such as "*duty*, [...] *patriotism* [... and] *love of freedom*" (*Travesties* 40) in an unstoppable civilising process. Even wars have their function: "Wars are fought to make the world safe for artists. It is never quite put in those terms but it is a useful way of grasping what civilised ideals are all about. The easiest way of knowing whether good has triumphed over evil is to examine the freedom of the artist" (39).

Carr considers it "the duty of the artist to beautify existence" (37). Therefore, contrary to Tzara's opinion, to him art is not indispensable to life:

> TZARA: Because man cannot live by bread alone.
> CARR: Yes, he can. It's *art* he can't live on. (46)

However, Carr attributes to it a certain pragmatism when he remarks that "a great deal of what we call art has no such function and yet in some way it gratifies a hunger that is common to princes and peasants" (74). According to David K. Rod, he assumes "a position which rejects the various idealisms of Tzara, Joyce, and Lenin in favor of a practical consideration of what art has been and what it has accomplished" (Rod 1983: 541). In his differentiation between art and politics he replies to Tzara that "[r]evolution in art is in no way connected with *class* revolution" (*Travesties* 46). With regard to politics, Carr is not as indifferent as Joyce, but he is not as involved in it as Lenin, either. Shultz sees in him the representation of a liberal democrat of a capitalist society (cf. Shultz 1984: 148ff.).

The concepts of history of all four characters show that *Travesties* offers two kinds of historical concepts. Both are diametrically opposed in terms of causality, finality and historical meaning. But in themselves also, they represent different positions. In *Travesties*, not only the causal analyses of Marxist linear philosophy of history are criticised, but also their teleology and allocation of meaning. Nonetheless, fundamental parts in Cecily's lecture about Lenin's biography and the development of Bolshevism do not result from a pro-Marxist point of view, although she is Lenin's disciple. In fact, she admits to historical misinterpretations made by Marx, such as wondering about the Russian translation of *Das Kapital* because the "conditions for a socialist revolution as he [Marx] saw it did not exist in Russia at all" (*Travesties* 66); or to the contradictory behaviour of the Social Democrats who argued for war, although they perceived it as a bourgeois-capitalist manipulation (cf. 69). Nevertheless, criticism of the Marxist philosophy of history does not imply that its opposite, the bourgeois position, is favoured. Carr, in contrast to Tzara's nihilism, accepts causal explanations for the outbreak of World War I. However, he confuses the causes of the outbreak of the First World War with the causes of Great Britain entering the war, speaking of "brave little Belgium" (36), and "[r]emember plucky little Poland – not Poland, the other one" (82). And when he is at a loss for causes himself, he finishes his arguments with the chant "We're here because we're here..." (40). Carr's conviction that history is a process moved by bourgeois ideals is deconstructed when his belief in historical causality is reduced to a causeless infinite loop. Again it is Tzara who exposes bourgeois faith in the meaning of history as wishful thinking. He reveals the fiction behind ideals such as *"patriotism, duty, love, freedom*, king and country, [...] and honour" (39, dialogue omitted) by implying that these words can be ascribed arbitrarily with whatever meaning according to political necessity.[92] The cheap clichés of companionship in the trenches (cf. 41) and the reduction of war activities to concerns about clothes (cf. 37) undermine Carr's position in the play (cf. Wolf 1986: 348f.). However, Carr can gain some ground in the historical discussion with Tzara, for example when he exposes the illogicality of Tzara's reasons for rejecting reason:

> TZARA: But, my dear Henry, causality, is no longer fashionable owing to the war.
> CARR: How illogical, since the war itself had causes. (*Travesties* 36)

Thus, Carr's position in *Travesties* is not as clear as that of the other three. His prismatic function in the play and his role as the dialectical counterpart of his respective interlocutors for progressing and teasing

---

[92] Charles Kay Ogden and Ivor Armstrong Richards address this issue in their study *The Meaning of Meaning*: "'Throughout the whole history of the human race,' wrote the late Dr Postgate [in 1896], 'there have been no questions which have caused more heart-searchings, tumults, and devastation than questions of the correspondence of words to facts. The mere mention of such words as 'religion,' 'patriotism,' and 'property' is sufficient to demonstrate this truth'" (Ogden/Richards 1969: 2).

out their arguments, make for some ambiguity in the presentation of his position.

Joyce's concept of history is of similar ambiguity. With his cyclical interpretation of history he questions historical meaning and concurs with Tzara's opinion. As Wolf points out, there are formal similarities between the two artists as well. Joyce's reflection on an ancient myth for his novel resembles Tzara's ideal concept of a regressive primitivism and his partial regress to stylistic devices of past epochs that of the Dadaist collage technique. At the same time, it is Tzara who most vehemently opposes Joyce's aesthetic concept of history, because to him the purpose of art lies in provoking the recipients with "anti-art" (39), and not to enrich them aesthetically. In return, Joyce parodies Tzara's "fashionable magic" (63). With reference to Tzara's poem out of a hat (cf. 17) and anticipating his remark about haphazard history, Joyce *"produces a rabbit out of his hat"* (63). Tzara is debunked by the artistic magic of Joyce into a second-rate magician, who follows the *Zeitgeist* of art and politics and is merely of entertaining value. Tzara himself undermines his Dadaistic-nihilistic *Weltanschauung* when he takes a Marxist position with an economic cause analysis of bourgeois-imperialistic wars, from which history can be interpreted meaningfully (cf. 39f.). At the same time, he opposes the demand of an "[i]nternational revolutionary union of all creative men and women on the basis of radical Communism – expropriation of property – socialization" by the "right to urinate in different colours" (61; cf. Wolf 1986: 349f.).

Teleological concepts are dissolved on many levels in *Travesties*. Temporal continuity is destroyed and the dogmatic insistence of Marxist dialectical and historical materialism is mocked by means of *time slips*. The idea of a general narrative teleology is demolished, as in the scene in which Carr and Bennett exchange war news (cf. *Travesties* 26ff.). While the historical events progress chronologically, the course of the scene between Carr and Bennett is repeated over and over again. The simultaneity of historical progress and cyclical repetition seems absurd. On the level of the historical and biographical drama, teleology is destroyed by ignoring the Russian Revolution and Lenin's part in it on stage. Lenin's speech, visually an imitation of the famous photograph *"which Stalin had re-touched so as to expunge Kamenev and Trotsky who feature prominently in the original*" (84),[93] is accordingly not about the revolution, but rather about the socialist understanding of art. And even on the level of the drama of ideas, the play is inconclusive. While in his closing lines Old Carr may summarise the argument between art and revolution, its nonsensical structure exposes a teleological ending:

> I learned three things in Zurich during the war. I wrote them down. Firstly, you're either a revolutionary or you're not, and if you're not you might as well be an artist as anything else. Secondly, if you can't be an artist, you might as well be a revolutionary...
> I forget the third thing.
> (BLACKOUT.) (98f.)

There are no final words to close the play, no denouement, and it is suspended in an absence of meaning. Carr only presents the thesis and the antithesis in his dialectical conclusion without being able to formulate the synthesis, "the dialectical transcendence of art and revolution" (Whitaker 1999: 63).

In *Travesties*, Stoppard criticises "the materialist inhumanity of Lenin, the spurious artistic arrogance of Joyce, the cavalier socialism of Tzara and the aristocratic hauteur of Carr", his detachment slipping only once or twice (Bigsby 1976: 27). The arguments between the positions are often enough "interactional cul-de-sacs", which do not allow for synthetical progress, so "the only way out is to have a 'time lapse' at each of these points" (Tan 1993: 217). Carr's last remark summarises the way the play progresses. It does not so much stop at a certain point of argument, declaring it the final one, but rather advances dialectically by thesis and antithesis, or "Firstly, A. Secondly, minus A" (Stoppard in Hayman 1982: 10), without stopping at a final synthesis, i.e. "contrast is not there only as a means towards something else, but can be present for its own sake" (Tan 1993: 218). Or as Stoppard put it himself:

> [T]here is very often *no* single, clear statement in my plays. What there is, is a series of conflicting statements made by conflicting characters, and they tend to play a sort of infinite leap-frog. [...] [T]here is never any point in this

---

[93] Ironically, Stoppard retouched his own text: this description which features prominently in the original is missing in the 1993 edition (cf. *Travesties* 1993: 58).

intellectual leap-frog at which I feel *that* is the speech to stop it on, *that* is the last word.[94] (Hudson/Itzin/Trussler 1974: 6)

The only constitutional level which, formally as well as thematically, seems to be attributed a teleological vanishing point is the plot level of the comedy. However, Wolf is right to point out that the implied double marriage at the end following the Wildean pattern seems so artificial that Stoppard appears to discard intentionally *the* concept of teleology *par excellence* through a self-exposing artificiality (cf. Wolf 1986: 353 and Berninger 2006: 269). Although Klein vehemently disagrees with Wolf about the deconstructionist notion in *Travesties*, viewing the plot's discontinuities and start-overs as Stoppard's approach of forming meaning (cf. Klein 1998: 386), it is this overtly artistic and constructive character which makes the idea of historiography and biography seem exactly this: an artificial construct. Hence, the ending of *Travesties* is what Londré calls "a travesty of the well-made play's ending" (Londré 1981: 85), and thus of conventional biographical drama. Stoppard self-reflexively exposes the construction of his own fiction, which is literally well-made, i.e. artistically constructed.

4. Recapitulation: *My memoirs, is it, then?*

Travesties is a *memory*, or rather, *memoir play*, which is constituted by Old Carr's personal and highly subjective memory. The historical events to which the play refers parallel the fictional events, which in turn follow Wilde's *The Importance of Being Earnest*. History and biography appear saturated by fiction and the play engages the proximity between literature and historiography. *Travesties* is a metabiographical drama, because it broaches the issue of how biography is constructed. With its two time levels, it reflects upon subjectivity, (in)coherence and the construction processes behind biography. The historical parody emphasises the process of historical construction and the relationship between art and history. This relationship is also omnipresent in biographical recon-

---

[94] On the colliding and diametrically opposed worlds in Stoppard's drama, cf. Morris 1987.

struction, which renders the historical parody a biographical one. Old Carr's senility partly leads to postmodern manifestations of disintegration in the narrative. The self-aggrandisement caused by vested interest and the subjectively distorted perception of the past manifest themselves in the stereotypes which influence Old Carr's historical views and his depiction of the biographees. Through his biographical depiction, the audience learns more about Old Carr's attitude towards the subjects of his reminiscences than about historical personalities or events. The plot of *Travesties* does not follow the conventional Aristotelian criteria of relevance concerning a conclusive story in which the ending refers to the beginning. The plot structure, the use of certain narrative forms and the language serve the deconstruction of meaning and not the construction of a reasonable biographical narration. The plot reductions, the destruction of narrative forms and some of the monologues by Carr and Tzara, which are partly devoid of meaning, all aim at the illustration of the impossibility of biographical renarration. Thus, *Travesties* is not only from the point of view of theme, but also of form, a drama depicting a world in which all epistemological models are exposed as fictional. At the same time, the play is traditional enough to tell a story with an anti-dogmatic, anti-Marxist purpose. This purpose, however, does not refer to the historiographical and biographical difficulties, but to the relationship between art and political revolution (cf. Wolf 1986: 356).

VI. *Arcadia*: Accenting the Epistemological Process of Biography

Arcadia is in so far a continuation of Stoppard's biography plays as, again, the best known and only authentic historical character, Lord George Gordon Noel Byron, is not the protagonist of the play, just as Hamlet and Joyce *et al.*, respectively, were not in *Rosencrantz and Guildenstern are Dead* and *Travesties* (cf. Niederhoff 2001/02: 43). This biographical marginalisation literally affects the staging of *Arcadia*, since Byron is never actually on stage, but always moving on its margins. The "real" protagonists, in turn, are purely fictitious. The plot revolves around a child prodigy, Thomasina Coverly, the thirteen year old daughter of Lord and Lady Croom, her tutor, Septimus Hodge, and two literary biographers, Bernard Nightingale and Hannah Jarvis. *Arcadia* shuttles between two time periods, the first being the early nineteenth century (1809 and 1812), the second the present day. Its plot integrates literary biography, landscape gardening, thermodynamics, chaos theory and fractal geometry. In the play, Stoppard employs modern mathematics and physics to question requirements of conventional drama and biography. *Arcadia* breaches neither historical authenticity nor scientific principles, while at the same time self-reflexively emphasising its own artificiality. Stoppard succeeds in combining many seemingly ambiguous, chaotic and antithetical topics and strands into one plot. Therefore, to arrive at the presentation of biography in *Arcadia*, its themes as well as its structure and character presentation have to be examined. This elaborate approach is necessary to place *Arcadia* in line with Stoppard's biography plays and to give due consideration to its metadramatic and metabiographical complexity.

1. Ideological landscapes

a. Landscape gardening: The change from Classicism to Romanticism

The "[p]eg" or "[e]piphany" (*Arcadia* 27) for Hannah's historical research for her new book on "the nervous breakdown of the Romantic Imagination" and "landscape and literature 1750 to 1834" (25) is a hermit who lived in Sidley Park until 1834. This hermit was described as "a savant among idiots, a sage of lunacy" (26) as he lived for more than twenty years in the hermitage created out of a gazebo by the "landskip architect" (2) Richard Noakes. There, the hermit covered sheets of paper "with cabalistic proofs that the world was coming to an end" (27) of which was "[m]ade a bonfire" (28) after his death. For Hannah, this hermit symbolises the "decline from thinking to feeling", as she explains to her colleague:

> The whole Romantic sham, Bernard! It's what happened to the Enlightenment, isn't it? A century of intellectual rigour turned in on itself. A mind in chaos suspected of genius. In a setting of cheap thrills and false emotion. The history of the garden says it all, beautifully. There's an engraving of Sidley Park in 1730 that makes you want to weep. Paradise in the age of reason. By 1760 everything had gone [...] the whole sublime geometry was ploughed under by Capability Brown. The grass went from the doorstep to the horizon and the best box hedge in Derbyshire was dug up for the ha-ha so that the fools could pretend they were living in God's countryside. And then Richard Noakes came in to bring God up to date. (27)

Hannah's description of the changes in the landscape garden reflects the discourse on whether man lives in a world of regularity or irregularity. The Italian, and also French, gardens which dominated Sidley Park with their geometrical patterns until 1740 are seen as the epitome of the Classicist principle of reason, according to which the universe is structured in an orderly way. The human hand is necessary to create structures in the haphazard appearance of nature. For Hannah, the rational and regular patterns of the landscape garden are her personal Arcadia, a paradise in the Age of Reason. Her *Weltanschauung* is emphasised by her name – a palindrome – which is reversible just like Newton's equations and the first law of thermodynamics (cf. Sternlieb/Selleck 2003: 493). When Hannah talks about the English landscape garden as an imitation of "God's countryside" in a derogatory manner, she rejects the notion dominant in the late eighteenth century that nature is the image of the perfection created by God, as formulated by Lady Croom: "it is nature as God intended" (12). As John Dixon Hunt comments, Lady Croom's remark

> nicely captures the late eighteenth-century English confidence, well expressed by [... Horace Walpole] in his *A History of the Modern Taste in Gardening*, that the English landscape garden under Brown's supreme and God-given control was exactly as nature should have been. (Hunt 1996: 59)

Although the world picture which is reflected in English landscape gardens is no longer strictly symmetrical and regular, there is still order. *Le jardin anglais* (cf. Fischer-Seidel 1997: 95) was claimed to be wholly natural, although Lancelot "Capability" Brown (1715-1783), its most famous creator, was a formalist himself – he claimed to be merely presenting the forms of nature (cf. Hunt 1996: 62). These forms go so far that there are "meadows on which the right amount of sheep are tastefully arranged" (*Arcadia* 12). The undulating arranged lines of the landscape garden are still seen as an expression of divine will in a meaningful universe (cf. Antor 1998: 329ff.). That is why Lady Croom approves of geometry (cf. *Arcadia* 83) and why she rejects Noakes's remodelling of the garden according to picturesque Romantic examples (cf. 9f.). The creation of free, untamed nature is for Lady Croom unsubstantiated artificiality because he creates "ruins where there was never a house" and has "water dashing against rocks where there was neither spring nor stone I could not throw the length of a cricket pitch". Noakes, on the other hand, defends his gardening plans by stating that "[i]rregularity is one of the chiefest principles of the picturesque style" (12). Hence, Thomasina ironically calls him later the "Emperor of Irregularity" (85). Like Hannah, but in a different way, she rejects the fallacy of the English landscape garden: "the one prefers the 'sublime geometry' of the pre-1740 Sidley gardens, and the other lauds the artifice of the picturesque as antidote to fake naturalism, while brushing aside any one style as the ideal mode of representing the natural world" (Hunt 1996: 62).

The landscape garden in *Arcadia* has undergone a change from absolute geometrical symmetry to moderate, fluent harmony, to artificial irregularity, and it represents three different *Weltanschauungen*. Although Noakes's garden is not chaotic but meticulously planned and thought-out, he emphasises discontinuity and non-linearity. Lady Croom, however, desires harmony and order. Noakes's suggestions are unsettling for her and she is overall too unRomantic to appreciate them. Hannah, with her classicist frame of mind, is even less able to accept Noakes's aesthetic and philosophical implications (cf. Antor 1998: 332f.).

As "[n]othing much need be said or seen of the exterior beyond" (*Arcadia* 1), the device to represent the landscape garden on stage is Noakes's sketch book, an allusion to the 'Red Books' by the landscape gardener Humphrey Repton (1752-1818), who became Brown's successor in the leadership of the profession (cf. Hunt 1996: 59):

> The sketch book is the work of MR NOAKES, who is obviously an admirer of Humphrey Repton's 'Red Books'. The pages, drawn in watercolours, show 'before' and 'after' views of the landscape, and the pages are cunningly cut to allow the latter to be superimposed over portions of the former, though Repton did it the other way round. (*Arcadia* 10)

In her seminal study of 'representations' in *Arcadia*, Müller-Muth correctly points out that, by reversing Repton's original order, Noakes's sketch book takes on the mechanisms of a palimpsest. Noakes overlays older landscape garden concepts with his visions, transforming them into a condition of alleged originality. This alleged original condition, however, turns out to be a layer over yet another pre-condition, which is another cultural construct of nature and so on (cf. Müller-Muth 2001: 183). The mechanism of the palimpsest opposes the idea of any possible authentic primitive state of the landscape garden and of nature *per se*.[95]

---

[95] In his study *The Making of the English Landscape* (1955), the local historian W.G. Hoskins implicitly views English landscape as a palimpsest. In the introduction to the 1977 edition, he writes that "one can sum it [English landscape] up safely in the phrase *Everything is older than we think*" (Hoskins 1977: 12). Hoskins ends his original study by describing a landscape in Oxfordshire upon which the "cultural humus of sixty generations or more lies [...]. But most of England is a thousand years old, and in a walk of a few miles one would touch nearly every century in that long stretch of time" (303).

In the present, it is the landscape archaeologist Hannah who is aware of the fact that the landscape garden is constituted by an accumulation of layers:

> English landscape was invented by gardeners imitating foreign painters who were evoking classical authors. The whole thing was brought home in the luggage from the grand tour. Here, look – Capability Brown doing Claude, who was doing Virgil. Arcadia! And here, superimposed by Richard Noakes, untamed nature in the style of Salvator Rosa. (*Arcadia* 25)

Here Hannah comments on the relationship between art and nature. Hanna Scolnicov explains:

> This aesthetic ideal of making the landscape look more "picturesque" turns around the logical priorities of nature and art, so that it is no longer clear whether art imitates nature, or nature, art. The established, and intuitively accepted, idea of art as a mirror of nature is thus upended, and our image of reality is seen as a mere imitation of art. In this vast hall of mirrors, every new work of art necessarily imitates other works, and the works already displayed are likewise to be understood in relation to the new additions. Ontology falls victim to intertextuality. (Scolnicov 2004: 487f.)

This description also becomes true for the historical reconstructions in the time line of the present insofar as the present is always superimposed on the past. In analogy to Noakes's sketch book, the search for a historical state of origin, a fixed moment in time, must turn out to be an illusion, as each layer represents a superimposition on yet another cultural construct (cf. Müller-Muth 2001: 183f.). The time shuttle in *Arcadia* thus achieves not only a comparison of two historical epochs, but also the comparison of "the former with the reconstruction of its image by the latter" (Scolnicov 2004: 496).

At the same time, the landscape garden becomes a metaphor for chaos theory because, as much as its growth is planned, controlled and maintained, one year "sets up the conditions for the next, the smallest variation blows prediction apart, and the weather is unpredictable the same way, will always be unpredictable" (*Arcadia* 48; cf. Hunt 1996: 63). Any garden style is always a representation of the understanding of the natural world by its own culture, as "each epoch speaks its values and ideas through its gardens" (Hunt 1996: 62). However, as with nature, landscape gardens must be tamed in order not to get out of control and form. In the same manner, the garden, as Alison Wheatley notes, "is identified with unrestricted sexuality because, according to prevailing patriarchal notions, both always 'need' to be reformed and controlled" (Wheatley 2004: 179). In an analogy to the garden of Eden, Mrs Chater is ultimately expelled from Sidley Park after Lady Croom sees her coming from Lord Byron's bedchamber. Here, landscape gardening draws another connection to chaos theory as it is sexuality, "[t]he attraction that Newton left out" (*Arcadia* 74), a so-called 'strange attractor' which disrupts the order of Arcadia or Eden. In the same context, Prapassaree and Jeffrey Kramer point out that entropy capsulises the concept of the Fall, and the consequent reign of *thanatos*, as being connected to sexuality (cf. Kramer 1997: 4).

b. Apposing universes: 'Classical' Newtonian physics and 'Romantic' chaos theory

It is well-known that Stoppard's main source on chaos theory was James Gleick's *Chaos: Making a New Science* (1987; cf. Nathan 1993), which is also a paean on Romanticism. Romanticism challenges and reverses the assumptions of Classicism and the Enlightenment. It seeks out gloom, pursues irregularity and prefers untamed landscapes (cf. Hunter 2000: 169). In his book, Gleick quotes the German physicist Gert Eilenberger, who points out that while "the silhouette of a storm-bent leafless tree against an evening sky in winter is perceived as beautiful, […] the corresponding silhouette of any multi-purpose university building is not" (Gleick 1987: 117). The opinion Gleick presents here is thus the diametrical opposite to Lady Croom's and even more so to Hannah's. Their attitudes about landscape gardens are similar in their contrast to the one Gleick quotes John Fowles's as criticising:

> The period [of eighteenth-century England] had no sympathy with unregulated or primordial nature. It was aggressive wilderness, an ugly and all-invasive reminder of the Fall, of man's eternal exile from the Garden of Eden. … Even its natural sciences … remained essentially hostile to wild nature, seeing it only as something to be tamed, classified, utilised, exploited.   (Gleick 1987: 117)

The character explaining all chaos mathematical and physical issues in the play is Valentine Coverly, the son of the present day Crooms and a mathematics student at Oxford, who is trying to find an equation to represent the apparently haphazard fluctuations in the grouse population at Sidley Park. In the past, Thomasina provided him with such an equation, and after Valentine feeds it into his computer, calling it the "Coverly set", he describes the patterns which emerge from the dots in an almost Romantic manner: "In an ocean of ashes, islands of order. Patterns making themselves out of nothing" (*Arcadia* 76). Valentine's description is reminiscent of Jean-François Lyotard's answer to the debate between stable and unstable systems, determinism and nondeterminism: "All that exist are 'islands of determinism'. Catastrophic antagonism is literally the rule: there are rules for the general agonistics of series, determined by the number of variables in play" (Lyotard 1994: 59).[96] In the phenomenon of chaos, Stoppard found a metaphor for his play that incorporated questions he had already asked in *Rosencrantz and Guildenstern are Dead*: the dialectic of free will and determinism. This becomes clear when we consider how the scientist Doyne Farmer describes the phenomenon of chaos: "On a philosophical level, it struck me as an operational way to define free will, in a way that allowed you to reconcile free will with determinism. The system is deterministic, but you can't say what it's going to do next" (Gleick 1987: 251).

Arcadia deals with the paradigm shift from Enlightenment rationality to Romanticism in science, in the past as well as in the present. Similar to the way Classicist landscape gardens are shaped by symmetry and geometry, Newton's universe is also made symmetrical by geometry. It is a structured, determined universe, and in principle one can predict future changes and reconstruct past conditions through calculations based on the knowledge of forces and masses which influence events (cf. Edwards 2001: 178):

> If you could stop every atom in its position and direction, and if your mind could comprehend all the actions thus suspended, then if you were really, *really*

---

[96] "Il n'y a donc que des 'îlots de déterminisme'. L'antagonisme catastrophique est la règle, au sens propre: il y a des règles de l'agonistique générale des séries, qui se définissent par le nombre des variables en jeu" (Lyotard 1979: 96).

good at algebra you could write the formula for all the future; and although nobody can be so clever to do it, the formula must exist just as if one could.
(Arcadia 5)

Anachronistically, Thomasina formulates here what became known as *Laplace's demon*, named after Pierre-Simon Laplace, who first formulated the notion in the preface to his *Philosophical Essay on Probability* (*Essai Philosophique sur les Probabilités*, 1814).[97] In the world of physics, *Laplace's demon* was refuted first by the theory of relativity, then by quantum physics, and lastly by chaos theory, as Valentine explains:

> It makes me so happy. To be at the beginning again, knowing almost nothing. People were talking about the end of physics. Relativity and quantum looked as if they were going to clean out the whole problem between them. A theory of everything. But they only explained the very big and the very small. The universe, the elementary particles. The ordinary-sized stuff which is our lives, the things people write poetry about – clouds – daffodils – waterfalls – and what happens in a cup of coffee when the cream goes in – these things are full of mystery, as mysterious to us as the heavens were to the Greeks. [...] The future is disorder. (47f.)

In *Arcadia*, it is Thomasina who outlines chaos theory as a rebuttal of *Laplace's demon*, ahead of her time and by observation only. However, her anachronistic discovery of chaos mathematics is not an unlikely phenomenon if we are to believe Farmer: "The phenomenon of chaos could have been discovered long, long ago. [... I]f you just look, there it is. It brought home the point that one should allow oneself to be guided by the physics, by observations, to see what kind of theoretical picture one could develop" (Farmer in Gleick 1987: 25). Accordingly, for Jernigan, Thomasina is the epitome of the Romantic genius, "toiling alone and in obscurity, creating success with limited means" (Jernigan 2003: 25) and at the same time the personification of Gleick's assessment of chaos theorists as described in his book (cf. 30).

---

[97] "Nous devons donc envisager l'état présent de l'univers, comme l'effect de son état antérieur, et comme la cause de celui qui va suivre. Une intelligence qui pour un instant donné, connaîtrait toutes les forces dont la nature est animée, et la situation respective des êtres qui la composent, si d'ailleurs elle était assez vaste pour soumettre ces données à l'analyse, embrasserait dans la même formule, les mouvements des plus grands corps de l'univers et ceux du plus léger atome: rien ne serait incertain pour elle, et l'avenir comme le passé, serait présent à ses yeux" (Laplace 1814: 3f.).

With her innocent question whether "God is a Newtonian" (*Arcadia* 5), Thomasina expresses her disaffection with Newton's laws and their incapability to explain inconsistencies in the world. She believes in a more complex world than Newton's mechanistic universe, which in turn demands a more complex kind of mathematics: "God's truth, Septimus, if there is an equation for a curve like a bell, there must be an equation for one like a bluebell, and if a bluebell, why not a rose?" (37). Later on, she claims to have discovered this kind of equation: "I, Thomasina Coverly, have found a truly wonderful method whereby all the forms of nature must give up their numerical secrets and draw themselves through number alone". At the same time she, like the French mathematician Pierre de Fermat, writes that the margin of her primer is too mean for the proof of her so-called "New Geometry of Irregular Forms" (43).

The first law of thermodynamics states that "[i]n any process, the energy of the universe is conserved" (Kaufman 2002: 49). Hence, this universe must be a self-preserving system which does not move in a certain direction, as is explained by Thomasina: "Newton's equations go forwards and backwards, they do not care which way" (*Arcadia* 87). Septimus adheres to the classical Newtonian belief that all processes are reversible or that at least the initial conditions can be restored. To him, this does not only apply to physical processes, but to life in general:

> We shed as we pick up, like travellers who must carry everything in their arms, and what we let fall will be picked up by those behind. The procession is very long and life is very short. We die on the march. But there is nothing outside the march so nothing can be lost to it. The missing plays of Sophocles will turn up piece by piece, or be written again in another language. [...] Mathematical discoveries glimpsed and lost to view will have their time again. (38)

The march of life, to Septimus, is a closed system as in the first law of thermodynamics, in which nothing, in the long run, gets lost, and everything is restored in the future. In this scene, Thomasina is translating a Latin text into English. However, she does not know that her Latin text is already a translation by Septimus, namely from Domitius Enobarbus's speech from Shakespeare's *Antony and Cleopatra* (1607; cf. Shakespeare 1974: 1357 [II.ii.191-199]), which in turn comes from Thomas North's translation of Jacques Amyot's translation of the Vatican text of Plutarch's "The Life of Marcus Antonius" from his *Parallel Lives* (cf.

Skeat (ed.) 1972: vii and 174). As in Noakes's sketch book and the mechanism of the palimpsest, we have layer over layer of hypotext: Thomasina translating into English Septimus's Latin translation of Shakespeare's treatment of North's English translation of Jacques Amyot's French translation of a Latin translation of Plutarch's description in Greek of Cleopatra in his biographical sketch of Marc Antony. In accordance with Septimus's statement, Thomasina is working with a text "written again in another language". However, her unpoetic retranslation efforts attest that life is not imperatively a closed system. They are proof of the irreversibility of certain processes, such as the re-creation of lost art (cf. Edwards 2001: 179).

Before her unwilling discovery of the irreversibility of translation processes, Thomasina makes some physical discoveries which also imply irreversibility, for example that you cannot "unstir" the jam in the rice pudding: "When you stir your rice pudding, Septimus, the spoonful of jam spreads itself round [...]. But if you stir backward, the jam will not come together again. [...] You cannot stir things apart" (*Arcadia* 4f., dialogue omitted). While Septimus sees in her observation an explanation for "free will or self-determination" (5), Thomasina's innocent and playful discovery implicates something more important, namely that God is not a Newtonian. Roughly 180 years later, Hannah realises that Thomasina predicted certain physical discoveries. Valentine explains the phenomenon implied by his ancestor by reference to a cooling cup of tea:

> Your tea gets cold by itself, it doesn't get hot by itself. [...] Heat goes to cold. It's a one-way street. [...] What's happening to your tea is happening to everything everywhere. The sun and the stars. It'll take a while but we're all going to end up at room temperature. (78, dialogue omitted)

Although ignorant about the maths, Thomasina deduces, through her discoveries, the second law of thermodynamics, actually first articulated in 1824 by the French military engineer Sadi Carnot and later restated by the German physicist Rudolf Clausius (cf. Ulanowicz 1986: 17). The latter also introduced the concept of entropy for describing the quantification of the distributed heat in a given environment. Thus, entropy is a measure of disorder in a system. The second law of thermodynamics provides information on the direction of processes. Contrary to the first law, it states that "[i]n any real process, there is net degradation of energy", meaning that "[e]nergy is degraded to less useful forms as we use it" (Kaufman 2002: 73f.). Thomasina realises this with regard to Noakes's steam engine: "the heat equation [...] goes only one way. That is the reason Mr Noakes's engine cannot give the power to drive Mr Noakes's engine" (*Arcadia* 87). From this she reasons that the universe will eventually cool down and return to a state of maximum entropy.[98] When all the energy is used up, it will be a distributed amount of irrecoverable energy, i.e. chaos (cf. Edwards 2001: 179f.). Or, as Septimus puts it: "So the Improved Newtonian Universe must cease and grow cold. Dear me" (*Arcadia* 93). Nonetheless, despite the universe growing cold, chaos theory "allows for pockets of self-organizing systems", i.e. out of entropy, "order is continuously being born in local settings" (McKinney 2003: 397).

Valentine explains to Hannah that if reversibility was true for the entire universe, it would be possible to watch a film backwards without realising whether it was not running in the right direction. There are some phenomena in the universe which pass such a test of reversal, e.g. a swinging pendulum. Other phenomena, however, do not, such as a ball breaking a window because "[y]ou can put back the bits of glass but you can't collect up the heat of the smash. It's gone" (*Arcadia* 93). The same is true of objects which incinerate: these processes are irreversible (cf. Edwards 2001: 178f.). *Arcadia* is full of incidents which document the irreversibility of time: props age, the landscape garden undergoes dramatic changes, letters by Byron and Septimus's entire calculations are burnt, and also, Thomasina falls prey to a fire on the night of her seventeenth birthday.

---

[98] In his ecological study *Growth and Development*, Robert E. Ulanowicz writes: "Evidence that something was gravely amiss with Laplace's demon began to appear in the 1820s. Engineers such as Sadi Carnot were experimenting with the new steam engines and exploring how efficiently they could be run with a given quality of steam. They discovered empirically that some of the the energy in the steam was inaccessible. This implied that the whole process of running the steam engine could not be reversed" (Ulanowicz 1986: 3).

Edwards points out that the idea of entropy can also be applied to information theory.[99] An increase in entropy, i.e. noise, amounts to a loss of information (cf. Edwards 2001: 180f. and Chung 2005: 698). In the context of his study on the grouse population, Valentine compares the increase of entropy with a piano playing in the next room:

> Distortions. Interference. Real data is messy. [...] It's all very, very noisy out there. Very hard to spot the tune. Like a piano in the next room, it's playing your song, but unfortunately it's out of whack, some of the strings are missing, and the pianist is tone deaf and drunk – I mean, the *noise*! Impossible!
>
> (*Arcadia* 46)

Analogically, the piano playing of Thomasina, who is the summoner of chaos mathematics and entropy in *Arcadia*, is described in the stage directions as the "*noise* [... *of*] *a badly played piano in the next room*" (41). The opposite of Thomasina's chaotic noise would be melody, which stands for harmony and structure (cf. Antor 1998: 346). This melody is what Valentine tries to find:

> You start guessing what the tune might be. You try to pick it out of the noise. You try this, you try that, you start to get something – it's half-baked but you start putting in notes which are missing or not quite the right notes... and bit by bit... (*He starts to dumdi-da to the tune of 'Happy Birthday'.*) Dumdi-dum-dum, dear Val-en-tine, dumdi-dum-dum to you – the lost algorithm!   (*Arcadia* 46)

Music and noise are also present on the time level of the past. Lady Croom plays a waltz[100] on the piano with the Polish Count Zelinsky. Only when the playing becomes more and more passionate does it suddenly break off in mid-phrase. Sexual tension disturbs the order, or, as Chloë has it: "The universe is deterministic all right, just like Newton said, I mean it's trying to be, but the only thing going wrong is people fancying people who aren't supposed to be in that part of the plan" (*Arcadia* 73). Similarly, Thomasina establishes an analogy between the real and the mathematical world when she wittily comments on thermodynamics, explaining to her mother what rebuts determinism in

---

[99] On information theory and its application to ecosystems as done by Valentine, cf. Ulanowicz 1986: 81ff.

[100] As Stern points out, the waltz was invented in the Romantic period and was satirised by Lord Byron in his poem *The Waltz: An Apostrophic Hymn* (1813; cf. Stern 1996: 156).

Newton's universe: "The action of bodies in heat" (84). In the course of the scene, "*[t]he piano is heard again, under the noise of the steam engine*" and Lady Croom complains about the "unendurable noise" and "[t]he ceaseless dull overbearing monotony of it" (82). While piano music represents Lady Croom's need for harmony and order, as in the landscape garden, Noakes's steam engine stands for the noise of technological progress and modern science and the resulting increase in entropy. Its monotony already hints at the homogeneity of the final state of maximum entropy and absolute amorphousness predicted by theorists of thermodynamics (cf. Antor 1998: 346).

Disorder, chaos and increasing entropy are also manifested in many of the dialogues of *Arcadia*. The noise with regard to communication is here polysemy and different frames of references, which make for semantic entropy and misunderstandings, indicating the twofold structure of *Arcadia*.

2. The twofold structure: Semantic doublings and varying characteristic repetitions

The play opens in "*a very large country house in Derbyshire in April 1809. Nowadays, the house would be called a stately home*" (*Arcadia* 1). The emphasis on describing the edifice as a large country house in 1809 and as a stately home nowadays is the first indication of the twofold perspective of the play, separated by and formed over time. In the opening dialogue, in which Septimus explains to Thomasina the meaning of "carnal embrace" and Fermat's last theorem in a single breath, after wittily dodging her rather direct but innocent questions about his seduction of Charity Chater, wife to the poet and guest at Sidley Park, Ezra Chater, the twofold discourse of the play again becomes apparent:

> THOMASINA: If *you* do not teach me the true meaning of things, who will?
> SEPTIMUS: Ah. Yes, I am ashamed. Carnal embrace is sexual congress, which is the insertion of the male genital organ into the female genital organ for purposes of procreation and pleasure. Fermat's last theorem, by contrast, asserts that when x, y and z are whole numbers each raised to power of n, the sum of the first two can never equal the third when n is greater than 2.

> (*Pause.*)
> THOMASINA: Eurghhh!
> SEPTIMUS: Nevertheless, that is the theorem.
> THOMASINA: It is disgusting and incomprehensible. Now when I am grown to practice it myself I shall never do so without thinking of you.   (3)

As Fischer-Seidel points out, arithmetic explanations and sexual innuendos are associated with each other, and the semantic doubling gives a first insight into the structure of the play (cf. Fischer-Seidel 1997: 96). The same semantic doubling occurs in the conversation between Lady Croom and Noakes. Sexual innuendos are intermingled with the "improvements" of the landscape garden. While Septimus thinks that Lady Croom, her brother Captain Brice, Noakes and Mr Chater are talking of his seduction of Mrs Chater in the gazebo, they are actually thinking of the "rape" of Sidley Park by Noakes (cf. *Arcadia* 9ff.).

The semantic ambiguities in the mentioned dialogues provide examples of the theme of twofold reality. Throughout the play, we encounter doublings with regard to the two shuttling time levels, until both time periods merge on stage in the final scene and the props exist "*doubled by time*" (93). According to the stage directions, the props can be present in both time periods throughout the entire play:

> The general *appearance of the room should offend neither period. In the case of the props – books, paper, flowers, etc., there is no absolute need to remove the evidence of one period to make way for another. However, books, etc., used in both periods should exist in both old and new versions.* [...]
> *During the course of the play the table collects this and that, and where an object from one scene would be an anachronism in another (say a coffee mug) it is simply deemed to have become invisible.*   (15)

There are, for example, two tortoises "whose actions are", according to Michele Ronnick, "a metaphor for our concepts of linear motion in relation to time and speed, to tell us that the world is not necessarily linear, nor predictable, nor evenly paced" (Ronnick 1996: 179).[101] The name of Septimus's tortoise is Plautus, named after the Roman comedian, Titus Maccius Plautus (*c*254-184 B.C.), whose surname in Umbrian dialect means 'flatfoot' and whose most famous comedy, *Menaechmi*, is about twin brothers and was the plot inspiration for Shakespeare's *Comedy of*

---

[101] On further 'representations' of the turtle, cf. Müller-Muth 2001: 278ff.

Errors (cf. Fort/Kates 1935: 22). The name Plautus is, thus, on the one hand an allusion to the twin structure of the play, on the other to the slowness of the animal "which is sleepy enough to serve as a paperweight" (*Arcadia* 1). The slowness in turn stands for the early nineteenth century (cf. Fischer-Seidel 1997: 98f.). There are no computers yet, with which Thomasina might be able to solve her iterative algorithms, or, as Valentine Coverly remarks in the present: "There wasn't enough time before. There weren't enough *pencils*!" (*Arcadia* 51). The static performance of the tortoise, and its function to keep Septimus's desk-top in order, represent the ordered and elaborate Newtonian universe, with all its patterns and structures, which dominated physics at that time. The theodolite (cf. 1) and, later on, the apple on the table (cf. 35) – an allusion to Newton, but also to the computer company of the same name, the Judgement of Paris and Eden (cf. Melbourne 1998: 562) – support this reading (cf. Antor 1998: 349). That Septimus "*cuts a slice of the apple, and while he eats it, cuts another slice which he offers to Plautus*" (*Arcadia* 35) is seen by Bernhard Reitz as the foreshadowed deconstruction of Newton's universe (cf. Reitz 1996: 174). Conversely, the tortoise's name in the present is "Lightning", and it thus represents the period of fast information processing computers (cf. Fischer-Seidel 1997: 99). This animal represents a universe of irregularities and of constructed patterns and structures ready to be dissolved any minute. Everything is in motion, just as Lightning, who sometimes hides and needs to be taken for his run (cf. *Arcadia* 18).

The characters – or rather certain of their characteristics – are another element doubled by time in *Arcadia*. Character traits of the past reappear with a variation in contemporary characters. For example, Chloë and Thomasina emanate a youthful unconcern and dynamic. In an almost identical text passage, both formulate a new theory about Newton's deterministic universe (cf. 5f. and 73f.), but while Chloë's actions mainly revolve around sex, Thomasina at first chooses knowledge over love (cf. 38). Only shortly before she turns seventeen does she turn to love. She has a crush on Byron and real feelings for Septimus. Chloë's and Thomasina's brothers, Gus and Augustus, respectively, also correspond to each other and were even played by the same actor in the première. But while Augustus is an arrogant and self-conscious teenager, Gus stopped talking at the age of five and is an autistic genius. Septimus's scientific mind is represented in the present by the mathematician Valentine. Both explain to the recipients the theoretical issues of the play, such as Fermat's last theorem (cf. 3), chaos theory, iterative algorithms and fractal geometry (cf. 43ff.) and Thomasina's cogitations about thermodynamics (cf. 78, 81 and 93f.). Septimus's world view is questioned by Thomasina's insights in the end, and Valentine uses her equations for his research on the grouse population in Sidley Park. As regards chaos – in Septimus's world, of course, still within the boundaries of Newton's deterministic universe – and the course of (life) time, both depict life as an irreversible "mixing" (5 and 94) until the end of time. Even the tutor-pupil relationship is doubled, Septimus teaching Thomasina and Valentine explaining modern physics to Hannah. Septimus's role as a reviewer of Mr Chater's lyric is taken up by the literary critic Bernard, whose aversions against science in turn resemble Captain Brice's, and who is as conceited as the poet Chater. Hannah, like Lady Croom, rejects the refashioning of the landscape garden by Noakes and the ideology behind it. Noakes in turn remodels Capability Brown's gazebo into the hermitage where Septimus practices "carnal embrace" with Mrs Chater and where he retreats to as the hermit after Thomasina's tragic death by fire, in order to calculate her equations, and so on.

As Müller-Muth points out, the characters can reach a certain multi-dimensionality despite their type-like conception. This is due to multifarious intertextual allusions to other characters, figures or discourses inherent in them (cf. Müller-Muth 2001: 123).[102] Thus, character depiction in the play resembles the conception of the subject as construct, repeatedly defining itself anew according to its interconnectedness or contextualisation, which never reaches a status of unity (cf. 127). Here, in the context of biography, the play considers the afore-mentioned notion of the non-unified and non-unique biographical subject as represented in poststructuralism, deconstructivism and New Historicism (cf. II.2.e). The depiction of characters as types and not as individuals denies

---

[102] On 'intertextual types' in *Arcadia*, cf. Müller-Muth 2001: 122-130; on Thomasina as a 'character of quotations', especially of the daughter of the historical Lord Byron, Augusta Ada Lovelace, cf. 141-148 and Clayton 2003: 118ff.

them a certain uniqueness and irreproducibility. The uniqueness which constitutes the autonomous subject of traditional biography is thus rejected in the play. The character depiction as an intertextual intersection suggests the renunciation of the Romantic notion of the genius (cf. 129), a key element of conventional biography and, in the context of *Arcadia*, 'Byrongraphy'.

3. 'Byrongraphical' constructions

Lord Byron is the only authentic historical character in *Arcadia*. Although he stands out on account of his physical absence from the stage, literally enacting what Susanne Schmid describes as "Byron's play with his audience [which] consisted in his successful literary hide-and-seek, a deliberate game confounding the public and the private spheres" (Schmid 2002: 86), he nevertheless is actively engaged in the events around Sidley Park and partially the cause for the complications in both time periods. While in 1809, Lord Byron actually interacts with the characters offstage – he is the reason why Chater learns about Septimus's harsh review of his first book (cf. *Arcadia* 36) and partly the cause for the Chaters and Captain Brice having to leave Sidley Park (cf. 68f.) –, he becomes the topic of voyeuristic interest circa 180 years later. As regards biographical research, his life is the matter of dispute between the two literary biographers, Hannah and Bernard, who for Müller-Muth represent a parody of literary criticism and literary history (cf. Müller-Muth 2001: 127).

Hannah is the author of a popular biography about Lady Caroline 'Caro' Lamb, Byron's former mistress and herself the author of *Glenarvon* (1816), a Byronic *roman à clef* (cf. Huber 1999: 460). The reaction to Hannah's feminist revisionist biography by the academic "Byron gang" was that they "unzipped their flies and patronized all over it". The second literary biographer in *Arcadia* is the conceited Bernard, who tries to shed light onto a dark area of Byron's life, namely why he suddenly left England in 1809. Bernard is one such a member of the "Byron gang" and he reviewed her book, "a thousand words in the *Observer* to see [... Hannah] off the premises with a pat on the bottom"

(*Arcadia* 22). He calls her biography a "novelette", denying its status as "a work of historical revisionism" as she "got them backwards": "Caroline was Romantic waffle on wheels with no talent, and Byron was an eighteenth-century Rationalist touched by genius" (59f.). With the help of the time shuttle, both biographers' hypotheses are put to the test in front of the audience. Hannah's theory about the hermit proves at the beginning to be an erroneous construct, reducing him to an oversimplified symbol for her theory of cultural decline. Bernard's theory about Byron is also refuted, discredited and shown to be purely fictitious. Chance occurrences in the past are instilled with meaning in the present and thus lead to false conclusions (cf. Huber 1999: 460). In 1809, for example, Thomasina draws the picture of a hermit in Noakes's sketch book in order to complete the hermitage in it. In the twentieth century, Hannah misinterprets this hermit as the symbol of the Romantic spirit of Noakes's creation, "[d]rawn in by a later hand, of course. The hermitage didn't yet exist when Noakes did the drawings". She is not aware of the fact that the drawing of her "Sidley hermit", which Bernard hence correctly describes as "[v]ery biblical" (*Arcadia* 25), does not take after an authentic model, but after Salvator Rosa's painting, *St. John the Baptist in the Wilderness* (c1640). Thomasina's drawing in the book is of pure coincidence and done with childlike unconcern in accordance with Salvator Rosa, "the very exemplar of the picturesque style" (11):

> THOMASINA: There. I have made him like the Baptist in the wilderness.
> SEPTIMUS: How picturesque. (14)

This shows that Hannah's initial theory about the hermit is caused by a haphazard action, the caprice of a young girl. By the end of the play, however, she has uncovered the true identity of the hermit, realising that it must have been Septimus. Thomasina showed him the dark future of the world through the second law of thermodynamics: "it was Frenchified mathematick[103] that brought him to the melancholy certitude of a world without light or life... as a wooden stove that must consume itself until ash and stove are as one, and heat is gone from the earth" (65). Living as a hermit, Septimus tried, for twenty-two years, to (dis)prove Thomasina's pessimistic notions that, through a continuous

---

[103] This refers to Sadi Carnot and the second law of thermodynamics.

process of disintegration and increasing chaos, the world is on its way to an entropic heat death. He feedbacks her equations again and again in order to reinstitute islands of order in an ocean of ashes. Thus Septimus becomes a Romantic, something which the classicist Hannah at first does not understand. This is why she thinks him a lunatic. However, Septimus's story goes deeper. Between Thomasina and him, there is love, as both have just begun to realise. The pain of losing her in a fire, the initial flame of which he lit himself by lighting her candle (cf. 96) is his true torment. *Contrary* to the first law, and *according* to the second law of thermodynamics, Thomasina is irrecoverable, just as Septimus's personal reasons for becoming a hermit cannot be reconstructed.

Hannah's *post-hoc* fallacy of Thomasina's drawing is similar to Bernard's of Byron's killing of Ezra Chater in a duel. According to his theory, Lord Byron visited Sidley Park on an April weekend in 1809, slept with Ezra Chater's wife and killed him in a duel, which resulted from the adultery. To Bernard, this is the explanation why Byron suddenly left England. However, the literary biographer turns out to be wrong. While it is true that Byron was in Sidely Park that weekend and did seduce Mrs Chater, there was no duel, and the challenge was directed at Septimus, who was the first to sleep with Mrs Chater the same weekend, and who was the author of the devastating reviews of Ezra Chater's lyrical work. On her own way to Byron's bed-chamber, Lady Croom encountered Mrs Chater leaving the same and, hence, threw both the Chaters and Lord Byron out. All of Bernard's efforts to reconstruct the events around Byron are doomed to failure as he misinterprets the historical data. It proves to be an incorrect, melodramatic construction. In the course of his speculations, Bernard bends historical fact in order to construe a fantastic story that is in accordance with the Byron myth of the rake, 'mad, bad and dangerous to know' – the famous description of Lord Byron by Caroline Lamb. Even so-called hard historical facts such as the data in the game book, which documents Byron shooting a hare, turns out to be unreliable when we learn that he is not good with guns and that "[h]is lameness […] is entirely the result of his habit from boyhood of shooting himself in the foot" (41). Augustus explains later in the play that it was actually he who shot the hare (cf. 79).[104]

Bernard celebrates the personification of the rake in Byron throughout the play and in his theory:

> HANNAH: Nobody would kill a man and then pan his book. I mean, not in that order. So he must have borrowed the book, written the review, *posted it*, seduced Mrs Chater, fought a duel and departed, all in the space of two or three days. Who would do that?
> BERNARD: Byron. (59)

While the biographical discourse's linchpin in the present is the historical Byron, the time line of the past presents a different picture of the poet because of the "hero's" constant stage absence. What takes his place is a 'Byron' figure, an ideal fictional representation made up of myths, traditions and contradictions: a "Biography Fiction", as Peter Paul Schnierer calls it (Schnierer 1999: 159). This 'Byrongraphy' is contrasted with the "real", albeit fictitious, hero Septimus. It is he who sleeps with Mrs Chater first, has feelings for Lady Croom, wittily ridicules Mr Chater in two reviews, accepts the challenges to a duel by him *and* Captain Brice, shoots a hare and finally falls in love with Thomasina. It is Septimus whom Bernard actually describes when talking of Byron.[105] The canon of the hero and poet is thus debunked as a myth, the biographical reconstruction on behalf of Bernard as a fictional construct (cf. Müller-Muth 2001: 129).

Bernard hopes to earn himself a name in literary criticism. Seen from this point of view, he interprets historical facts with a personal agenda. Because of his desire for fame he has "left out everything which doesn't fit" (*Arcadia* 59). He ignores any inconsistencies in his theory, which falls to pieces when Hannah discovers that "Ezra Chater of the Sidley Park connection is the same Chater who described a dwarf dahlia in Martinique in 1810 and died there, of a monkey bite". Even his alleged literary discoveries – "two completely unknown Byron essays – *and* [...] the] discovery of the lines he added to 'English Bards'" – were written

---

[104] On the epistemological question of who shot the hare in *Arcadia*, cf. Niederhoff 2003/04: 171-174.

[105] The likeness between Septimus and Byron goes so far that in one performance of *Arcadia*, the former was made to look like the latter (cf. Graham 1995: 318).

by Byron "as sure as he shot that hare" (89), i.e. not at all. It was Septimus who penned the two reviews in the *Piccadilly Recreation* (the editor of the newspaper being his brother; cf. 88), and it was probably he who added the lines, inspired by Lady Croom's remark to Mr Chater that Lord Byron "intends to include [... his] name in the second edition of his *English Bards and Scotch Reviewers*" (40).

Bernard explicitly states that he is "not a scientist" (59). He adheres to a Romantic epistemology, i.e., to him "truths are privately constructed; they are to be pursued for their own sake rather than with the intent of accurately describing the world at large" (Jernigan 2003: 24). This becomes clear when Bernard says to Valentine: "If knowledge isn't self-knowledge it isn't doing much, mate. Is the universe expanding? Is it contracting? Is it standing on one leg and singing 'When Father Painted the Parlour'? Leave me out. I can expand my universe without you" (*Arcadia* 61). Conversely, Hannah conducts her research using a method which Daniel Jernigan calls Enlightenment epistemology, i.e. she is committed "to a rationality as the means by which truth is discovered". She applies this form of epistemology and Karl Popper's scientific method of falsification (cf. Popper 1979: 104f.) when she continually subjects her theories "to a method of conjecture and refutation" (Jernigan 2003: 23):

> VALENTINE: It may all prove to be true.
> HANNAH: It can't prove to be true, it can only not prove to be false yet.
> VALENTINE: (*Pleased*) Just like science.   (*Arcadia* 74)

In turn, "[k]nowledge as construction is at least partially rebutted since theories that began as interpretive constructions are reconstructed to mirror the truth more accurately" (Jernigan 2003: 23f.). Ironically, however, Hannah only succeeds in arriving at the truth about her hermit by also relying on "gut instinct" and intuition (cf. *Arcadia* 66). As Bernard points out to her, she is also a romantic for "[i]t takes a romantic to make a heroine of Caroline Lamb" (63). On the other hand, Bernard also applies classic scientific methods when he construes his picture of Byron according to the principles of linearity and order, "[b]ecause time is reversed. Tock, tick goes the universe and then recovers itself" (50). By referring to the *tick-tock* of a clock, Bernard shows that he believes in temporal order and the ability to reverse this order just like Newton's equations in the form of his research. However, Frank Kermode points out that "[t]he fact that we call the second of the two related sounds *tock* is evidence that we use fictions to enable the end to confer organization and form on the temporal structure". To Kermode, the clock's *tick-tock* is "a model of what we call a plot, an organization that humanizes time by giving it form; and the interval between *tock* and *tick* represents purely successive, disorganized time of the sort that we need to humanize" (Kermode 1968: 45). Hence, Bernard "emplots" the disorganized historical events through a narrative. In a simplified Newtonian fashion, he starts off with a theory, collects the data that fit it and then moulds them into a cause-and-effect pattern, creating an idealised account. Both Hannah and Bernard embody "Stoppard's notion that classical and romantic temperaments are not mutually exclusive, but rather coexist in people. Again, it is a matter of life being understood via a both/and paradigm as opposed to an either/or model" (Fleming 2001: 201).

In his book on *Theatre of Chaos*, William Demastes summarises what both researchers should have learned at the end of their reconstruction attempts:

> In the process of individual awakening, Hannah learns the value of "feeling", and Bernard learns that a "logical" reconstruction of the past reveals unforeseen trackings on his graph of reconstruction. What their minds have been configured to expect is fractally undermined by nature and reality itself. At different levels, they both learn something of the value of chaos, of the truth that unexpected order rises out of moments of unpredictability. (Demastes 1998: 99)

For Jernigan, too, chaos theory in *Arcadia* becomes a metaphor for the difficulties of biographical research (cf. Jernigan 2003: 17). He even draws a connection to the postmodern theories which have criticised traditional life-writings in the twentieth century such as New Criticism and poststructuralism, as described above (cf. II.2.e): "By implication, chaos theory complements those contemporary theories which suggest that biographical interpretation results in the construction of its subject, since true recovery is impossible" (21). In terms of chaos theory, it is the so-called 'butterfly effect' which hinders the biographer's accurate reconstruction of the past: "it is impossible to foresee what seemingly slight and inconsequential inputs will be widely magnified over time until their effects overwhelm and bury the thread which connects us to the past (or future)" (Kramer 1997: 6). By ignoring seemingly inconsequential input, Bernard can only achieve a subjective construction of his biographee, as he cannot fathom the idea that life and personalities are subject to chaotic and unpredictable influences.

The only character in the time line of the present who has some sort of access to the past is Gus, who stopped talking when he was five. He gives Hannah the apple (cf. *Arcadia* 34) – reversing the biblical relationship of Adam and Eve – which is cut into slices by Septimus (cf. 35) and whose leaf Thomasina and Valentine use as an example to illustrate fractal geometry (cf. 37 and 47). It is Gus who pointed out the foundations of Capability Brown's boat-house right away (cf. 48), and it is he who brings Hannah the final proof that Septimus was the hermit (cf. 96f.).[106] To bolster Gus's connection to the past, he and Augustus are played by the same actor, and at the end of the play "[*i*]*t takes a moment to realize that he is not Lord Augustus*" (96). Lisa Sternlieb and Nancy Selleck see Gus as "a perpetual reminder that what has been lost are words" and that "without speech, he […] will always call attention to something that is missing" (Sternlieb/Selleck 2003: 497). However, it is not so much the loss of words but their imprecision and arbitrariness, particularly with regard to a renarration of the past, which Gus emphasises by their absence, i.e. his muteness. As Ludwig Wittgenstein renownedly pointed out in his *Tractatus Logico-Philosophicus*: "Whereof one cannot

---

[106] The character of Gus bears similarity to the character of Ralph Moore in E.M. Forster's novel *A Passage to India* (1924), one of the key hypotexts for *In the Native State* and *Indian Ink* (cf. VII.2). Ralph first appears "to be almost an imbecile" (Forster 1978: 297), but soon Dr. Aziz must discover that he is "extraordinary" (299) and even calls him "an Oriental" because Ralph can always tell when a stranger is a friend (301). The meeting with Ralph leads to the reconciliation between Aziz and Fielding. On the water, Ralph points out to Aziz right away "the chhatri of the Rajah's father": "There was only one spot from which it could be seen, and Ralph had directed him to it. Hastily he pulled away, feeling that his companion was not so much a visitor as a guide" (303). At the end, Fielding and Aziz agree that Ralph is a wise boy and Aziz partly loves him because he brought him back to Fielding to say goodbye (cf. 309).

speak, thereof one must be silent" (Wittgenstein 1962: 189).[107] In fact, Gus is the embodiment of the knower as described in Lao Tse's saying which opens the discussion on the influence of language upon thought in *The Meaning of Meaning*: "He who knows does not speak, he who speaks does not know" (Ogden/Richards 1969: 1). Gus knows and is able to bridge the gap between present and past because he does *not* rely on words, as all the literary biographers and historical researchers do. Rather, he becomes a perpetual reminder that any presentation of a past in words is a subjective construction and not a recovery of the same – just like Stoppard's play.

To Antor, the misinterpretations of both scholars represent a general scepticism towards man's attempts to understand the world and to create patterns in order to explain what one perceives as true (cf. Antor 1998: 348). Similarly, to Palmer *Arcadia* "deconstructs the idea of history. [...] Stoppard shows the historians' misconstructions, based on surviving documents, of events that the audience has observed" (Palmer 1998: 176). Derek Alwes disagrees, since to him "one of the main points of the play is that the past is *not* inaccessible. The modern day researchers sometimes get their 'facts' wrong, but they often get them right" (Alwes 2000: 398). Burkhard Niederhoff must agree with Alwes when he writes that *Arcadia* "does allow for a reconstruction of the past, and that it does distinguish between true and false theories" (Niederhoff 2001/02: 56). He sees the emphasis on the process of research. While both are right in pointing out that Hannah finally succeeds in reconstructing Thomasina's discoveries and the true identity of the hermit, it cannot be denied that Bernard does not, and that Hannah is not able to uncover all the reasons for Septimus's existence as a hermit, because certain personal truths remain lost. What Stoppard tries to achieve by presenting two different outcomes of historical research in *Arcadia* is, on the one hand, the notion of chaos insofar as it incorporates both determinism and unpredictability of the future *and* the past, and on the other hand (and here, Niederhoff is correct), the emphasis on the epistemological process and not so much on the result of the research. As Elison Wheatley writes, *Arcadia*'s "self-conscious interleaving of past

---

[107] "Wovon man nicht sprechen kann, darüber muss man schweigen" (Wittgenstein 1962: 188).

and present evolves into an aesthetic version of the human tendency to create an order out of the unintended and the unexpected" (Wheatley 2004: 173). For her, Stoppard offers consolation in what she calls "the human effort, the 'procession', 'the march', the struggle to know and the creative impulse" (175). Similarly, to Ronald McKinney, the playwright "acknowledges that the ultimate 'product' of this universe will be the sheer nothingness of entropy" while "what matters is the 'process' of forming 'islands of order' along the way, however tentative they may be" (McKinney 2003: 402). Fleming also sees in *Arcadia* the "celebration of the human struggle to obtain knowledge, with meaning arriving as much out of the process as the product". To him, it stresses the point "that despite all the indeterminacy, people can use their intellect and intuition to gain knowledge" (Fleming 2001: 200). In a response to Niederhoff, Müller-Muth points out that the many intertextual allusions to Arcadia, landscape gardening, chaos theory and Lord Byron undermine notions of determinate knowledge and account for the uncertainties of the play (Müller-Muth 2002/03: 282).[108]

4. Chaotic structure and design

Valentine uses chaos mathematics to find a pattern in the development of the grouse population in Sidley Park. Although it appears irregular, there is regularity at work in nature. This applied mathematics can create complex patterns, but also natural and organic forms which contradict Newton's geometry. In theory this means that information and nature itself can overcome the tendency towards increasing entropy (cf. Edwards 2001: 181f.). The time shuttle in *Arcadia* suggests chaos at first glance, but, as Fleming describes, underneath this alleged randomness of alternating scenes there is a dramatic order:

> There are seven scenes – three in the past, three in the present, and the chaotic seventh scene where the periods mix. Within that scene there are six subscenes: two of only the past, two of only the present, and two where the different

---

[108] For a more thorough account of the intertextual allusions and their functions in *Arcadia*, cf. Müller-Muth 2001: 149-177 (on Arcadia), 177-226 (on landscape gardening) and 226-277 (on chaos theory).

periods share the stage. Thus, as with chaotic systems in the physical world, there are a series of bifurcations and even within the chaotic region there are pockets of order; and so overall, this nonlinear play exhibits a fine, underlying structure. (Fleming 2001: 195)

According to Alwes, Stoppard encourages and enables "the audience to adopt a godlike perspective on the human events of the play" (Alwes 2000: 394). This perspective, however, is only godlike to a certain limit, as it only lasts for the duration of the play and as even gods can be fooled when, for example, as Berninger points out, at the end of the first act the audience hears a pistol shot and thus expects a duel to have taken place (cf. Berninger 2006: 231f.). To Berninger, the shuttle of alternating scenes between the past and present implies a questioning of the linearity of time and its associated principle of cause and effect. The chronological course of events is opposed to the drama's narrative order. This in turn achieves an equilibrium between the time levels, as the present is liberated from its post-position and it actually begins to interact with the past (cf. 234 and Guaspari 1996: 231). Time is presented as a "give-and-take relationship, not one-way-traffic" and its common rules are undermined: "the viewers often know the answers even before they are given the status of answers, i.e. before the questions are formulated" (Brandejská 2002: 9 and cf. Brater 2005: 163). This is especially evident in Bernard's implied rhetorical questions in his lecture: "Is it *likely* that Hodge would have lent Byron the book without first removing the three private letters?" (*Arcadia* 56), "is it likely that the man Chater calls his friend Septimus Hodge is the same man who screwed his wife and kicked the shit out of his last book?" (57). The recipients already know that it is likely because it was Septimus's book Lady Croom gave to Byron, and it did contain the three letters (cf. 41), and that it was Septimus who slept with Mrs Chater, wrote bad reviews about Chater's books and was nevertheless called "friend" in the dedication (cf. 9). Only the simultaneity of both time frames of 'before' and 'after', forming a constant theatrical 'present', leads to a full comprehension on the part of the audience (cf. Melbourne 1998: 563). At the same time, the "here and now of theatrical presence makes the past doubly fictitious" (Boireau 1995: 102), which constitutes a condition only perceivable in the theatre.

What we encounter in the twofold time frame is reappearance or repetition with a variation, as described above for the characters, and as in a fractal image of an iterative algorithm. Valentine explains:

> The left-hand pages are graphs of what the numbers are doing on the right-hand pages. But all on different scales. Each graph is a small section of the previous one, blown up. Like you'd blow up a detail of a photograph, and then a detail of the detail, and so on, forever. (*Arcadia* 43)

As Susanne Vees-Gulani writes, "in natural fractals, self-similarity does not imply exact equality, but rather a similarity of structure on different scales" (Vees-Gulani 1999: 416). While the blown-up section of the (photo)graph may resemble the larger (photo)graph, it is still not identical, and this also holds true not only for the character traits in *Arcadia*, but also for other dimensions in the play, as Demastes points out:

> In the play, we have instances of self-similar repetition between 1809 and 1993, between leaf and park, between the formation of Thomasina's leaf and Bernard's Byron story, between Septimus's hermit project and Valentine's computer calculations. Even the algorithmic graphing of the leaf (the smallest-scaled system in the play) finds self-similar parallels in the very nonlinear, seemingly chaotic structure of the play (the largest-scaled system), wherein each scene is separately graphed with little concern for linearly presented chronology but so as collectively to reveal, scene by scene, a whole picture. We ultimately have before us a self-similar pattern of the accumulated totality of the nineteenth- and twentieth-century cast of characters and stream of events (though the latter time frame is not yet completed). (Demastes 1998: 102)

Fractal geometry thus becomes a metaphor for the twofold reality of the structure of *Arcadia*, i.e. the encounter of a thematic likeness in the structure of the play, and vice-versa.

To Reitz, the last scene becomes an "imaginative re-enactment" of past events (Reitz 1996: 173). In the earlier scenes incidents of the past influenced discussions in the present. The past was shown to be a diffusion of ideas leading to a higher understanding in the present. In the same way, Valentine's explanations about the effects of the past is linked with Thomasina's complex research, which in turn prefigures modern physics. Thomasina's metaphor of jam stirred in rice pudding becomes the symbol for the structure of the play. Or, as both the Newtonian scientist Septimus and the chaos theorist Valentine tell us, respectively:

"we must stir our way onward mixing as we go, disorder out of disorder into disorder" (*Arcadia* 5) "[a]nd everything is mixing the same way, all the time, irreversibly [...] till there's no time left. That's what time means" (94, dialogue omitted). Two clearly disconnected systems, past and present, classical and chaos mathematics, which, transferred to the world of physics, are in a condition of absolute order, mix to a point of maximum entropy. While Hannah's and Gus's future is unpredictable, depicted by them dancing "*rather awkwardly*", i.e. chaotically, Septimus and Thomasina dance "*fluently*" (97), i.e. in a structured way, making clear that their future is already predetermined and cannot be reversed. As Valentine says, "[t]he unpredictable and the predetermined unfold together to make everything the way it is" (47). *Arcadia* turns into such an irreversible process, and the last scene depicts the final thermodynamic condition of the universe (cf. Reitz 1996: 173), a universe in which determinism and free will exist side by side.

5. Recapitulation: *It's wanting to know that makes us matter*

Stoppard applies modern mathematics and physics to his play in order to show that requirements of conventional art such as causality, rationality and mimesis are not valid as absolutes any more. These concepts derive from Aristotelian drama and Newtonian physics, and just as Bernard explains that Newton's notion of the cosmos superseded Aristotle's (cf. *Arcadia* 61), Stoppard's biography play ironically supersedes conventional biographical drama and thus Aristotelian concepts of tragedy: "Stoppard here leaves behind the old 'Newtonian theatre' of the well-made play not merely *pour épater* the theatregoing *bourgeois*, but in order to discover new truths about how dramatic literature and theatre can present a complex and chaotic reality" (Melbourne 1998: 557f.). The Aristotelian idea of the logical progress of the plot through a cause-and-effect chain is questioned in *Arcadia* by bifurcations and strange attractors. Both disturb the linear progress while leading to order at the same time (cf. Berninger 2006: 239f.). This, however, again stands in harsh contrast to the action taking place in one and the same room in both time periods in accordance with the unity of place (cf. Scolnicov 2004: 482). While Stoppard's play thus depicts the limitations of the stage realism of conventional biography plays, it nevertheless applies a form of realism which considers new scientific insight as an explanation for the world. Stoppard points out that Aristotelian tragedy, the well-made play and conventional biographical drama, although ascribing itself to the concept of mimesis, do not mirror nature, just as "nature must be molded to fit the model" (Demastes 1998: 95) in Newtonian physics. This is explained by Valentine:

> When your Thomasina was doing maths it had been the same maths for a couple of thousand years. Classical. And for a century after Thomasina. Then maths left the real world behind, just like modern art, really. Nature was classical, maths was suddenly Picassos. But now nature is having the last laugh. The freaky stuff is turning out to be the mathematics of the natural world. (*Arcadia* 44f.)

Stoppard's applied realism, however, is exemplary, just as a plotted leaf is not a real leaf, but a mathematical object. This mathematical object, however, is a more apt artificial depiction than any classical geometrical form:

> HANNAH: [...]
> (*She picks up an apple leaf from the table. She is timid about pushing the point.*)
> So you couldn't make a picture of this leaf by iterating a whatsit?
> VALENTINE: (*Off-hand*) Oh yes, you could do that. [...] It wouldn't *be* a leaf, it would be a mathematical object. (47, dialogue omitted)

This form of realism – Demastes calls it "a renaturalizing of human experience and thought" (Demastes 1998: 103) – combines fact and fiction insofar as it is based on physical phenomena. It is presented in a way contrary to traditional dramatic conventions and human perception by self-reflexively considering its own artificiality. Accordingly, Moon-young Chung, who reads *Arcadia* in the context of the ideas of Gilles Deleuze and Félix Guattari, describes it as "a revolutionary theatre that is waiting for the birth of a new theatre, a becoming theatre" (Chung 2005: 702). Objective reality becomes a relativistic presentation of different historical constructions, scientific models and blurred references, because the play takes its position between the poles of fiction and fact just as biography does. *Arcadia* neither breaches historical authenticity nor scientific principles while at the same time emphasising its own artificiality. Thus, it displays the relativity of the principle of authenticity and the idea of science (cf. Berninger 2006: 241).

The 'Byrongraphic' intertext acts as a metanarrative and metabiography and assumes a central role by pointing out the irreversibility of time – "a persistent theme throughout the whole play" (Brandejská 2002: 6) – and the meaning of chance and chaos. Byron, his biography and the myth of the rake all function as the illustration of a multiplicity of paradigms addressed in *Arcadia*, which in turn reveal the principle of indeterminableness or the relativity of truth in life-writing. Thus, with its time shuttle, its reflection on subjectivity involved in biographical writing and the discourse about a paradigm shift, *Arcadia* is a metahistorical and metabiographical drama *par excellence* (cf. Huber/Middeke 1996: 142, Huber 1999: 461 and Berninger 2006: 236). A complete reconstruction of one's life is presented as a haphazard undertaking and can only be an approximation of a "truth". While Bernard fails in his reconstruction attempts, Hannah reaches a hypothesis which, albeit incomplete, turns out to be true in the end. This is also due to the fact that she corrects her original hypothesis when new evidence emerges. The metahistorical and metabiographical discourse in *Arcadia* aims at questioning the notion of objective historical authenticity, just like the metascientific discourse questions the notion of absolute truth and the possibility of an understanding of nature. Both levels of discourse show the dependence of explanations of the world and historical concepts on the interpreting person. Nevertheless, the implied criticism towards meaning does not lead to a complete deconstruction of the same. It is the epistemological process and the consideration of its bifurcations and indeterminacies that becomes the leitmotif of *Arcadia*. Or as Hannah puts it: "It's wanting to know that makes us matter" (*Arcadia* 75).

VII. *Indian Ink*: The Relationship between Biographical Facts and Art

Indian Ink is literally a fictional biography play: the poetess Flora Crewe, its protagonist and the subject of desire for the American academic and biographer Eldon Pike, is purely fictitious. The play is about the short time Flora spent in the (equally fictitious) Indian native state Jummapur in 1930 and the reconstruction attempts of that life episode in the mid-1980s by Pike, but also by Flora's younger sister Mrs Eleanor Swan and the Indian Anish Das, the son from the second marriage of Nirad Das, who painted Flora in Jummapur. Flora's fictitious biography is interconnected with authentic historical personalities such as Amedeo Modigliani and events such as Mahatma Gandhi's Salt Satyagraha, also known as the Salt March to Dandi. The audience, however, learns about these historical personalities and events only through letters written by Flora to her younger sister, reports by the characters and Pike's footnotes. As in *Arcadia*, authentic historical personalities do not appear on stage, and the authentic historical events are not enacted. Berninger also points out that the structure of *Arcadia* and *Indian Ink* is similar, for "both plays work on two time-levels, as scenes from an historical past interact with scenes situated in present-day surroundings. The scenes often overlap and comment on each other" (Berninger 2001: 44). *Indian Ink* is based on Stoppard's radio play *In the Native State*, which was first broadcast in 1991.[109] The stage version was written after *Arcadia* and first performed in 1995. Fleming sees the satire on academic literary criticism and the time shuttle of *Arcadia* indebted to the radio play (cf. Fleming 2001: 293). And as Terry Hodgson observes, in *Indian Ink*, as in *Arcadia*, characters from both time levels come together in the final scene,[110] although in *In the Native State* and *Indian Ink*, the scenes alter-

---

[109] On *In the Native State*, cf. Andretta 1994.

[110] Cf. also Brater 2005: 164, although it mistakes *In the Native State* for *Indian Ink*. The difference between radio and stage play with regard to the time shuttle in the final scenes is that in *In the Native State*, Mrs Swan remembers home, i.e. India,

nate in place and time, whereas in *Arcadia* they only alternate in time (cf. Hodgson (ed.) 2001: 161).

Thematically, *Indian Ink* does not differ significantly from *In the Native State*. The stage play incorporates the plot and most of the dialogue from the radio play, while adding some material. However, there are two major changes. Firstly, the sequence of scenes is rearranged. The scenes in *In the Native State* alternate regularly between the past and the present, with the exception of Scene xiii and xiv. Additionally, the scenes in the past present the events not in a strictly chronological order: Flora's arrival in Jummapur is not enacted before Scene ix. In *Indian Ink*, however, each time level is presented chronologically for itself while the play fluently shuttles between the past and the present, giving up the idea of demarcated scenes entirely. Thus, Stoppard structurally realises his own stage directions, as Laurie Kaplan explains:

> Stoppard modifies the episodic structure of the radio play into a more organic structure that capitalizes on the single frame of the set: stage directions for *Indian Ink* indicate that "It is not intended that the stage be demarcated between India and England, or past and present" [...]. Juxtaposition of scenes simulates chronology/simultaneity, and Stoppard extends the smaller geographical scale of the radio play by including scenes set in present-day India. (Kaplan 1998: 340)

Secondly, while in the radio play the character of Pike is merely a "disembodied voice" (Fleming 2001: 211), "a flat character representing Lit Crit at its most fatuously oracular" (Kaplan 1998: 338), he has become a fully developed character in the stage version. Pike becomes a vital part in presenting the construction processes of biography as the recipients witness his academic research quest in England and now also in India, including resultant over- and misinterpretations: "it is Pike's quest for the details rather than the larger picture that provides the catalyst for the decoding of the past" (338).

In the following chapter, I will concentrate on *Indian Ink* and not so much on *In the Native State*, as this study deals primarily with Stoppard's biography plays for the stage. Fleming identifies three main thematic issues in *Indian Ink*: "(1) divergent views surrounding the positive

---

in Scene xvii, but when her younger *alter ego* Nell and Eric are at Flora's grave, it is clearly marked as a new scene, namely Scene xviii (cf. *ItNS* 81f.). Thus, there is no explicit mixing of time levels as in *Arcadia* and *Indian Ink*.

and negative effects of Britain's colonization of India; (2) the nature of cultural identity; and (3) the difficulties and fallibility involved in trying to reconstruct the past" (Fleming 2001: 212). However, what connects all three topics listed by Fleming is the question of identity formation and construction. This applies to the characters in the play, to the author's creative process and to biographical reconstruction in *Indian Ink*, because the presentation of the biographee's identity is the key issue of life-writing, an undertaking which Stoppard, at least partly, views as ambiguous.

1. The post/colonial debate

By fluently shuttling between two time periods and two locations, Stoppard achieves the opposition of colonial and postcolonial Anglo-India, India and England. In the Leninist terms in which Josephine Lee describes it, the play broaches the issues of "the increasing need for natural resources and labor in the capitalistic expansion of modern industrial European nations" and the former colonies' "dependence on foreign capital even after their later independence" (Lee 2001: 40). The political confrontations, however, appear mainly marginally: "momentous events, it seems, keep calling to be addressed, but then only obliquely" (Hunter 2005: 85). According to Antoinette Burton, the mere renarration of the historical and political events by the characters on stage "further distances the audience from [… them] and makes it easier and indeed more pleasurable to read decolonisation as a highly individual, personal process" (Burton 2001: 225). However, Burton criticises Stoppard's approach as it neglects the historical processes:

> By moving political questions into the bedroom, *Indian Ink* effectively domesticates the end of empire and arguably depoliticises the whole 'affair'. More accurately, the play repoliticises the last days of the Raj as a comfortable, consumable tale which does little to disrupt dominant narratives of empire's end in India as the 'granting' of autonomy, rather than as the concession of independence in the face of a popular anti-imperialist movement that was, by 1947, several decades old. (225f.)

While Burton may be right in pointing out that Stoppard de-emphasises the political actions which in the end led to India's independence, it is important to note that the playwright's concern is more with the individual in history. This is one reason why his play mainly takes place in a fictitious state in India, and not in an authentic geographical location which has its own history and representatives. *Indian Ink* focuses not so much on historical events and on representative human beings from the epoch of the end of Empire, but emphasises personal relationships in a post/colonial world, and it is limited to individual life sketches, making it a biographical rather than a historical drama. For this reason Stoppard concentrates on Flora's and Das's artistic and emotional relationship in the past, which also becomes the topic of biographical dispute between Mrs Swan and Anish and Dilip and Pike in the present, additionally providing a metabiographical dimension to the play.

To Lee, *Indian Ink* is another of Stoppard's dramatized debates, this time "on colonial history, where characters provide a series of cogent arguments" (Lee 2001: 41). This debate, however, is not dominated by political arguments, but "by an interest in the paradoxes which the conflicting views present" (Berninger 2001: 47). The characters debate in both time periods and in both places:

> The conflicted relationship between England and India is mirrored in and reflected by the complex Anglo-Indian relationships that evolve between Flora and Das, between Mrs. Swan and Anish, and between Pike and Dilip. England's role in the creation of hyphenated identities thus becomes part of Stoppard's concern with the ethics of empire. (Kaplan 1998: 342)

In this section, I will concentrate on the main relationships of these three dialectic pairs in *Indian Ink*, on the way they determine the post/colonial debate in the play and on the role the topic of art plays in their arguments.

a.   Flora Crewe and Nirad Das

For Burton, "Flora is a basically apolitical person, as careless about politics as she is about posing nude" (Burton 2001: 224f.). That her interest is more in art and romance is undeniable, but what Burton considers apolitical is rather political opinion based on personal relations. Flora explains to Captain Durance that she came to India without informing the British representatives in Jummapur. Her reason was that taking advantage of the Resident's hospitality would automatically have offended her hosts of the Theosophical Society, who either think that Britain exploits India too much or too little (cf. *Indian Ink* 44), i.e. that the Empire keeps it industrially a minor power on purpose. At the same time her decision is also due to self-respect (cf. 22). In a letter to her then Communist sister, she describes the two sides of the colonial coin: "I felt like a carneval float representing Empire – or, depending how you look at it, the Subjugation of the Indian People, and of course you're right, darling, but I never saw anyone less subjugated than Mr Coomaraswami" (4). It seems that, in her letter, Flora agrees with her sister again in respect of her hosts, as her sister is the mistress of the Communist Joshua Chamberlain, who gave Flora letters of introduction "to a number of social clubs and literary societies" for her tour of the country to "speak on the subject of 'Literary Life in London'" (22). Flora is not a Communist herself, and she has her own theory on the way political opinions are formed. To her, "[p]olitical opinions are often, and perhaps entirely, a function of temperament" (36).[111] That this is true for her can be seen when Flora meets the Rajah. While discussing the Empire, she objects to his remark that "the loss of India would reduce Britain to a minor power" by pointing out that "one must consider India's interests, too". However, what the Rajah calls "the First Uprising" in 1857 is for Flora still the "Mutiny" (61). This dialogue presents the change in Flora's temperament. While in her present situation in Jummapur, she shows concern for India in contrast to the interests of the British Raj, her "historical" standpoint is still from a British perspective. Her new political and cultural concern for India stems from her relationship with the artist Nirad Das, i.e. it is a function of her temperament. When Das paints Flora, she thinks him too Indian, meaning

---

[111] Stoppard himself stated with regard to Lenin in an interview in 1974 that "ideological differences are often temperamental differences in ideological disguise" (Hudson/Itzin/Trussler 1974: 13).

he is "Englished-up" (12) because he is painting her in an English manner:

> You're enthralled. Chelsea, Bloomsbury, Oliver Twist, Goldflake cigarettes, Winsor and Newton... even painting in oils, that's not Indian. You're trying to paint me from my point of view instead of yours – what you *think* is my point of view. You *deserve* the bloody Empire! (43)

Flora wants Das to paint her "without thinking of Rossetti or Millais" or "Holman Hunt" (44), and she wants him to stick up for himself: "If you don't start learning to *take* you'll never be shot of us. Who whom. Nothing else counts. [...] It's your country, and we've got it. Everything else is bosh" (45).

Das is overenthusiastic about English culture. Chelsea is his favourite part of London although he has never been there. And it becomes clear that it is rather the Chelsea he knows from its painters such as J.M.W. Turner, Dante Gabriel Rossetti and William Holman Hunt of the Pre-Raphaelite Brotherhood (cf. 7). His expressions are stereotypically English (cf. 12) for Das received "a proper English education"; his family was "loyal to the British right through the first War of Independence" (17). His imaginary picture of England is inspired by the works of Charles Dickens, Robert Browning, Shakespeare and Agatha Christie. Nevertheless, it shows that Das is not one of 'Macaulay's children', the term derogatorily used to refer to people born of Indian ancestry who adopt Western culture as a lifestyle and thus were said to betray their country and heritage. When Das thanks Lord Thomas Babington Macaulay for his idea that English was to be taught in India, he does so because it made the language become the means of communication between the nationalists. Asked by Flora whether he is a nationalist himself, Das evades her question (cf. 19). Later, he explains to her the Indian concept of *rasa*, and when Flora compares the "Englished-up" part of his personality to Dr. Aziz from E.M. Forster's *A Passage to India*, he acknowledges that the character alters at the end of the novel (cf. 30), something which is also true for Das. Das may not agree with Chamberlain's theory of social imperialism (cf. 36), but he starts to see that the "bloody Empire finished off Indian painting" (44) and that it exploits India. At the end of the first act he elucidates why he likes the Pre-Raphaelites: their story-telling is similar to his Rajasthani cultural tradition of narrative art, a tradition which had artists long before Shakespeare (cf. 45). Over the course of the play and because of the confrontations with Flora, Das alters in terms of politics as well as of art. By recalling his traditional origins he creates a nude watercolour of Flora in the manner of Hindu symbolism (cf. 68), a "Rajput miniature", which Das himself calls a "quite witty pastiche" (74). Finally, Das also turns his back on Durance, disrespecting a British representative of the Empire, a fact which Flora comments on with "Oh! There's hope for him yet". Durance realises the potential threat in Das's behaviour, remarking that "[t]hey'll be throwing stones next" (77), and we learn in the time period of the mid-1980s that Das really did throw a mango at the Resident's Daimler, a deed for which he went to prison (cf. 57, 59 and 79).

The debate between Flora and Das on the British Raj is rooted in their personal relationship which at the end of the play even seems to turn towards the erotic like the Indian legend of Krishna and Radha (cf. 28 and 74). While Flora is in India following the footsteps of the Communist Chamberlain, who is also her sister's lover, she does not care much about abstract Indian politics. For example, her sister in England knows more about Gandhi's Salt March than Flora in Jummapur, and she is quick to change the topic in her letter to another possible object of romance, namely Durance (cf. 33). On account of her artistic relationship with the Indian portrait painter Das, her attitude changes. She starts to encourage him to stand up for his cultural heritage and to take sides against the British Raj. And her poetry changes, too, by incorporating Hindu art, especially its concept of *rasa*. Das, in turn, alters from apparently being one of 'Macaulay's children' to an Indian participating in political protests. Like his watercolour, the artist becomes a "quite witty pastiche" of British culture and Indian heritage. Through an aesthetic communion Das and Flora refashion Indian and English identities "predicated upon mutual trust and curiosity, not distrust or exploitation from either side" (Russel 2004: 6).

b. Mrs Eleanor Swan and Anish Das

When Anish refuses sugar for his tea at their first meeting, Mrs Swan counters: "Oh. I thought you'd be more Indian" (13). With Indian she actually means Anglo-Indian, i.e. "[o]f, pertaining to, or characteristic of India under British rule, or the English in India" (*OED*, s.v. "Anglo-Indian, *a.* and *n.*" A). The ambiguity of Indian identity is maintained in their ensuing dialogue:

> MRS SWAN: [...] You are a painter like your father.
> ANISH: Oh... yes. Yes, I am a painter like my father. Though not at all like my father, of course.
> MRS SWAN: Your father was an Indian painter, you mean?
> ANISH: An Indian painter? Well, I'm as Indian as he was. But yes. I suppose I am not a particularly *Indian* painter... not an Indian painter *particularly*, or rather...
> MRS SWAN: Not particularly an Indian painter.
> ANISH: Yes. But then, nor was he. Apart from being Indian.
> MRS SWAN: As you are.
> ANISH: Yes.
> MRS SWAN: Though you are not at all like him.
> ANISH: No. Yes. My father was a quite different kind of artist, a portrait painter, as you know... (*Indian Ink* 13f.)

What Mrs Swan and Anish confuse here is the question of ethnical, cultural and artistic identity, and the ethnical question alone seems too complicated to answer in the context of hyphenated identities. Anish has assumed such a postcolonial hyphenated identity. Born in India, which was "still 'home'" (67) when his father died, he now calls England his home as he has spent half his life there and married an English girl. It shows that he is familiar with English customs of hospitality when he accepts Mrs Swan's offer of cake, something which the American, Pike, at first fails to comply with (cf. 15 and 3 respectively). At the same time, Anish refers to what is commonly called the Indian Mutiny in Britain as the "first War of Independence" or "The Rising of 1857", and he defends Indian culture, foreshadowing his father's comparison between Indian and English art:

> *We* were the Romans! We were up to date when you were a backward nation. The foreigners who invaded *you* found a third-world country! Even when you

> discovered India in the age of Shakespeare, we already had our Shakespeares. And our science – architecture – our literature and art, we had a culture older and more splendid, we were rich! After all, that's why you came. (17f.)

Mrs Swan does not agree with Anish's view of colonial history. For her, the rising is "the Mutiny" (17) and the British were India's Romans, although they could have been their Normans. However, she was not always of this opinion. Mrs Swan's younger *alter ego* Nell was "working for a communist newspaper" (79) in 1930, and thus, she would have disapproved of a British Army Officer for her sister more than of an Indian painter. It was her opinion that India was subjugated by the Empire. But now, in the mid-1980s, she angrily replies to Anish's view: "We made you a proper country! And when we left you fell straight to pieces like Humpty Dumpty! Look at the map! You should feel nothing but shame!" (18). Her only explanation for her change of personality over the years is the commonplace that "[o]ne alters" (79). Mrs Swan is aware of the cultural disparities when having a Hindu guest at Christmas, but is unable to abandon her Christian standpoint when she comments on the time of the death of Anish's father's: "Oh, and at Christmas!" (67), which for a Hindu is of course irrelevant. Mrs Swan rejects Anish's symbolic Hindu interpretation of Nirad Das's nude drawing of Flora, agreeing rather with Muslim realism in saying that "sometimes a vine is only a vine" (68). She also sharply differentiates between colonial India and the native states. Jummapur was a native state in which the Rajah had his own justice and therefore it was not the British who imprisoned Nirad Das: "facts are facts. The Rajah put your father in the choky" (24). Her use of the Anglo-Indian word for 'lock-up', however, demonstrates that Mrs Swan is also Anglo-Indian, but with an emphasis on *Anglo*. This becomes clear when she describes her furniture in India and England:

> In India we had pictures of coaching inns and foxhunting, and now I've landed up in Shepperton I've got elephants and prayer wheels cluttering up the window ledges, and the tea-tray is Nepalese brass. One could make a comment about human nature but have a slice of Battenburg instead. (25)

She praises the water which "came straight off the Himalayas" and which does not compare to the water from a "reservoir near Staines"

(26). Finally, it is India which she calls home at the end of the play, and not England: "I always loved the fruit trees at home" (80).

In the characters of Anish and Mrs Swan, Stoppard presents two possibilities of postcolonial hyphenated identity, albeit with different emphases. Anish used to be a portrait painter like his father, but his work is now deconstructive rather than figurative (cf. 18) and his pictures are all like one another (cf. 25). Like his art, Anish is not figurative any more, i.e. he is not what may be understood as typically English or typically Indian, but he has deconstructed his ethnical background in England into a postcolonial Anglo-*Indian* identity. Conversely, Mrs Swan is the figurative representation of the British Raj. Her nostalgic memories of India are connected with reminiscences of Flora and her husband Eric, giving her an *Anglo*-Indian identity. Reflections about the nature of her identity formation are silenced by traditional English cake. Despite their different emphases of identity, the figurative colonial *Anglo*-Indian and the deconstructed postcolonial Anglo-*Indian* identities are reconciled through art. When Anish asks to sketch Mrs Swan, he repeats the act his father performed with Flora: "Only a little sketch with pencil. We must not resist when life strives to close one of its many circles! [...] It will make us friends" (18, dialogue omitted). As Russel writes:

> Anish's aesthetic act places this exchange, along with his father's painting of Flora and Anish's drawing of the woman who would become his wife, onto a continuum of artistic attempts at *rapprochement* between the two countries that together represent Stoppard's profound contribution to conciliatory Anglo-Indian relations. (Russel 2004: 17)

It is also their shared secret of the two drawings – Flora's nude by Das and the Indian watercolour from a volume of about 1790 of Jayadeva's poem *Gita Govinda* (late 12th century) – which unites Mrs Swan and Anish against the academic curiosity of Pike, who is excluded from their family bonds (cf. *Indian Ink* 66).

c.   Eldon Pike and Dilip

The last two characters representing the post/colonial debate in Stoppard's play are Pike and his Indian colleague Dilip of "the fellowship of teachers of English literature" (32). When Pike goes to Jummapur to find the watercolour for his biography of Flora, the stage directions describe him as staying at the best hotel and looking like it, staring around the place *"in a vaguely disappointed way"* (30). His entrance is accompanied by "[*m*]*odern street sounds, distinctly Indian*" (31). Pike is inexperienced when it comes to foreign cultures. While he refused Mrs Swan's cake because he was not hungry, he now refuses Dilip's "*Thumbs Up* Cola" (31) because it is not a proper American Cola (cf. 57). For him the term 'Partition' has no political or historical meaning at first (cf. 31f.), and he does not know the English customs in Jummapur, failing to wear jacket and tie to the club. Nor is he at ease with the Rajah and the present political situation in India, not knowing how to address a princely-ruler-turned-ordinary-politician and mistaking the Hindi word for goodbye for his Christian name, although the Rajah is not even Christian (cf. 66). Pike seems to have suffered a minor cultural shock in Jummapur when facing the beggars and poverty (cf. 57). His description depicts an India which fits Mrs Swan's view of a postcolonial country falling to pieces.

Dilip is Pike's personal guide to culture and customs in postcolonial India. He epitomises what Mrs Swan described as being "more Indian". For him, "begging is a profession" and when he calls Indian poverty "a higher stage of development" (58) as compared to America, he does not do so with Hindu wisdom, as Pike thinks, but with English wit. In order to explain the origin and meaning of the Theosophical Society[112] in India, he refers to the Northern Irish poet and playwright Frederick Louis MacNeice (1907-1963) and his "Bagpipe Music" (1937; cf. 58). Dilip advises against offering a reward leading to information about the watercolour as Pike's "hotel will be stormed by a mob waving authentic watercolour portraits of English ladies in every stage of undress" (33). He also holds Pike back from questioning their eyewitness right away in order to keep everyone's face: "Tomorrow there is time, there is reflection, there is... esteem..." (50). Like Das, Dilip is enthralled by everything English, and he gives a vivid description of postcolonial India:

---

[112] On Theosophy as the main metaphor in *Indian Ink*, cf. Russel 2004: 9ff.

(*Cheerfully*) Yes, it's a disaster for us! Fifty years of Independence and we are still hypnotized! Jackets and ties must be worn! English-model public schools for the children of the elite, and the voice of Bush House is heard in the land. Gandhi would fast again, I think. Only, this time he'd die. It was not for this India, I think, that your Nirad Das and his friends held up their home-made banner at the Empire Day gymkhana. It was not for this that he threw his mango at the Resident's car. (59)

Dilip represents an India that cannot shed its colonial past. He leaves when the Rajah's grandson comes to meet Pike "so he does not need to wear two hats", i.e. an 'English' and an 'Indian' one. Although the Rajah is now merely a representative of the Lok Sabha, the lower house of the Indian Parliament, with his ancestry he represents a part of Anglo-Indian colonial history, as can be seen by the circumstance that the same actor plays the Rajah in both time periods. Dilip advises Pike to address him as "Your Highness" although he is only an "ordinary politician" (60). In Stoppard's India, the colonial past and the postcolonial present are closely interwoven. This also becomes apparent in the stage directions, when Pike and Dilip wait for the Rajah *"in the garden/courtyard of the Jummapur Palace Hotel, which was formerly the Palace of the Rajah of Jummapur"*. Here, as in *Arcadia* (with its difference of large country house and stately home), the twofold perspective of India, again separated by and formed over time, is visualised: the waiter of the hotel is *"decked out in the authentic livery of the old regime"* and *"*[*t*]*hus, the* SERVANTS *operate freely between the two periods"* (57), representing the temporal as well as cultural fluency in the play.

Pike is at first unable to understand postcolonial India. Being neither British nor Indian, he cannot comprehend the influence of Jummapur's colonial past on its postcolonial present. Like Mrs Swan, he is unable to abandon his Christian Western standpoint and to adopt a historical view. The person explaining India to Pike is Dilip, another hyphenated identity in *Indian Ink*, who again emphasises the 'Anglo' part of Anglo-India. Like Das, he loves English literature and cheerfully acknowledges the grip of British culture on India even after Independence. At the end of the play, Pike also begins to alter. He starts improvising to "Bagpipe Music" (cf. 75), contradicting his former statement that he is not a poet (cf. 9). Again, it is art that bridges different cultures and historical periods.

The three character pairs of Flora and Das, Mrs Swan and Anish and Pike and Dilip present an account of post/colonial Anglo-India, England and India in the form of dramatic debates. For Lee, the difference between the Indian and English/American characters lies in the following: "While Stoppard's English characters are preoccupied with defining 'India', his Indian characters show the contradictions of their own colonial history" (Lee 2001: 46). However, the dramatic debate goes beyond defining India, as it also reflects on the question of identity formation. To Christopher Innes, the play becomes "a superior vision to the alienating absorption in the other's culture of the present-day characters" (Innes 2004: 190). All the characters alter by interacting with different cultural patterns, finding reconciliation through and in art, which "helped deconstruct past static notions of national identity" (Russel 2004: 15). Thus, *Indian Ink* is a biography play which stresses sociobiographical factors. Following Clifford (cf. II.3.b), it is also possible to differentiate between synchronic and diachronic aspects in the biographical presentation of the play. While all characters are portrayed in their time, the character of Mrs Swan is also portrayed over time, appearing in the play as her older and younger self in the form of the addressee of Flora's letters as well as a character named Nell in Mrs Swan's memories. Similarly, Anish Das has completed the process of cultural reconciliation begun by his father by marrying an English girl and by meeting Flora's sister to show her Nirad Das's painting. Stoppard does not present biographical identity as an integral whole. His characters are rather depicted as subjects which are constructed and deconstructed through continual relations of participation and opposition.

The dramatic debate in the context of the post/colonial debate in *Indian Ink* focuses on the problem of identity construction, especially in life-writing. Nirad Das, Anish Das and Dilip on the one hand and Flora, Mrs Swan and Pike on the other all struggle in some way with forming or realising their identity, either in colonial Anglo-India or in postcolonial India or England. In the presentation of his characters, however, Stoppard also reflects metafictionally on the process of identity construction in biography.

2. The construction of biographical identity

In an interview, Stoppard admitted to have read parts of fifty or sixty books for *In the Native State* and *Indian Ink*, most of them auto/biographies and histories. Fleming names some of the literary sources: Forster's *A Passage to India*, Nirad C. Chaudhuri's *Autobiography of an Unknown Indian* (1951), Mark Tully's *No Full Stops in India* (1991), several books by V.S. Naipaul and *Up the Country: Letters written to her Sister from the Upper Provinces of India by the Hon. Emily Eden* (1866; cf. Fleming 2001: 293*n*3). Susanne Peters also writes that *Indian Ink* reflects the plot as well as the characters of Forster's novel (cf. Peters 2003: 310), and for Innes, "the play is a positive re-writing of *A Passage to India*, echoing the major elements of Forster's plot, but reversing the fate of the main figures" (Innes 2004: 188). Even the idea of a fictitious native state can be found in English fiction about India. Ralph J. Crane names three novels which (re-)invent the name of Indian cities and states in the same way as Stoppard does with his fictitious Jummapur. His native state becomes one of those places which is not to be found on any map, but which is nevertheless a "true place" "because of the strange marriage between history and fiction, and because there is no single truth, no single India, no single Krishnapur" (Crane 2002: 2).

While Stoppard tends to list his secondary sources used in the writing of a play in its acknowledgements section (cf., for example, in *Travesties* and *The Coast of Utopia*), the characters in *Indian Ink* directly refer to some of his fictional intertexts: Joseph Rudyard Kipling's poem "Gunga Din" from his *Barrack-Room Ballads* (1892/96) is quoted by the Englishman (cf. *Indian Ink* 47), Flora refers to Forster's novel and the character of Dr. Aziz (cf. 30) and Emily Eden's collected letters feature as an object as well as a subject (cf. 16 and 68f.), the play even ending with a quotation from *Up the Country* (cf. 83). By making fiction about India the subject matter of the dialogue and setting the plot in India, Stoppard exposes his own characters and plot as fictional. The process of constructing the identity of a character, a country or history is put into the centre of attention when the characters in the play themselves become aware of their similarity with other fictional characters and their events. This is the case when, for example, Flora compares Das to Dr.

Aziz (cf. 30), when she says of herself at the club that she'll be going "up the country" (48) and when Durance remarks that Emily Eden reminds him of Flora (cf. 77).

A telling statement reveals Stoppard's preoccupation with the challenge of representing Anglo-Indian characters in *Indian Ink*:

> the difficulty, particularly in this decade by the way, is not to write Indians who sound like Indians, which is hard enough, but to avoid writing characters who appear to have already appeared in *The Jewel in the Crown* and *Passage to India*. I mean the whole Anglo-Indian world has been so raked over and presented and re-presented by quite a small company of actors who appear in all of them [...], and so I mean there is this slight embarrassment about actually not really knowing much about how to write an Indian character and really merely mimicking the Indian characters in other people's work. Because my own memory of living in India really hasn't been that much help because my conscious knowledge of how Indians speak and behave has actually been derived from other people's fictions. (Stoppard in Allen 1994: 242f.)

From this, Lee concludes:

> What Stoppard seems to be indicating here is not only the problem of writing believable characters from a different cultural background but also the degree to which these characters – particularly given his method of writing – are always already established in overdetermined ways, influenced by the pervasive images appearing in novels, television, and film. [... F]or Stoppard, [...] the "real" India is inseparable from the fictions influenced by the history of power and representation. (Lee 2001: 42)

Through his various intertextual allusions, Stoppard on the one hand discloses his biography play as a fictional presentation of the history of Anglo-India and of the life episodes of Anglo-Indian characters, whose presentation is influenced by and inseparably connected with other works of fiction. As Annette Kreis-Schink writes, the play utilises the many cultural intertexts, quotes and allusions to emphasise the constructed nature of the events (cf. Kreis-Schink 1998: 203). On the other hand, the characters in his play are "aware" of this influence and connection, reflecting on their constructed identity by comparing themselves and others with characters from different works of fiction. Stoppard presents biography therefore as saturated with fiction in a twofold manner: intrinsically by the characters' and extrinsically by the author's intertextual allusions. By incorporating different genres such as narrative texts (as in the letters), poetry (as in Flora's poems) and drama (as in *Indian Ink* itself), the play also reflects on the blurred boundary between fact and fiction in historiography and biography.

The notion of constructed and fluent identities is also taken up by the structure of the play. It has been mentioned before that the stage shows no demarcation between places and time levels, and that the play is not divided into scenes. As Fleming points out, "British and Indian cultures are inevitably partially entwined, overlapping like the divergent eras and settings that share the stage of the play itself" (Fleming 2001: 223). In the same way, identity is depicted not as a clear-cut, integral and unified whole, but as being in flux like the change of time and place. For this reason, biographical reconstruction cannot arrive at a certain single truth, a problem which Pike faces in the play.

3. Researching biographical truth

The topic of biography in *Indian Ink* is presented through the American scholar of English literature, Eldon Cooper Pike. He is the editor of Flora Crewe's collected poems and at the beginning of the play engaged in editing what later becomes *The Collected Letters* (cf. *Indian Ink* 14). His actual plan, however, is to write a biography of Flora. As Fleming rightly states, "[t]he larger presence of Pike is theatrically used to create a fuller integration of the two time periods" (Fleming 2001: 211). He is the inner cause of the origin of the play as the onstage events of Flora's arrival in Jummapur are actually the re-enactment of the letters which he and Mrs Swan read in her garden. Flora disappears from view when Mrs Swan turns the page of a letter (cf. *Indian Ink* 2) or when she stops reading (cf. 3), only to reappear when Pike continues to read (cf. 4). Flora resumes the description of her Jummapur home as soon as Mrs Swan has helped Pike to decipher her handwriting (cf. 2f.). Pike "*grunts approvingly*" (3) when the poetess makes a pun on a shower the size of a sunflower, and Mrs Swan explains to Pike the meaning of the Indian word *dak* when Flora makes another pun on the phonetic similarity with the English word 'duck' (cf. 3). The opening scene is what Peters describes as anti-mimetic recapitulative, because Flora writes the letter days after her arrival in Jummapur (cf. Peters 2003: 304). The letters are not only Pike's historical sources to reconstruct Flora's time in Jummapur, they are also a dramatic device to bridge the chasm between past and present plausibly on the stage. As Peters writes, the letters form the entrance to the past, which instantaneously becomes the present on stage. The temporal distance of the action represented in the epistolary style is quickly sublated by the onstage re-enactment of the past. The language of distance, i.e. the epistolary style, becomes the language of proximity, i.e. dialogue, and both complement each other (cf. 306).

Although Pike collects Flora's letters – he has been to the British Library, which has nothing to compare to Mrs Swan's letters (cf. *Indian Ink* 3), and also to the University of Texas, which has "Flora Crewe indexed across twenty-two separate collections" (4)[113] – his work and passion actually lie in the footnotes, as he exclaims gaily:

> The notes, the notes! The notes is where the fun is! You can't just *collect* Flora Crewe's letters into a book and call it 'The Collected Letters of Flora Crewe'. The correspondence of well-known writers is mostly written without a thought for the general reader. I mean, they don't do their own footnotes. [...] So this is where I come in, wearing my editor's hat. To lighten the darkness.   (4)

His example of editorship, however, fails miserably when he interprets Flora's dream about "the Queen's Elm" literally as being about a tree, while Mrs Swan corrects him that it is merely "a pub in the Fulham Road". This does not stop Pike's academic (and stereotypically American) zeal, and he debunks his own trade when he replies: "Thank you. This is why God made poets and novelists, so the rest of us can get published" (4). Here Pike gives away two reasons for writing his biography about Flora. On the one hand, he sees its purpose in bringing light to the dark areas in the life story of his biographee, on the other it means a possibility of survival in the academic game of 'publish or perish'. To Fleming and Burton, Pike's character does not merely represent academic satire, but rather a satire of the excessive American academic way of approaching history and biography and in the course failing to understand it (cf. Burton 2001: 218 and Fleming 2001: 221). In Pike's

---

[113] Stoppard here alludes to his own personal papers which he sold in 1991 and 1993 to the Harry Ransom Humanities Research Center at the University of Texas, Austin, after he balked at selling them to the British Library (cf. Nadel 2004: 394).

question "Is that *true*, Eleanor?", Mrs Swan realises Pike's ambition to write a biography, and she opposes it: "Now, Eldon, you are *not* allowed to write a book, not if you were to eat the entire cake. [... *B*]*iography* is the worst possible excuse for getting people wrong" (*Indian Ink* 5).

In the course of the play, Flora's letters are constantly interrupted by Pike's footnotes (cf. 6f., 31, 33f., 51, 63f., 68f. and 78). Mrs Swan has her own opinion about Pike's editorship, which is also reflected in the play: "Far too much of a good thing, in my opinion, the footnotes; to be constantly interrupted by someone telling you things you already know or don't need to know at that moment. There are pages where Flora can hardly get a word in sideways" (25f.). As regards *Indian Ink*, Mrs Swan is correct. All but one footnote contain information which has either already been or will be given in the regular course of the play, the exception being what happened to Captain Durance (cf. 78). At one point, the notes become so annoying that even Flora seems to be bothered, exclaiming from the past: "Oh, shut up! (*It is as though she has turned on* PIKE. *Simultaneously,* DAS, *losing his temper, is shouting in Hindi,* 'Get off! Get off!' [...])" However, the stage directions clarify that "*they are both shouting at a couple of unseen pi-dogs who have been heard yapping and barking and are now fighting under the verandah*" (34). While this dialogue across time is a theatrical device that "serves a thematic point of the subject getting to speak back to the scholar" (Fleming 2001: 294*n*6), it also exemplifies what Peters describes as a twofold time period of the present in *Indian Ink*: the epistolary level of the play, which *becomes* the present, and the present of Mrs Swan and Pike, who are reading Flora's letters together. From their perspective, the events in Jummapur are part of the past, but through the re-enactment they become the present. The letters are dramatised and thus transferred to the medium of the theatre, and the concept of a unified "past" is deconstructed to a direct audience participation at the present re-enactment (cf. Peters 2003: 306).

Despite their redundant character, the footnotes also often enlarge on information about Flora and help to artistically contextualise her historically. Thus, the footnotes also fulfil a twofold function. On the one hand they are a clever dramatic device for connecting Flora's fictitious biography with authentic historical characters and events such as

Mahatma Gandhi's Salt March, Amedeo Modigliani, H.G. Wells, J.C. Squire, Gertrude Stein and so on. With the latter two, the play refers to authors who engaged with the relationship between fact and fiction in their own works of historiography and auto/biography. J.C. Squire edited *If It Had Happened Otherwise: Lapses into Imaginary History* (1932), a collection of alternative histories featuring essays by Winston Churchill and G.K. Chesterton, among others. Gertrude Stein wrote the two auto/biographies *The Autobiography of Alice B. Toklas* (1933) and *Everybody's Autobiography* (1937).[114] Flora's fictitious biography also exhibits a similarity to Stein's, as both volunteered to be drivers in Paris during the First World War (cf. Stein 1990: 173ff. and *Indian Ink* 10). In filling a fictional life with factual figures and events, *Indian Ink* thus reflects on the relationship between fact and fiction in biography.

On the other hand, the footnotes are proof of Pike's obsession with the biographical interpretation of Flora's literary work and his indiscreetness and obtrusiveness. In *Indian Ink*, private correspondence between Flora and her sister Nell is made public by Pike, but also by the play itself. As Peters states, the audience is not the intended addressee of the letters, and the play thus focuses on the complex relationship between publicity and privacy (cf. Peters 2003: 305). This relationship is also a matter of dispute in biography, with regard to the question where public information ends and where the privacy of the biographee begins. This is exactly why Mrs Swan remarks that Pike is "waiting for [... her] to die so he can get on with Flora's biography" (*Indian Ink* 25), because she is the only living member of the family and thus the only person who can defend Flora's privacy.

Through Pike's reference to his own essay entitled "The Woman Who Wrote What She Knew" (51) it becomes clear that he is a literary critic who succumbs to the intentional fallacy of New Criticism of confusing personal with poetic studies (cf. II.2.e), because a short time later Flora explains to Durance that her remark to the magistrate that she wrote about what she knew was "just showing off" (54). However, Pike's biographical commitment sets him on the right track for his re-

---

[114] On the subject of alternative history, cf. Durst 2004 and Duncan 2003; on *The Autobiography of Alice B. Toklas*, cf. Goer 2003, on *Everybody's Autobiography*, cf. Curnutt 1999/2000; and on both, cf. Hoffmann 1992.

search. Like the dream about the Queen's Elm, he takes a line of Flora's letters literally, namely that "perhaps my soul will stay behind as a smudge of paint on paper, as if I'd always been here, like Radha who was the most beautiful of the herdswomen, undressed for love in an empty house" (82f.). He correctly reasons that a nude watercolour of Flora must exist. Mrs Swan, who does not know of the existence of the painting at first, sees the lines as poetic ambiguity:

> PIKE: Well, if it doesn't mean a portrait of Flora undressed, what do you think it means?
> MRS SWAN: As much or as little as you like. Isn't that the point of being a poet? (9)

Pike travels to Jummapur in order to find the alleged watercolour, and there Dilip also reads the letter with poetic ambiguity:

> PIKE: The other thing is, there was the watercolour. A lost portrait, a nude. That's the way it reads to *me*. Don't you think so?
> DILIP: (*Laughs*) Oh yes, I think that's the way it reads to you, Eldon, but she was a poet... and you're a biographer! A lost portrait would be just the ticket.
> (32f.)

Dilip explains to Pike that he reads into these lines what he wants as a biographer, i.e. an interpreter of Flora's artistic work through life facts and *vice versa*. But Dilip helps him nevertheless and even finds an eyewitness, Flora's punkah-wallah (cf. 42 and 50f.), who "saw Miss Crewe having her portrait painted" (50). The credibility of the witness, however, is at least to be questioned when Dilip says that the boy recalled receiving two annas for his job, although Das told Flora that he "will give him an anna" (46). From the eyewitness they learn the name of Nirad Das and that he went into prison for throwing the mango. But Pike's biographical speculations do not stop here. He now wonders whether Das and Flora had a relationship, something which is unthinkable for Dilip at that period. Again Dilip tells him that he is constructing Flora's biography from speculative "facts":

> DILIP: (*Recovering*) Well, we will never know. You are constructing an edifice of speculation on a smudge of paint on paper, which no longer exists.
> PIKE: It must exist – look how far I've come to find it. (59)

Pike makes his own edifice collapse when he talks to the Rajah. Flora's thank-you note recovered from the archive makes Pike come to the conclusion that the watercolour was not of Flora but actually a miniature watercolour from the *Gita Govinda* depicting the nude herdswoman Radha (cf. 65f.). Ironically, he was on the right track, because Das had painted a nude miniature watercolour of Flora. Conversely to Bernard's approach in *Arcadia*, Pike does not prove his own theory true, but only disproves it mistakenly, and it seems rather unlikely that he will succeed in finding Das's son Anish, as he is searching in India and not England:

> It's no go the records of the Theosophical Society, it's no go the newspaper files partitioned to ashes... All we want is the facts and to tell the truth in our fashion... Her knickers were made of crêpe-de-Chine, her poems were up in Bow Street, her list of friends laid end to end... weren't in it for the poetry. But it's no go the watercolour, it's no go the Modigliani... The glass is falling hour by hour, and we're back in the mulligatawny... But we will leave no Das unturned. He had a son. God, this country is so *big*! (75)

Pike cannot count on Mrs Swan's or even Anish's help as both have made a family pact not to tell him, the one in respect of his father, the other to fend off curious biographers. Mrs Swan is not interested either in knowing with whom Flora had a romance, and it remains the main question which is not answered, both in the past and in the present. The play spreads hints and invites the recipients to reconstruct the dark area in Flora's life themselves, without stating a certain truth about the alleged affair:

> ANISH: She had a romance with my father.
> MRS SWAN: Quite possibly. Or with Captain Durance. Or His Highness the Rajah of Jummapur. Or someone else entirely. It hardly matters, looking back. (79)

While truth is what Pike is after, and while large portions of Flora's life have been reconstructed, certain personal truths remain unknown, and certain events remain private, just like Septimus's and Thomasina's feelings for each other. This time, however, the audience does not find out the "truth", either. Unlike his colleague Bernard, Pike does not hastily publish his unsustainable conclusions, although his gut instinct was correct about the nude watercolour. His continuous zeal for knowledge emphasises the importance of the epistemological process in *Indian Ink*.

In his research he follows Flora's footsteps up to her grave without finding the truth. As regards the supposed romance between Flora and Das, Durance or the Rajah, the play ends on a note which is similar to the way Das describes the theft of the duck pâté: "Ah well... the whole thing is a great mystery. [...] The truth will never be known, only to God who is merciful" (27f., dialogue omitted).

4. The relation of art to life

In *Indian Ink*, the two time periods seemingly merge on stage. Quite often, characters from one time period stay onstage while characters from another enter; at times these characters even seem to communicate and interact with each other over time. Peters is right to make clear that within the two different time periods there emerges a new temporal arrangement, in which the plot is not aligned unidirectionally from Flora's past to the present of Mrs Swan and Pike. And although the play clearly has a beginning, middle and end, the Aristotelian chronological, causal progression of separate plot elements is not given (cf. Peters 2003: 308). The non-unidirectional temporal arrangement culminates at the end of the play when past and present, England and India and Mrs Swan and Nell all share the stage. In England, Mrs Swan remembers herself as Nell visiting Flora's grave in India. In the time line of the present, she is followed by Pike, who also visits the grave. After Flora has read aloud her last letter from Jummapur to Nell in England, which was the reason for Pike to search for the nude painting in India, we see Nell going through the contents of Flora's now duplicate suitcase, recovering all the objects which have survived the journey through time. These objects function as "visual reference points which allow the audience to follow the action across time and space and back again" (Burton 2001: 219). There is Flora's blue dress she is wearing in Das's unfinished painting, the unfinished painting itself, which also features on the dust jacket of *The Collected Letters*, which caught Anish's attention in the first place and made him visit Mrs Swan to show her the nude watercolour. There is also the copy of the Emily Eden book and the Rajah's gift (cf. *Indian Ink* 83). Burton thus sees Eleanor Swan as the "nexus of past and present" (Burton 2001: 218), and the objects she keeps "serve as witnesses to history" (219), giving "the narrative precisely the momentum it needs to negotiate the relationship between past and present, Britain and India, home and 'away'" (220).

All the objects are contained in the suitcase, which Mrs Swan told Pike she threw away because "one shed things" (*Indian Ink* 8). As Septimus proclaimed in *Arcadia*, Nell has picked up what might be described as a 'life container', as it conserves the personal things Flora shed on her march of life. Similarly, Anish found the nude watercolour in his father's tin trunk, which he had left to his son, full of personal belongings of no material value (cf. 67). Flora's suitcase ends up on the rack of the train where it lay in the beginning, and the play ends in an almost circular manner with a letter read by Flora. Only this time, the letter is not Flora's but Eden's, and it is not read on stage but via a recording of Flora while she "*is reading it to herself as we hear her voice*" (83). The paraphernalia in her suitcase are Flora's material belongings left after her death. This is similar to the recording, which is the last thing the audience hears from Flora. It is the artificial re-creation of a past voice, a reproducible historical echo. And the author of the letter read, i.e. Eden, has taken the same march as Flora, biographically as well as artistically. While the implied reference to Eden in a political context recapitulates the historical relationship between colonial and postcolonial India, it also stands for the major theme in *Indian Ink*, which can best be summarised as *vita brevis ars longa*. Eden's legacy is not a suitcase full of objects, but her collected letters in the book *Up the Country*.

What truly prevails over time in art is also one of the major topics in the dialogue between Flora and Das:

> DAS: [...] Well, the Empire will one day be gone like the Mughal Empire before it, and only their monuments remain – the visions of Shah Jahan! – of Sir Edwin Lutyens!
> FLORA: 'Look on my works, ye mighty, and despair!'
> DAS: (*Delighted*) Oh yes! Finally like the empire of Ozymandias! Entirely forgotten except in a poem by an English poet. You see how privileged we are, Miss Crewe. Only in art can empires cheat oblivion, because only the artist can say, 'Look on my works, ye mighty, and despair!' (44)

The notion of the relative immortality of and through art unites Das and Flora, and it is a motif Stoppard already referred to in *Travesties*, through the character of Joyce. For Das and Flora, it is not politics which outlasts the times, but monuments such as the Taj Mahal by the emperor Shah Jahan or the works by the English architect Edwin Lutyens. And this is even more true of works of literature, as is achieved by and alluded to in Shelley's sonnet "Ozymandias" (1818) and Flora's poems. Because paintings such as Das's are usually unique copies, his legacy is more fragile. This becomes apparent in the episode of the burned Modigliani (cf. 64) and when Das tears up his first pencil sketch of Flora (cf. 37): "Fear about the fragile state and possible loss of the [two remaining] paintings is shared by all the characters in the play" (Burton 2001: 221).This fear is the reason for Anish's excitement at seeing his father's painting of Flora reproduced on the dust jacket, as it means he has succeeded in cheating oblivion:

> I'm sure my father never had a single one of his paintings reproduced, and that is an extraordinary pleasure for an artist. I know! The painting under one's hand is everything, of course… unique. But replication! *That* is popularity! Put us on book jackets – calendars – biscuit tins! Oh, he would have been quite proud!
> (*Indian Ink* 14)

In Das's understanding, his painting has finally become a monument, albeit a minor one, which has outlasted the British Raj. It is also a result of Pike's research that the "Unknown Indian Artist" (14) is finally attributed with a name.

What Stoppard stresses in *Indian Ink* is the relationship between art and life facts, which proves to be ambiguous. This becomes most apparent in the discussion of the paintings. During the creation of his first portrait, Das comments on the idea of Flora being Indian:

> DAS: An Indian Miss Crewe! Oh dear, that is a mental construction which has no counterpart in the material world.
> FLORA: So is a *unicorn*, but you can imagine it.
> DAS: You can imagine it but you cannot mount it.
> FLORA: Imagining it was all I was asking in my case. (12f.)

Stoppard here refers to another intertext, one of his own, namely *Rosencrantz and Guildenstern are Dead*, where Guil also refers to the idea of a unicorn when discussing the construction of reality (cf. IV.2).[115] Das rejects imagination without reference to the material world. For this reason, his first proper portrait is too much like the Pre-Raphaelites for Flora's taste, i.e. lacking the artist's own imagination. In the present, however, Mrs Swan describes it as "fairly ghastly, like an Indian cinema poster", a "Technicolor Flora" (10). She cannot perceive the connection between the portrait and the Pre-Raphaelites although, at least characteristically, "Pre-Raphaelite art is composed of shallow spaces, *flat* planes, *luminous* or *cinematic* colour with clarity of definition, in thinly applied paint. Its content and meanings are *heightened* and *symbolic* rather than anecdotal or simply descriptive" (Marsh 1995: 14; emphasis added).[116] In the second portrait, the nude watercolour, Nirad Das has, according to Mrs Swan, still not made Flora Indian, i.e. "he hasn't painted her flat". Anish sees the reason for this in the obvious fact that "she was *not* Indian". Despite that, Mrs Swan comments on the picture:

> Everything else looks Indian, like enamel... the moon and the stars done with a pastry cutter. The birds singing on the border... and the tree in bloom, so bright. Is it day or night? And everything on different scales. You can't tell if the painter is in the house or outside looking in. (*Indian Ink* 68)

Anish sees the picture as an example of Hindu art: "everything is to be interpreted in the language of symbols".[117] He is convinced that his father knew that Flora was dying because the flowering vine "sheds its

---

[115] Stoppard applied the same image in his radio play *Artist Descending a Staircase* (1972). In it, Sophie, who is blind, explains: "I can improve on reality, like a painter, but without fear of contradiction. Indeed, if I hear hoofbeats, I can put a unicorn in the garden and no one can open my eyes against it and say it isn't true." To this, the artist Martello adds: "To the Incas, who had never seen a horse, unicorns had the same reality as horses, which is a very high degree of reality" (Stoppard 1990: 142f.).

[116] On the use of colour in Pre-Raphaelite paintings, cf. Prettejohn 2000: 148-152.

[117] As Milo Cleveland Beach writes in his study on Mughal and Rajpuit painting: "Hindu poetry continually presents forms and shapes as metaphors and symbols evoking other, quite different sensations. [...] These sometimes relentless poetic images serve to open out, to universalize, the subjects portrayed by showing their likeness to other forms, qualities, or aspects of existence. Hindu paintings too, although far less concretely, seek to generalize" (Beach 1992: 174f.).

leaves and petals, they are falling to the ground"; she "is not posing [...] but resting" in the picture and it "was painted with love". Mrs Swan, however, rejects Anish's symbolic interpretation:

> MRS SWAN: Now really, Mr Das, sometimes a vine is only a vine. Whether she posed for him or whether it's a work of the imagination...
> ANISH: Oh, but the symbolism –
> MRS SWAN: Codswallop! Your 'house within a house', as anyone can see, is a mosquito net. And the book is Emily Eden, it was in her suitcase. Green with a brown spine. You should read the footnotes! (68)

From the episodes of the past, the recipients are able to tell that the answer to the meaning of the painting is ambiguous as regards its relation to life facts. Das knew Flora was ill, because he witnessed one of her fits. While Flora did not pose for him, as she did for his first portrait, the miniature is not a work of pure imagination either, since Das also saw Flora resting naked on her bed cloaked by a mosquito net, which Flora described as her "Wendy house" (38): "That's what I love about my little house – you can see out better than you can see in" (44).[118]

In *Indian Ink*, the concept of India in art, as in history, is depicted as depending on the beholder, i.e. as being subjective. While to Flora, Das's first portrait is the imitation of the Pre-Raphaelite style, to her sister it is rather the vibrant style of Bollywood; while to Anish, the nude watercolour is a work of symbolism, to Mrs Swan it is rather a work of realism. With the different interpretations of the nude watercolour, Stoppard reflects on the ambiguity of art with regard to truth. He sublates the idea of defining art in binary oppositions and of interpreting it monolithically. Art is not to be understood through an either/or model (as in being either realistic or symbolic), but through a both/and paradigm. It carries truth which, however, is personal and subjective and not universal and factual. Pike draws a false conclusion in his biographical quest because he chooses alleged factual evidence over subjective "gut

---

[118] Das might actually have painted Flora in a more Indian style than Mrs Swan and Anish think. Flora describes the sculptures of Indian women she saw at the temples as having "breasts like melons, and baby-bearing hips", saying that Das must think her "ill-favoured". Das denies this, replying that his wife was also "slightly built" (*Indian Ink* 29). Thus, in painting her not flat(-chested), he might actually refer to Indian sculptures and Flora's own remark.

instinct", which actually turns out to be correct. And because his mind only works in an either/or model, he cannot fathom the idea that there might exist both a gift from the Rajah and a nude watercolour of Flora. As in *Arcadia*, *Indian Ink* sees life according to the both/and paradigm, which also reflects the aporia of the biographical genre, since true lifewriting must consist of both granite and rainbow.

5.   Recapitulation: *The truth will never be known*

Indian Ink is a biography play that concentrates on individual life sketches of fictitious characters in a fictitious native state in India, contextualised by authentic historical figures and events. As in Anish's remark to Mrs Swan that he "didn't come to give [... her] a history lesson" (17), Stoppard avoids giving a one-sided lecture, too, and rather considers the various relationships and dependencies of Anglo-Indian culture and history (cf. Berninger 2001: 47). As with the 1857 revolt, which was neither a mutiny nor a war of independence, but, as Crane describes it, "perhaps a mixture of all these things – the truth lying somewhere between the extremes of contemporary imperialist interpretation and more recent nationalist interpretation" (Crane 2002: 11), historical truth is presented as relative, depending on the cultural and personal standpoint. *Indian Ink* is a metabiographical play, because the plot incorporates two time levels and broaches the process of reconstructing a life. The play concentrates on the various artistic and emotional relationships in the past, in the present, and over time between people of different ethnicity. The dramatic post/colonial debate stresses personal relationships in the construction of the characters' identity. This leads to their depiction as subjects constructed and deconstructed through continual relationships of participation and opposition, as in sociobiography. Stoppard does not present identity as a clear-cut, integral and unified whole, but as being complex and in flux, like the change of time and place in *Indian Ink*. While his play does not breach historical authenticity in its own fictional context, it emphasises its own artificiality through intrinsic and extrinsic intertextual allusions and by incorporating different fictional genres. Through the fluent shuttling between time periods, the plot of the play does not follow Aristotelian chronological, causal progression. By breaking up the unities of time and space and by emphasising the meaning of works of art against politics, *Indian Ink* questions the relationship between art and life facts, which proves ambiguous. Art is not about facts, as in traditional biographical reconstruction, but rather carries subjective truth, which renders its possible interpretations manifold. Neither art nor life is to be interpreted by an either/or model, but only by a both/and paradigm. This also reflects the aporia of the biographical genre as poised between fact and fiction. Pike's character becomes the epitome of the biographer involved in his construction process. Through his biographical research, the deviating views on colonial history and the different interpretations of Das's paintings, *Indian Ink* continues to emphasise the epistemological process and the relativity of truth we have encountered in *Rosencrantz and Guildenstern are Dead*, *Travesties* and *Arcadia*. The emphasis of the epistemological process is the main difference between the radio play *In the Native State* and the stage play *Indian Ink*. And while in *Arcadia*, all the answers may not be clear to the biographers but at least to the recipients, *Indian Ink* is an ambiguous dramatic fiction that is both realistic and symbolic, providing no final answer to the question of the romance between Flora and Das. "The truth will never be known" (*Indian Ink* 28), neither to Pike, Anish or Mrs Swan, nor to the recipients who have to decide on their own subjective truth.

VIII. *The Invention of Love*: The Subordination of Biographical Facts to Artistic Truth

When Flora visits the Jummapur Club in *Indian Ink*, she and the Resident have a short exchange about poetry:

> RESIDENT: The only poet I *know* is Alfred Housman. I expect you've come across him.
> FLORA: (*Pleased*) Oh yes, indeed I have!
> RESIDENT: A dry old stick, isn't he?
> FLORA: Oh – come *across him* –
> RESIDENT: He hauled me through 'Ars Amatoria' when I was up at Trinity.
> FLORA: (*Pleased*) Oh, yes – the Art of Love!
> RESIDENT: When it comes to love, Housman said, you're either an Ovid man or a Virgil man – *omnia vincit amor et nos cedamus amori* – you can't win against love; we give in to it. That's Virgil. Housman was an Ovid man – *et mihi cedet amor* – 'Love won't win against me!'
> FLORA: I'm a Virgil man.
> RESIDENT: Are you? Well, you make friends more quickly that way.
> (*Indian Ink* 47f.)

In this witty exchange, which also features in *In the Native State* (cf. *ItNS* 55), the preoccupation of Stoppard's next biographical subject after *Indian Ink* is already foreshadowed. *The Invention of Love* has at its biographical core the (love) life of the classical scholar and poet, Alfred Edward Housman, Benjamin Hall Kennedy Professor of Latin at Trinity College, Cambridge. His scholarly *opus magnum* is a critical edition of Marcus Manilius's *Astronomicon* (1903-1930). However, A.E. Housman is most famous for his poetry collected in *A Shropshire Lad* (1896), *Last Poems* (1922) and the posthumous publications *More Poems* (1936) and *Additional Poems* (1939). From his marginal perspective, *The Invention of Love* outlines the height of the Victorian age and the aesthetic movement in Oxford as well as the time of Wilde's prosecution for 'gross indecency'. The depiction of his life episodes is interwoven with the "invention of love, the kind of love that dare not speak its name" (Huber 1999: 462).

In his biography play, Stoppard focuses on three main aspects of A.E. Housman's life: 1) his unrequited love for his best friend Jackson; 2) his classical scholarship; and 3) his poetry. Describing the play, Stoppard hints at its similarity to *Arcadia*:

> The play which I have written previously, *Arcadia*, derived from some sort of interest in a dichotomy which I felt was a rather simplified dichotomy between the romantic and the classical temperament. So I didn't feel that this play is a large step away from the previous play, but the succinct task – it was almost the same [...] which made me interested in a different play in the things which became *Arcadia*. It was this combination, perhaps, I detected in myself, maybe that we all detect in ourselves, of two competing, not conflicting, but slightly competing temperaments which take part of each other. (Stoppard 1997)

Again, the playwright's interest focuses on a dichotomy embedded in the human mind and the juxtaposition of alleged oppositions. Although one leitmotif of the play is textual criticism together with the translation process of classical texts, reminding one of Thomasina's and Septimus's Latin translations in *Arcadia*, *The Invention of Love* is concerned most immediately with A.E. Housman in the age of Wilde. Stoppard presents the former as a homosexual who did not live out his disposition as the latter did. He lived in an age which celebrated Wilde's flamboyant lifestyle but prosecuted him for his homosexuality. Thus, the contrast between A.E. Housman and Oscar Wilde, the way they lived and loved, becomes the central dichotomy of the play.

As in *Travesties*, *The Invention of Love* takes place in the memories of its protagonist, AEH.[119] Doris Mader, however, sees the difference between Old Carr and AEH in that the former appears as an unreliable and shallow character, while the latter's epic and epistemic point of view bestows the inner-fictional world presented with a higher truth as regards individual life and suffering (cf. Mader 2003: 61). In addition, while *Travesties* is a *memory/memoir play*, *The Invention of Love*, according to Fleming, could rather be termed a *dream-memory play* (cf. Fleming 2001: 227). In a surrealistic manner, the river in the opening scene of AEH's oneiric reminiscences represents the Styx, the boundary

---

[119] In order to avoid confusion, 'A.E. Housman' applies to the historical person and, as in *The Invention of Love*, 'AEH' to his older and 'Housman' to his younger character in the play.

between the world of the living and Hades. Later, however, it also becomes the Isis/Thames. The river is a symbol for the progress of time; it connects the past with the present, a picnic place with Hades and AEH with Housman (cf. Seeber 1999: 367). Although AEH exclaims at the beginning of the play "I'm dead, then. Good" (*TIoL* 1), he later corrects himself: "Not dead, only dreaming!" (5). In the course of the play, he makes further comments on his own dreaming in the Evelyn Nursing Home, the place where A.E. Housman "lapsed into unconsciousness" and died on 30 April 1936 (Graves 1981: 265). Hence, AEH seems to be in abeyance between life and death: "Neither dead nor dreaming, then, but in between" (*TIoL* 101; cf. Pankratz 2005: 109).

While Archie Burnett, the editor of *The Poems of A.E. Housman*, commends *The Invention of Love* for attracting larger audiences than a biography or a scholarly edition about A.E. Housman (cf. Wren 2002), Stoppard hastened to point out that his play does not constitute a biography proper: "It's not biographical. Things happen that never happened. The whole thing never happened – it all goes on in Housman's head" (Stoppard in Fleming 2001: 227). As in *Rosencrantz and Guildenstern are Dead* and *Travesties*, some of the lines of the characters of the play are *verbatim* quotations from their works.[120] This again, however, does not aim at a realistic depiction of the truth about a biographical subject. On the contrary, Stoppard applies metafictional and metadramatic means in order to emphasise the constructed nature of his play, as well as of biography.

1. The dichotomous structure: Metadramatic and metabiographical disclosure

When the mythical ferryman Charon belays the painter in order to fetch AEH from Styx's shore, the audience learns about AEH's dichotomous nature, which becomes a structuring device for the whole play:

---

[120] Stoppard, for example, quotes from Ruskin's *Lectures on Art* (1870), especially from "The Relation of Art to Morals" and "The Relation of Art to Use" (cf. *TIoL* 15 with Ruskin 1903: 80ff. and 115ff.), or from Pater's *The Renaissance: Studies in Art and Poetry* (1873; cf. *TIoL* 19 with Pater 1980: 188ff.).

AEH [...] Are we waiting for someone?
Charon He's late. I hope nothing's happened to him. [...]
AEH [...] *(looking out) Doubly* late. Are you sure?
Charon A poet and a scholar is what I was told.
AEH I think that must be me.
Charon Both of them?
AEH I'm afraid so.
Charon It sounded like two different people.
AEH I know. (*TIoL* 1f., emphasis added)

Charon is confused at the idea that AEH is to represent scholar and poet in one person. Evidently, his personality cannot be described in an either/or, but only through a both/and pattern. As Jon Volkmer points out, this is not an original treatment, as the titles of quite a few A.E. Housman biographies show (cf. Volkmer 2001: 90). There is Percy Withers's *A Buried Life* (1940), George L. Watson's *A Divided Life* (1957), Maude M. Hawkins's *Man Behind a Mask* (1958), Norman Marlow's *Scholar and Poet* (1958) and Richard Perceval Graves's *The Scholar-Poet* (1979). Christopher Ricks begins his introduction to a collection of A.E. Housman's poems and prose in the same tone by exposing the scholar-poet's dichotomous character:

> A.E. Housman had integrity, and he was deeply divided. Housman the poet thrives upon division. Sometimes he sets classical form against romantic impulse; [...] sometimes he newly lays bare an age-old conflict between head and heart [...]. A.E. Housman the classical scholar appears so intransigently different a figure as to have made people in his lifetime deny that this could be one and the same Housman. (Ricks 1989: 7)

Ricks continues by quoting the poet John Berryman for whom "there was a total split between Housman the 'absolutely marvellous minor poet' and Housman the 'great scholar'. 'You are dealing with an absolute schizophrenic'" (Berryman in Ricks 1989: 7f.).[121]

The principle of dichotomy, which many contemporaries observed in A.E. Housman's personality, structures the play, with the division between the two acts functioning as an axis of reflection: in the first act

---

[121] On Hawkins's and Graves's biographies and Ricks's edition of poems and prose, cf. Naiditch 1995: 173-180, 180-185 and 150-156 respectively, which itself was a source for Stoppard, as Paul Naiditch pointed out to me (private communication, 4 November 2006).

AEH is picked up by Charon, who returns to fetch Wilde in the second. Housman, Pollard and Jackson (and a dog) row a boat in the first act, repeating a dialogue:

> **Pollard** Pull on your right, Jackson.
> **Jackson** Do you want to take the oars? (*TIoL* 4, cf. 13 and 47)

This exchange is again echoed in the second act by Chamberlain and Jerome K. Jerome (cf. 84 and 86), who in turn is the author of *Three Men in a Boat (To Say Nothing of the Dog)* (1889), rowing on the Thames with Frank Harris, and repeated by the three Oxford students on the Isis (cf. 100). In the first act it is the three Oxford lecturers John Ruskin, Walter Pater and Benjamin Jowett, and in the second, the three London journalists Henry Labouchere, Frank Harris and W.T. Stead, who act as the chorus of the play. And while in the first act, AEH meets his younger ego Housman, in the second act he encounters Wilde. Both acts, too, end with a soliloquy by AEH.

While, on the whole, *The Invention of Love* progresses chronologically as regards A.E. Housman's biography, it is, as Raimund Borgmeier remarks, "by no means – as can be expected from Stoppard – a 'well-made play'" (Borgmeier 2002: 151). The reason is that *The Invention of Love* does not follow the three unities of space, time and plot. The plot takes place in AEH's dream-memory, and it fluently alternates without scenic division between various places such as Oxford, Worcestershire, London, the Thames at Reading and a place near Dieppe, France, with both acts returning at the end to Styx's shore. From AEH's retrospective, the play presents A.E. Housman's life from his matriculation in Oxford until his death in the Evelyn Nursing Home, stressing incisive biographical moments by the devices of time lapse and temporal deceleration. However, although the play thus has a beginning and an ending, and with Housman's disclosure of his love for Jackson an emotional and structural climax, the recurrence of certain moments and dialogue, the surreal presentation of the plot, and the dichotomous structure of the play negate an Aristotelian chronological, causal progression. Accordingly metaphorically speaking, *The Invention of Love*, as Mader states, presents a curvilinear time in which past and present coexist, refractorily mirroring each other. Temporal linearity is dissolved:

> Die zeitlich variabel referenten Erinnerungsfragmente, intermittierenden Traumsequenzen und teilweise delirienhaften Rückblenden konstituieren das im engen Sinn Dramen-Innere. Damit löst sich die temporale Linearität hinter den szenisch realisierten inneren Bildern in einem Zugleich von Vergangenem und Gegenwärtigem auf. Keine Zeitenthobenheit entsteht dadurch, sondern eine Kontraktion bzw. mehrfache Brechung der Zeit im dramatischen Perspektivzentrum, nämlich im Bewußtsein und in der Erinnerung der Zentralfigur A.E. Housman.[122] (Mader 2003: 66f.)

This temporal distortion is commented on by AEH himself in his penultimate soliloquy:

> Which is not to say I have remembered it right, messing about in a boat with Moses and dear old young Pollard on a summer's day in '79 or '80 or '81; but not impossible, not so out of court as to count as an untruth in the dream-warp of the ultimate room, though the dog is still in question. And yet not dreaming either, wide awake to all the risks – archaism, anachronism, the wayward inconsequence that only hindsight can acquit of *non sequitur, quietus interruptus* by monologue incontinent in the hind leg of a donkey class (you're too kind but I'm not there yet), and the unities out of the window without so much as a window to be out of: still shaky, too, from that first plummet into bathos, Greek for depth but in rhetoric a ludicrous descent from the elevated to the commonplace, as it might be from Virgil to Jerome K. Jerome if that is even a downward slope at time of speaking, and when is *that*? – for walking on water is not among my party tricks, the water and the walking work it out between them. Neither dead nor dreaming, then, but in between, not short on fact, or fiction [...].
> (*TIoL* 100f.)

AEH here gives a metadramatic and metabiographical comment on Stoppard's biography play. He admits that his memory is unreliable, that the presentation might have fallen victim to archaisms, anachronisms and *non sequiturs*, that *The Invention of Love* does not observe the three unities of time, place and plot, that it is serious entertainment and that it

---

[122] "The drama's core in a more narrow sense is composed of the temporally variable fragments of memory referring to each other, the intermittent dream sequences and the partly delirious flashbacks. For this reason, temporal linearity dissolves behind the scenically realized interior images in a simultaneity of things past and things present. This does not cause a sense of temporal displacement, but a contraction or the repeated refraction of time in the dramatic centre of perspective, *viz.*, in the consciousness and memory of the central character A.E. Housman" (my translation).

consists of a mixture of fact and fiction. AEH continues his soliloquy with a factual renarration of how it came that Wilde was prosecuted, beginning with Jerome's attack on *The Chameleon*. It is a demonstration of the fact that he knows when his dream-memories are factual and when fictional: "Which goes to show, I know what I'm doing even when I don't know I'm doing it" (101). In almost exactly the same way, Stoppard comments on his own biographical drama:

> Well, you wouldn't go to a play for the authentic biography – there'd be no point, either for the audience or the playwright. It's a difficult one. I mean Housman is maniacally accurate in some degrees and quite cavalier in others, in different places. [...] And what I try to do is to know everything, so that when I'm straying from strict chronology or sequential fact, I know I'm doing it and I know why I'm doing it. (Stoppard in Cott 2001)

Thus, it is consistent that Stoppard has AEH disclose *The Invention of Love* at its end as a biographical and dramatic construct, almost like a ventriloquist speaking through his puppet. In his last, dying words, AEH even seems to address the audience directly, seemingly describing the performance of the day before:

> You should have been here last night when I did Hades properly – Furies, Harpies, Gorgons, and the snake-haired Medusa, to say nothing of the Dog. But now I really do have to go. How lucky to find myself standing on this empty shore, with the indifferent waters at my feet. (*TIoL* 102)

AEH's closing soliloquy is given in the form of an interior monologue which is similar to Old Carr's closing lines in *Travesties*. Like Old Carr, AEH, too, recapitulates place, time and the ideological contradictions of the play (cf. Fleming 2001: 242f.). He stands "on this empty shore", and it seems AEH has found all the mysteries and lost all the meaning. At least if we are to believe Septimus, who also declared at the end of *Arcadia* that, "[w]hen we have found all the mysteries and lost all the meaning, we will be alone, on an empty shore" (*Arcadia* 94). With his last words, however, *The Invention of Love* returns to its biographical topic and AEH passes away, "indifferent waters at my feet" implying that the urethral sphincter relaxes (cf. Hunter 2005: 96). Stoppard's biographical presentation of A.E. Housman classically ends with the death of the biographee.

Now that the structural principles of *The Invention of Love* have been pointed out, it is necessary to consider the afore-mentioned thematic dichotomies of the play in more detail. There are three central dichotomies which can be identified in the play: the dichotomy of the Oxford lecturers and London journalists, of AEH and Housman and of AEH and Wilde.

2. Oxford lecturers and London journalists: Vice *vs.* virtue

The Oxford scenes in Act I, which lead uo to the encounter between AEH and Housman, serve to characterise Housman, Jackson and Pollard and to depict Oxford. The different *Weltanschaungen* prevalent at the university are presented at an imaginary croquet match by Ruskin, Pater and Jowett. With regard to art, morality and social order, Ruskin favours the Medieval Gothic, Pater the Renaissance and Jowett classical Greece as archetypes for the education of the young students. Their discussion also juxtaposes the Victorian and the aestheticist views of taste and beauty and what is beautiful in art and life.

Ruskin rejects aestheticism because its devotees dress like "the London Fire Brigade". To him, aestheticism in Oxford is "connected in some way with that excessive admiration for male physical beauty which conducted to the fall of Greece" (*TIoL* 10). In Ruskin's opinion, the true meaning of life is that "[t]here is nothing beautiful which is not good, and nothing good which has no moral purpose" (15). Mimetic art which avoids rampant sensuality, is for him ethical by nature, and this medieval Christian notion has been undermined by aestheticism: "Conscience, faith, disciplined restraint, fidelity to nature – all the Christian virtues that gave us the cathedral of Chartres, the paintings of Giotto, the poetry of Dante – have been tricked out in iridescent rags to catch the attention of the moment" (18).

Conversely, according to Pater's creed, life is not to be lived according to moral utilitarianism. Man should not aspire to the fruits of experience, but experience itself. Pater represents a *carpe diem* mentality in his lecture:

208

> The Renaissance teaches us that the book of knowledge is not to be learned by rote but is to be written anew in the ecstasy of living each moment for the moment's sake. Success in life is to maintain this ecstasy, to burn always with this hard gem-like flame. Failure is to form habits. To burn with a gem-like flame is to capture the awareness of each moment; and for that moment only. To form habits is to be absent from those moments. How may we always be present for them? – to garner not the fruits of experience but experience itself? – [...] to catch at the exquisite passion, the strange flower, or art – or the face of one's friend? For, not to do so in our short day of frost and sun is to sleep before evening. The conventional morality which requires of us the sacrifice of any one of those moments has no real claim on us. The love of art for art's sake seeks nothing in return except the highest quality to the moments of your life, and simply for those moment's sake. (19, stage directions omitted)

Although Pater was Ruskin's student, he has become his polar opposite as regards the meaning of art and life. He represents the aestheticist attitude of *l'art pour l'art*, as underlined by his appearance as *"a dandy: top hat, yellow gloves, blue cravat"* (9), who is later rebuked by Jowett for his homoerotic relationship with a handsome Balliol student (cf. 21ff.).

Jowett is the third lecturer proclaiming a golden age: "Nowhere was the ideal of morality, art and social order realized more harmoniously than in Greece in the age of the great philosophers. [...] Buggery apart" (17, dialogue omitted). His main complaint is that classical antiquity addressed homosexuality quite openly in its literature, and therefore Jowett conceals it in his translations:

> A Platonic enthusiasm as far as Plato was concerned meant an enthusiasm of the kind that would empty the public schools and fill the prisons where it is not nipped in the bud. In my translation of the Phaedrus it required all my ingenuity to rephrase his depiction of paederastia into the affectionate regard as exists between an Englishman and his wife. Plato would have made the transposition himself if he had the good fortune to be a Balliol man. (21)

For Jowett as for Ruskin, homosexuality is the "canker that brought low the glory that was Greece", and it "shall not prevail over Balliol!" (22).

With the three Oxford lecturers, Stoppard once again broaches the issue of the function of art, as he did in *Travesties* and *Indian Ink*. This is most evident in the confrontation between Ruskin and Pater. As Fleming points out, their ideological opposition represents the polarities of Wilde's and A.E. Housman's ways of life: "Pater's art-for-art's-sake aestheticism was lived to the full by Wilde, while Housman lived similarly to Ruskin's axiom of austerity" (Fleming 2001: 230). However, Ruskin, Pater and Jowett are so convinced of their theoretical views that they do not realise their own hypocrisy. As Stoppard comments: "My chorus of old Oxford wrinklies, who bang on about 'beastliness' in the play, consists of Pater who wanted to have sex but never dated, Jowett who didn't want to, and Ruskin who couldn't [.] 200 combined years of celibacy and impotence!" (Stoppard in Conrad 1998). Ironically, the three play croquet with an imaginary ball (cf. Zeifman 2001: 194), commenting on their actions with sportsmanlike phrases such as "Check. Play the advantage", "Deuce" and "Leg-before" (*TIoL* 17f.). These terms, however, are not from croquet, but from football, tennis and cricket respectively (cf. Carle/Steen 2000: 19f.). The malapropisms emphasise their ignorance of sports (cf. *TIoL* 10) and their impotence and incompetence in talking about the subject of sexuality, which they do not know, are not able to perform or do not understand: "Ruskin, along with Pater and Jowett, represents [...] the sublimation of sexuality for erudition and aesthetics" (Weltman 2002: 90).

Similar to the way this discussion during a game of croquet gives a picture of Oxford's cultural milieu and its intellectual oppositions in the first act, the conversation between the three journalists Labouchere, Harris and Stead during a game of billiards in the second act characterises Victorian London society in 1885 and ten years later, shortly after Wilde's conviction. The audience learns about Wilde's rise to fame and the circumstances of "the invention of crime [...] that brought about Wilde's downfall" (Emilsson 2003: 139). As in the earlier *Night and Day* (1978), Stoppard's depiction of the journalists also critically considers the power and moral duty of the press.

Labouchere complains that while it was the press that made Wilde, it is impotent to unmake him:

> We invented Oscar, we bodied him forth. Then we floated him. Then we kited the stock. [...] But now he's got away from us. No matter where we cut the string, the kite won't fall. The ramp is over and the stock keeps rising. [...] Up, up, up... It shakes one's faith in the operation of a moral universe by journalism.
> (*TIoL* 57f., dialogue omitted)

In the scene taking place in 1885, Labouchere comments on the Criminal Law Amendment Act that it "is badly drawn up and will do more harm than good" (59). The Labouchere Amendment clause was attached to the Criminal Law Amendment Act in this year on the proposition of its namesake. While the latter was "designed to protect young girls from sexual exploitation and the slave trade", the former "made "gross indecency" between men punishable by up to two years' imprisonment with or without hard labour" (Carle/Steen 2000: 33). According to the character of Labouchere, the Labouchere Amendment had "nothing to do with the Bill". The intention was not "to address a contemporary evil", as assumed by Stead, but "to make the Bill absurd to any sensible person left in what by then was a pretty thin House" (*TIoL* 61). Ten years later, however, Labouchere contradicts his former statement. He now boasts that he introduced the clause because "Stead happened to tell [... him] just before the debate that in certain parts of London the problem of indecency between men was as serious as with virgins" and that instead of two years he actually wanted "a maximum of *seven* years", but the "Attorney General of the day persuaded [... him] that two years was more likely to secure a conviction from a hesitant jury" (83).

Stead is a manic upholder of moral standards in this journalistic triumvirate. His scoop in the *Pall Mall Gazette* called "The Maiden Tribute of Modern Babylon" (Carle/Steen 2000: 35) about his purchase of a thirteen-year-old virgin for five pounds made Parliament pass the Criminal Law Amendment Act: "I gave virtue a voice Parliament couldn't ignore" (*TIoL* 60). For him, "[i]n the right hands the editor's pen is the sceptre of power" (58), and his work implies the higher duty to influence public opinion and to set moral standards, for "journalists have a divine mission to be the tribunes of the people" (59). The stage directions describe him as having "*a full beard and the fanatical gleam of a prophet*" (57). Accordingly, he exclaims that the *Pall Mall Gazette* "is testament enough that the Lord is at my elbow" (58), and he occasionally hears "the clear call of the voice of God" (59).

The third journalist, Harris, cares more about sales figures than about the truth: "When I took over the *Evening News* I edited the paper with the best in me at twenty-eight. The circulation wouldn't budge. So,

I edited the paper as a boy of fourteen. The circulation started to rise and never looked back" (58). Overall, Harris has a rather ambiguous relationship to truth, claiming to have been "with General Skobeleff at the battle of Plevna" (59), to have built Brooklyn Bridge in 1870 (cf. 61) and to have met the German archaeologist Schliemann in Greece in 1880 (cf. 62). Consequently, Labouchere asks him: "Harris, do you *ever* tell the truth?" (cf. 62). Ten years later, when for once he is actually not lying about Labouchere's original reasons for introducing the Amendment, Labouchere rebukes him with the words: "Who's going to believe *you*?" (83). Harris's relationship with truth reflects on the historical Harris's autobiography *My Life and Loves* (1922-29), which is notorious for its exaggerations. It also reflects on the fact that he wrote diverse biographies, most notably *The Man Shakespeare and his Tragic Love Story* (1909), *Bernard Shaw* (1931) and *Oscar Wilde: His Life and Confessions* (1916/18) and even two biography plays, namely *Shakespeare and his Love* (1910), after his own biography, and *Joan La Romée* (1926). In a review of Harris's autobiography, Samuel L. Hynes appropriately describes his life-writings as follows:

> Harries's biographies have been called impressionistic sketches, and this is a fairly accurate description, but one should add that in each frame there are always *two* faces at once, like a double-exposed negative: one is the ostensible subject, the other Harris's small-town-seducer's face, saying "Look at me. I'm more interesting, more important, a better writer and a better lover than my subject ever was". Such portraiture can scarcely be called objective, but it is often extremely entertaining, in the way that indiscreet gossip is. (Hynes 1964)

In the character of Harris and his ambiguous relationship with truth, Stoppard depicts the journalist, but also the author of auto/biographies and the playwright of biography plays, as a person who does not represent the life of his subjects objectively. On the contrary, Harris becomes the prototype of a biographer whose life-writings, as already remarked by Woolf, reveal more about the biographer than about the biographee. Harris functions as a metabiographical as well as metadramatic character insofar as he combines in one person the notion of subjective biographer and fictional biography playwright, who has no obligation to historical facts.

In the dichotomous structure of the play, the three Oxford lecturers find their counterparts in the three London journalists. In fact, they were played by the same actors in the first production of *The Invention of Love*. Labouchere wants to bring down Wilde, dismissing him "as an effeminate phrase-maker" (*TIoL* 57), who tells the people in the provinces that they are provincial (cf. 58). In a similar way, Jowett dismisses the "Balliol bugger" (21) from university; he describes Wilde (when actually addressing Housman) to be of "Irish provincialism" and reproaches him with "making affected remarks" (22). Just as Labouchere complains that "Oscar himself has never done anything" (58), Ruskin complains about his project of a flower-boarded road sinking into the swamp because Wilde, "an Irish exquisite, a great slab of a youth with white hands and long poetical hair who said he was glad to say he had never seen a shovel [...] rose at noon to smoke cigarettes and read French novels" (15).[123] Accordingly, Stead finds "[t]here is a scepticism of what is morally elevating, a taste for the voluptuous and the forbidden in French literature" (62). Like Ruskin, he represents Christian virtues, which are undermined by aestheticism and homosexuality, the latter being for Stead, Ruskin, as well as for Jowett, that which caused the fall of Greece (cf. 62, 10 and 22 respectively). In turn, Harris and Pater defend homosexuality as a vital part of Greek culture (cf. 21f. and 62).

In *The Invention of Love*, in which Stoppard continuously alludes intertextually to ancient Greek and Roman works, Ruskin, Pater and Jowett on the one hand and Labouchere, Stead and Harris on the other take on the function of a Greek chorus. As Aristotle describes it, "[t]he Chorus should be regarded as one of the actors; it should be a part of the whole, and should assume a share in the action" (Aristotle 1977: 57). According to Fleming, the main function of the chorus in Stoppard's play is explain the social and historical context to the audience (cf. Fleming 2001: 299n20). However, especially with the journalists, it assumes a share in the offstage action because it is the journalists who are presented as partly responsible for Wilde's prosecution. The chorus,

---

[123] While Ruskin here does not identify Wilde explicitly, Lucia Krämer points out the allusion to *The Importance of Being Earnest* and thus to its author in these lines (cf. Krämer 2003: 146), because in the play Gwendolen satirically remarks to Cecily: "I am glad to say that I have never seen a spade" (Wilde 1976: 364).

particularly Jowett's corruptions of ancient texts in order to preserve Victorian morale and Harris's ambiguous relationship to truth as a journalist, auto/biographer and biographical playwright, reflects on the composition of biography and the difference between "facts" and "truth". In *The Invention of Love* the topic of life-writing is closely connected with the leitmotif of textual criticism and with the Wilde myth. Both topics are taken up in the encounters between AEH and Housman and AEH and Wilde.

3. AEH and Housman: Identity formation in a divided self

Charon calls the place AEH and he are reaching Elysium, i.e., according to the *OED*, the "supposed state or abode of the blessed after death in Greek mythology". Additionally, the term figuratively describes a "place or state of ideal or perfect happiness" (*OED*, s.v. "Elysium" 1 and 3 respectively). It is the latter meaning which AEH implies when he describes the place:

> **Charon** [...] Here we are. Elysium.
> **AEH** Elysium! Where else?! I was eighteen when I first saw Oxford, and Oxford was charming then, not the trippery emporium it has become. There were horse-buses at the station to meet the Birmingham train; and not a brick to be seen, before the Kinema and Kardomah. The Oxford of my dreams, re-dreamt.(*TIoL* 26)

In this dream place within a dream, AEH meets his younger *alter ego*. This encounter constitutes the central focus of the first act, and Adam Phillips calls it

> both a good conceit and a brilliant dramatic device because the poetry [of A.E. Housman] gives the impression that the young Housman had always been in some kind of dialogue with an imagined older self, and often with a dead one; that he was always old before his time.   (Phillips 2000: 277)

AEH and Housman continue the nostalgic enthusiasm for the past:

> **AEH** [...] I did Greats, too. Of course, that was more than fifty years ago, when Oxford was still the sweet city of dreaming spires.
> **Housman** It must have been delightful then.   (*TIoL* 30)

Similar to Ruskin, Pattison and Jowett (cf. 9, 14 and 16 respectively), AEH is nostalgic for a past which is actually Housman's present. This is also the subject of the Newdigate poetry prize, for which Housman wants to submit a poem:

> **Housman** [...] The subject this year is from Catullus – the lament for the Golden Age when the gods still came down to visit us, before we went to the bad.
> **AEH** An excellent topic for a poem. False nostalgia. (44)

AEH is aware of how the past is transfigured in one's personal memory and in art – unlike Housman, who is too young to have a past. It can only be romanticised with hindsight, as then it has dissolved into a subjective reminiscence. The golden age is yet to come for Housman, and AEH explains: "We're always living in someone's golden age" (44).

At first, AEH does not recognise his younger *alter ego*. When he does, AEH remarks: "Well, this is an unexpected development. Where can we sit down before philosophy finds us out. I'm not as young as I was. Whereas you, of course, are" (30). These lines indicate in how far Stoppard has developed his technique of the time shuttle from *Arcadia* to *The Invention of Love*. In *Arcadia*, characters from different time levels share the stage only at the end of the play. In *Indian Ink*, characters from different time levels mix onstage from the very beginning. With Mrs Swan and Nell, an old and a young incarnation of the same character, who in the course of the play has undergone the change from Communist to reactionary, share the stage for a short moment at the end. But in these two plays, the characters interact only indirectly in the space of the stage. In *The Invention of Love*, Stoppard blends the different time levels so that AEH and Housman engage in actual dialogue, "thereby dramatically representing the divided self by having two incarnations of one character simultaneously present" (Fleming 2001: 232).

The enacted temporal schizophrenia visualises the process of biographical identity formation and construction. When AEH quotes parts of *More Poems* V: "Diffugere Nives", Housman mentions Theseus and Pirithous. In this same spirit, he describes the feelings for a person of the same sex as virtue. The reason for this is that he has not come to terms with his homosexuality yet:

Housman Companions in adventure! *There* is something to stir the soul! Was there ever a love like the love of comrades to lay down their lives for each other?
AEH Oh, dear.
Housman I don't mean spooniness, you know.
AEH Oh – not the love of comrades that gets you sacked at Oxford –
Housman (No! –)
AEH – not as in the lyric poets – 'when thou art kind I spend the day like a god: when thy face is turned away, it is very dark with me' –
Housman No – I mean friendship – virtue – like the Greek heroes. (*TIoL* 39f.)

Housman differentiates between homosexual love, as alluded to by AEH with the line from Theocritus's *Idyll* XXIX, and virtue, as in the friendship between Theseus and Pirithous, because he has not fallen in love with Jackson yet. He is waiting for his friends to pick him up for their fateful boat trip, in the course of which he will discover his feelings for his best friend (cf. 77). The classical scholar AEH, however, knows about the exact meaning of words and is not taken in by circumlocutions: "Love will not be deflected from its mischief by being called comradeship or anything else" (43).

In the construction of Housman's life, Stoppard apposes socio- and psychobiographical factors. As regards sociobiography, Housman's process-like identity is formed by his admiration for ancient texts, their homoerotic subtext and the culture they derive from. This culture accepted the homosexuality thematised in the texts, unlike Victorian society. In a similar way, Aestheticism and New Paganism refer to ancient culture as a protective model against Christian moral concepts (cf. Seeber 1999: 373). New Paganism is explicitly mentioned by Wilde at the end of the play (cf. *TIoL* 96). Aidan A. Kelly describes it

> as a religious concept [...] based on a desire to recreate the pagan religions of antiquity, usually not as they actually were, but as they have been idealized by romantics ever since the Renaissance. [...] Fascination with the classics was a major theme of Romanticism, and the idea of reviving some sort of classical religion gained strength and became programmatic during the late nineteenth century, at which time attention was divided between Greco-Roman and Norse paganism. (Kelly 2001: 310)

As Hans Ulrich Seeber explains, identifying with the 'other' of Greco-Roman antiquity was a common way of coming to terms with one's true identity. In Stoppard's play, Housman, too, draws on these cultures in his identity formation process:

> Stoppard enacts Housman's fascination with (erotic) ancient texts precisely in order to demonstrate this mechanism of subversive cultural identification with the other. Instead of translating the cultural other into Victorian and Christian terms as Jowett does, Housman's intellectual and physical *eros*, in an act of cultural emancipation, translates him 'out' of his cultural heritage. (Seeber 1999: 373)

Housman creates a 'homosexual identity' for himself by dissociation from Victorian and Christian norms via Greek and Roman love poetry and prose. Hence, as in sociobiography, Housman is presented as being influenced by ancient cultural patterns in demarcation from Victorian moral concepts.

With regard to Stoppard's psychobiography, Housman's personal development is affected by his unrequited love for Jackson to such an extent that the scene in which he confesses his unanswered feelings to his friend marks the split between younger and older self, i.e. literally between Housman and AEH. Stoppard achieves this by incorporating A.E. Housman's *Additional Poems* VII into the most emotional scene of the play in combination with simple but effective light effects:

> *Jackson puts out his hand.*
>   *Darkness, except on Housman.*
> **Housman**
> He would not stay for me; and who can wonder?
> He would not stay for me to stand and gaze.
> I shook his hand and tore my heart in sunder
> *Light on AEH.*
> And went with half my life about my ways.
> *Darkness on Housman.*
>   *AEH is at a desk among books, inkpot and pen.* (*TIoL* 78)

First, Housman is isolated by darkness from his love Jackson, who does not requite his feelings and to whom the poem refers in Stoppard's context.[124] Before the last line, on the theme of dichotomy, is recited, AEH is illuminated, thus presenting the two versions of younger and older

---

[124] Burnett, in his exceptional edition of A.E. Housman's collected poems, also comments on the poem's addressee: "*He*. Probably AEH's 'greatest friend', M[oses] J[ohn] J[ackson]" (Housman 1997: 468).

217

self simultaneously for a brief moment. After the last line is spoken, marking the end of one half of AEH's life, i.e. of his youth, Housman is blacked out, and the following scene concentrates on AEH's scholarly work as textual critic and his appointment to the chair at University College London. Thus, this following scene seems to imply that AEH sublimates his unrequited feelings for Jackson through his scholarly work. This is reminiscent of Freud's description of the sublimation of the sexual drive in his *Leonardo da Vinci and a Memory of His Childhood*:

> Observation of men's daily lives shows us that most people succeed in directing very considerable portions of their sexual instinctual forces to their professional activity. The sexual instinct is particularly well fitted to make contributions of this kind since it is endowed with a capacity for sublimation: that is, it has the power to replace its immediate aim by other aims which may be valued more highly and which are not sexual. We accept this process as proved whenever the history of a person's childhood – that is, the history of his mental development – shows that in childhood this over-powerful instinct was in the service of sexual interests. We find further confirmation if a striking atrophy occurs in the sexual life of maturity, as though a portion of sexual activity had now been replaced by the activity of the over-powerful instinct.[125] (Freud 1989: 26)

Following Freud, AEH, too, directs his unrequited feelings for his best friend to textual scholarship, which he values more highly than anything else. Up to Housman's adolescence, the "over-powerful instinct" of the study of classical texts was in service of Housman's homosexuality. And when the play depicts the change from Housman in emerging adulthood to a mature AEH, it appears that Housman's preoccupation with Jack-

---

[125] "Die Beobachtungen des täglichen Lebens der Menschen zeigt uns, daß es den meisten gelingt, ganz unsehnliche Anteile ihrer sexuellen Triebkräfte auf ihre Berufstätigkeit zu leiten. Der Sexualtrieb eignet sich ganz besonders dazu, solche Beiträge abzugeben, da er mit der Fähigkeit der Sublimierung begabt, das heißt imstande ist, sein nächstes Ziel gegen andere, eventuell höher gewertete und nicht sexuelle Ziele zu vertauschen. Wir halten diesen Vorgang für erwiesen, wenn uns die Kindergeschichte, also die seelische Entwicklungsgeschichte, einer Person zeigt, daß zur Kinderzeit der übermächtige Trieb im Dienste sexueller Interessen stand. Wir finden eine weitere Bestätigung darin, wenn sich im Sexualleben reifer Jahre eine auffällige Verkümmerung dartut, gleichsam als ob ein Stück der Sexualbetätigung nun durch die Betätigung des übermächtigen Triebes ersetzt wäre" (Freud 1995: 46f.).

son has been replaced by AEH's scholarly activity. Psychobiographically speaking, the oneiric encounter between AEH and Housman describes an intrapsychic conflict connected to Housman's sexuality on the subconscious level of AEH's dream-memory, which is made conscious on-stage in front of the audience.

By considering, on the one hand, the role of cultural patterns in antiquity in contrast to Victorian society, and on the other hand sexuality and the subconscious in the presentation of the formation and construction of Housman's identity, Stoppard apposes socio- and psychobiographical factors. With these different approaches of interpretation of the biographical subject, *The Invention of Love* debunks the myth of personal coherence, presenting the biographee not as an integral whole, but literally as a fragmented self, a notion which is also applied to the interpretation of another dark area of the subject's life.

At the end of the first act, we learn that AEH did not even receive a pass degree in Oxford, although everybody thought he was an absolutely safe First (cf. *TIoL* 45). Because there is no first-hand explanation why A.E. Housman failed his exams, Stoppard considers a dark area of his biographee. On the one hand, the play presents internal reasons, hinting at the possibility that Housman failed because of his love for Jackson. After university, both start working in the Patent Office and share a house, while Housman continues his classical textual criticism after work. In his explanation for his failure to Jackson, he betrays a sense of happiness:

> I didn't get what I wanted, that's true, but I want what I've got. [...] But here we are, you and I, we eat the same meals in the same digs, catch the same train to work in the same office, and the work is easy, I've got time to do classics... and friendship is all, sometimes I'm so happy, it makes me dizzy –
>
> (54, dialogue omitted)

Meeting Jackson at Oxford and the fateful picnic have changed Housman's desires and wishes. He has chosen a life which resembles the Greek idea of brothers in arms as in the legend of Theseus and Pirithous, and he makes no effort to win Jackson's affection, for he is content with their platonic relationship. This suppression of sexual desire stands in contrast to Wilde, who was the topic of Gilbert and Sullivan's operetta *Patience, or Bunthorne's Bride* (1881), from a performance of which they have just returned in the above scene. Jackson rejects the aesthetic movement, and especially Wilde, because "all that posing and dressing up, it's not manly" (56). He does not understand why Wilde attracts so much attention with the public because, according to Jackson, he has not done anything worthwhile. Jackson represents the creed also represented by Ruskin and Labouchere, i.e. emphasising practical utility and despising idleness. This stands in contrast to the aesthetes' *l'art pour l'art* and Housman's knowledge-for-knowledge's-sake. Accordingly, as Michael R. Schiavi points out, Jackson reacts to Housman's 'outing' in a "genuine crisis of knowledge": "He had thought, via Wilde, that he knew how to read "beastliness" in other men – only to find his sexual criteria insufficient" (Schiavi 2004: 417).

Later in the play, however, in the second encounter between AEH and Housman, Stoppard presents a different explanation for Housman's failure, which has nothing to do with his love for Jackson, but rather with his love for textual criticism and initial scholarly ambitions:

> **AEH** Propertius!
> **Housman** The first of the Roman love elegists. Actually, Propertius is not set for Finals. I should be cramming, everybody expects me to get a First, you see. My family, too. I'm the eldest and I've always been... a scholarship boy... I ought to put Propertius aside now, but we're already all of us so late! – and there's someone with his Propertius coming out next year, Postgate he's called. Who knows how many of my conjectures he'll anticipate?   (*TIoL* 97f.)

Here, the play presents external reasons for Housman's failure. It seems to be his ambitious project of editing Propertius which stopped him from studying for his finals, paired with first academic pressure of expectations by friends and family and the race for a first publication on a certain topic. With the two contrasting explanations for Housman failing his final exams at Oxford, Stoppard reflects again on the dichotomy of scholar and poet in his biographical subject. He also questions the notion of depicting the subject as an integral whole according to an either/or model, which can arrive at a singular truth. In his biographical rendition, Stoppard shows that there is a difference between the facts and the truth about a biographee, a notion which is most clearly expressed in the imaginary encounter between AEH and Wilde.

The Invention of Love: The Subordination of Biographical Facts to Artistic Truth

4. AEH and Wilde: The Apollonian and Dionysian

A second, even more significant encounter with regard to the structure and the theme of the play occurs near the end when AEH meets Wilde. Appropriately, the entrance of the most "revolutionary" artist of his time is accompanied by "[t]*he faint sound of children singing the 'Marseillaise'* " (92), the rallying call of the French Revolution. Wilde enters reciting *A Shropshire Lad* XLIV. In AEH's words, it is about a "Woolwich cadet" who "blew his brains out so that he wouldn't live to shame himself, or bring shame on others" (93). Although after his imprisonment of two years' hard labour Wilde is physically in bad shape, he does not share AEH's cynicism. Wilde's love for life stands in marked contrast to AEH's aloofness. As Fleming points out, their lives reflect the Apollonian and the Dionysian: "Wilde lived the sensual, Dionysian life, while Housman opted for the critical-rational mode of the Apollonian. Each man's tragedy resulted from not balancing the two impulses" (Fleming 2001: 241). This perceived dichotomy is worth considering in more detail.

In *The Birth of Tragedy* (*Die Geburt der Tragödie*, 1872), Friedrich Nietzsche draws on the dialectic of the Apollonian and Dionysian in order to explain the advancement of art. According to him, in ancient Greece there existed an opposition in the origins and purposes of visual (plastic) arts, the Apollonian, and the non-visual art of music, the Dionysian. Through a marvellous metaphysical act of Hellenic 'will' they are paired to create Attic tragedy, both an Apollonian and Dionysian work of art. Nietzsche attributes each aspect to a separate artistic world: the Apollonian to the world of dream and the Dionysian to the world of intoxication. The oneiric world is seen as a perfect state and a higher truth in contrast to the incomplete understanding of daily reality. At the same time, it is the symbolic analogy to the ability to prophesy and to art in general. By contrast, the Dionysian world of intoxication is summoned by narcotic drink or the coming of spring, dissolving the principle of individuation. Man ceases to be an artist but instead becomes a work of art (cf. Nietzsche 1995: 1ff.). Thus, nature's art-impulses are expressed in two ways:

first, on the one hand, in the pictorial world of dreams, whose completeness is not dependent upon the intellectual attitude or the artistic culture of any single being; and, on the other hand, as drunken reality, which likewise does not heed the single unit, but even seeks to destroy the individual and redeem him by a mystic feeling of Oneness.[126] (5)

Accordingly, there are three types of artists:

With reference to these immediate art-states of nature, every artist is an "imitator", that is to say, either an Apollonian artist in dreams, or a Dionysian artist in ecstasies, or finally – as for example in Greek tragedy – at once artist in both dreams and ecstasies: so we may perhaps picture him sinking down in his Dionysian drunkenness and mystical self-abnegation, alone, and apart from the singing revelers, and we may imagine how now, through Apollonian dream-inspiration, his own state, *i.e.*, his oneness with the primal nature of the universe, is revealed to him in a *symbolical dream-picture*.[127] (5)

If we apply Nietzsche's dichotomy to AEH and Wilde, it becomes clear that the classification in the play goes further than indicated by Fleming: it is not only AEH's critical-rational character, but also his oneiric condition in the play which associates AEH with the Apollonian. In the same manner, it is not only Wilde's sensual characterisation, but also his, admittedly mild, condition of intoxication – he, for example, enters *"drinking brandy"*, a narcotic drink, *"and smoking a cigarette"*, and comes from a *"children's party"* (*TIoL* 92) – that associates him with the Dionysian.

---

[126] "[E]inmal als die Bilderwelt des Traumes, deren Vollkommenheit ohne jeden Zusammenhang mit der intellectuellen Höhe oder künstlerischen Bildung des Einzelnen ist, andererseits als rauschvolle Wirklichkeit, die wiederum des Einzelnen nicht achtet, sondern sogar das Individuum zu vernichten und durch eine mystische Einheitsempfindung zu erlösen sucht" (Nietzsche 1972: 26).

[127] "Diesen unmittelbaren Kunstzuständen der Natur gegenüber ist jeder Künstler 'Nachahmer', und zwar entweder apollonischer Traumkünstler oder dionysischer Rauschkünstler oder endlich – wie beispielsweise in der griechischen Tragödie – zugleich Rausch- und Traumkünstler: als welchen wir uns etwa zu denken haben, wie er, in der dionysischen Trunkenheit und mystischen Selbstentäußerung, einsam und abseits von den schwärmenden Chören niedersinkt und wie sich ihm nun, durch apollinische Traumeinwirkung, sein eigener Zustand, d.h. seine Einheit mit dem innersten Grunde der Welt in einem gleichnisartigen Traumbilde offenbart" (Nietzsche 1972: 26).

Correspondingly, Wilde is not presented as an artist, but as his own work of art. As Müller-Muth puts it, "*The Invention of Love* does not stage Oscar Wilde, but the creation of the Wilde myth" (Müller-Muth 2002: 219). In the Oxford scenes, he becomes a stereotype through his constant stage absence in combination with his description by others. Jowett, who for a moment mistakes Housman for Wilde – the former's first year was the latter's final one –, addresses the differences between the two alleged antipodes of the play:

> If you can rid yourself of your levity and your cynicism, and find another way to dissimulate your Irish provincialism than by making affected remarks about your blue china and going about in plum-coloured velvet breeches, which you don't, and cut your hair – you're not him at all, are you? (*TIoL* 22)

The mix-up introduces the later topic of a binary opposition between Wilde and AEH, but it also questions it at the same time. While the enumeration of Wildean stereotypes helps to distinguish Housman from Wilde, the mere possibility of a confusion of identities between the two shows that what is taken for eventually Wildean might be nothing but a myth, something only possible through the stage absence of its actual manifestation. This myth is bolstered even further by Pollard:

> Wilde is reckoned the wittiest man at Oxford. His rooms at Magdalen are said to be completely bare except for a lily in a blue vase. [...] He went to the Morrell's ball in a Prince Rupert costume which he has absentmindedly put on every morning since, and has been seen wearing it in the High. Everyone is repeating his remark that he finds it harder and harder every day to live up to his blue china. Don't you think that's priceless? (16, dialogue omitted)

Through Wilde's stage absence in the Oxford scenes, Stoppard ironically plays on Wilde's remark rephrased here by Pollard, because any onstage manifestation of Wilde would not live up to his myth. As with Byron in *Arcadia*, absence once again becomes the highest form of presence, a presence which emphasises that what the recipients conceive as 'Wilde' is only a stereotypical construction of the aestheticist homosexual poet. Or, in Wilde's own words, uttered by his character at the end of the play: "Wickedness is a myth invented by good people to account for the curious attractiveness of others" (102). Appropriately, Wilde's first actual onstage manifestation is Bunthorne, a Wildean parody. Only at the end of the play does the characterisation through others apparently give way to the appearance of a Wilde character proper. Nonetheless, this Wilde is still filtered through AEH's dream-memory and Stoppard's play. He is "nothing more than another role or mask – presumably a parody of sorts – one of the many facets, constructions and representations of Wilde that are equally fictitious and unreliable" (Müller-Muth 2002: 220). By retelling Wildean anecdotes (cf. *TIoL* 93f.) and rephrasing Wildean aphorisms (cf. 102) he is presented in a "cliché-ridden language – a veritable *déjà lu* for those familiar with Wilde's works" (Müller-Muth 2002: 220). It is this presentation which in Nietzschean terms dissolves and destroys any individuality in Wilde's character. Wilde has become his own work of art. As Beatrix Hesse writes: "The overall impression is that Wilde has in his lifetime so thoroughly invented himself that there was nothing left for later authors to re-invent" (Hesse 2002: 193f.). Hence, Wilde not only becomes the embodiment, but also the organ of central concerns and modes of presentation of Stoppard's art (cf. Krämer 2000: 300).

Nonetheless, *The Invention of Love* rather apposes than opposes AEH and Wilde, as Stoppard himself emphasised (cf. Stoppard in Cott 2001). Their tension and the tension between the dialogue and the form of representation respectively resists a final resolution (cf. Müller-Muth 2002: 221). In their encounter, then, which forms the focal point of *The Invention of Love*, Stoppard achieves a combination of the Apollonian and Dionysian in his drama. AEH is Stoppard's 'A' and Wilde his 'minus A', visualising not only the advancement of art through Nietzschean dichotomies, but metadramatically also the advancement of Stoppard's play and his drama in general. The Apollonian and Dionysian dialectic also reflects on the discrepancy between the world of dream images and the world of intoxicating reality in *The Invention of Love*. The *dream-memory play* refers to the Apollonian notion that the oneiric condition and art in general claim for themselves a higher truth, as the character of Wilde also formulates: "Truth is quite another thing [than fact] and is the work of the imagination" (*TIoL* 93).

In the play, Wilde differentiates between fact and truth. With this aspect in mind, he describes his relationship with Lord Alfred Douglas, his beloved Bosie:

> The betrayal of one's friends is a bagatelle in the stakes of love, but the betrayal of oneself is lifelong regret. Bosie is what became of me. He is spoiled, vindictive, utterly selfish and not very talented, but these are merely the facts. The truth is he was Hyacinth when Apollo loved him, he is ivory and gold, from his red rose-leaf lips comes music that fills me with joy, he is the only one who understands me. [...] [B]efore Plato could describe love, the loved one had to be invented. We would never love anybody if we could see past our invention. Bosie is my creation, my poem. In the mirror of invention, love discovered itself. Then we saw what we had made – the piece of ice in the fist you cannot hold or let go.
> (94f.)

Wilde here describes the tendency of lovers to romanticise the loved one, which also reflects on the title of *The Invention of Love*. This title describes, on the one hand, the invention of the love poem by the Roman poet Catullus in the first century B.C., because "[l]ike everything else, like clocks and trousers and algebra, the love poem had to be invented" (13). On the other hand, it describes the condition that in love, the beloved is invented, too, and the person created is not fact but becomes subjective truth. Housman "invented" Jackson in the same way, with the difference that for him, the classical poets are "[r]eal people in real love, baring their souls in poetry that made their mistresses immortal!" Their love poems are for him "love as it really is" (99). The poems, however, as AEH comes to realise, resemble rather the Apollonian world of dream images as they are "only" art. They are no substitute for the actual experience of love, the Dionysian world of intoxicating reality.

AEH pities Wilde and wishes for him that he could have lived at a time when and a place where homosexuality was accepted, referring again to ancient Greece and its poetry:

> I'm very sorry. Your life is a terrible thing. A chronological error. The choice was not always between renunciation and folly. You should have lived in Megara when Theognis was writing and made his lover a song sung unto all posterity… and not *now*! – when disavowal and endurance are in honour, and a nameless luckless love has made notoriety your monument. (96)

Wilde, however, sees AEH as the actual victim when he counters:

> Better a fallen rocket than never a burst of light. Dante reserved a place in his Inferno for those who wilfully live in sadness – sullen in the sweet air, he says. Your 'honour' is all shame and timidity and compliance. Pure of stain! (96)

Wilde will not be remembered for his affair with Bosie alone. His monument is his art, which has been of great influence to this day, especially for Stoppard's drama:

> The blaze of my immolation threw its light into every corner of the land where uncounted young men sat each in his own darkness. What would I have done in Megara!? – think what I would have missed! I awoke the imagination of the century. [...] I made art a philosophy that can look the twentieth century in the eye. I had genius, brilliancy, daring, I took charge of my own myth. I dipped my staff into the comb of wild honey. I tasted forbidden sweetness and drank the stolen waters. (96)

The realisation that Wilde's life of excess is the real success must be even more bitter for AEH as Wilde uses his own words against him: "stolen waters" is an allusion to *More Poems* XXII (cf. Zeifman 2001: 197). The topic of this poem is *carpe diem*, as that of Horace, *Odes* I.11, to which AEH referred earlier in his conversation with his younger self (cf. *TIoL* 39). AEH is the first to admit that he lived a taciturn life and sees his life-work in his textual criticism:

> My life is marked by long silences. [...] Meanwhile I defended the classical authors from the conjectures of idiots, and produced editions of books by Ovid, Juvenal and Lucan, and finally of Manilius, which I dedicated to my comrade Moses Jackson, and that will have to do, my sandcastle against the confounding sea. Classics apart, my life was not short enough for me to not do the things I wanted to not do, but they were few [...]. (95)

Wilde, however, reminds AEH that he also has his poems: "You didn't mention your poems. How can you be unhappy when you know you wrote them? They are all that will still matter" (97). Wilde here hints at the theme of *ars longa vita brevis*. For him, art is the triumph of the artist over life, a concept which is similar to Joyce's in *Travesties* and Flora's and Das's in *Indian Ink*. Art alone, and not scholarship about art, will endure. Although AEH spent much more time and energy editing his Manilius, his poems became what Housman, in reference to Horace, *Odes* III.30, calls "a monument more lasting than bronze [...], higher than the pyramids of kings, unyielding to wind and weather and the passage of time" (35).

5. The difference between biographical facts and artistic truth

A leitmotif in *The Invention of Love* is the question of the nature of truth. AEH is a classical scholar who sees his purpose in establishing the original wording of ancient texts: "The only reason to consider what the ancient philosophers meant about anything is if it's relevant to settling corrupt or disputed passages in the text" (31). Housman, too, sees the purpose in the mastery of Greek and Latin in exactly this field: "But isn't it of use to establish what the ancient authors really wrote?" (24). The question is put to Jowett who, in a lengthy explanation, instructs Housman that it is a rather futile exercise, since over the centuries the texts have been corrupted. He conveniently forgets his own contribution to the corruption through his translations in accordance to Victorian morals:

> In other words, anyone with a secretary knows that what Catullus really wrote was already corrupt by the time it was copied twice [...]. Think of all those secretaries! – corruption breeding corruption from papyrus to papyrus, and from the last disintegrating scrolls to the first new-fangled parchment books, with a thousand years of copying-out still to come, running the gauntlet of changing forms of script and spelling, and absence of punctuation – not to mention mildew and rats and fire and flood and Christian disapproval to the brink of extinction as what Catullus really wrote passed from scribe to scribe, this one drunk, that one sleepy, another without scruple, and of those sober, wide-awake and scrupulous, some ignorant of Latin and some, even worse, fancying themselves better Latinists than Catullus – until! – finally and at long last – mangled and tattered like a dog that has fought its way home, there falls across the threshold of the Italian Renaissance the sole surviving witness to thirty generations of carelessness and stupidity: the *Verona Codex* of Catullus; which was almost immediately lost again, but not before being copied with one last opportunity for error. And there you have the foundation of the poems of Catullus as they went to the printer for the first time, in Venice 400 years ago.   (24f.)

Textual corruptions as described by Jowett are omnipresent in *The Invention of Love* on at least three levels. Firstly, they can be found on an explicit thematic level. Housman and Pollard explain to Chamberlain that the task of the textual critic is to decide between "hushing it up" and "hashing it up", and eventually between "lashing it up", "mashing it up" and "washing it up" – "only in Latin, of course" (67f.). Secondly, textual corruptions feature on an implicit intertextual level. In the lecture that concludes the first act, AEH draws on a biblical metaphor in order to rebuke an imaginary student:

> If Jesus of Nazareth had had before him the example of Miss Frobisher getting through the Latin degree papers of the London University Examinations Board he wouldn't have had to fall back on camels and the eyes of needles, and Miss Frobisher's name would be a delightful surprise to encounter in Matthew, Chapter 19; as would, even more surprisingly, The London University Examinations Board. (48)

Even in his dream-memory lecture, Stoppard has AEH interlace textual criticism because the word 'camel' (κάμηλον) in Matthew 19:24 can be read as a mistranslation of the word 'rope' (κάμιλον) in the Greek original (cf. Nestle (ed.) 1963: 51). Finally, textual corruptions can also be found on an implicit textual level. Sylvia Tomasch hints at deliberate errors in the play text on the side of Stoppard (cf. Tomasch 2004: 460n9), e.g. AEH's remark on the peril of poetical feelings for scholarship: "There are always poetical people ready to protest that a corrrupt [sic] line is exquisite" (*TIoL* 36).[128]

In the conversation between AEH and Housman, the young student himself dreams of compiling a definitive, text-critical edition of Propertius because "(there's) the feeling that between the natural chaos of his writing and the whole hit-or-miss of the manuscripts, nobody has got the text anywhere near right" (32f.). AEH knows of the problems of textual criticism, and to him being human is "an impediment to editing a classic" (33). The scholar's duty is to add to knowledge and "the only thing that makes it knowledge is that it is true" (37). It is again the human factor which opposes these ends, as already realised by Housman with respect to homosexual allusions in ancient texts and the moral dilemma of their translators: "The passion for truth is the faintest of all human passions" (40). And when the translators equate moral with textual corruption, they not only corrupt texts but also life's meaning and truth. As in his aspiration for a definitive Propertius, Housman

---

[128] It is interesting to know in this context that Stoppard translated the Greek and Latin texts used in the play himself, as the playwright kindly pointed out to me (private communication, 3 May 2007).

The Invention of Love: The Subordination of Biographical Facts to Artistic Truth

believes in a single true meaning to life, but AEH disagrees: "You think there is an answer: the lost autograph copy of life's meaning, which we might recover from the corruptions that have made it nonsense. But if there is no such copy, really and truly there is no answer. It's all in the timing" (41).

Because AEH believes that there is no ultimate reconstructable truth to life, he distrusts biography, which bestows meaning on life with hindsight. He calls biographers "jackals" (1) who "will find it [his life] hard scavenging" (95). One reason for this is that AEH has arranged to have his papers burned when he is dead (cf. 46). When his colleague Chamberlain reasons that AEH started writing poetry in the first five months of 1895 because it was the beginning of the Oscar Wilde trials, AEH rebukes this *post-hoc* fallacy with the words: "Oh, really, Chamberlain. You should take up biography" (88). And when Chamberlain metabiographically asks the dreaming AEH "What happened to me, by the way?", he answers: "How should I know? I suppose you became a sort of footnote" (91). Stoppard here discloses his biography play as an artistic construct poised between fact and fiction, just as his biographee is poised between scholar and poet.

For Tomasch, Housman and AEH represent the antagonism of different schools of textual editing, believing that its goal is either to arrive at transcendent truth or at contingent accuracy. In the play "these two perspectives turn out to be not quite as contrary as they seem, for each is predicated on a yearning to recapture lost perfection" (Tomasch 2004: 458). The character of AEH himself sublates this apparent binary opposition because he mediates between scholarly fact and artistic truth, as is evident from his remark about scholarship: "To be a scholar is to strike your finger on the page and say, 'Thou ailest here, and here'" (*TIoL* 37). AEH apparently credits the scholar with the authority and the need to identify errors, to correct them and thus to add to knowledge, but he does so with an intertextual allusion to Matthew Arnold's "Memorial Verses" (1850).[129] In the poem, Arnold has Goethe speak the words *"Thou ailest here, and here"*, and has him continue a few lines

---

[129] A.E. Housman delivered an obituary for Matthew Arnold at University College London, to the College's Literary Society, in the 1890s (cf. Housman 1989: 275f.).

229

later: *"Art still has truth, take refuge there"* (Arnold 1945: 162). In the context of Arnold's poem, then, it is not only scholarship, but also art which is again associated with truth. Hence, the character of AEH implies and at the same time sublates the dichotomy between scholarly fact and artistic truth.

That the notion of subjective truth in and through art also applies to Stoppard's own play can be seen in the case of Wilde's age. In the stage directions, it says: *"Wilde, aged forty-one"* (*TIoL* 92). Since he was born in 1854, the scene with Wilde would thus be set in 1895, the year in which he was imprisoned. But it is also Queen Victoria's Jubilee, which is correctly dated to June 1897 in the stage directions (cf. 86) and to which Wilde himself refers (cf. 94). Because he is also listed as aged forty-one in the character list, a misprint can be ruled out. Seeber conjectures that the discrepancy with regard to Wilde's age may be Stoppard's intentional hint at Wilde's contempt for facts (cf. Seeber 1999: 370). However, while in his essay Seeber emphasises Stoppard's inclination to use biographical facts in *The Invention of Love*, he himself does not consider the fact that the playwright actually reflects on the historical Wilde's own account of his age. At the first testimony of his trials on 3 April, 1895, Wilde stated: "I am thirty-nine years of age" (Hyde (ed.) 1960: 116). To this, the counsel for the prosecution, Edward Carson, responded in the cross-examination:

> [Carson:] You stated that your age was thirty-nine. I think you are over forty. You were born on 16th October, 1854? – [Wilde:] I have no wish to pose as being young. I am thirty-nine or forty. You have my certificate and that settles the matter.
> [Carson:] But being born in 1854 makes you more than forty? – [Wilde:] Ah! Very well. (120)

When Stoppard uses Wilde's self-proclaimed age, i.e. thirty-nine plus two years as two years have passed since the trials, he turns Wilde's fiction into a fact of his own fiction, which is *The Invention of Love*. This confirms what Wilde says to AEH about the artist: "The artist must lie, cheat, deceive, be untrue to nature and contemptuous of history. I made my life into my art and it was an unqualified success" (*TIoL* 96). Stoppard is contemptuous of history, but true to Wilde. He makes Wilde's life into his art, and by not following the factual account but Wilde's own invention, Stoppard emphasises that art, despite its lack of facts, is nevertheless true. Hence, the Wilde character assumes a metadramatic and metabiographical function. As Krämer points out, the Wilde character stresses the circumstance that in biography, "reality" is created only through the individual recipient who instils life with meaning, and that truth is to be found beyond facts for "[n]othing that actually occurs is of the smallest importance" (102; cf. Krämer 2003: 233). According to Wilde, scholarly factual biography which tries scrupulously to reconstruct the life of its biographee would negate her/his exceptionality and degrade her/him to a type: "Art deals with exceptions, not with types. Facts deal only with types". Only artistic treatment emphasises what is of importance and consists of subjective truth: "I was said to have walked down Picadilly with a lily in my hand. There was no need. To do it is nothing, to be said to have done it is everything. It is the truth about me. [… S]incerity is the enemy of art". In the same manner, Stoppard takes the biographical facts and subordinates them to his art, i.e., his play. By further developing this notion of subjective truth in and through art, which we have also seen in *Indian Ink*, he shows in *The Invention of Love* that while conventional biography may be a compilation of facts, it holds no truth about its biographee. This can only be achieved by art: "Art cannot be subordinate to its subject, otherwise it is not art but biography, and biography is the mesh through which our real life escapes" (all quotations *TIoL* 93).

6. Recapitulation: *Biography is the mesh through which our real life escapes*

The structuring principle of *The Invention of Love* is the principle of dichotomy, which Stoppard obtains from his biographical subject. A.E. Housman's biography is presented through a *dream-memory play* that underlines the unreliability of his reminiscences. AEH's memory again and again returns to poetic expressions of desire coming from classical authors such as Sappho, Catullus, Horace and Vergil. The references to these classical authors deconstruct any objective claim to biography, but, at the same time, they depict AEH's inmost truth (cf. Seeber 1999:

368). This reminds one of Old Carr in *Travesties*, where it was not classical Greco-Roman poetry but *The Importance of Being Earnest* and *Ulysses* which affected his biographical reconstructions.

The play features a beginning, a climax and an ending, but the repetition of certain scenes and parts of dialogue, the surreal presentation of the plot and the dichotomous structure of the play negate any Aristotelian chronological, causal progression. *The Invention of Love* presents a curvilinear time in which past and present co-exist, mirroring each other in a refractory way. Thus, *The Invention of Love* is a metabiography play. While it also consists of scenic presentations of historical events, conducted by the chorus of lecturers and journalists, it deals primarily with the self-reflexive retrospective construction process of AEH's biography and Housman's identity. In his characterisation, Stoppard apposes socio- and psychobiographical factors, rejecting the myth of personal coherence. He questions the notion of depicting the subject as an integral whole according to an either/or model. However, *The Invention of Love* is also in parts a postbiography play, since it considers the difference of biographical fact and artistic truth. The play gives two very different reasons for Housman failing his final exams. By presenting the biographical subject as a divided self, it also visualises AEH's varying conceptions of himself, in the past and in the subconscious of his mind. In the play, the Wilde character takes on a metabiographical function and becomes a work of art instead of a biographically reconstructed subject. Stoppard takes biographical facts and subordinates them to his art. With regard to Wilde, he underlines that, while conventional biography may be a compilation of facts, it holds no deeper truth about its biographee.

Finally, AEH can be seen "as a more enlightened version of previous Stoppardian characters" (Müller-Muth 2002: 221). Although AEH acknowledges the impossibility of retrieving an authentic original, both with regard to textual criticism and to life-writing, his scholarly side and its principle of knowledge-for-knowledge's-sake represent the importance of the epistemological process in the retrieval of facts because "[l]ife is in the minding" (*TIoL* 48). This, in turn, is reminiscent of Hannah's exclamation that "[i]t's wanting to know that makes us matter" (*Arcadia* 75; cf. Müller-Muth 2002: 221*n*7). These retrieved facts, however, are not what constitute life. By apposing AEH's scholarly and artistic side and by confronting Wilde and AEH, Stoppard sublates the binary opposition of (intoxicating) fact and (oneiric) fiction, underlining the relevance of aesthetic notions for the interpretation of someone's life.

IX. *The Coast of Utopia*: The 'Causal-Realistic' Presentation of Biography

Stoppard's monumental *The Coast of Utopia* trilogy consists of the three plays *Voyage*, *Shipwreck* and *Salvage*. In them, he depicts life episodes of the Russian intelligentsia. The trilogy is set between 1833 and 1868 and covers, geographically, six European countries. It seems beyond question that *The Coast of Utopia* is a history and biography play *par excellence*, merely by considering the vast historical and biographical material Stoppard processed. Historically, it deals with the development of Russia in contrast to the "enlightened" West, the failure of the European revolutions of 1848/49, German Idealism and Romanticism, Marxism, the emancipation of the Russian serfs and the generation gap between the 'superfluous men' (*lishnye lyudi*) – individuals of talent and capability, who do not fit into the state-centred pattern of employment – and the 'nihilists' – here simply meaning 'new men'.[130] Biographically, *The Coast of Utopia* has at its centre the interwoven lives of Michael Bakunin, Vissarion Belinsky, Alexander Herzen, Ivan Turgenev and friends, with many additional historical characters such as Karl Marx, Guiseppe Mazzini, Alexandre Ledru-Rollin and Louis Blanc. *The Coast of Utopia* apposes and opposes different historical concepts on the levels of structure, theme and character. In the trilogy, Stoppard reflects on the idea that life is less the assertion of a single will than the product of innumerable and shifting relationships and he considers the relationship between personal history and socio-historical forces.

---

[130] The historical Herzen described this generation gap in his essay *The Superfluous and the Jaundiced* (1860; cf. Herzen 1982: 619-628).

1. The macroscopic level: *The Coast of Utopia* as a conventional and realistic biography play

Before we concentrate on the biographical aspects of *The Coast of Utopia*, it should be categorised in terms of the history play. The trilogy displays many features of a conventional and realistic history play. In *The Coast of Utopia*, Stoppard uses a mixture of documented material and fictional elements. He draws, for example, on Alexander Herzen's memoirs *My Past and Thoughts* (*Byloe i dumy*, 1861–67) and *From the Other Shore* (*S togo berega*, 1850) and on Ivan Turgenev's *Literary Reminiscences and Autobiographical Fragments* (*Literaturnye i zhiteiskie vospominaniia*, 1874/80), even partly quoting from them in the stage directions (cf. *Salvage* 92 and *Shipwreck* 52) and throughout the text. His main secondary sources, as described by Stoppard in the "Acknowledgements" section at the beginning of the plays, are E.H. Carr's *Romantic Exiles* (1933) and his biography *Michael Bakunin* (1937), Isaiah Berlin's *Russian Thinkers* (1978) and the writings of Aileen Kelly, one of the leading scholars of nineteenth- and early twentieth-century Russian intellectual history, who wrote her doctoral thesis under Berlin's direction. As with the autobiographical writings quoted in the stage directions, Stoppard sometimes even quotes *verbatim* from these texts, too.[131] With such a vast basis in, and similarity to, primary and established secondary sources, the trilogy can be said to follow the dominant interpretation of the events of its main characters and thus does not contradict historical knowledge. *The Coast of Utopia* aims at historical stage realism as well, the London production using "96 wigs and 40 'face-sets' of

---

[131] To Herbert F. Tucker, *Russian Thinkers* "stands to the epic dramaturgy [...] of the trilogy] in a relation like that borne by Epicurus's teachings to the *De Rerum Natura* of Lucretius or by Aquinas's philosophy to the theological architecture of *The Divine Comedy*" (Tucker 2005: 156). In the case of Stoppard's presentation of Herzen, Thomas Harlan Campbell views *The Coast of Utopia* as "the latest contribution to what we might call a 150-year-long tradition of English 'Herzenism'" (Campbell 2007: 215). To him, the "thesis of Berlin/Kelly and the antithesis of Carr produce the unique synthesis of Stoppard's *Coast of Utopia*" (222). On the influence of Berlin's, Kelly's and Carr's view of the historical Herzen on the trilogy, cf. 216-223.

moustaches and beards. There are 416 costumes: 271 for the actors, 60 for the understudies and 85 for the stage hands" (Peter 2002). Additionally, *The Coast of Utopia* is a biography play because it does not so much concentrate on history represented through personalities, but rather on certain personalities in history, their interdependent and connected lives, as well as, thematically, the quest for the self in history. More precisely, because of the observed elements of the realistic history play present in the trilogy, *The Coast of Utopia* can be read on a macroscopic level – i.e. taking all three plays as a sequential unit – as a conventional and realistic biography play. The trilogy observes the Aristotelian unity of plot, uses language as a means for realistic presentation, incorporates intermedial and intertextual allusions which, however, do not disrupt mimesis, and is mainly of a non-comic tone.

a. The Aristotelian plot of the trilogy

The trilogy follows the Aristotelian plot with beginning, complication, middle, denouement and end (cf. Aristotle 1977: 41 and 56), or the pyramidal plot as suggested in Gustav Freytag's *Technique of the Drama* (*Die Technik des Dramas*, 1863) with a) introduction; b) rise; c) climax; d) return or fall; and e) catastrophe (cf. Freytag 1896: 115).

The beginning to (or introduction of) the trilogy is *Voyage*, as the title already gives away. "*Premukhino, the Bakunin estate, a hundred and fifty miles north-west of Moscow*" represents the traditional Russia of aristocratic landowners. Alexander Bakunin, whose "*rule is benign despotism*", calls himself a liberal who argues for the education of women – all his daughters "have been educated in five languages" (*Voyage* 3). He, nevertheless, stands for a system in which a "landowner's estate is reckoned not in acres but in adult male serfs" (59). He is planning to marry his oldest daughter to Baron Renne, a cavalry officer, although she does not love him. Alexander's paternal authority is shaken by his son Michael, who is fascinated with the ideas of German Idealism, infecting his sisters with it and intervening on their behalf.

The four main characters of the trilogy are introduced in *Voyage*. The future revolutionary and anarchist Michael Bakunin, who dominates Act

I, is visited at Premukhino by the future critic Vissarion Belinsky and by the future writer Ivan Turgenev, who both represent Russia's new literary generation. Herzen and the political (as opposed to the philosophical) perspective of the trilogy are also introduced in *Voyage*, in the first scene[132] of Act II, set in Moscow. The progressive philosophical and political circles of the city are diametrically opposed to traditional-minded Premukhino. Like Michael, Herzen dissociates himself from the old-fashioned conservative generation (cf. *Voyage* 58). The first appearances of Michael Bakunin, Belinsky, Turgenev and Herzen, respectively, strike in *Voyage* what Freytag calls "a clearly defining keynote" (Freytag 1896: 121):[133]

> Now certainly this note, sounded at the beginning, is not necessarily a loud unison of the voices of different persons; brief but deep emotions in the chief characters may very well indicate the first ripple of the short waves which has to precede the storms of the drama.[134] (119f.)

The four main characters set the particular dichotomising tone of revolutions and (generational) conflicts of the trilogy and they make the audience realise that in and through them, "[d]awn has broken" (*Voyage* 9). Their appearances indicate the first ripple of the short waves which precede the storms of the drama they will encounter on their voyage to the coast of utopia and from which shipwreck and salvage will follow.

The exciting force or moment in the trilogy, in which the plot is set into motion, the main characters reveal their nature and their participation is prompted (cf. Freytag 1896: 125), is achieved by the introduction of the main characters. Michael arrives in the Russian idyll of Premukhino, his head full of "German thoughts" about the 'Universal Idea' and the 'Absolute' and considers it his duty to intervene in his family's affairs. Belinsky follows him by literally stumbling into the same idyll

---

[132] Although Stoppard does not divide the plays into scenes, I have counted those sections beginning with a date as scenes to enable the reader to follow the suggested structure.

[133] "[S]charf bezeichnender Akkord" (Freytag 1975: 107).

[134] "Nun ist allerdings dieser Akkord des Anfangs nicht notwendig ein lautes Zusammentönen verschiedener Personen, sehr gut mögen auch kurze Seelenbewegungen der Hauptpersonen das erste Kräuseln kleiner Wellen andeuten, welches die Stürme des Dramas einzuleiten hat" (Freytag 1975: 106).

The Coast of Utopia: The 'Causal-Realistic' Presentation of Biography

with his own conviction about Russian literature, which, in a nutshell, is that there is none (cf. *Voyage* 35). Turgenev, in a quieter manner, announces at Premukhino that "our situation in Russia isn't hopeless while we've still got twelve days to catch up" (52),[135] and Herzen describes what is wrong with the Russian picture. He calls his circle "revolutionaries with secret arsenals of social theory" (58), suggesting political reform and renouncing German Idealism. Michael Bakunin, Belinsky, Turgenev and Herzen all stand for the beginning of the ideological, philosophical, political as well as physical departure from a Russia which seems to be literally behind the times, towards the coast of utopia.

The rising movement takes place during the first four scenes of *Shipwreck*. According to Freytag, during this movement the main characters need to be given room and opportunity to act (cf. Freytag 1896: 125), and

> the scenes of this rising movement [...] have to produce a progressive intensity of interest; they must, therefore, not only evince progress in their import, but they must show an enlargement in form and treatment, and, indeed, with variation and shading in execution [...].[136] (128)

The newly named Russian intelligentsia is given this room to identify and define itself as a "uniquely Russian phenomenon, the intellectual opposition considered as a social force" (*Shipwreck* 17) that is distinct from traditional Russia and the West. The first scene of *Shipwreck* is the last time in the trilogy that the action takes place in Russia. Afterwards, the trilogy changes places by following Belinsky and Turgenev first to Salzbrunn and then to the alleged capital of free thinking, namely Paris. The ideological and political preparation for the climax takes place at the

---

[135] Turgenev here refers to the time difference of twelve days between the Julian Calender used in Russia and the Gregorian Calender used in West Europe. Russia replaced the Julian with the Gregorian Calender in 1917, after the Russian Revolution.

[136] "Für die Szenen der Steigerung gilt der Satz, daß sie eine fortlaufende Verstärkung der Teilnahme hervorzubringen haben; sie müssen deshalb nicht nur durch ihren Inhalt den Fortschritt darstellen, auch in Form und Behandlung eine Vergrößerung zeigen, und zwar mit Wechsel und Schattierungen in der Ausführung" (Freytag 1975: 113).

Herzen residence, where the main characters discuss their different political convictions. Belinsky compares Paris to a zoo "where the seals throw fish to the public", as it is there possible to publish anything without worrying about censorship. In his opinion, this makes writing in Russia more truthful. Bakunin plays the anarchist who expects the Russian revolution soon and prefers action to ideas (cf. 37). His revolutionary Romanticism is defused by Herzen, who perceives that there has to be a European revolution first (cf. 32). Turgenev stands between these three poles. When Belinsky despairs over a children's puzzle which is supposed to form a square, Turgenev remarks: "Perhaps it's a circle" (37), suggesting the impossibility of finding a consensus on the topic of personal freedom and revolution.

The whole of *Shipwreck* forms the middle or climax in this Aristotelian plot, with the title of the play again hinting at the crisis of the trilogy. On the one hand, this is true of the political events in the trilogy: the outbreak of the European Revolutions of 1848, especially in Paris with the establishment of the Second Republic, followed by "omnibuses full of corpses" and the drowning of the Marseillaise "*in volleys of rifle fire*" (53). On the other hand, it also holds true for the personal events in the lives of the protagonists, which make up the tragic forces or incidents in the trilogy. The close connection of these (political and personal) tragic forces with the climax gives to the drama a magnitude and expanse of the middle part, which alters Freytag's pyramidal form into one with a double apex (cf. Freytag 1896: 132f.). The pyramidal double apex begins with Belinsky's death and continues with Bakunin's imprisonment, the adultery committed by Herzen's wife Natalie with George Herwegh and the death by drowning of Herzen's mother and deaf son Kolya. It ends with Natalie's and her newborn's deaths as retold by Herzen to Bakunin. Thus, *Shipwreck* forms "the middle point of a group of forces, which, darting in either direction, course upward and downward" (130).[137]

The denouement, or return or fall, consists of Herzen settling down in London and his engagement with the other political émigrés. How-

---

[137] "[D]eshalb bildet die Hauptszene des Höhepunktes gerne den Mittelpunkt einer Gruppe von Momenten, welche nach beiden Seiten anschließend auf- und abwärts laufen" (Freytag 1975: 114).

ever, the attacks of the opponents as described by Freytag (cf. 133) do not come from them, but from the nihilist generation of Russian revolutionaries, namely Chernyshevsky and Sleptsov, and from his friends Bakunin and Turgenev, who partly agree with the political views of the new generation. The return also takes place on a personal level, in the affair Herzen starts with his best friend's wife (also called Natalie) and the rupture in the relationship with his children.

The forces of the final suspense consist of the so-called emancipation of the serfs and its severe consequences, Bakunin's revolutionary network operating from Herzen's house and its collapse, and Olga's and Tata's departure with their tutor Malwida von Meysenbug to Italy. The revolutionary generations become separated for good because of their differing opinions about the assassination attempt on the Tsar by the nihilists. These moments are "a slight hindrance, a distant possibility of a happy release, [...] thrown in the way of the already indicated direction of the end" (136).[138]

In consequence, *Salvage* as a whole forms the end or catastrophe of the trilogy. The revolutionary émigrés of Europe have washed up on the English shore "forever going over the past, living on recrimination and fantasy" (*Salvage* 16), and Herzen has lost every illusion dear to him (cf. 18). His (by now old) generation of Russian revolutionaries quarrel with the nihilists about how to achieve the emancipation of the serfs: by reform from above or by revolution from below, i.e. 'abolition by the axe'. The achieved emancipation backfires, the revolutionary network collapses, *The Bell*'s circulation goes down and the assassination attempt shatters the last hopes for reform in Russia. The generational conflict of *Voyage* is thus mirrored in *Salvage*. While in *Voyage*, Herzen and his circle disapprove of the position of "reform from above, not revolution from below" (*Voyage* 57), it is this very same position which Herzen later defends in *Salvage*. The generational conflict was foreshadowed by Polevoy: "Well, it will happen to you one day... some young man with a smile on his face, telling you, 'Be off with you, you're behind the

---

[138] "Dies geschieht durch eine neue kleine Spannung, dadurch, daß ein leichtes Hindernis, eine entfernte Möglichkeit glücklicher Lösung, der bereits angedeuteten Richtung auf das Ende noch in den Weg geworfen wird" (Freytag 1975: 119).

times!'" (59).[139] Herzen's children become estranged from their father and Russian culture, abandoning Russian for other European languages, leaving the father's house to live with the German tutor, and his son even marrying an Italian proletarian woman. In the end, the ideas of the main characters have not reached their desired goal, which can be seen as a failure in terms of tragedy: "The more profound the strife which has gone forward in the hero's soul, the more noble its purpose has been, so much more logical will the destruction of the succumbing hero be" (Freytag 1896: 137).[140]

b.   Language as a means of realism

In the sequential unit of *The Coast of Utopia*, language becomes a means for the plausible presentation of the characters in terms of the realistic biography play. In the stage directions of the trilogy, it is made clear that "*'English' dialogue is spoken with a Russian accent*" (*Voyage* 3) or "*[s]peech is without accent except when inside quotation marks*" (*Salvage* 3). Thus, "Stoppard has his aristocrats speaking Russian, albeit in English" (Beye 2002), i.e. the presentation of Russian life through language follows a "realistic" presentation as much as is possible in front of an English-speaking audience. Interwoven in this Russian-English dialogue are passages in 'English', French, German, Italian and Russian. Alexandra presents her knowledge of English by not only speaking in this tongue, but also by citing English cliché phrases as perceived by a

---

[139] Herzen's question "what is to be done?" (*Voyage* 59) only a few lines later also anticipates the conflict between him and Chernyshevsky in *Salvage*. It is the same question which the historical Chernyshevsky posed as a rebuttal to Turgenev's *Fathers and Sons* (*Otcy i deti*, 1862) with the title of his political novel *What is to be done? Tales About New People* (*Čto delat'? Iz rasskazov o novych ljudjach*, 1863; cf. Yacowar 2003: 84n6). Lenin and his wife were inspired by Chernyshevsky's novel to write their book *What is to be done? Burning Questions of Our Movement* (*Čto delat'? Nabolevsie voprosy nasego divizenija*, 1902) which propounds the main features of Leninism.

[140] "Je tiefer der Kampf aus ihrem innersten Leben hervorgegangen und je größer das Ziel desselben war, desto folgerichtiger wird die Vernichtung des unterliegenden Helden sein" (Freytag 1975: 120).

foreigner: "(*In 'English'*) 'How do you do, Baron Renne! I say! charming weather, you do not think!'" Tatiana takes the cue and misquotes a line from *The Merchant of Venice*: "(*in 'English'*) 'The quality of mercy is not strained, it dropping like the gentle dew from heaven!'" (*Voyage* 4).[141] Varenka explains to her mother what the English governess said in French (cf. 5), Michael later quotes a part of Mignon's song from Goethe's *Wilhelm Meister* when he proclaims his plan to go to Moscow: "*Dahin! Dahin! Lass uns ziehn!*" (23), and entire conversation passages between Herwegh, Emma and Herzen are in German (cf. *Shipwreck* 38). The Herzens talk with their Italian servant in his mother tongue, and in *Salvage*, the stage Russian becomes real Russian – offstage (cf. *Salvage* 44) and onstage (cf. 26 and 115). This mix of languages can be explained by considering Russian history:

> The Russian aristocracy that followed Peter the Great's exhortation to make themselves European had per force to speak French or German. French was the common language of aristocratic households, cultured people knew German as well. It was not uncommon for aristocrats to speak Russian poorly or not at all.
> (Beye 2002)

Thus, as far as the medium of drama allows, Stoppard gives a taste of how Russian aristocrats communicated in the nineteenth century, leaving the audience literally in the dark, since only the printed versions of the trilogy gives translations in brackets. This Babel of languages throughout the trilogy also helps to explain the social milieu of the main characters, namely that they come from a Russia which since Peter the Great has been influenced by western thought and culture, and in which a uniquely Russian national identity has yet to be moulded.

c. Intermediality and intertextuality as non-disturbing elements

Anna Muzna points out that the Russian style of the trilogy and especially of *Voyage* is derived on the one hand from the historical setting

---

[141] The original lines read: "The quality of mercy is not strain'd, / It droppeth as the gentle rain from heaven / Upon the place beneath" (Shakespeare 1974: 276 [IV.i.184-186]).

and its "Russian" main characters, but on the other hand mainly from Chekhov's drama:

> *The Coast of Utopia* contains not only such 'generic' Russian elements as family estates, gardens, verandas, and "doleful piano music", but also numerous specific allusions to Chekhov's dramatic canon: four sisters and a brother, a beginning writer and a foreign governess, fishing rods, a cry "To Moscow!" and, neither last nor least, the recurring sound of a "distant thunder", echoing, of course, the sound of a broken string.[142]
> (Muza 2003)

This Russian or rather Chekhovian style does not undermine the presentation of *The Coast of Utopia* in terms of realism. On the contrary, it is accepted by the theatre audience as dramatic reality because of their familiarity with it from Chekhov's drama:

> If Stoppard mocks his public's (as well as his own) anticipation that a play from Russian life will feature a country estate, a large family, a russified German Baron, a garden and a lake, he also grants the audience the (partly Freudian) pleasure of recognizing the familiar in the unknown. The Chekhovian element mediates the reader/viewer's transition into a vast, remote and alien world.
> (Muza 2003)

Nadel sees it in a similar way and even views Stoppard's style, in the context of Brechtian epic drama, as a stylistic means for creating historical realism:

> Historicizing his work provides both the political validity and the dramatic authenticity necessary to convince the audience to believe in the illusion (and romance) of the social actions represented on stage. [… B]y rooting his drama in the historically valid, Stoppard ensures that the audience will find the stage an appropriate site of Russian life and European exile. History, dramatized authentically (although not always accurately), meets their expectations. To create this authority, Stoppard not only draws in detail from his sources but balances a panoramic, Brechtian view of Russia with a Chekhovian focus on domestic drama.
> (Nadel 2004a: 504f.)

Other intermedial and intertextual allusions such as Edouard Manet's painting *Le Déjeuner sur l'herbe* (*Luncheon on the Grass*, 1863; cf. *Shipwreck* 73f.) or Ivan Turgenev's conversation with Bazarov, the protagonist from his novel *Fathers and Sons* (cf. *Salvage* 84ff.) are recognisable, but do not disturb the unity of the historical world presented.

---

[142] I am indebted to Anna Muza for sending me her unpublished paper.

The Coast of Utopia: The 'Causal-Realistic' Presentation of Biography

The scandal of the Manet painting of an undressed woman in the company of two fully dressed men is enacted onstage, as can be seen on page 325.[143] The dramatic scandal does not so much refer to stage nudity, which would hardly be scandalous to a contemporary theatre audience any more, but rather to the conceivable first steps of the soon-to-be-committed adultery between Natalie and Herwegh:

> The marriages' turmoil will prove the real human cost when fervid idealists abandon themselves to an abstraction, whether it is art (*pace* the Manet) or political philosophy (the radical free love and spiritualism by which Natalie rationalizes her affair with Herwegh). (Yacowar 2003: 80f.)

Similarly, Turgenev's conversation with the nihilist doctor does not disturb the historical realism presented if one keeps in mind that the historical Turgenev apparently based his protagonist Bazarov on the personality of a young provincial doctor, who had much impressed him, and that he conceived the first draft of his novel in Ventnor on the Isle of Wight (cf. Freeborn 1998: xiif. and Turgenev 2001: 193f.), the very place the scene is set. Turgenev comments on his main character's name to Semlov: "It's quite simple, I called him Bazarov because Bazarov was his name" (*Salvage* 94) – Stoppard here implying a biographical reality behind his conversation between Turgenev and the Doctor. On the macroscopic level, this episode rather helps to develop the character of the nihilist, who disagrees with Herzen's generation in terms of politics. Although intermedial and intertextual elements are present throughout the text and the performance, they do not heavily disturb the biographical and historical illusion or the mimetic presentation of the historical and biographical subject matter, and they conform to the tradition of the realistic biography play as described above.

The overall tone of the trilogy is also quite serious. The climax, tragic moment and moment of last suspense as called for by an Aristotelian plot are met with by historical and personal tragedies such as the deaths of friends and children, adultery and the bloody suppression of democratic uprisings in Paris and Russia. The most tragic scene is probably when Herzen tells his friend Bakunin what has happened to his son

---

[143] On the scandal of *Le Déjeuner sur l'herbe* at its presentation in the Salon des Refusés, cf. Körner 1996: 65f., McCauley 1998 and King 2006: 86-89.

Kolya, his mother, his wife Natalie and her newborn baby, which almost makes Herzen break down (cf. *Shipwreck* 100). This dominantly tragic tone, together with the Aristotelian plot, the use of language in a realistic manner, as well as the non-disturbing intertextual and intermedial references all make *The Coast of Utopia* a realistic biography play. That this is only true with respect to the macroscopic level of the trilogy and that, examining the plays *Voyage*, *Shipwreck* and *Salvage* separately, a different picture emerges, will become clear in the following.

2. The microscopic level: *Voyage*, *Shipwreck* and *Salvage* as innovative biography plays

So far we have examined *The Coast of Utopia* as a trilogy, with the three plays considered as a sequential unit. However, as Stoppard has stressed from the first staging of *The Coast of Utopia*, the three plays *Voyage*, *Shipwreck* and *Salvage* can also be seen as self-contained. The question is in how far the criteria of the conventional and realistic history and biography play still work if the plays are not seen as a trilogy, but separately.

a. *Voyage*: The reversal of the Aristotelian cause-and-effect chain

Voyage is divided into two acts, the first one set entirely at Premukhino, the second one in Moscow and St. Petersburg with the exception of the last scene, which returns the play to Premukhino. What is most striking about the structure of *Voyage* is that, chronologically the scenes of the second act more or less take place between the scenes of the first one, as figure 1 on page 326 illustrates.[144] To Maurice Yacowar, "[d]omestic

---

[144] In chronological order, the sequence of the scenes in *Voyage* would be I.i (Summer 1833); II.i (March 1834); II.ii (March 1835); II.iii (March 1835, a week later); I.ii (Spring 1835); II.iv (Summer 1835); I.iii (Autumn 1835); II.v (Spring 1836); I.iv (Spring 1836); I.v (August 1836); I.vi (Autumn 1836); II: Inter-Scene (November 1836); II.vi (December 1836); II: Inter-Scene (January 1837); I.vii (January 1837); II.vii (February 1837); II.viii (March 1838); II.ix (April 1838); I.viii

situations or personal impulses limned in act I are explained or redefined in act II" (Yacowar 2003: 78). However, the chronological interlocking of the scenes of both acts is more than a delay of explanations or a redefinition of events. The plot of *Voyage* is not presented following the principle of cause and effect, but rather in the opposite way as the recipients usually learn about the effect *before* its cause. It exemplifies Aristotle's differentiation between "what happens as a result of something else and what merely happens after it" (Aristotle 1977: 45). The farce surrounding Belinsky's penknife becomes a metaphor for this reversal of cause and effect. In Act I, he retrieves his lost penknife in the belly of a carp. This penknife he will have lost in Act II at the Soirée when Stankevich tries to prevent Belinsky from fleeing the scene, ripping his coat pocket (cf. *Voyage* 68f.). It will then have been found by Liubov, who takes it for Stankevich's. He is looking for it in order to return it to its owner (cf. 72f.). Thinking herself a fool on realising that it is not actually Stankevich's penknife (cf. 22f.), Liubov must have thrown it into the fish pond, where it was gobbled up by a carp, which in turn is fished by Belinsky. Later, he gives his retrieved penknife to his mistress, Katya (cf. 95). Belinsky aptly describes the circumstances surrounding the lost penknife already in Act I: "Lost objects from another life are restored to you in the belly of a carp" (36). The farce surrounding the penknife exemplifies the fact that *Voyage* does not follow the dramatic unities of time, place and plot, as the cause-and-effect chain is reversed in the play. This is illustrated in the following table:

(Spring 1838); II.x (June 1840); II.xi (July 1840); I.ix (Autumn 1841); II.xii (Spring 1843); II.xiii (Autumn 1844).

effect	cause
I.ii: the four sisters read a letter by Natalie Beyer	II.iii: Natalie writes the letter to the four sisters
I.ii: Alexander is angry as Michael has deserted the army	II.i: Michael has left his regiment
I.ii: Varenka, meanwhile married to Dyakov, is pregnant	II.i: Varenka is engaged to Dyakov
I.ii: the newly-weds are not Liubov and Baron Renne, as one might assume after I.i, but Varenka and Dyakov	II.i: Varvara tells Mrs Beyer that Liubov has rejected Baron Renne
I.ii: Tatiana and Alexandra tell Liubov that Stankevich fancies her and not Natalie, and that "he led Natalie up the garden" (11)	II.ii: Natalie confronts Stankevich about her mistaken affections and tells Tatiana and Alexandra that Stankevich "led [... her] up the garden" (71)
I.iii: Liubov returns "Stankevich's" penknife; I.vi: Belinsky's penknife is restored to him in the belly of a carp	II.ii: Belinsky loses his penknife, which is picked up by Liubov, who mistakes it for Stankevich's
I.iii: Kant's philosophy has taken Schelling's place in the philosophical circle	II.ii: Stankevich introduces Michael to the works of Kant
I.iv: Michael has his first article published in *The Telescope*	II.v: Michael submits his first article to *The Telescope*
I.iv: Michael says he heard Count Sollogub was a fop	II.v: Asked by Michael what he thinks of Sollogub, Belinsky calls the count a fop
I.iv: Tatiana complains about a horrible letter written by Michael	II.v: Michael writes a letter to his sister Tatiana

The Coast of Utopia: The 'Causal-Realistic' Presentation of Biography

I.v: Belinsky arrives at Premukhino	II.v: Michael invites Belinsky to stay at Premukhino
I.vi: *The Telescope* has been banned and closed down; Michael tears out chapters of a German history book and gives them to his sisters for translation	II.v: Nadezhdin is arguing over an article at the censor's office; Michael is hired by Count Strogonov to translate a German history book
I.vi: Belinsky discusses his article about Russian literature	II.ii: Shevyrev is quoting from and objecting to Belinsky's article in *The Telescope*
I.vii: In a letter to Varenka, Michael calls Dyakov "an animal" (44)	II.vi: As Varenka "has weakened" on the matter of Dyakov, Michael felt obliged to write to her "about that animal Dyakov" (94)
I.viii: Alexander wants Michael to study agriculture; Michael has broken off relations with Belinsky	II.ix: Michael has to leave for Premukhino as his father calls him back to study agriculture; Belinsky and Michael quarrel

The reversal of the Aristotelian cause-and-effect chain in *Voyage* negates, on the one hand, the dramatic unities of time, place and plot, and on the other the archetypical biographical plot of conventional biography, which views life as a chronological cause-and-effect succession. Thus, the reversal of causality in *Voyage* is diametrically opposed to the Aristotelian plot of *The Coast of Utopia*.

By setting Act I entirely at Premukhino and Act II in Russia's cultural capitals, Stoppard achieves the apposition of two opposing worlds. One is the traditional world of the Russian aristocracy, embodied by Alexander Bakunin. The other, like "another life", is progressive Russia, with its philosophical and political circles, embodied by Michael Bakunin, Belinsky, Turgenev and Herzen. This opposition becomes most obvious when the young revolutionary minds enter Premukhino. Although the likes of Michael and his friends stand out in this old-fashioned world, they nevertheless seem to be drawn towards it, too. As much as Michael argues with his father, at one time even renouncing his parents and exclaiming that they will never see him again (cf. 24), "[h]e talks about home all the time" (50) and often misses it (cf. 85), because his roots are at Premukhino (making him an aristocrat at heart), and because it is the home of his four beloved sisters. Belinsky says that being at Premukhino is "like being in a dream" (36), and Turgenev tells Tatiana that "if you can't write a poem here [at Premukhino], there's no hope. And not much if you can" (52). Alexander himself comments on these opposing worlds and the change from one to the other while embracing his eldest daughter Liubov: "How the world must have been changing while I was holding it still" (24). This statement is underlined by the transition to the next scene: while a year has passed between the scenes, "*Alexander and Liubov are where they were*" (25). This opposition of worlds, however, is also given in the dichotomy of idealism and realism, and of illusion and truth.

b.   Idealism *vs.* realism: Schelling, Kant, Fichte and Hegel

With his allusions to Schelling, Kant, Fichte and Hegel, Stoppard refers to the period in the history of philosophical thought usually termed German Idealism or Romanticism, a *Weltanschauung* the playwright already discussed in *Arcadia* (and indirectly in *The Invention of Love*). However, A. Robert Caponigri distinguishes sharply between sentimental and theoretical/speculative/philosophical Romanticism, the latter being the terminological equivalent of German Idealism. For him, sentimental Romanticism

> embraces and exhibits all those extravagances and contradictions which the romantic intuition of man, when not developed with philosophical rigor, is prone to. The openness of man's nature to the infinite, when it is not fortified with clear philosophical concepts, gives rise to that utopianism and nostalgis [sic], that vanity and despair with which romantic literature is replete. [...] The importance assigned to the passions, to spontaneity, to the individual and his personality, easily gives rise to the extravagances of indulgence in passion for its own sake [...], to the cult of personality, spontaneity and the individual which rejects all law and society and becomes the prefigured anarchist, a law to himself and an outlaw from all forms of community.   (Caponigri 1963: 474f.)

Philosophical Romanticism or German Idealism, on the other hand,

> is the revolt against and criticism of the philosophical intellectualism which had dominated the age of the Enlightenment. [...] It thrust back into their normal limits the natural and mathematical sciences, which rationalism had tended to make the measure of science itself and even of the highest form of science, philosophy. Finally, it rescued history and the concept of history from speculative oblivion and with history all of the sciences and disciplines which depend on historical data. (474)

German Idealism opposed the rational belief of the Enlightenment "that the principal causes of human misery, injustice, and oppression lay in men's ignorance and folly" (Berlin 1978: 83f.). According to Berlin, the creed of the Enlightenment was that complying with the laws of Newtonian physics meant living as happily as possible in the world as it was (cf. 83f.). Even God was fathomed as a clockmaker, someone who arranged and organised the universe to a benevolent purpose. Man, automatically carrying out the divine plan through his actions, was then able to live as he wanted (cf. Sandkühler (ed.) 2005: 230). Or as Michael Bakunin, who has just discovered German Idealism for himself, puts it:

> Idealism is concerned with questions that lie outside reasoning, it's quite simple. Reason has triumphed over all the ancient problems of natural science, so the clever fools in France thought they could solve the problem of society – of morality, art – in the same way, by reason and experiment, as if God our Maker was a chemist, an astronomer, a clockmaker... (*Voyage* 37)

Hans Jörg Sandkühler summarises the three main characteristics of German Idealism: 1) as ontology, it claims the existence of spiritual entities (ideas) which are not reducible to material entities; 2) as epistemology, it states that the outer world which appears to men is not independent from the imagination of cognitive subjects; 3) as ethics, it commits itself to normative concepts of grounds and justification of actions out of principles of reason. Sandkühler also emphasises that 'idealism' cannot be conceived without its diametrically opposed concept of 'materialism' or 'realism' (cf. Sandkühler (ed.) 2005: 1). It is especially this antithesis of 'idealism' and 'realism' which is of central concern to the first part of the trilogy. An elaborate analysis of the theme of German Idealism in *Voyage* is necessary in order to present the way the play progresses structurally.

From the very beginning, the topic of German Idealism can be found in *Voyage* and from the very beginning it is questioned through the play's presentation of the contrast between idealism and realism. Michael, on leave from his duty with the Artillery, introduces his sisters to German Idealism in the first scene of Act I. As he realises that Liubov does not love Baron Renne and that the marriage is their father's will, he explains with implicit reference to Schelling's work why his sister ought not to marry the Baron: "To give oneself without love is a sin against the inner life. The outer world of material existence is mere illusion" (*Voyage* 9). In the introduction to his *System of Transcendental Idealism* (*System des transzendentalen Idealismus*, 1800), Friedrich Wilhelm Joseph von Schelling (1775-1854) distinguishes between two necessary basic sciences: *Natur-Philosophie*, which deduces the subjective (*the self* or *the intelligence*) from the objective (*nature*), and *Transzendental-Philosophie*, which deduces the objective from the subjective. The topic of transcendental philosophy stands in the centre of Schelling's disquisition, and in it he questions the existence of an objective world; the concept of things outside of the self is seen as a fundamental prejudice (cf. Schelling 1993: 5ff.). Nevertheless, Michael contradicts Schelling's philosophy and yields to material need by concluding with a mundane "God, I'm starving!" (*Voyage* 9). This preaching of Schellingian philosophy (while at the same time contradicting it) is continued in the next scene. Michael's four sisters read the letter which Natalie Beyer has written "as a duty to myself, to you, and to the Universal Idea" and in which she complains that Michael is frustrated by his sisters' "limited progress in transcending the objective reality in which you see him only as your brother" (11). Michael repeats: "Illusion… it's only illusion", demanding the return of the letter, although it was to his sisters, because the "letter is to you but the paper and ink were only on loan" (13). Again, Michael contradicts Schelling because the intellectual content of the letter (the subjective) is for him worth less than the paper and ink used to write it (the objective).

Schelling's transcendental philosophy is set against Kant's critical idealism in the following scene. Stankevich contrasts Schelling's "cosmos, the totality of Nature struggling towards consciousness" with Kant's idea that "we are the only government of our real lives, the ideal is to be discovered in *us*, not in some book of social theory written by a Frenchman. Idealism – the self – the autonomous will – is the mark of God's faith in his creations" (18). Stankevich explains the difference between the two philosophers to Michael as well as to the audience: while Schelling has it that the "inner life is more real, more complete, than what we call reality – which has no meaning independent of my observing it", Kant says that one "cannot have the experience without there being something out there to *cause* the experience":

> what I perceive as reality includes concepts *which I cannot experience through the senses*. Time and space. Cause and effect. Relations between things. These concepts already exist in my mind, I must use them to make sense of what I observe. And thus my existence is necessary to a complete description of reality. Without me there is something wrong with this picture. (19)

In the course of his *System of Transcendental Idealism*, Schelling tried to achieve the synthesis of *Natur-* and *Transzendental-Philosophie*, of spirit and nature, of realism and idealism (cf. Sandkühler (ed.) 2005: 5f.). He ascribed predicates to nature which had been attributed only to man before, namely being out of itself (productive) teleological. Hitherto, the natural sciences had been looking to solve the mechanism or the question *how* and according to what laws nature worked. The analysis of the mechanism explained nature through causal relations and denied it a teleological character. It rather followed Kant's dictum that nature is "the existence of things so far as it is determined by general laws" (Kant 1952: 268).[145] Nevertheless, for Schelling, causal-mechanic explanations only scratched the surface of nature and only concentrated on the objective part of it while neglecting its subjective core (cf. Gamm 1997: 193f.). Nature is to be seen as the visible spirit, and the spirit as invisible nature.

Kant, on the other hand, was epistemologically engaged with the problem of the status of the objects of knowledge. He solved this problem by introducing the dualism of a phenomenal and a noumenal world, which became a matter of dispute for Fichte, Schelling and Hegel. For Kant, things are not given to perception by the noumenal reality of the

---

[145] "*Natur* im allgemeinsten Verstande (der Form nach) [… ist] das Dasein der Dinge, […] sofern es nach allgemeinen Gesetzen bestimmt ist" (Kant 1977a: 51).

things in themselves (*Dinge an sich*); rather, they are constituted as objects of knowledge in the process of perception within the limits of the appearing (phenomenal) world. These objects of knowledge are the representations of our senses (cf. Sandkühler (ed.) 2005: 87f.). However, its true correlative, i.e. the thing-in-itself, is not known, nor can be known by these representations, nor is it of any concern for the daily experience: "things as objects of our senses existing outside us are given, but we know nothing of what they may be in themselves, knowing only their appearances, i.e., the representations which they cause in us by affecting our senses" (Kant 1987: 33).[146]

According to Kant, all experience is achieved by the understanding, impressing its thought-process on the raw material provided by sensibility and therefore in all experience we will encounter this thought-process again. This thought-process, however, is subject to the standpoints of the twelve *a priori* categories.[147] These categories do not apply to the things-in-themselves and the *a priori* forms of sensibility, i.e. space and time, but generally and necessarily to the things as they *appear* to us. There cannot be an experience which, for example, does not correspond with the law of causality, because all experience only comes into being via the forming action of the understanding by applying the twelve categories. Through the faculty of judging (*Urteilskraft*), the intellect knows which category to apply (cf. Störig 1999: 458f.).

Stankevich's theoretical lecture about Schellingian and Kantian epistemology, however, is put to the test by the appearance of Liubov. While summarising Schelling, Stankevich watches a "young woman in a chair reading a book", touching "her hair where it's come undone" (*Voyage* 19). So far, no reaction stirs in Stankevich as he continues his

---

[146] "[E]s sind uns Dinge als außer uns befindliche Gegenstände unserer Sinne gegeben, allein von dem, was sie an sich selbst sein mögen, wissen wir nichts, sondern kennen nur ihre Erscheinungen, d.i. die Vorstellung, die sie in uns wirken, indem sie unsere Sinne affizieren" (Kant 1977: 152).

[147] These twelve categories are 1) of Quantity: Unity, Plurality, Totality; 2) of Quality: Reality, Negation, Limitation; 3) of Relation: of Inherence and Subsistence (*substantia et accidens*), of Causality and Dependence (cause and effect), of Community (reciprocity between the agent and patient); 4) of Modality: Possibility – Impossibility, Existence – Non-existence, Necessity – Contingency (cf. Kant 1952: 42).

philosophical lecture. But as he arrives thematically at Kant's category of cause and effect and Liubov comes inside to meet him, he suddenly gets nervous, begging Michael not to leave. For Roberta Barker, this merely means that "Stoppard's men idealize, in theory, women they cannot cope with in practice" (Barker 2005: 713). However, Barker neglects the intertext of German Idealism. In Schelling's philosophy of nature, causality has no deeper meaning, and therefore, Stankevich does not need to react to it. However, in the world of Kant, the outer world is real and has effects on the perceiving subject, i.e. Stankevich, who gets nervous because of Liubov, the woman he holds feelings for. The understanding of the objective alters in terms of the system which is applied to its understanding. It is Michael who mocks the alleged illusionary world while he makes to leave, showing his discontent with the philosophical constructs: "Father's looking for me anyway... (*gloomily*) I've had to ask him to settle a few debts here and there in the world of appearances, so now he's been busy getting me a job" (*Voyage* 20). Transcendental philosophy and subjective explanations for an objective world become less satisfying for Michael. The protagonists are up against something which cannot be explained with philosophical concepts.

Stankevich makes this discovery during his conversation with Liubov. Kant, or rather his system of ethics, is challenged by the French novelist George Sand (1804-1876), the "philosopher of love". Liubov defends Sand's creed that "love is the highest good" against Kant's moral code that "the only good actions are those performed out of a sense of duty, not from instinct... like passion or desire..." Liubov shows Stankevich that Kant's philosophical constructs must collapse when applied to passion, and that he has not understood the least bit about the other sex:

> **Stankevich** (*insistently*) In the system of Kant a man is judged only by his intention.
> **Liubov** (*still timidly*) A *fool* can mean well.
> **Stankevich** (*bursts out*) And usually does! How was I to know that Natalie Beyer mistook my intentions? I only talked to her about philosophy!
> **Liubov** Yes. Only another fool would make that mistake.   (22)

The German philosopher's ethical system of moral actions and intentions does not work in the complex world of passion and love, since love destroys logic: "*omnia vincit amor et nos cedamus amori*" (*Indian Ink* 47). Kant cannot win against Sand, and rational philosophical constructs have to give in to romantic needs. Constructs shipwreck on real needs and desires. This is why Michael flees even from Premukhino, his peaceful haven, this time to leave for Moscow: "*Dahin! Dahin! Lass uns ziehn!*" (*Voyage* 23). Nevertheless, in the next scene, Michael has already returned and as a comfort he has brought a new philosophy with him. Fichte has taken Schelling's place and is directly commented on by Alexander, who calls him "another German windbag" (26) and Varvara, who "wouldn't give thirty kopecks for it" (27).

While Kant saw as the source of perception the things-in-themselves, which existed independently of the subject and which were the cause of the objects of perception, Johann Gottlieb Fichte (1762-1814) allowed reason to place (*setzen*) itself and its objects from itself and free from outer determination. The perceiving subject (the self, *Ich*) is able, through the simultaneous process of intellectual action in self-determination and self-negation, to constitute reality (not-self, *Nicht-Ich*). For Fichte, the two concepts of *idealism* and *dogmatism* compete with each other directly. The dogmatist abstracts from the intelligence in favour of the thing-in-itself, the idealist from the real objects in the interest of the salvation of the freedom of intelligence. Thus Fichte writes: "the thing-in-itself is a pure invention and has no reality whatever" and he introduces a self-in-itself (*Ich an sich*), "not as an object of experience, for it is not determined [by an outer world] but will only be determined by me [...] as something that is raised above all experience" (Fichte 1982: 10).[148] The idealist searches for the cause of experience in the self-in-itself and not in the thing-in-itself, as would the dogmatist/realist. S/he deduces the objectivity of the world from the self-in-itself and shows that in consciousness, the self is something real, which is in the self-de-

---

[148] "[D]as Ding an sich ist eine bloße Erdichtung, und hat gar keine Realität"; "nicht als Gegenstand der Erfahrung, denn es ist nicht [durch eine äußere Welt] bestimmt, sondern es wird lediglich durch mich bestimmt [...] als etwas über alle Erfahrungen erhabenes" (Fichte 1845/46: 428).

termination of thinking. Thus, subject and object are not separated in consciousness but are one and the same (cf. Sandkühler (ed.) 2005: 101).

Belinsky, arriving at Premukhino, however, is still preoccupied with Schelling. Asked about Russian literature, Belinsky answers that Russia has none. Although it may have a small number of masterpieces, it has no unique national literature, because its authors mostly imitate the western style. To have a national literature, the 'Spirit' must talk through the artists:

> The universal idea speaks through humanity itself, and differently through each nation in each stage of its history. When the inner life of a nation speaks through the unconscious creative spirit of its artists, for generation after generation – then you have a national literature. That's why we have none. (*Voyage* 40)

For Schelling, art becomes the possibility of experiencing the 'Absolute', i.e. the 'Idea' or 'Spirit' of which all that exists is an expression. Art is the medium of the 'Absolute' because in the person of the artist, i.e. the genius, nature and spirit, liberty and necessity, the finite and the infinite, are identical. In the work of the genius, consciously free construction and unconsciously "natural" inspiration come together. Nature's impulse to create is spiritualised in the artist, and art reveals the meaning of the absolute process of the world (cf. Gamm 1997: 210ff.). That is why art is so important for Schelling, as he proclaims at the end of his *System of Transcendental Idealism*:

> Art is paramount to the philosopher, precisely because it opens to him, as it were, the holy of holies, where burns in eternal and original unity, as if in a single flame, that which in nature and history is rent asunder, and in life and action, no less than in thought, must forever fly apart. The view of nature, which the philosopher frames artificially, is for art the original and natural one. What we speak of as nature is a poem lying pent in a mysterious and wonderful script. Yet the riddle could reveal itself, were we to recognize in it the odyssey of the spirit, which, marvelously deluded, seeks itself, and in seeking flies from itself; for

through the world of sense there glimmers, as if through words the meaning, as if through dissolving mists the land of fantasy, of which we are in search.[149]
(Schelling 1993: 231f.)

For Belinsky, art and literature are manifestations of the 'Absolute', as in Schelling's idealism, and thus he concludes: "Every work of art is the breath of a single eternal idea breathed by God into the inner life of the artist" (*Voyage* 41). Only when Russia has come to terms with the meaning of Schelling's idealism can its literature reach the status of a national literature. Belinsky's agitated speech has moved Varenka and Liubov: Varenka rewrites her letter to her husband, Liubov asks Michael to take her to Moscow so she can meet Stankevich. Belinsky has reminded them of what Michael said in the first scene of the play, that "[t]o give oneself without love is a sin against the inner life" (9), or, in the case of Liubov, that if one is in love, one has to give oneself unconditionally. But Michael, by now jealous of Belinsky, questions all these philosophical constructs again, despairing that "[n]one of it's any use – the outer world worms itself into my heart like a serpent!" (41). Enter reality, or rather re-enter Belinsky, who, after his agitated speech, went into the house to read a letter, and now returns as the bearer of bad news: "O my prophetic soul! – The *Telescope* has been banned! Closed down! They've arrested Nadezhdin!" Michael can only remark "(*ironically*) Illusion! – It's only illusion –" and Belinsky, Michael and Liubov leave "to Moscow!" (42). The sound of a gunshot, symbolising the death of Pushkin, and thus the grimmest part of reality, carries over into the next scene.

---

[149] "Die Kunst ist eben deswegen dem Philosophen das Höchste, weil sie ihm das Allerheiligste gleichsam öffnet, wo in ewiger und ursprünglicher Vereinigung gleichsam in Einer Flamme brennt, was in der Natur und Geschichte gesondert ist, und was im Leben und Handeln, ebenso wie im Denken, ewig sich fliehen muß. Die Ansicht, welche der Philosoph von der Natur künstlich sich macht, ist für die Kunst die ursprüngliche und natürliche. Was wir Natur nennen, ist ein Gedicht, das in geheimer wunderbarer Schrift verschlossen liegt. Doch könnte das Rätsel sich enthüllen, würden wir die Odyssee des Geistes darin erkennen, der wunderbar getäuscht, sich selber suchend, sich selber flieht; denn durch die Sinnenwelt blickt nur wie durch Worte der Sinn, nur wie durch halbdurchsichtigen Nebel das Land der Phantasie, nach dem wir trachten" (Schelling 1907: 302).

Reality and death worm their way into Premukhino in the form of tuberculosis, as Liubov has fallen ill since she left for Moscow. Varenka, disillusioned with Michael's talk about the 'inner life' and the 'ideal' and angry about his attitude towards Dyakov, criticises her younger sisters, Tatiana and Alexandra, about still defending their idealist brother. She is the first to break the spell of idealism by confronting Liubov with her sickness and Stankevich's inability to marry her: "Why can't he marry you and take you with him? You need to go to the spas just as much as he does". But when Liubov suffers a small fit because of this sudden confrontation with reality, Varenka soothes her right away and explains that everything will be all right: "*(embracing her)* Liuba... Liuba... I'm sorry... ssh... there, there, my lamb, I'm sorry for all the things I said. You'll be well and Nicholas will come back and marry you... I know he will..." (45). Michael has also come to terms with reality by reading Hegel, who has taken Fichte's place, because

> Fichte was trying to get rid of objective reality, but *Hegel* shows that reality can't be ignored, on the contrary, reality is the interaction of the inner and outer worlds [...] and harmony is achieved by suffering through the storms of contradiction between the two. (46)

Georg Wilhelm Friedrich Hegel (1770-1831) described Fichte's subject centred idealism as 'subjective idealism', and Schelling's philosophy of identity, which sees nature in the self and the unconscious creative spirit in nature, as 'objective idealism'. Hegel's own philosophy can be seen as the synthesis of these two antitheses: Hegel's 'absolute idealism' sublates subjective and objective idealism, the absolute spirit sublates the subjective and the objective spirit (cf. Störig 1999: 522). According to Hegel, the spirit is "the 'Idea' entered on possession of itself. Here the subject and object of the Idea are one – either is the intelligent unity, the notion". It is "the self-knowing, actual Idea" (Hegel 2003: 8).[150] Absolute idealism objects to all forms of subjective causes for knowledge about objects of knowledge. As an ontological *dialectic*, it conceives the thought process as a *progress of contradictions*, as the self-creating and

---

[150] "In dieser Wahrheit ist die Natur verschwunden, und der Geist hat sich als die zu ihrem Fürsichsein gelangte Idee ergeben, deren *Objekt* ebensowohl als das *Subjekt* der *Begriff* ist". Es ist "die sich selbst wissende wirkliche Idee" (Hegel 1970c: 17).

self-regressive movement of the objective spirit (cf. Sandkühler (ed.) 2005: 111). Hence, Hegel's Method is "no-ways different from its object and content; – for it is the content in itself, *the Dialectic which it has in itself*, that moves it on" (Hegel 1966: 65).[151] Dialectic, then, is "not an activity of subjective thinking applied to some matter externally, but is rather the matter's very soul" (Hegel 1952: 19).[152] "[T]hought in its very nature is dialectical" (Hegel 1975: 15) and there exists a "Dialectical influence in logic" (78).[153]

As if to underline his dialectic "storms of contradiction", Michael remarks about Belinsky in his contradictory style: "He's turned out to be a complete egoist. But my estate is self-fulfilment and the future of philosophy in Russia" (*Voyage* 47). And although Michael despairs at his own reality – the discussion with his father about lending him money ends in an argument, shattering his hopes to study Hegel in Berlin – it is Varenka who knows what is to be done: "Well, we mustn't let it show. Everything must be happy" (49). She desperately tries to uphold the illusion of happiness at Premukhino, but it is too late. In the last scene of Act I, Turgenev summarises the changes which have occurred at Premukhino. Realism, in the form of death, has confronted and disproven Schellingian and Fichtian idealism:

> But the White Death that slips into the breast of the young and brave, blind to sense as a slow-worm, and makes itself at home, feeding on blood and breath… How do they like it now, those fine catchwords which sound even nobler in German? – the Universal, the Eternal, the Absolute, the Transcendent? How they must blush and shift about when they bump up against death by wasting and coughing […]. (50f.)

The confrontation between idealism and realism becomes visible on stage in the form of a brief flashback, recalled by Tatiana: "It was the last time we were all together, and somehow we were happy!" However,

---

[151] "Dies erhellt für sich schon daraus, daß sie [die Methode] von ihrem Gegenstande und Inhalte nichts Unterschiedenes ist; – denn es ist der Inhalt in sich, *die Dialektik, die er an ihm selbst hat*, welche ihn fortbewegt" (Hegel 1970: 50).

[152] "Diese Dialektik ist dann nicht *äußeres* Tun eines subjektiven Denkens, sondern die *eigene Seele* des Inhalts" (Hegel 1970a: 84).

[153] "[D]ie Natur des Denkens selbst [ist] die Dialektik" (Hegel 1970b: 55); "das *dialektische* Moment des Logischen" (128).

"[t]he past fades" (51) and Turgenev comments on the non-reality, the illusion, but also the necessity, of Premukhino:

> At Premukhino the eternal, the ideal, seems to be in every breath around you, like a voice telling you how much more sublime is the unattainable, imagined happiness of the inner life, compared with the vulgar happiness of the crowd! And then you're dead. There's something missing in this picture. Stankevich was coming round to it, before the end. He said: 'For happiness, apparently, something of the real world is necessary.' [...] Oh yes, we're all Hegelians now. 'What's rational is real, and what's real is rational.' (52, dialogue omitted)

It is Hegel's, and not Schelling's and Fichte's, idealism which becomes the background for the second act of *Voyage*, although the process from Schelling to Hegel via Kant and Fichte is repeated in it. While in Act I idealist Premukhino was the background of the transition process from idealism to realism, in Act II it is Moscow and St. Petersburg.[154] Reality is pinpointed right away by Herzen, who comments at length on the question "What is wrong with this picture?" (53), although his descriptions display no hint of idealism. He gives an ample description of Tsarist Russia and especially of the way the philosophical topic of 'realism' is discussed at Moscow University:

> Professor Pavlov, with a twinkle in his eye, has taken to button-holing us with philosophy – 'You wish to understand the nature of reality? Ah, but what do we mean by reality? By nature? What do we mean by understand?' So that's philosophy, well, well, and at Moscow University teaching philosophy is forbidden as a threat to public order. Professor Pavlov's class is physics and agriculture, it's only by centrifugal force that he goes flying off from crop rotation to Schelling's philosophy of nature..." (54)

According to Herzen, in Russia the political reality is ignored even, or especially, at university. Life is an illusion as the people ignore the reality behind it, which is censorship, banishment to Siberia (cf. 56) or forced conscription and political arrests (cf. 57). Herzen's political circle mocks the idealist viewpoints of the likes of Stankevich. Sazonov, for example, making fun of Schellingian philosophy, tells Stankevich that "tea has made a phenomenal appearance" (57), and calling the change on

---

[154] On the impact of German Idealism on St. Petersburg and Moscow and the role the historical Stankevich and Bakunin played in it, cf. the chapter "German Romanticism in Petersburg and Moscow" in Berlin 178: 136-149.

the table "[t]en absolute kopecks" (58). Stankevich, defending his idealist viewpoint, answers to Herzen's political thoughts that "[p]olitical arrangements are merely changing forms in the world of appearances" (59). Political reality is non-existent for him, or rather just a phenomenon which has no meaning for the inner world or the 'Absolute':

> Reform can't come from above or below, only from within. The material world is nothing but the shadow on the wall of the cave. The convulsions of whole societies in their frantic adjustment of advantage, are the perturbed, deformed spirit objectified on the wall of the cave. (60)

For Stankevich, political actions are unimportant. The only two things that can make a difference are art and philosophy, as he suggests to Belinsky: "Everything now depends on artists and philosophers. Great artists to express what can't be explained, philosophers to explain it!" (61).

However, even for Stankevich, realism as before is reached via Hegel in this second act. Belinsky is the first to pinpoint the difference between idealism and realism. Having returned from Premukhino, he describes the estate in Schellingian terms to his mistress Katya:

> **Belinsky** And the place itself, Premukhino in the freshness of the early morning, everything chirping and croaking, whistling, and splashing, as if Nature was having a conversation with itself, and the sunsets breathing, as alive as fire... You understood how the Eternal and Universal are more real than your everyday life, than this room and the world lying in wait outside the room, you believed in the possibility of escape, of transcendence, of raising your soul to the necessary height, and living high above your own life, folded into the mind of the Absolute.
> **Katya** (*impatient with him*) Tell me what happened properly.
> **Belinsky** It was awful. (91f.)

Belinsky has realised that Schelling and Fichte cannot compensate for personal disappointments and misery and the idealist house of cards collapses:

> **Belinsky** (*recovered*) Don't you bother with reading, Katya, words just lead you on. They arrange themselves every which way with no can to carry for their promises they can't keep, and off you go! 'The objective world is the still unconscious poetry of the soul.' What do these words mean? 'The spiritual communion of beautiful souls attaining harmony with the Absolute.' What do they mean?

> **Katya** I don't know.
> **Belinsky** Nothing, and I understood them perfectly! – my everyday life, which was banal, meaningless, degrading, was merely illusion... In my real life, my inner life, there was no cause for misery and humiliation. But when it turned out the necessary height was a metre or two above my reach, and all those fine phrases burst like bubbles, there was nowhere to go except back home feeling worthless and now without even a job...   (92)

Reality has caught up with Belinsky, and Schelling and Fichte cannot make up for it. The idealist bubble has burst. But help arrives in the form of Michael, who recommends an answer to Belinsky's dilemma: "You must read Hegel. Hegel is the man! Fichte tried to argue the objective world out of existence" (94). Belinsky takes to Hegel right away, not realising that he uses the same ambiguous words as Schelling and Fichte, and we hear again *"the sound of an other-worldly distant pistol shot"* (95), symbolising once more Pushkin's death in a duel and proclaiming the advent of Hegelian realism to recipients and characters alike.

Hegelian dialectic – in *Hamlet* and in Pushkin's death – becomes the topic of discussion, but also of misunderstanding, between Stankevich and Belinsky in the next scene.[155] While to Stankevich, Hamlet's "moral and spiritual despair is what comes from refusing to face up to the rationality of the objective world" (95), and while he sees in the duel between Hamlet and Laertes the duel "between knowledge and denial, the dialectic dramatised" (96), Belinsky talks about Pushkin's death, which in his opinion was caused by his wife's flirtatiousness. Whether it is fiction, as in *Hamlet*, or fact, as in the death of Pushkin, everything has by now turned real:

> **Belinsky** So, the objective world is not an illusion?
> **Stankevich** No.
> **Belinsky** The laundry, the blacksmith, everything that Fichte said was just the shapes left by the impress of my mind... is real?
> **Stankevich** Yes. Everything rational is real, and everything real is rational.

---

[155] The historical Belinsky wrote an essay on *Hamlet* in 1837 which, according to the editor of the Soviet edition of his collected works, was not only of great importance in the history of the Russian theatre and literature, but also in the history of Shakespeare scholarship (cf. Poljakow 1952: 168).

Belinsky Poverty, injustice, censorship, whips and scorns, the law's delay? The Minister for Public Instruction? Russia?
Stankevich Real.
Belinsky How did we miss it?
Stankevich Not just real but necessary.
Belinsky Why's that?
Stankevich Necessary to the march of history. The dialectical logic of history.
Belinsky Really? So, to... worry about it... deplore it... is...
Stankevich Unintelligent. A vulgar error. (97)

Via Hegel, the characters in the play have not only come to terms with reality, but also with history. For Hegel, History appears as a drama of passions and is to be conceived of as "the slaughter-bench at which the happiness of peoples, the wisdom of states, and the virtue of individuals have been victimized" (Hegel 1952: 162).[156] But if this is the case, then there has to be a final purpose to history to explain the suffering. According to Sandkühler, Hegel's philosophy of history has six main points to explain this purpose: 1) history is not unified by a divine being outside of the worldly goings-on, but by something *acting*, which is the Spirit fulfilling itself in history. World history itself is the Last Judgement; 2) history is a history of single steps, of which each – as in the life of a plant or any other organic life form – consists of periods of growth, followed by standstill and apparent regression. Only the perspective of the Spirit allows for discovering a single, reasonable line of progress in the apparent irreconcilable conflicts and discontinuities of history; 3) history is not only a diachronic, but also a synchronic unity. The Spirit expresses itself in the form of certain spirits of nations (*Volksgeistern*); they arrange the unity which is the basis of all state forms; 4) according to Hegel, history is good because it is progressive and providential. Over time, it fulfils a purpose which is recognised by individuals as generally reasonable. However, this purpose – contrary to the position of the Enlightenment – is not progress towards the greater happiness of man. The providential character of history is connected with its nature

---

[156] "Aber auch indem wir die Geschichte als diese Schlachtbank betrachten, auf welcher das Glück der Völker, die Weisheit der Staaten und die Tugend der Individuen zum Opfer gebracht worden, so entsteht dem Gedanken notwendig auch die Frage, wem, welchem Endzwecke diese ungeheuersten Opfer gebracht worden sind" (Hegel 1970d: 34f.).

as the realisation of reason; in relation to this, happiness itself is irrelevant: *"What is rational is actual and what is actual is rational"* (Hegel 1952: 6);[157] 5) history has for Hegel what Sandkühler calls a subject-object character. This means that history is not only the history of change in social reality, but also the history of the ways this social reality is perceived; these ways primarily determine the character of a given society; therefore, 6) philosophy itself must be understood as a historical process. At the end of this process, the unity behind the philosophical diversity will be recognised and, finally, the existence of a single, unified philosophy will come about (cf. Sandkühler (ed.) 2005: 238f.).

The opposition between Schellingian and Fichtian idealism, which dominates Act I, and Hegelian realism, which dominates Act II, and which constitutes a central topic of *Voyage*, is best put in the prompt script, in an extension of the dialogue between Belinsky and Stankevich:

Stankevich [...] Belinsky... tell Liubov she's too good for me!
Belinsky She's not! She's not! I mean, you're good too. You can make each other happy!
Stankevich Happiness is a love token. It's the ideal we've talked about a thousand times, to be in harmony with the whole of nature.
Belinsky Stankevich, have you never felt desire?
Stankevich I know I experienced a powerful feeling when she knelt down to take off Natalie's skate...
Belinsky That's it!
Stankevich But marriage is so...
Belinsky Real?
Stankevich In its illusionary way, yes. And all the setting up house together...
Belinsky Real!
Stankevich And... you know (sex)... and children.
Belinsky Real.
Stankevich Family life, sitting round the fire on winter evenings...
Belinsky Real.
Stankevich Then what is the Shadow on the wall of the cave?
Belinsky That's philosophy.[158]   (*Voyage* Prompt Script 98)

---

[157] "Was vernünftig ist, das ist wirklich; und was wirklich ist, das ist vernünftig" (Hegel 1970a: 24). Hegel defends these statements in the introduction to his *Encyclopaedia of the Philosophical Sciences in Outline* (*Enzyklopädie der philosophischen Wissenschaften im Grundriss*, 1830), because they "have given rise to expressions of surprise and hostility" (Hegel 1975: 9).

Philosophy, i.e. Schellingian and Fichtian idealism – Stankevich's escape from a reality of commitment –, has become the world of illusion, which for him used to be the "convulsions of whole societies in their frantic adjustment of advantage" (*Voyage* 60). The wall of the cave and the shadow have switched sides. The whole philosophical constructs of Schelling and Fichte have given way to Hegel's explanation and reason for the grim reality which it would be unwise not to accept, since it is necessary for the progress of history. Idealism has given in to realism in the form of another philosophical construct, namely Hegel's absolute idealism, which differs in that it does not accept subjective causes for knowledge and thus, according to Stankevich, would be another shadow on the wall.

The Dialectical Spirit becomes the "Moloch that eats his children" (106), personified by "a six-foot ginger cat" raising "its glass to Absolute Subjectivity" (104). In Stoppard's own words, the Ginger Cat is essentially "an arbitrary purposeless malign or mischievous force/fate which deflects the individual life within the overarching Hegelian Law of History ('the Moloch') to which populations are subject" (Stoppard in Lemon 2006/07). After Turgenev has given Belinsky his first poem and calls him "our only critic", it is the Ginger Cat which has the last words in this "real" Russia, only answering "Of course" (*Voyage* 111) to Belinsky's introduction. In the teleological progress of history represented by the Ginger Cat, this answer foreshadows the important role Belinsky is going to play in the literary history of Russia. It also foreshadows the dominating conflict between Hegelianism/Marxism, with their teleological progress of history, and the free will of man in *Shipwreck* and *Salvage* – but not before *Voyage* returns to Premukhino one last time.

The first act of *Voyage* takes place at Premukhino, which stands for the manifestation of the 'Absolute'. There, the protagonists engage critically with Kant's critical, Schelling's objective and Fichte's subjective idealism, only to arrive at "realism" in the form of death and the break-up of the Bakunin family. The act concludes with the acceptance of real-

---

[158] In 2007, a revised edition of *The Coast of Utopia* was published which includes the changes made in the prompt script. For this extended dialogue, cf. Stoppard 2007: 104.

ity via Hegel's absolute idealism. This reality becomes the antithetical background to the sheltered life at Premukhino in the form of a politically oppressed Russia in Act II, where the critical debate with German Idealism by the characters is repeated and which returns to Premukhino. This return, however, is not a return to the beginning but to an end. The sun has set over the estate and the Bakunin family, as hinted at by the by now old and blind Alexander Bakunin: "Sun's gone. Has it? [...] I saw it go down" (114, stage directions omitted). The structure of *Voyage* becomes the visualisation of Hegel's diachronic and synchronic unity of history, and not so much an allusion to cyclical time (as remarked on by Barker). What Barker calls the rewinding of the second act in order to show the events of the first act in Moscow and St. Petersburg (cf. Barker 2005: 715) is rather a diachronic and synchronic shift in focus. In a dialectical manner, idealism – the thesis – is contrasted with realism – its antithesis: diachronically, as regards the sequence of the action with the detachment from idealist Premukhino to realistic Moscow and St. Petersburg; synchronically, as regards the arrangement of the plot by parallelizing the teleological progress from Schelling to Hegel.

c. Illusion *vs.* truth: Deconstructing Chekhov through Chekhov

The dichotomy between idealism and realism becomes the dichotomy between illusion and truth in the light of the Chekhovian subtext. The dramatic contrast between Act I and Act II in *Voyage* does not only refer to content as regards the generation gap and German Idealism. It also refers to structure as regards the allusion to Chekhovian drama. I have already referred to the influence of Chekhov on the trilogy in the context of the conventional and realistic biography play. Stoppard adapted *The Seagull* in 1997, and he always "had a very abstract desire to write a play in the manner of Chekhov" (Stoppard in Cavendish 2002). Muza points out that "the Chekhovian framing of these people [the mid-nineteenth century Russian intelligentsia] underscores not their 'reality' or historicity but their theatrical roots" (Muza 2003). Thus the alleged realism of the history play becomes a Russian illusion, which is the stereotypical presentation of a Russian subject matter derived from Chekhovian drama.

This Chekhovian framing is most dominant in Act I of *Voyage*, as there, the afore-mentioned Chekhovian elements can be identified best. Act II, on the other hand, shows a different Russian picture, one which is the opposite of Chekhovian life in the country and atypical of his drama: "the Chekhovian world in *The Coast of Utopia* may seem an illusion that ultimately needs to be cast away for the sake of what one is tempted to call 'reality'" (Muza 2003). The transition from the Chekhovian world to a different reality is again made by Turgenev, in the last scene of the first act. As he talks to Tatiana about Premukhino, he remarks that somehow it is not *real*: "There is something missing in this picture" (*Voyage* 52). Herzen picks up Turgenev's line as the first words spoken in Act II. "What is wrong with this picture?", he asks, giving a description of the political situation in Russia at the time:

> Someone sitting next to you in class disappears overnight, nobody knows anything. In the public gardens ice creams are eaten, in all the usual flavours. What is wrong with this picture? The Kritski brothers disappeared for insulting the Tsar's portrait, Antonovich and his friends for forming a secret society, meaning they met in somebody's room to read a pamphlet you can buy on the street in Paris. Young men and women are pairing off like swans on the skating ground. A crocodile of Poles goes clanking by in leg-irons on the Vladimir road. There is something wrong with this picture. Are you listening? You're in the picture.
> (54)

The answer to his question lies in the singularity of his mother country: "What is wrong with this picture? Nothing. It's Russia" (59). Through the entire second act, Stoppard presents a different, un-Chekhovian version of Russia, in which the protagonists have to worry about Tsarist oppression, censorship, editorship and making ends meet. It is this "reality" from which Michael continuously escapes, first by returning to Premukhino during Act I and then by leaving for Berlin in Act II. The contrast between the dream world of the first act and its harsh opposite in the second one is picked out as a central theme when Belinsky criticises Michael's character:

> **Belinsky**   ...and above all your permanent flight into abstraction and fantasy which allows you not to notice that the life of the philosopher is an aristocratic

> affair made possible by the sweat of Premukhino's five hundred souls who somehow haven't managed to attain oneness with the Absolute.
> **Michael** Right. I don't remember you saying any of this when you had your snout in the trough.
> **Belinsky** I wasn't even thinking it. I was in the dream myself. But reality can't be thought away – what's real is rational, and what's rational is real. (101f.)

The end of Act II returns again to Premukhino, which by now does not resemble its own version in the first act. Alexander reads an official letter ordering his son Michael to return home as "[b]y imperial decree, former Ensign Michael Bakunin has been condemned to loss of his noble rank and to banishment to Siberia for an indefinite period, with hard labour" (114). It is again Alexander who summarises the changes which have occurred during the play and in Chekhov's world:

> Michael isn't coming home again. Premukhino knows it, too. The spirit has left it. You grew up in Paradise, all of you children, in harmony that was the wonder of all who came here. Then, in the time of Liubov's betrothal to that cavalry officer – what was his name? …and what was the point in the end? Michael… (*Pause*.) Or a new spirit, which is worse… (113)

The "new spirit" Alexander names is Hegel's World-Spirit. While the sun has set over Premukhino – Alexander gloomily exclaiming "[a]nother sunset, another season nearer God" (111) –, "[d]awn has broken" for Michael and his generation. He has set sail to Germany, where "the sun is already high in the sky" (9).

In an essay about Chekhov's leitmotifs, Ralph Lindheim identifies "the complex relationship between mask and face" and "the conflict between appearance and reality, between illusion and truth" (Lindheim 1985: 56) as one of the playwright's major themes. By way of example, he refers to the two plays *Three Sisters* (*Tri Sestry*, 1900) and *The Cherry Orchard* (*Veshnevyi Sad*, 1900) and the short story "Gusev" (1890):

> *Three Sisters* traces the loss of dreams and illusions and the gradual acceptance of the hard, cold, often painful facts of reality. […] The marvelous short story "Gusev" and his last play, *The Cherry Orchard*, suggest a necessary antidote to facts that endanger rather than promote survival. Both works glimpse the possibility that human beings are helpless puppets in a brutal, hostile universe of natural and unnatural forces. (56f.)

It is no accident that Lindheim refers to *Three Sisters* and *The Cherry Orchard* in this context, and it is no coincidence, either, that allusions to them can be found in all three plays, but structurally they affect *Voyage* most.

Muza has already hinted at the cry "Moscow! Moscow! To Moscow!" in *Three Sisters* (Chekhov 2001: 278), which is echoed by four sisters and a brother in *Voyage*: "to Moscow!" (*Voyage* 42). Thanks to their father, Chekhov's three sisters, just like Stoppard's four, were "oppressed [...] with education" and they "know French, German, and English, and Irina knows Italian besides" (Chekhov 2001: 248). As in the trilogy, some passages in Italian and French also feature in *Three Sisters* (cf. 264 and 270) and in *The Cherry Orchard* (cf. 354f. and 360). Fedotik gives Irina first a top (cf. 255) and later a penknife (cf. 267) as a present. Herzen's son Kolya's spinning top becomes one of the leitmotifs in *Shipwreck* (cf. 26, 29, 39, 46 and 58) and Belinsky also gives Katya a penknife as a present (cf. *Voyage* 95). The death of Baron Tuzenbach in a duel is indicated by the *"faint sound of a gunshot [...] in the distance"* (Chekhov 2001: 309) just as is Pushkin's death – twice – in *Voyage*,[159] or the assassination attempt on the Tsar in *Salvage*. Like Kolya in *Shipwreck*, Lyubov Andreyevna's seven-year-old son died by drowning in *The Cherry Orchard*, and Pishchik and Michael Bakunin are constantly asking for money, the latter squandering it as much as Lyubov Andreyevna. *The Cherry Orchard*'s characters gather on a meadow to watch the sunset (cf. 347) which is Stoppard's leitmotif for change (cf. *Voyage* 31, 41 and 114). As already mentioned before, a distant sound *"like the sound of a snapped string mournfully dying away"* (Chekhov 2001: 348) becomes the *"distant sound of thunder"* (*Shipwreck* 104), another Stoppardian leitmotif (cf. 21 and 39). Paris is the civilised opposite to Russian rural backwardness, for Yasha (cf. Chekhov 2001: 361) as for the Russian intelligentsia in *Shipwreck*, and Chekhov's dramatised boredom of life in the country in all of his plays is for Natalie Herzen "part of the attraction" in the country (*Shipwreck* 3). The emancipation of the serfs is reached in *Salvage*; some of its consequences are depicted in *The Cherry Orchard*. Chekhov's Trofimov

---

[159] Stoppard creates a similar effect in *Arcadia*, when Septimus's distant pistol shot is also repeated (cf. *Arcadia* 52 and 67).

and Stoppard's Michael Bakunin are alike in many respects. The latter would agree with the eternal student when he says: "Mankind goes forward, perfecting its powers. Everything that is now unattainable will some day be comprehensible and within our grasp, only we must work, and help with all our might those who are seeking the truth" (Chekhov 2001: 346). Like Michael, Trofimov is "above love" (350), but neither understands, respectively, that Natalie in *Voyage* and Anya in *The Cherry Orchard* want to actually love, spiritually as well as physically. Lyubov Andreyevna criticises Trofimov for this (cf. 359), causing the student to leave the room screaming agitatedly "All is over between us!" (359) and falling down the stairs. Soon thereafter Lyubov Andreyevna dances with him in order to apologise. This is similar to Michael renouncing his parents but lying in the hammock in the next scene at Premukhino, as if nothing had happened (cf. *Voyage* 24ff.). They both, too, make some money by translating books (cf. 88 and Chekhov 2001: 369f.) and see themselves in the front ranks of "[m]ankind [...] advancing toward the highest truth, the highest happiness attainable on earth" (Chekhov 2001: 370) because "[t]he age has arrived at its reversal, and we were born to be the turning point" (*Salvage* 37).

The characters of Tuzenbach, Vershinin and Chebutykin in *Three Sisters* all have different views on life. Chebutykin questions reality and existence itself altogether: "Maybe I didn't break it [a china clock], and it only appears to have been broken. Maybe it only appears that we exist, but, in fact, we are not here" (Chekhov 2001: 285). "It only seems so. ... We are not here, there is nothing in the world, we do not exist, but merely seem to exist. ...And it really doesn't matter!" (301). For Tuzenbach, on the other hand, as much as the future progresses, "life will remain just the same – difficult, full of mysteries, and happy. A thousand years from now man will still be sighing: 'Ah, how hard life is!' – Yet he will fear death, exactly as he does now, and be unwilling to die" (265). Contrary to this opinion of life remaining static, Vershinin, the man from Moscow, sees life as progressing little by little. For him, "[h]appiness is something we never have, but only long for" (269). The purpose of existence is to work, to suffer and to create a new, happy life in which the present generation, however, will have no share (cf. 265). The following generations will outlive the present one and "people will appear who will be better than you" (286). His opinion is shared by the three sisters Masha, Irina and Olga at the end of the play. This apposition of views on life is taken up by Stoppard. Chebutykin's notion is similar to the Schellingian and Fichtian concepts of an illusionary objective world, represented by Michael, and Tuzenbach's opinion resembles the Hegelian perspective throughout the trilogy, the nihilists being the new people who think themselves better than the superfluous men, as pictured in *Salvage*. *The Cherry Orchard* is about the problems caused by the generation gap between inexperienced youth, which is starry-eyed about the future, and the experienced older generation, which tries to push away its failures by clinging on to the past and not accepting change. It is about the conflict between former masters and serfs and at the end of the play, Lopakhin buys the estate where his father and grandfather were slaves (cf. 366). Similarly, Stoppard's trilogy depicts the generation gaps between Michael and Alexander Bakunin, aristocrats and political progressives, superfluous men and nihilists. It is exactly the contrast between illusion and truth, between idealism and realism that Lindberg identifies in Chekhov's plays that we also find in *The Coast of Utopia*, especially in *Voyage*.

Nonetheless, the events presented in *The Coast of Utopia* pre-date Chekhov and his art by almost half a century. Muza sees the use of "Chekhov before Chekhov" as a "part of the complex dialectic, underlying the trilogy, of reality, art, and historical consciousness". While *The Cherry Orchard* and *Three Sisters* came after Bakunin, Herzen and the like, Stoppard's *The Coast of Utopia* comes after Chekhov. This is true for all inter- and intramedial allusions: "What seems to be life imitating art turns into art imitating life and ultimately, into art imitating other art at the expense of the dissolving historical reality". Muza assumes that Stoppard probably wants to expose "the limitations of the modern mind that perceives history as an anachronistic collection of ready-made tableaux" (Muza 2003). In this context, the contrast between Act I and Act II is important. In the first act of *Voyage*, with its frequent use of Chekhovian motifs and intertextual allusions to Chekhovian drama, Stoppard discloses the artificiality and referentiality behind drama and biographical depictions of historical personalities. This Chekhovian style is contrasted by a Russian reality of life in Moscow and St. Petersburg. Stoppard thus deconstructs the Chekhovian world of Act I by giving an anti-Chekhovian presentation of the events in Act II. Or as Muza formulates:

> Thus, somewhat paradoxically, the Chekhovian vocabulary in Stoppard's trilogy refers not to the "organic flow of life" but to a theatrical language, a theater of masks and situations, a Russian commedia dell'arte which subverts rather than sustains any notion of verisimilitude. (Muza 2003)

This confrontation, however, is at the same time another leitmotif of the Russian playwright Chekhov, namely the conflict between appearance and reality, between illusion and truth. Typical Chekhovian elements are done away with by depicting an antithetical world which is un-Chekhovian because it has never been presented onstage in any of Chekhov's drama. Nonetheless, this alleged reality is again artificial, i.e. theatrical, because it is still part of Stoppard's drama and because it is the opposite, or rather the supplement, which actually completes the Chekhovian leitmotif of the contrast between illusion and truth. What Stoppard achieves, then, is the deconstruction of Chekhovian drama, its style and characteristics, by apposing it with another un-Chekhovian dramatic world which, in turn, complements the Chekhovian major theme of illusion and truth.

So far we have concentrated on the structure of *Voyage* which proved to be the diametrical opposite to the macroscopic Aristotelian plot of the trilogy. In the following two sections I will now consider *Shipwreck* and *Salvage*. It will be shown that their structure hints at a development back to the macrostructure of the trilogy.

d.   *Shipwreck*: *Reprise* and *continuation* – The swirl of history

Unlike *Voyage*, the second part of the trilogy, *Shipwreck*, has a more or less linear structure with the exception of two scenes. Both acts of the play end with some form of a flashback, Act I with a 'reprise' of Scene iv and Act II with a 'continuation' of the first scene of Act I. Both flashbacks are triggered off by personal loss. In the scene before the reprise, Herzen learns of Belinsky's death from a letter:

> **Herzen** (*with Granovsky's letter, cries out*) Who is this Moloch who eats his children?
> **Turgenev** Yes, and your taste for melodramatic, rhetorical –
> **Herzen** Belinsky's dead.
> **Turgenev** No, no... oh, no, no, no... No!... No more blather please. Blather, blather, blather. Enough. (*Shipwreck* 56)

The news of Belinsky's death makes the political discussion between Herzen and Turgenev seem irrelevant and unimportant. The reprise that follows is the repetition of the end of the gathering at the Herzens' in Paris. Nonetheless, while Scene iv runs for a while in *"a continuum of word-noise"* (37) with simultaneous conversations taking place (cf. 38f.), during the reprise

> [t]*he rest of the scene now repeats itself with the difference that instead of the general babel which ensued, the conversation between Belinsky and Turgenev is now 'protected', with the other conversations virtually mimed. At the point where the babel went silent before, nothing now alters.* (57)

The reprise also ends differently from the original scene, with deaf Kolya pronouncing his name for the first time (cf. 58) instead of being drowned out by a thunder of historical noise (cf. 39).

In the scene before the continuation, Herzen has just given Michael Bakunin and the audience a summary of the events of the last year. It is, on the one hand, the deaths of his son Kolya, his mother and his wife Natalie, and on the other hand the disappointment with the western civilisation because of the failed revolutions that make Herzen reach his gloomy conclusion about West Europe at the end of the scene:

> Nobody's got the map. In the West, socialism may win next time, but it's not history's destination. Socialism, too, will reach its own extremes and absurdities, and once more Europe will burst at the seams. Borders will change, nationalities break up, cities burn... the collapse of law, education, manufacture, fields left to rot – military rule and money in flight to England, America... And then a new war will begin between the barefoot and the shod. It will be bloody, swift and unjust, and leave Europe like Bohemia after the Hussites. Are you sorry for civilisation? I am sorry for it, too.
>   *Natalie's voice – from the past – is heard distantly calling repeatedly for Kolya. Distant thunder.*
> He can't hear you. I'm sorry. I'm so sorry, Natalie. (103f.)

The following scene, the one that concludes *Shipwreck*, is the continuation of the reunion of Kolya and his mother Natalie brought about by Ogarev (cf. 22): "*Sokolovo as before: a continuation. Distant thunder*" (104). At the end, Ogarev tells Herzen's other son, Sasha, how the two met and became best friends and revolutionaries:

> No, my *happiest* day was another day, before that, up on the Sparrow Hills, just where the Cossack had come running down, and your daddy and I... we climbed up to the top where the sun was setting on Moscow spread out below us, and we made a promise to... to be revolutionaries together. I was thirteen then. (*He gives a little laugh and looks up.*) The storm has missed us. (105)

In Stoppard's play, reprise and continuation both have the function of putting into perspective the present through reflections of the past. Over their heated political conversation about the outcome of the western revolutions and their different attitudes towards it, Herzen and Turgenev have forgotten about the individual in history, of which they become painfully aware through Belinsky's death. Without the "general babel", the reprise refocuses on Belinsky and Kolya and the creed that answers are not to be found in abstract utopias, but rather in art and personal happiness. This is similar to the continuation. After the failure of the European revolutions and his personal loss, Herzen remembers the idealism and enthusiasm which made him a revolutionary in the first place: "The high hopes and enthusiasm with which the Herzens set off for Europe we now know are rendered ironic both in historical and in personal terms" (Rzhevsky 2003).[160] The continuation amplifies the disappointment and personal tragedies Herzen had to go through during *Shipwreck* and the contrast between the idealist view of the future in the past and the real present in the course of the play.

The reprise establishes a connection between the scenes in the first act: from the time shortly after the failed revolution in Paris back to the time shortly before. The continuation arranges the whole of *Shipwreck* into a plot: from Herzen leaving the European continent for England back to the beginning of Herzen receiving permission to travel to Europe with his family. The flashbacks are foreshadowed by Natalie's remark to Ogarev in the first scene of *Shipwreck* to which the play returns

---

[160] I am indebted to Nicholas Rzhevsky for sending me his unpublished paper.

with its last scene: "But don't you ever have the feeling that while real time goes galloping down the road in all directions, there are certain moments... situations... which keep having their turn again?... Like posting stations we change horses at..." (*Shipwreck* 4). Both, reprise and continuation, are also connected with Kolya, who is either playing with a spinning top or becoming aware of the sound of distant thunder. Spinning top and distant thunder become the leitmotifs for the structure of *Shipwreck*. The top symbolises recurrence, the thunder the noise of historical events. If we imagine now that the reprise and the continuation arch back over the chronological plot of *Shipwreck*, that these two arches were set on a top, and that this top was spun, we would receive the impression of a swirl, as figure 2 on page 326 illustrates. This swirl is similar to what the historical Turgenev described as the 'torrent of history':

> Only the few chosen ones are able to leave for posterity not only the content, but also the *form*, of their ideas and opinions, their personality, to which, generally speaking, the mob remains entirely indifferent. Ordinary individuals are condemned to total disappearance, to being swallowed up by the torrent; but they have increased its force, they have widened and deepened its bed – what more do they want? (Turgenev 2001: 203)

The characters in *Salvage* may be able to stem this torrent, the historical swirl, for a short while, but it will seize most of them sooner or later. The flashbacks in the form of reprise and continuation show that the past and its memories are not identical, but that the past has undergone slight alterations through retrospection, which in turn is due to the traumas of the remembering characters. The meaning of the past for the present is thus presented, not as an unchangeable constant, but rather as a limited variable, whose focus can change, depending on personal experiences and the emotional state of the mind of the person remembering.

e. *Salvage*: Reflecting on the macrostructure –
The Aristotelian plot

The structure of *Salvage* is much more conventional compared to that of *Voyage* and *Shipwreck*. Brian Mullin points out that "[i]t has a generic 'historical drama' structure" (Mullin 2002: 6): contrary to that of the two other plays in the trilogy, the plot of this play progresses linearly without any exceptions from February 1853 to August 1868. As in the trilogy's macrostructure, the Aristotelian plot with introduction, exciting force or moment, ascent, climax, falling action, force or motive of last suspense and catastrophe can again be found in *Salvage*. The first half of its first scene constitutes the introduction. Through Herzen's dream the recipients learn that he and his family have by now settled in London, and that England's capital has become the place of exile for many former European revolutionaries. The plot is set into motion on a personal level when Malwida is hired as tutor for Herzen's children (cf. *Salvage* 10f.) and on a political level when Herzen and Worcell establish the Free Russian and Polish Press (cf. 18). These incidents constitute the exciting force or moment. The close relationship between Tata, Olga and Malwida and her move into Herzen's house (cf. 24), the quarrel about the press (cf. 29f.), the arrival of the first Russian edition of Herzen's *From the Other Shore* on New Year's Eve of 1854 (cf. 33f.), the death of the Tsar in 1855 (cf. 39) and the arrival of Ogarev and his wife Natalie one year later (cf. 43) constitute the ascent of *Salvage*. The climax is reached when Herzen and Natalie kiss at Worcell's funeral (cf. 56), an event foreshadowed by Herzen's broken wedding ring (cf. 43). The tolerated adultery between Herzen and Natalie (cf. 61), Ogarev's love affair with the prostitute Mary (cf. 70f.) and Chernyshevsky's visit to the Herzen's house make up the falling action. The forces or moments of last suspense are provided by the Russian Emancipation (cf. 88f.) and its bloody consequences (cf. 89f.), the formation of Michael Bakunin's revolutionary network (cf. 92ff.) and its collapse (cf. 104f.) and the failed assassination attempt on the Tsar by Karakozov (cf. 108). The catastrophe is realised in the last meeting of the remaining protagonists. Herzen's children have distanced themselves from their father, not speaking their mother tongue any longer. Their father has become an old and weak man, whose visions have failed. Even Bakunin has finally settled down for a quiet cigarette. However, in a final dream, Herzen argues against Marx's historical vision, holding on to his convictions of personal liberty. His youngest daughter Liza *"kisses him like a tomboy"*, which is followed by *"[s]ummer lightning... and cheerful responses of fright... then thunder and further responses... and a quick fade"* (119).

Although *Salvage* is structurally designed as progressing in a linear manner, the first act of the play hints at the theme of recurrence from *Shipwreck* through the motif of the loss and recovery of a glove. Maria, the German nanny of the Herzen children, complains first that two-year old Olga has lost a glove, only to find it in her pocket (cf. 4). In the same scene, Malwida finds a child's glove on the floor and Herzen says that it is his (cf. 11). When later in the play Worcell, who is ill, is about to leave Herzen's house, he realises that he seems to be "a glove short". Herzen is puzzled, but Worcell only answers: "No matter. Last time I had three. That probably explains it" (42f.). The last time a glove is mentioned is at Worcell's funeral, where Natalie and Herzen kiss for the first time. Herzen comments: "I'm always at the wrong funeral. Kolya's body was never found. There was a young woman rescued from the sea, my mother's maid. For some reason one of Kolya's gloves was in her pocket. So that's all we got back. A glove" (56).[161]

The missing and finding of a glove becomes a metaphor for death and the continuation of life respectively. Like Kolya, who lost a glove before his death in (a) *Shipwreck* as it was in the pocket of his grandmother's maid, Worcell has also lost a glove. And it is at his funeral that Herzen recalls the story of Kolya and the glove. This story is anticipated by the nanny, who finds not Kolya's but Olga's glove in her pocket. Olga is Herzen's youngest child, born after Kolya's birth (cf. *Shipwreck* 86) but before his death, and evidence that life continues even after personal tragedy. Malwida, who also finds a child's glove, is later told by Herzen that "a German once did a great evil in my life... which you, in your way, are making good" (*Salvage* 28). Herzen is moving on in life,

---

[161] The glove featured prominently in the New York production of *The Coast of Utopia* at the Lincoln Center for the Performing Arts in 2006/07. Each part of the trilogy began with a tableau of Herzen, sitting alone in an armchair and holding Kolya's lost glove.

and Malwida helps him cope with the memories of Herwegh's and Natalie's adultery. At the funeral he finds a new partner in his best friend's wife. Nonetheless, this mistress is also named Natalie and she repeats the adultery of her namesake, although it is somehow tolerated by Ogarev. That Natalie Ogarev should take Natalie Herzen's place is also evident from the list of characters: while Natalie Ogarev, then Tuchkov, was called Natasha in *Shipwreck*, she is now called Natalie in *Salvage*.[162] Conversely, in the description of her relationship towards Olga, Natalie Herzen is referred to as Natasha. Yacowar has rightly pointed out that the doubling of character names can be found throughout the whole trilogy, even if his enumeration is slightly imprecise. There are two Alexanders – Bakunin and Herzen – and even a third if we count Herzen's son Sasha, his name being the Russian diminutive of Alexander (cf. 47). Ogarev's first unfaithful wife was called Maria and his devoted prostitute's name is Mary. *Voyage* features five characters named Nicholas: Stankevich, Sazonov, Ketscher, Polevoy and Ogarev, and *Salvage* adds Chernyshevsky to that list. To Yacowar it suggests on the one hand "the lack of individuation among the radical 'thinkers'", and, on the other hand, that the presence of one character evokes the absence of her or his namesake (Yacowar 2003: 83). This is especially the case with Natalie/Natasha and Natasha/Natalie, and it is also what the symbol of the glove implies. A glove always needs its counterpart to fulfil its function. The presence of an uneven number of gloves, whether it is one or three, always implies the absence of another. As much as Herzen tries to go on with his life by letting a new Natalie into it and living on with the rest of his children, it is their presence which makes him aware of Kolya's and especially his first Natalie's absence:

Herzen (*weeps*) Oh, Natalie…!
Natalie comes forward but hesitates.
Natalie! It's your Tata grown up!

---

[162] Probably in order to reduce complexity, Natasha remained Natasha in the New York production of *Salvage* (cf. Stoppard 2007: 235). It also hints at the fact that the director of the trilogy, Jack O'Brien, aimed at abiding continuity between the three plays. This would comply to the New York audience which is much more a membership or subscription audience. The nine so-called 'marathon days' – day-long performances of the entire trilogy – were also fully booked almost immediately.

> *Tata kisses Herzen and runs out, stopping to hug Natalie.*
> *Natalie comes forward. Something has tipped in her.*
> **Natalie** *(jeers)* 'Oh, Natalie! It's your Tata grown up!'
> *Herzen is frightened.* (*Salvage* 103f.)

Natalie Ogarev, too, is caught between the past and the present, as she loves Herzen, but at the same time feels guilty, thinking that their affair is the reason why Ogarev became an alcoholic (cf. 68), and she occasionally becomes hysterical. This hysteria about the past is what the young Olga implies when she remarks about Natalie to Malwida: "I like her sometimes, when she's not historical. When she gets historical the only thing that calms her down is intimate relations" (84). Thus, *Salvage* demonstrates that 'presence through absence' evokes the past, and that the past determines the present as well as the presence of certain characters. This is also true in the larger context of *The Coast of Utopia*, as the presence of the plot of *Salvage*, with its references to the the other plays, evokes the absence of its prequels *Voyage* and *Shipwreck*. Thus, all three plays become part of a larger (historical and dramatic) design, a design that constitutes the trilogy. As Daphne Merkin writes: "what links everything and everyone [in *The Coast of Utopia*] is a feeling of untold loss and undwelled-on heartache" (Merkin 2006: 43). *Salvage* does not only establish its relationship to the trilogy's macroscopic level through the plot, but through the doubling of its Aristotelian macrostructure as well.

f. *The Coast of Utopia*: The apposition of characters – Bakunin, Herzen, Belinsky and Turgenev

Isaiah Berlin, Stoppard's main inspiration for the trilogy, writes in *Russian Thinkers* that "Chekhov once said that a writer's business was not to provide solutions, only to describe a situation so truthfully, do such justice to all sides of the question, that the reader could no longer evade it" (Berlin 1978: 303). While the apposition of ideas and characters is a trademark of Stoppard's drama, with *Travesties* as a prime example, it becomes quite important in *The Coast of Utopia* when considered in a

Chekhovian context. J.L. Styan describes the structural relationship between characters as a part of Chekhov's dramatic technique:

> Character, however deceptively realistic, is in this way part of a guiding pattern. It is first a pattern of checks and balances achieved by carefully setting one character off against another. [...] This device of implicit character comparison and contrast both undermines and controls the sentiment and emotionalism in each play, and encourages a subtle ambivalence in the action played out before the audience. (Styan 1985: 110)

This notion of checks and balances achieved by the apposition of characters is most aptly demonstrated in *The Coast of Utopia* through the four main characters Michael Bakunin, Alexander Herzen, Vissarion Belinsky and Ivan Turgenev, and it is the concern of this section. Emphasis will be laid on their different concepts of history because, as Muza rightly points out, a "debate that lies at the core of the trilogy concerns the meaning and purpose of history, the future, progress, and teleology" and the different concepts are "constantly debated by Stoppard's highly articulate and self-conscious characters" (Muza 2003).

Michael Bakunin epitomises the Hegelian dialectical and teleological concept of history, despite "his propensity to go round in circles" (Barker 2005: 712). In *Voyage*, his character represents a maturing revolutionary and anarchist. He changes philosophies like underwear, taking what he requires from Schelling, Kant, Fichte and Hegel, until he discovers revolution (in terms of Hegelian historical progress) as his "new philosophy of self-fulfilment" (*Voyage* 109). His affection for Hegelianism already becomes evident when he begins to doubt idealism, describing himself as the epitome of man standing between transcendental freedom and the objective determination of action: "You see, Liubov, I'm one of those who are born for their time. I will do such things I know not, but I must sacrifice everything to that sacred purpose, to strengthen my resolve until I can say, 'Whatever I want, that's what *God* wants'" (20). Bakunin here foreshadows his self-understanding in terms of what Hegel calls 'World-Historical individuals':

> This principle is an essentiel phase in the development of the *creating* idea, of truth striving and urging towards itself. Historical men – w*orld-historical individuals* – are those in whose aims such a general principle lies. [...] Such individuals had no consciousness of the general idea they were unfolding, while pros-

ecuting those aims of theirs; on the contrary, they were practical, political men. But at the same time they were thinking men, who had an insight into the requirements of the time – *what was ripe for development*. [...] World-historical men, the heroes of an epoch, must, therefore, be recognized as its clear-sighted ones; *their* deeds, *their* words are the best of that time.[163]   (Hegel 1952: 166f.)

Bakunin sees himself as one of Hegel's World-Historical individuals. "Transcending to the Universal Idea" already assumes another meaning for him, namely "to put a bomb under our submission to habit and convention [...] to release the passion of our nature" (*Voyage* 77). This reinterpretation of Schellingian philosophy indicates the anarchistic character Michael is to become in *Shipwreck* and *Salvage*, where he turns to action, i.e. revolution, because "[t]he mistake is to put ideas before action. Act first! The ideas will follow, and if not – well, it's progress" (*Shipwreck* 37). His concept of history is of a naïvely dialectical kind, as is his inner nature, contradicting himself as he goes:

> **Bakunin** He's right, madame!
> **Herzen** But you just said the opposite!
> **Bakunin** (*unabashed*) He's right again!   (*Shipwreck* 35)

His revolutionary goal is not personal liberty but universal egalitarianism: "The liberty of each, for the equality of all! [...] I am not free unless you, too, are free! [...] Freedom is a state of mind" (36, dialogue omitted). Stoppard has Bakunin anticipate Karl Marx, who, with Friedrich Engels, stated in the *Manifesto of the Communist Party* (*Manifest der kommunistischen Partei*, 1848) that "the free development of each is the condition for the free development of all" (Marx/Engels 1952: 429).[164] This kind of freedom, however, implies the exchange of personal liberty for the future good of mankind. Bakunin seems to have

---

[163] "Dies Allgemeine ist ein Moment der produzierenden Idee, ein Moment der nach sich selbst strebenden und treibenden Wahrheit. Die geschichtlichen Menschen, die *welthistorischen Individuen* sind diejenigen, in deren Zwecken ein solches Allgemeines liegt. [...] Solche Individuen hatten in diesen ihren Zwecken nicht das Bewußtsein der Idee überhaupt, sondern sie waren praktische und politische Menschen. Aber zugleich waren sie denkende, die die Einsicht hatten von dem, was nicht und was *an der Zeit ist*. [...] Die welthistorischen Menschen, die Heroen einer Zeit, sind darum als die Einsichtigen anzuerkennen; ihre Handlungen, ihre Reden sind das Beste der Zeit" (Hegel 1970d: 45f.).

finally reached his goal in life after the fall of the monarchy of Louis Philippe, when he also encounters Marx:

> **Bakunin** Marx! Who'd have thought it!?
> **Marx** It was bound to happen. I was expecting it.
> **Bakunin** Why didn't you tell me? (*Shipwreck* 40)

In a nostalgic manner, Bakunin romanticises his past depicted in *Voyage* as a teleological journey to the present:

> This is what it was all for, from the beginning... studying Kant, Schelling, Fichte [...]. We were on a journey to this moment. Revolution is the Absolute we pursued at Premukhino, the Universal which contains all the opposites and resolves them. It's where we were always going. (43, dialogue omitted)

The journey that was depicted in *Voyage* seems to have reached its final destination, which for Bakunin is the revolution in Paris, and which is to spread to the whole of Europe, including Russia. He wants to carry the spirit of revolution there, i.e. he wants to invade Russia with a Polish army. And even after the bourgeois revolution has failed in the West because "the Germans and French, they were all for getting rid of aristocratic privilege, but they closed ranks to defend their property" (101), he still optimistically believes in the revolution of the Russian peasants:

> I couldn't wait to get to the West! Twenty Cossacks couldn't have held me back in my yearning for the other shore. But the answer was behind me all the time. A peasant revolution, Herzen! Marx bamboozled us. He's such a townie, to him peasants are hardly people, they're agriculture, like cows and turnips. Well, he doesn't know the Russian peasant! There's a history of rebellion there, and we forgot it. (103)

To Bakunin, "[d]estruction is a creative passion" (103), and he believes in the teleological progress of history, in which the failed revolutions of Europe are only a minor setback: "Reaction is only the optical effect of the river running backwards on the tide, while the river runs always to the sea, which is liberty boundless and indivisible!" (*Salvage* 36). He conceives of the history of mankind in a dialectical and teleological manner:

---

[164] "An die Stelle der alten bürgerlichen Gesellschaft mit ihren Klassen und Klassengegensätzen tritt eine Assoziation, worin die freie Entwicklung eines jeden die Bedingung für die freie Entwicklung aller ist" (Marx/Engels 1959: 482).

Bakunin No – listen! Once – long ago, at the beginning of history – we were all free. Man was at one with his nature, and so he was good. He was in harmony with the world. Conflict was unknown. Then the serpent entered the garden, and the name of the serpent was – Order. Social organisation! The world was no longer at one with itself. Matter and spirit divided. Man was no longer whole. He was riven by ambition, acquisitiveness, jealousy, fear... Conflict became the condition of his life, the individual against his neighbour, against society, against himself. The Golden Age was ended. How can we make a new Golden Age and set men free again? By destroying everything that destroyed their freedom.
Herzen (*nostalgically*) Ah, the zig and the zag.
Bakunin I knew you understood. The age has arrived at its reversal, and we were born to be the turning point. The year of revolution cracked the foundations of the old world. Things will never be the same again. (37)

Social organisation, i.e. any form of government, is the thesis, and its destruction (i.e. revolution) its antithesis, which then creates the synthesis. Of this, however, even Bakunin has no concept, because action has priority over ideas. That is why he is immediately in favour of supporting the young revolutionaries Chernyshevsky and Sleptsov in Russia. At the end of *Salvage*, the historical Bakunin's conflict with Marx is foreshadowed. He talks of undermining "Marx's International Working Men's Association" in order to "destroy authority" because "[t]o be answerable to authority is demeaning to man's spiritual essence. All discipline is vicious". In Bakunin's contradictory style, however, he wants to achieve this with "a dedicated group of revolutionaries under iron discipline, answerable to [... his] absolute authority" (113f.).[165]

Bakunin is diametrically opposed to Herzen, who epitomises man's free will in contrast to historical necessity. Bakunin reaches his view on life by inducing the composition of the world from his egotistical search for his transcendental self. Herzen, on the other hand, deduces the possibilities of man from the political reality in Russia.[166] He is the spokes-

---

[165] In the introduction to the 2007 edition of *The Coast of Utopia*, Stoppard states that he "adopted Alexander Herzen's perspective of his old comrade". The playwright describes Michael Bakunin as "courageous, inspiring, big-hearted and tireless", but also as "jumping from one enthusiasm to another" and displaying an "erratic pursuit of mutually contradictory goals" (Stoppard 2007: xiii-xiv).

[166] This contrast between Bakunin and Herzen, which Stoppard employs throughout the trilogy, is very similar to the antithesis between utopia and reality Carr describes in his *The Twenty Years' Crisis*: "The antithesis of utopia and reality –

man of a political circle, which stands for republicanism, socialism and anarchism. However, he and his circle "are revolutionaries with secret arsenals of social theory" (*Voyage* 58). Ideas precede their actions. For Herzen, it is "almost unforgivable" that the turning point of Stankevich's life should have been "reading Schelling's *System of Transcendental Idealism*" (60), because it reduces the individual to a mere shadow on the wall of the cave. For the same reason, he criticises the Dialectical Spirit of History when he comments on Belinsky's Hegelianism:

> You've got Hegel's Dialectical Spirit of History upside down and so has he. People don't storm the Bastille because history proceeds by zigzags. History zigzags because when people have had enough, they storm the Bastille. When you turn him right way up, Hegel is the algebra of revolution. The Dialectical Spirit of History would be an extravagant redundancy even if one could imagine what sort of animal it was supposed to be... a gigantic ginger cat, for example. Belinsky!... Belinsky! We are not the plaything of an imaginative cosmic force, but of a Romanov with no imagination whatsoever, a mediocrity. (104)

Herzen does not only oppose Hegel and the idea of the teleological progress of history, he also believes in the free will of man and chance as historical patterns of explanation: "But about the *Cat*... the Cat has no plan, no favourites or resentments, no memory, no mind, no rhyme or reason. It kills without purpose, and spares without purpose, too. So, when it catches your eye, what happens next is not up to the Cat, it's up to you" (105). For him, the future is open to the actions of individuals, rather than to mere historical necessity. But just as Michael contradicts his idealist philosophy, Herzen also contradicts himself. The rhyme in his lines (*too* and *you*) cancels his statement that the Cat, the progress of history, has "no rhyme or reason".

Herzen opposes any abstract concept, such as "the Spirit of History, the ceaseless March of Progress", which does not consider the individual and reduces people to supernumeraries: "Oh, a curse on your capital let-

---

a balance always swinging towards and away from equilibrium and never completely attaining it – is a fundamental antithesis revealing itself in many forms of thought. The two methods of approach – the inclination to ignore what was and what is in contemplation of what should be, and the inclination to deduce what should be from what was and what is – determine opposite attitudes towards every political problem" (Carr 1940: 16).

ters! We're asking people to spill their blood – at least spare them your conceit that they're acting out the biography of an abstract noun!" He pinpoints the question which is at the bottom of social organisation: "why should anyone obey anyone else?" (*Shipwreck* 18). This includes theist beliefs:

> **Granovsky** Without faith in something higher, human nature is animal nature.
> **Herzen** Without superstition, you mean.
> **Granovsky** Superstition? Did you say superstition? [...]
> **Herzen** Superstition! The pious and pitiful belief that there's something outside or up there, or God knows where, without which men can't find their nobility.
> **Granovsky** Without 'up there', as you call it, scores have to be settled down here – that's the whole truth about materialism.
> **Herzen** How can you – how dare you – throw away your dignity as a human being? You can choose well or badly without deference to a ghost! – you're a free man, Granovsky, there's no other kind.   (19, stage directions omitted)

For Herzen, personal liberty is the only foundation for life and social change. Any abstract theory, including theism, deprives mankind of autonomy. By comparing God to a ghost, Herzen also alludes to the famous first line of the *Manifesto of the Communist Party* which names "the ghost of Communism" (41): "A spectre is haunting Europe – the spectre of Communism" (Marx/Engels 1952: 419).[167] And as before, Herzen partly undermines his argument by actually referring to God, whom he questions ("God knows where"). Nevertheless, to him, as to Rousseau, freedom implies that man does not have to do what he does not want to do, rather than that he has the liberty to do what he wants:

> **Herzen** [...] What freedom means is being allowed to sing in my bath as loudly as will not interfere with my neighbour's freedom to sing a different tune in his. But above all, let my neighbour and I be free to join or not to join the revolutionary opera, the state orchestra, the Committee of Public Harmony... [...]
> **Sazonov** An orchestra is a very good metaphor. There is no contradiction between individual freedom and duty to the collective –
> **Herzen** I'd like to be there when they play.
> **Sazonov** – because being in the orchestra is the individual right.
> **Herzen** We all missed it, Plato, Rousseau, Saint-Simon, me...
>   (*Shipwreck* 36f., dialogue omitted)

---

[167] "Ein Gespenst geht um in Europa – das Gespenst des Kommunismus" (Marx/Engels 1959: 461).

Herzen is disappointed with the revolution in Paris because the Second Republic behaves like the monarchy it displaced, i.e. it does not share its new freedom: "But it turns out the Republic makes revolution unnecessary, and, in fact, undesirable. Power is not to be shared with the ignoramuses who build the barricades. They're too poor to have a voice" (47). His attitude towards abstract solutions to social problems, as suggested by German Idealism and Hegelianism, becomes apparent when he disappointedly talks to a *"'Blue Blouse', an old workman in tattered clothes"* (49):

> What do you want? Bread? I'm afraid bread got left out of the theory. We are bookish people, with bookish solutions. Prose is our strong point, prose and abstraction. But everything is going beautifully. Last time – in 1789 – there was a misunderstanding. We thought we had discovered that social progress was a science like everything else. The First Republic was to have been the embodiment of morality and justice as a rational enterprise. The result was, admittedly, a bitter blow. But now there's a completely new idea. History itself is the main character of the drama, and also its author. We are all in the story, which ends with universal bliss. Perhaps not for you. Perhaps not for your children. But universal bliss, you can put your shirt on it which, I see, you have. Your personal sacrifice, the sacrifice of countless others on History's slaughter-bench, all the apparent crimes and lunacies of the hour, which to you may seem irrational, are part of a much bigger story which you probably aren't in the mood for – let's just say that this time, as luck would have it, you're the zig and they're the zag. (51f.)

The 'Blue Blouse' is *"invisible to Natalie and Natasha"* and George (49), i.e. he is a figment of Herzen's imagination. Only he can see him, as his character emphasises the individual in history. In his monologue, he sarcastically settles old scores with Enlightenment and German Idealism, especially Hegelianism. Abstract concepts leave no room for the individual or any practical applicability. Rather, they aim at some artificial higher cause, such as universal bliss, which holds no personal answers and in which the individual plays no direct part as conceived by Schelling and Hegel. Schelling, for example, depicts history as a drama, in which man is a character as well as co-author:

> If we think of history as a play in which everyone involved performs his part quite freely and as he pleases, a rational development of this muddled drama is conceivable only if there be a single spirit who speaks in everyone, and if the

playwright, whose mere fragments (*disjecta membra poetae*) are the individual actors, has already so harmonized beforehand the objective outcome of the whole with the free play of every participant, that something rational must indeed emerge at the end of it. But now if the playwright *were to exist* independently of his drama, we should be merely the actors who speak the lines he has written. If he *does* not exist independently of us, but reveals and discloses himself successively only, through the very play of our own freedom, so that without this freedom even he himself *would not be*, then we are collaborators of the whole and have ourselves invented the particular roles we play.[168]

(Schelling 1993: 210)

According to Schelling, historical progress cannot be described or predicted in terms of Newtonian mechanics. The historian must find the pattern of progress and providence in the alleged non-conformity and diversity of history (cf. Sandkühler (ed.) 2005: 231ff.). Similarly, for Hegel, as has been mentioned before, History is a drama of passions and a slaughter-bench at which the happiness of the people is victimized (cf. Hegel 1952: 162). The individual has no priority in this universal scheme: "For the fancies which the individual in his isolation indulges, cannot be the model for universal reality; just as *universal* law is not designed for the units of the mass. These as such may, in fact, find their interests decidedly thrust into the background" (Hegel 1952: 169).[169]

---

[168] "Wenn wir uns die Geschichte als ein Schauspiel denken, in welchem jeder, der daran Teil hat, ganz frei und nach Gutdünken seine Rolle spielt, so läßt sich eine vernünftige Entwicklung dieses verworrenen Spiels nur dadurch denken, daß es Ein Geist ist, der in allen dichtet, und daß der Dichter, dessen bloße Bruchstücke (disjecti membra poëtae) die einzelnen Schauspieler sind, den objektiven Erfolg des Ganzen mit dem freien Spiel aller einzelnen schon zum voraus so in Harmonie gesetzt hat, daß am Ende wirklich etwas vernünftiges herauskommen muß. *Wäre* nun aber der Dichter unabhängig von seinem Drama, so wären wir nun die Schauspieler, die ausführen, was er gedichtet hat. *Ist* er nicht unabhängig von uns, sondern offenbart und enthüllt er sich nur sukzessiv durch das Spiel unserer Freiheit selbst, so daß ohne diese Freiheit auch er selbst nicht *wäre*, so sind wir Mitdichter des Ganzen, und Selbsterfinder der besonderen Rolle, die wir spielen" (Schelling 1907: 276).

[169] "Denn was das Individuum für sich in seiner Einzelheit sich ausspinnt, kann für die allgemeine Wirklichkeit nicht Gesetz sein, ebenso wie das Weltgesetz nicht für die einzelnen Individuen allein ist, die dabei sehr zu kurz kommen können" (Hegel 1970d: 52).

Herzen's criticism is directed against any form of determinism. After the failed revolutions, this is manifest in Marx's dialectical materialism, which for Herzen deprives man of self-control, too: "But how can Communism catch on? It asks a worker to give up his... aristocracy. [...] A minimum of control over your own life, even to make a mess out of it, is something necessarily human" (*Shipwreck* 60). Even when it comes to the death of his own child Kolya, Herzen rejects the teleological progress of history as a means to vent his grief about his son's early death:

> Because children grow up, we think a child's purpose is to grow up. But a child's purpose is to be a child. Nature doesn't disdain what lives only for a *day*. It pours the whole of itself into the each moment. We don't value the lily less for not being made of flint and built to last. Life's bounty is in its flow, later is too late. Where is the song when it's been sung? The dance when it's been danced? It's only we humans who want to own the future, too. We persuade ourselves that the universe is modestly employed in unfolding our destination. We note the haphazard chaos of history by the day, by the hour, but there is something wrong with the picture. Where is the unity, the meaning, of nature's highest creation? Surely those millions of little streams of accident and wilfulness have their correction in the vast underground river which, without doubt, is carrying us to the place where we're expected! But there is no such place, that's why it's called utopia. The death of a child has no more meaning than the death of armies, of nations. Was the child happy while he lived? That is a proper question, the only question. If we can't arrange our own happiness, it's a conceit beyond vulgarity to arrange the happiness of those who come after us. (100f.)

Seen teleologically, Kolya's life was ended before it could fulfil its destiny, and this would devalue his existence before death. The future, however, is not to be known, as is the meaning of history. To Herzen, life has no final purpose; every theory which views life and history in this way is utopian, i.e. it projects a place that does not exist. With these lines about Kolya, Herzen addresses Bakunin who, just like the 'Blue Blouse', is only present in his imagination. Bakunin becomes Herzen's imaginary interlocutor in *Salvage*, too. Throughout the play, he functions as his counterweight: Bakunin's revolutionary Hegelianism on one side and Herzen's personal liberty and free will on the other. However, it is Herzen who, at the end of the play, answers to Marx in his dreams:

> **Herzen** *(to Marx)* But history has no culmination! There is always as much in front as behind. There is no libretto. History knocks at a thousand gates at every moment, and the gatekeeper is chance. We shout into the mist for this one or that one to be opened for us, but through every gate there are a thousand more. We need wit and courage to make our way while our way is making us. But that is our dignity as human beings, and we rob ourselves if we pardon us by the absolution of historical necessity. What kind of beast is it, this Ginger Cat with its insatiable appetite for human sacrifice? This Moloch who promises that everything will be beautiful after we're dead? A distant end is not an end but a trap. The end we work for must be closer, the labourer's wage, the pleasure in the work done, the summer lightning of personal happiness...
>   *Marx and Turgenev ignore him and stroll away.*
>   *Herzen half-falls out of his chair. Ogarev sees him and comes to him.*
> *(awake)* Nothing, nothing... The idea will not perish. The young people will come of age.
> **Ogarev** Whose fault is it we didn't carry them with us? We knew what we were aiming for, but how were we supposed to get it? – by revolution? – by Imperial decree? – a constitution? What do you believe? I ask you seriously because I no longer understand.
> **Herzen** We have to open men's eyes and not tear them out... and if we see differently, it's all right, we don't have to kill the myopic in our myopia... We have to bring what's good along with us. People won't forgive us. I imagine myself the future custodian of a broken statue, a blank wall, a desecrated grave, telling everyone who passes by, 'Yes – yes, all this was destroyed by the revolution.'
>
> (*Salvage* 118)

And it is Bakunin who for once seems to agree with him at the end: "*(lighting a cigarette)* At last, the happy moment" (119). Herzen sees history as a haphazard succession of events, which man must cope with by relying on his humanity. Man's ignorance of life is also his great chance, because it means that man does not have to follow or recognise a set path, but can choose his own way and direct his fate according to free will. Art and personal happiness are the only factors which console him in this life.

While Bakunin represents the teleological progress of history and Herzen non-determinism and man's free will, the character of Belinsky represents recurrent change. For him, understanding the meaning of art can give insight into life and history. It is the double duty of the critic to discover an explanation for the creation of art and to explicate what it implies for its recipients: "If something true can be understood about art, something will be understood about liberty, too, and science and politics and history – because everything in the universe is unfolding together with a purpose of which mine is a part" (*Voyage* 39). According to Belinsky, whose thoughts are suffused with Schellingian philosophy: to understand art is to understand history. Because of this, art is important to such a degree that he is convinced that it can actually represent Russia:

> No! Let social purpose hang itself unhindered! No – I mean, literature can *replace*, can actually *become*... Russia! It can be greater and more real than the external reality. It only has to be true. Art is true or false. [...] Not true to the *facts*, not true to appearances, but true to the innermost of the innermost doll, where genius and nature are the same stuff. The moment an artist has a thesis he is merely a huckster, maybe talented but that's not it, it won't help us when every time we say 'Russia' we have to grin and twitch like half-wits from the embarrassment of a mother country that has given nothing to the world and taken nothing from it. 'Russia! Yes, I'm afraid so – you've got it – the backwoods – no history but barbarism, no law but autocracy, no glory but brute force, and all those contented serfs!' – we're nothing to the world except an object lesson in what to avoid. But a great artist can change all that, make it irrelevant [...]. When the word Russia makes you think of great writers *and almost nothing else*, the job will be done [...]. (80f.)

In Belinsky's opinion, art, i.e. literature, can become synonymous with 'Russia', can provide it with historical identity. This art only has to be true – not true to the facts, but true to the 'Absolute'. However, this changes when Belinsky turns to Hegel and when he comes to terms with reality:

> But reality can't be thought away – what's real is rational, and what's rational is real. I can't describe to you my feelings when I heard those words. They were my release from my weary guardianship of the human race. I grasped the meaning of the rise and fall of kingdoms, the ebb and flow of history, the petteness of my miserable anxiety about my life. Reality! I say it every night when I go to bed and every morning when I awake [...]. (102)

Belinsky has accepted reality in the form of historical necessity and the dialectical logic of history. But even faster than Bakunin changes philosophies, Belinsky changes his opinion again. At the end, he renounces the idea of historical necessity because "the life and death of a single child weighs more than your whole construction of historical necessity" (107). Stoppard puts into Belinsky's mouth the argument which the character of Ivan Karamazov in Fyodor Dostoevsky's *The Brothers Karamazov* (*Bratja Karamazovy*, 1879-80) uses as an argument against God.[170] With this anachronistic allusion to Dostoevsky, Belinsky credits literature with a social as well as an artistic purpose: the reflection on man's existence and the appreciation of the individual. For him, not Schellingian art (as the manifestation of the genius' age through which the 'Absolute' speaks) is of importance any more, but realistic, i.e. political prose, which reflects on the suffering of the individual in the world:

> I always believed that the artist expresses his age by singing with no more purpose than a bird. But now we need a new kind of song, a different singer. [...] Well, the man and the artist can no longer pass each other in the doorway taking turns to be at home: there's only one person under the roof, he can't be separated from himself, and must be judged all together... (108f.)

Apparently, the age of Pushkin is over, an age in which art did not need to represent social reality, in which the artist and the real person behind him were separate entities. However, Belinsky cannot give up the idea of art for art's sake:

> **Chaadaev** If I could bring Pushkin back to life by reducing George Sand to a fine powder and sprinkling it on his grave, I'd leave for Paris tonight with a coffee grinder in my luggage.
> **Belinsky** Oh God, you're right, you're right! (108)

If literature is to become synonymous with Russia, it needs to do the work that is done elsewhere by parts of society: "In other countries, the advance of civilised behaviour is everybody's business. In Russia, there's no division of labour, literature has to do it all". It seems that Belinsky

---

[170] "'Tell me yourself, I challenge you – answer. Imagine that you are creating a fabric of human destiny with the object of making men happy in the end, giving them peace and rest at last, but that it was essential and inevitable to torture to death only one tiny creature – that baby beating its breast with its fist, for instance – and to found that edifice on its unavenged tears, would you consent to be the architect on those conditions? Tell me, and tell the truth.' 'No, I wouldn't consent,' said Alyosha softly" (Dostoevsky 1952: 126f.). Interestingly, in her study on the historical Herzen, Vera Piroschkow draws on exactly this passage from Dostoevsky's novel to emphasise the belief Herzen was occupied with at his time, namely that personal happiness is not to be sacrificed for the bliss of future generations. Man must not be a means to an end, but an end in himself (cf. Piroschkow 1961: 140f.).

has changed his opinion. He used to see art as "aimless, pure spirit": "I was a young ruffian from the provinces, with the artistic credo of a Parisian dandy. Remember Gautier? – 'Fools! Cretins! A novel is not a pair of boots! [...] A play is not a railway!'" (*Shipwreck* 23f., dialogue omitted). Belinsky's former artistic creed was influenced by Théophile Gautier, who wrote in the famous preface to his *Mademoiselle de Maupin* (1834) that "tout ce qui est utile est laid", everything that is useful is ugly (Gautier 1966: 23). Now, however, Belinsky apparently favours the practical utility of literature: "Well, we have no railways, so that's another job for literature, to open up the country" (*Shipwreck* 24). This new creed is the reason why Belinsky declines staying in Paris, to publish unhindered by censorship, because "[i]t wouldn't mean anything... [...] it's like a zoo where the seals throw fish to the public. None of it seems serious. At home the public look to writers as their real leaders. The title of poet or novelist really counts with us" (30f.). Belinsky prefers political oppression and censorship in Russia to the freedom of opinion in Paris, because only in this way can literature fulfil its purpose to make Russian history.

Belinsky's realisation about himself, i.e. that he is constantly changing his opinion, is important with regard to his view on art. He admits that his motto is that "[i]t's not too late to change your mind" (58) and that the reconciliation of contradictory interests, such as Bakunin's universal bliss for mankind and Herzen's personal happiness, is like squaring a circle:

> **Belinsky** I can't fit the pieces together to make a square – it's a children's puzzle and I can't do it...
> **Turgenev** Perhaps it's a circle. [...]
> **Belinsky** Turgenev's got a point...   (37, dialogue omitted)

Turgenev's remark shows that Belinsky has not abandoned his standpoint of art for art's sake. His change of opinion from pure to purposeful art over the course of *Voyage* and *Shipwreck* becomes rather recurrent. This is underlined by the structural device of the reprise, which reconstructs a conversation between Belinsky and Turgenev. Belinsky argues on the one hand that literary criticism has no practical application to life: "The poetry of practical gesture. Something unknown to literary criticism!" On the other hand, he is convinced that only literature can make Russia a great nation: "People are going to be amazed by Russian writers. In literature we're a great nation before we're ready" (57). Belinsky suffers shipwreck by trying to square the circle; he wants to reconcile art's transcendental purity with its practical utility, realising that adhering to one side implies excluding the other, which he just cannot do. Turgenev comments: "You're going round again, Captain" (58). Belinsky's concept of history is connected with his recurrent argument about art. When he was viewing *l'art pour l'art* as the medium to transport the transcendental truth of mankind, it was the teleological progress of history that dominated his ideas. With the awareness of the significance of a single child's life, however, his concept of art has also changed: he has realised art's meaning and duty to the people and for the formation of a national identity. At the same time, he remains lovesick for literature all his life, relating to its manifestations on a highly personal level. Thus, for Belinsky, history is a recurrence of irreconcilable ideas. The individual who tries to find a meaning to history will realise that this understanding is as futile as trying to square a circle, and s/he will end up by going around in circles.

While the character of Belinsky represents the recurrence of arguments, the character of Turgenev represents historical ambiguity. As with Belinsky, a great deal about Turgenev's concept of history is revealed in his attitude towards art. In the presence of Tatiana, who is in love with him but whose love he does not requite, he calls himself a sportsman rather than a writer and he vehemently revokes Schelling's and Fichte's idealism, admitting that "we're all Hegelians now" (*Voyage* 52). Two years later, he presents Belinsky with the first work in his own voice, *Parasha* (1843), leaving it to the critic as to whether he is to be called a poet (cf. 110f.). A poet he becomes, describing to Natalie how the deaf Kolya perceives the world and at the same time describing poetry: "The names for things don't come first, words stagger after, hopelessly trying to become the sensation" (*Shipwreck* 8). By then, however, he sees himself rather as a novelist, and as much as he finds it impossible for words to describe sensations, he also refuses to assume a standpoint in his novels:

> I'm not pure spirit, but I'm not society's keeper either. [...] People complain about me having no attitude in my stories. They're puzzled. Do I approve or dis-

approve? Do I want the reader to agree with this man or the other man? [...] Where does the author stand? Why doesn't he come clean with us? Well, maybe I'm wrong, but how would that make me a better writer? What has it got to do with anything? (24)

Turgenev does not deem it necessary for literature to provide an opinion, to give reader (and society) a clear idea of what is good and what is bad. He expresses this view in his *A Sportsman's Sketches* (*Zapiski Okhotnika*, 1852), the later title of the collected narrations he refers to here. Nonetheless, Turgenev becomes the first in the trilogy to criticise Marx and Communism by ridiculing the first line of the *Manifesto of the Communist Party*. Marx asks Turgenev about the beginning paragraph: "You're a writer. Do you think there's something funny about 'the ghost of Communism'? I don't want it to sound as if Communism is dead" (41), and Turgenev plunges right in to give alternative versions for it:

> Let me see... (*in 'English'*) 'A ghost... a phantom is walking around Europe...' [...] (*thoughtfully*) 'A spook... a spectre...' [...] (*jogged*) 'A *spirit*... a spirit is haunting Europe...' [...] (*taps the book, triumphantly satisfied*) 'A hobgoblin is stalking around Europe – the hobgoblin of Communism!'
>
> (41ff., dialogue omitted)

Eloquent as he is, Turgenev gives a plethora of synonyms for 'ghost', which have less and less in common with the intended meaning of the original. Marx's dialectical and historical materialism is reduced to an ugly, fantastic creature. By the end of Turgenev's translation attempts, Marx has already left the stage, pursuing the Herweghs because they want to interfere in the economic struggle by marching on Baden. Similar to his neutral position in his novels, Turgenev's position in the Paris revolution becomes that of a tourist: he observes the action but does not participate in it. Herzen is angry about Turgenev remaining aloof to the failure of the revolutions: "All you liberals are splashed with blood no matter how you tried to keep your distance" (54). Turgenev's self-image is rather West European, and to him, "taking everything to extremes" is something typically Russian. Herzen agrees, although he rejects Turgenev's detached standpoint:

> Single-minded conviction is a quality of youth, and Russia is young. (*pointedly*) Compromise, prevarication, the ability to hold two irreconcilable beliefs, both

with ironic detachment – these are ancient European arts, and a Russian who finds them irresistible is, I would say, exceptional. (55)

Herzen affronts his friend by denying him a Russian character. What makes Turgenev European, however, is that he should hold irreconcilable beliefs while at the same time distancing himself from them. Turgenev agrees with Herzen's analysis, but he sees the negative side in the Russian character:

> Putting yourself in another's place is a proper modesty, and, yes, it takes centuries to learn it. Impatience, pigheaded stubbornness to the point of destruction – yes, these are things to be forgiven in the young, who lack the imagination to see that almost nothing in this life holds still, everything is moving and changing – (56)

Turgenev positions himself between opinions, between the democratic revolution in Paris and the failure of the Second Republic, which did not turn out to be a democracy after all. While Herzen is disappointed with the outcome of the revolution, Turgenev accepts it as it is, because "[f]or all the venality you see around you, France is still the highest reach of civilisation" (48).

The notion of seeing no version as the better alternative can also be found in his play *A Month in the Country* (*Mesiats v Derevne*, 1850), the ending of which he describes to Emma Herwegh:

> **Turgenev** It takes place over a month in a house in the country. A woman and a young girl fall in love with the same man.
> **Emma** Who wins?
> **Turgenev** Nobody, of course. (78)

His refusal to state his opinion even goes so far as to give answers without knowing the question:

> **Emma** I want to ask you something but you might be angry with me.
> **Turgenev** I'll answer anyway. No.
> **Emma** But how do you know the question?
> **Turgenev** I don't. You can apply my answer to any question of your choice. (78)

To be in balance, his next answer is of course "Yes". However, as much as Turgenev tries to detach himself from any side, his dignity and artistic principles still make him defend his opinion about art:

> I was the one who defended Chernyshevsky, you know, when he made his debut with the discovery that you can't eat a painted apple, so art is merely life's poor relation; paintings of the sea are only useful for people living in the middle of Russia who don't know what the sea looks like. I stood up for him. 'Yes,' I said, 'yes, these are the ravings of an infantile bigot, the stinking vomit of a vulture without the first understanding of art – but,' I said, 'there is something here which shouldn't be ignored; the man has made a connection with something vital in the times.'[171]
>
> (*Salvage* 64)

The utilitarian doctrine of art is opposed by Turgenev, but at the same time, he shows sympathy for the standpoint of the next generation of revolutionaries. It is the beginning of the conflict between Herzen's generation and nihilists such as Chernyshevsky and Sleptsov. Although Turgenev tries to win their favour, to bridge the generation gap by considering all sides, they take his detached standpoint for opposition:

> The word 'liberal' has now entered the scatological vocabulary, like 'halfwit' or 'hypocrite'... It means anyone who supports peaceful reform over violent revolution. Our generation of repentant gentry comes off very badly, lumped in with indecisive lovers and slugabeds from Onegin to Oblomov – we're all examples of the same disease, an egotistical upper-class weakness with its roots in the social corruption of a society based on serfdom. (*Pause*.) Well, that makes sense, probably. (64)

Herzen's circle is considered liberal, but while for Herzen and Chernyshevsky "freeing the serfs is an absolute", either by "reform from above or revolution from below", Turgenev does not share their belief in the Russian peasantry, since for him "they're no different from Italian, French or German peasants. Conservatives *par excellence*" (65). The generation conflict is best expressed in the novel *Fathers and Sons*, which Stoppard takes up in the conversation between Turgenev and the Doctor. The Doctor's name is Bazarov, the protagonist of the novel:

---

[171] Stoppard's Turgenev refers here to the historical Chernyshevsky's master's thesis *The Aesthetic Relations of Art to Reality* (*Esteticheskiye otnosheniya iskusstva k deyatel'nosti*, 1855). Its essence was "[t]o defend reality against fantasy, to demonstrate that works of art cannot possibly be compared with living reality [...]". For the historical Chernyshevsky, "art is *lower* than real life – is less perfect than real life": "Let art not be ashamed to say that its goal ... is to reproduce reality and explain it for the benefit of man" (Chernyshevsky in Donaldson 1986: 107).

> **Turgenev**: I don't know what to call you.
> **Doctor**: Bazarov. [172] (*Salvage* Prompt Script 87)

During the conversation, Turgenev again takes the standpoint between the superfluous men and the nihilists, without, however, abandoning the position of the artist and novelist. While his purpose with *Fathers and Sons* "was to write a novel", while he takes "every possible side" (*Salvage* 96), and while he agrees with everyone a little "up to a point" (98), he is also aware that one is expected to make a choice:

> At home we had an English clock with a little brass lever that said, (*accented*) 'Strike – Silent'... It was the first English I knew... 'Strike – Silent'. You had to choose. Even then I thought it was unreasonable... Someone has a headache, someone has an appointment..." (99)

That is why, despite his balancing of sides, his own apposition of ideas, Turgenev takes a side simply by presenting ambiguity in his art. He sees "western civilisation transmitted by an educated minority" (102) as Russia's only hope, and centres his novels, as well as his *Weltanschauung*, on the individual, just like Herzen and Belinsky. But while Herzen epitomises personal liberty in history and Belinsky the dilemma of recurrently trying to reconcile contradictory beliefs, Turgenev represents the ambiguity of history. His notion is that history has no meaning, or rather every possible meaning at the same time, while emphasising the exceptional position of art and the individual in it.

The four main characters of Bakunin and Herzen, Belinsky and Turgenev work in a pattern of checks and balances with regard to the presentation of historical concepts in *The Coast of Utopia*. While Bakunin represents the teleological progress of history and historical necessity, Herzen balances this viewpoint with his emphasis on non-determinism and personal liberty, politically as well as historically. And while Belinsky stands for the perpetual change of historical concepts, one irreconcilable with the other, Turgenev checks this standpoint by accepting the existence of various historical concepts, which belief leads to historical ambiguity. Isaiah Berlin himself contrasts the historical Bakunin with the historical Herzen, and he even centres the essay "Herzen and Bakunin on Individual Liberty" on their opposition (cf. Berlin 1978:

---

[172] Cf. also Stoppard 2007: 318.

82-113). In general, Stoppard's characterisation closely follows Berlin's in *Russian Thinkers*,[173] but it is in the Chekhovian context and with regard to the topic of history that the apposition of characters is of significance. While *The Coast of Utopia* may favour Herzen just by the sheer stage presence of his character in the trilogy, the idea to "do such justice to all sides of the question" is not only Chekhovian, but also represented in the character of Turgenev throughout the plays. Thus, *The Coast of Utopia* is centrally concerned, at least with regard to its *dramatis personae*, with the ambiguity of history. It is in these terms that Ketscher in *Shipwreck* describes 'the intelligentsia' which the diverse characters are a part of:

> **Ketscher** It means us. A uniquely Russian phenomenon, the intellectual opposition considered as a social force.
> **Granovsky** Well...!
> **Herzen** The... intelligentsia!...
> **Ogarev** Including Aksakov?
> **Ketscher** That's the subtlety of it, we don't have to agree with each other.
>
> (*Shipwreck* 17)

g. *Voyage*, *Shipwreck* and *Salvage*: Mediating the ambiguity of language through language, and identity formation through language

Lindheim names additional major Chekhovian themes which can also be found in *The Coast of Utopia*. One of them is the "lack of communication", meaning that "[t]he inability of people to talk to one another in the same language or to make themselves understood across differences in temperament, status, and values, produces a confusion in communication or even its breakdown" (Lindheim 1985: 59).[174] Nadel has also

---

[173] On Bakunin, cf. Berlin 1978: 102 and 105; on Herzen, cf. 86f., 90ff., 112 and 194ff.; on Belinsky, cf. 157f., 160, 167ff., 179, 181f. and 184; on Turgenev, cf. 129f., 134, 148, 182f. and 202f.

[174] Among other stories, Lindheim names Chekhov's "The Requiem" ("Panikhida"), "Difficult People" ("Tiazhelye Liudi"), "Excellent People" ("Khoroshye Liudi) and "Misery" ("Neschast'e", all 1886), as well as his play *Uncle Vania* (*Diadia Vania*, 1899) as examples (cf. Lindheim 1985: 59f.).

pointed out that "[l]anguage competes with history as the core theme of the trilogy" (Nadel 2004a: 515) and I have already discussed the use of language in the context of realism in the trilogy. Moreover, the Chekhovian "inability of people to talk to one another in the same language" – as well as in different ones – is amply demonstrated in the first scene of *Voyage*. Hunter has identified linguistic misunderstandings as Stoppard's typical way of opening a play (cf. Hunter 2005: 32). *Voyage*, too, begins in *medias res* and with the topic of language: "Speaking of which" (*Voyage* 3), and the table talk quickly becomes a pandemonium of misunderstandings – for the participants as well as for the audience. This is due to the simultaneity of some conversations and to the mixture of languages. Alexander proudly announces that his liberalism does not just mean "piano lessons and Russian grammar *pour les filles*", but also educating his daughters in different languages, contrasting Russian/English here with French. Present at the table, besides the Bakunin family, are also the English governess Miss Chamberlain, who cannot follow the Russian conversation, because she only speaks English, and Varvara, Alexander's wife, who does not understand the governess as Varvara does not speak 'English'. When Miss Chamberlain asks what Alexander has just said, it is Varvara's turn to ask her daughters – partly in Russian/English and partly in French – what the governess has said: "I mean Miss Chamberlain, *qu'est-ce qu'elle a dit*? [*What did she say?*]" When Varenka answers her in French as well, Varvara replies in Russian/English, commenting on the impossibility of teaching her daughters without being able to speak their language: "How can you teach them anything if you can't talk to them?" By doing so, she unwittingly resolves another misunderstanding between Alexander and the Baron about "the philosophy of *worms*", her husband taking his wife's remark as an affirmation of his statement that "[w]orms have no philosophy". Again, Miss Chamberlain asks the daughters what their mother has said and they lie to her about tomorrow's lessons in 'English'. In his paternal fashion, Alexander ends this parody of the Chekhovian lack of communication by stating in Russian/English: "That's enough English for now" (all quotations 5). Ironically, the play of course continues in this very language, i.e. in Russian/English.

The Coast of Utopia: The 'Causal-Realistic' Presentation of Biography

On the one hand, Stoppard, who also involves the audience in this communicational pandemonium by only giving translations in the printed version of the play, makes use of Chekhov's leitmotif of lack of, or unsuccessful, communication. The opening scene at the dining table is a metaphor for the misunderstandings to come between the older generation and the new radical one, and the dichotomy between illusion and truth, again pointedly put by Alexander, who criticises his son's philosophical viewpoints:

> I myself am a Doctor of Philosophy. My dissertation was on worms. We did not chatter about some inner life. Philosophy does not consist in spinning words like tops till the colours run together and one will do as well as another. Philosophy consists in moderating each life so that many lives will fit together with as much liberty and justice as will keep them together – and not so much as will make them fly apart, when the harm will be the greater. I am not a despot. For Michael to have fallen in with my wishes would have been praiseworthy and, yes, philosophically fitting; for me to fall in with his would be absurd and despicable. (24)

On the other hand, Stoppard deconstructs Chekhov's major theme of "lack of communication" by literally going over the top and by parodying Chekhovian drama. There is the misunderstanding between Baron Renne and Alexander, the non-understanding between Varvara and Miss Chamberlain, the historically founded mixture of Russian, English and French, as well as the dramatic mixture of Russian/English as means of communication between the "Russian" characters and the English-speaking audience, and 'English' and French as means of communication between the "Russian" and non-Russian characters. Later on, Belinsky also comments on the arbitrariness of language when he complains about the non-reality of idealist phrases:

> **Belinsky** (*recovered*) Don't you bother with reading, Katya, words just lead you on. They arrange themselves every which way with no *can* to *carry* for their promises they *can't keep*, and off you go! (92, emphasis added)

The irony is obvious. Belinsky wants to convince Katya that words carry no truth as they can be arranged in every which way, in this case to the stylistic effect of an alliteration. This he does by using words which, according to Belinsky's argument, "lead you on", i.e. they do not carry truth, either. Hence, in *Voyage*, Stoppard deconstructs the historical "truth" presented on stage by questioning the utility of language as a means for presenting history and the life of the subjects in biography. The depiction of any historical reality must already fail at utilising language for this purpose, as it does not lead to a single understanding of the subject, but to multifarious meanings and misunderstandings.

A similar mixture of conversations and languages is evident from *Shipwreck*, I.iv. Kolya, Herzen's deaf son, his name itself ('call ya') onomatopoeic with regard to language, is present at the opening of the scene, his brother Sasha *"'speaking' face to face with Kolya, saying 'Kolya, Kol-ya' with extra enunciation. Kolya has a spinning top"* (*Shipwreck* 26). In *Voyage*, Alexander Bakunin describes his son's philosophising as "spinning words like tops till the colours run together" (*Voyage* 24), and it is the spinning top which is taken up in *Shipwreck*, literally as well as metaphorically. During this scene, *"there are separate conversations going on. They take turns to occupy the vocal foreground, but they are all continuous"* (*Shipwreck* 27). When Kolya goes offstage, he leaves his top behind and Bakunin enters announcing "The Russians are here!" (29). Like a top spinning faster and faster, in a crescendo of a simultaneity of topics of conversations and spoken languages, the scene unfolds until the social gathering ends in a hubbub of English, German and French (cf. 38f.). When Kolya re-enters *"in search of his top"*, *"[a]ll the conversations cut off into silence simultaneously, but 'continue'"* (39). With the appearance of the little boy, the goings-on on stage continue in silence, i.e. they lose their textual meaning as Kolya is deaf. He is only disturbed by thunder, which already startled him in I.i (cf. 22): *"There is distant thunder, which Kolya doesn't hear. Then there is a roll of thunder nearer. Kolya looks around, aware of something"* (39). The sound turns to the sound of rifle fire, symbolising the fall of the monarchy of Louis Philippe (cf. 40). Stoppard here alludes to the contrast between historical progress and the individual in history. Kolya becomes the child whose life and death matters more to Belinsky than historical necessity. He is unaware of the distant thunder, i.e. the distant goals of historical progress, but he is affected by the nearby sound, i.e. the direct consequences of the fall of the monarchy and the establishment of the Second Republic, which also ends in bloodshed and rifle fire. Words and languages become replaceable in this context, means of representing abstract constructs such as politics, revolution and love, used up to a state of insubstantiality. When in I.vi Kolya leaves behind his top again, this time it is Sazonov who speaks to Herzen on behalf of historical necessity: "*history is being made*! [...] You can laugh... but the stage is now bigger than your little articles for the *Contemporary*" (46, dialogue omitted). Again, the words swirl as Sazonov wants to convince Herzen that their time has come in a Russia which does not want to be left behind by a progressive Europe. However, the people turn against the Second Republic and it comes to bloodshed. The political situation calms down in I.ix, and it is Kolya with his top who is once again sitting onstage at the opening of the scene, while Herzen and Turgenev discuss the outcome of the revolution. Accordingly, Turgenev understands life as being similar to the figure of a spinning top, seeing "that almost nothing in this life holds still, everything is moving and changing" (56). Act I concludes with a reprise, the resumption of I.iv which Turgenev metadramatically comments on: "You're going round again, Captain" (58). However, Kolya stays on stage, the deaf boy speaking his first words and playing with his top. This time, no historical noise drowns his words, and no historical events cut him short.

Kolya becomes the centre of another linguistic mix-up in the second act. By now the Herzens have settled in Nice where Kolya speaks his first full sentences, although confusing Russian with German and 'English':

> **Herzen** *Was moechtest du denn?* [*What do you want, darling?*]
> *Kolya looks back to Mother for assurance. She smiles him on.*
> **Kolya** *Ich spreche Russisch!* [*I speak Russian!*] (*in 'English'*) 'Sunny day! My name is Kolya!'
> **Herzen** *Wunderbar!* [*Wonderful!*]
> *Great delight, made physical, on all sides.*
> *Jetzt sprichst du Russisch!* [*Now you speak Russian!*]
> **Kolya** *Ich spreche Russisch!* [*I speak Russian!*] (81f.)

Where Herzen and Kolya say they are speaking Russian, they are actually speaking German or 'English', the whole business taken to the extreme by the translations given in English in the text. With all the travelling around Europe and the constant change of languages, it seems impossible to keep track of the language one is speaking, especially when one is deaf. The use of German and 'English' instead of Russian represents a loss of Russian identity in a Europe which is convinced that "the Russian people are not human, because they are devoid of moral sense" (83). Herzen here quotes from a paper written by Jules Michelet, "a distinguished historian famous for his humanitarian views, writing for intelligent Frenchmen". And it is because of him that he shouts: "It's about time to acquaint Europe with Russia, don't you think?" (84).[175] Language thus becomes a means of identity formation, which after the failure of the European revolutions seems more important than ever for Herzen. That is why Herzen previously wanted to consult the best doctors so that Kolya would learn how to speak, and why for him the worst thing about his son's death is that it happened at night, because Kolya "couldn't hear in the dark. He couldn't see your lips" (100). This is also why, after 1848, Herzen turns his back on Europe: "After the farce of 1848, I was in despair. My life meant nothing. Russia saved me…" (103).

The quest for the Russian soul begins in the first act of *Shipwreck*, where Herzen ironically describes his fragmented national identity: "Being half-Russian and half-German, at heart I'm Polish, of course… I often feel quite partitioned, sometimes I wake up screaming in the night that the Emperor of Austria is claiming the rest of me" (12). Herzen travels to Paris because a "country like this [Russia] will never see the light if we turn our backs to it, and the light is over there. (*He points.*) West. (*He points the other way.*) There is none there" (15). Herzen distances himself from the Slavophiles like Aksakov, who have a starry-eyed vision of a Russia isolated from the West. For Beye, this distancing constitutes a *cæsura* in the trilogy:

> Aksakov's arrival and dismissal by the others is therefore a moment of renunciation for the drama, and indeed the rest of the play's action takes place in Europe, strictly speaking, because Herzen finally receives permission to leave Russia and later on disobeys an imperial command to return. (Beye 2002)

Herzen leaves his mother country, never to return again; and when the European model proves a reactionary failure, he orientates himself again towards Russia and a Russian national identity, this time, however, from

---

[175] The historical Herzen answered Michelet in an open letter titled *The Russian People and Socialism* (*Du Developpement des Idées Revolutionnaires en Russie*, 1851; cf. Herzen 1982: 651-655).

West Europe. This Russian identity turns out to be different from the Slavophiles', as it is constituted in opposition to his locations of exile.

In *Shipwreck*, abstract language is shown to be an empty shell without any meaning for the individual. In the metaphor of a spinning top as the toy of a deaf child, Stoppard shows that words can be "swirled" and twisted to such an extent that they lose their actual relevance to the subject. Instead, they only tend to describe distant, unreachable goals as *ersatz* concepts, which are actually empty of meaning. But on the other hand, language also has the function of bestowing a national identity on the individual; and the loss of one's mother tongue entails the loss of this identity. Thus, in *Shipwreck*, Stoppard presents an ambiguity of language: on the one hand its postmodern arbitrariness, on the other its vital function in the formation of identity.

The idea of language as a constituting factor of national identity becomes the major linguistic theme in *Salvage*. When Malwida von Meysenbug arrives and enquires whether she is to teach in French or in German, Herzen answers: "Undoubtedly! – We speak Russian *en famille*" (*Salvage* 10). He means to tell Malwida that she will be teaching in French as well as in German while the family itself communicates in Russian, his answer echoing Alexander Bakunin's remark about "Russian grammar *pour les filles* Bakunin" (*Voyage* 3). Malwida and Herzen are probably meant to converse in German or French here, since Malwida does not speak Russian, and it cannot be 'English' because of the missing quotation marks in the text. To settle their deal about Malwida's tutorship, however, they "shake hands on it like Englishmen", Herzen commenting that "[a]t home we used to call Englishmen 'Eyseyki' – 'I say-ki!'" (*Salvage* 11). It is one of many remarks about English culture from the perspective of the political émigrés in London, because "[t]he only thing that unites the émigrés is criticising the English" (13). Ledru-Rollin complains about English restaurants, Blanc about the country's disorder, calling England "one enormous shroobbery", i.e. shrubbery, and Herzen summarises why, for all their discontent with England, the émigrés still come there:

> The English take us up with cries of interest and delight as if they've discovered a new amusement, like an acrobat or a singer, but it's a noise, an energy, to cover their instinctive aversion to foreigners. We're amusing when we wear a hat we

brought from home, and even funnier when we put on a hat we bought in St James's. There's no way round it. But their coarseness is the sinew of some kind of brute confidence which is the reason England is home to every shade of political exile. They don't give us asylum out of respect for the asylum-seekers but out of respect for themselves. They invented personal liberty, and they know it, and they did it without having any theories about it. They value liberty because it's liberty. (14)

It becomes clear why Herzen has found a new home in England. It is here he sees personal liberty realised to its fullest extent. Herzen also fashions a Russian identity by emphasising the differences between English and foreign national identities, and he wishes his children would take after him. It is in England that he finally manages to have his book *From the Other Shore* published in Russian, and he would like to pass on his revolutionary legacy to his eldest:

> Sasha… this is a book I wrote in the year of revolution, six years ago now. It was only ever published in German. But here it is at last in Russian as I wrote it. […] Don't look for solutions in this book. There are none. Anything which is solved is over and done with. The coming revolution is the only religion I pass on to you, and it's a religion without a paradise on the other shore. But do not remain on this shore. Better to perish. Go in your time, preach the revolution at home to our own people. There they once loved my voice, and will perhaps remember me. (34)

Stoppard here quotes bits from the actual introduction of the historical Herzen's book, which is dedicated to his son (cf. Herzen 1969: 41f.). Herzen wishes his children to follow in his footsteps, to follow his political thought and return to Russia one day. However, as Herzen and his generation did before, his children orientate themselves towards western culture. Sasha addresses his father in German and finds it difficult to read what Herzen wrote in the first edition of the "Free Russian and Polish Press in London" (cf. *Salvage* 20f.). Tata is curious about Malwida's national classification, because she, too, is an émigré from Germany and asks her in an English lesson whether she thinks Germany or England greater. Malwida answers that "at Lord Wellington's funeral they played Beethoven's 'Funeral March'. I think that's all that needs to be said" (23). Conversely, Malwida would "like to learn Russian" (10) and shows first signs of having done so when she has moved into the Herzen's house (cf. 25f.). To make her feel more comfortable, Herzen confesses that on his mother's side he is half-German: "Luckily, the bottom half". Malwida counters that she herself is "half-French", which Herzen comments on that "I might have guessed" (25), referring to her enlightened pedagogical principles. When Herzen tells Tata and Sasha that it is "good to be talking Russian together", and when he recalls Natalie teaching Kolya Russian words, Tata closes the book on her Russian past: "They're both dead, and that's all. Well, they are. We can't help it. (*She frees herself without a fuss and goes away.*)" (35). The children are constantly distancing themselves from their father's Russian heritage and feel much more at home in Europe. The cultural divide becomes wider when Ogarev and Natalie arrive, indicated by the language spoken: "*Offstage, the language is Russian and on re-entry remains theoretically in Russian*" (44). When Malwida greets Natalie in Russian/English, Natalie responds in French and then continues in Russian/English. However, Malwida cannot follow, and Herzen asks his friends to speak French, which Malwida rejects out of politeness (cf. 44). Herzen is so overwhelmed with nostalgia that for a moment he converses in Russian with the parlourmaid, who does not understand him (cf. 46). Ogarev, out of distaste, rejects Brown Windsor soup (cf. 48), and Natalie undermines Malwida's pedagogic principles to such an extent that she leaves the household (cf. 48 and 51f.). But Herzen's daughters also leave his house. Tata first goes to Germany and later with Olga to Italy, to live with Malwida. Herzen is aware that he is losing them, because he asks them not to forget their Russian (cf. 80 and 103). For Herzen, the language his children speak is an important factor with regard to their national identity; they, however, are drawn towards Europe instead and become alienated from Russia. Sasha marries an Italian proletarian woman, and when Olga arrives back from Italy with Malwida, she has forgotten her Russian: "Malwida and I are fluent Italians now!" (115). Only Liza, Herzen's youngest daughter, speaks to him in Russian. She represents Herzen's hope in the generations to come, personally as well as politically: "The idea will not perish. The young people will come of age" (118). And *Salvage* ends on an optimistic note, Liza saying to Herzen in Russian: "*Da!* [*Yes!*]" (119) followed by summer lightning and thunder.

In search of the "Russian soul" (14), Herzen defines his cultural identity by contrasting his otherness with English culture, which he reduces at the end to "Colman's mustard" (106). By speaking Russian, he differentiates his national identity from a Europe which let him down politically; by not speaking Russian, his children detach themselves from their father's national identity, which is not their own, since they all grew up in Europe. Thus, for Stoppard, the Russian language becomes of importance to his central characters in the way described by the historical Turgenev:

> [G]uard our Russian tongue, our beautiful Russian tongue, that treasure, that trust handed down to you by your predecessors, headed again by Pushkin! Treat this powerful instrument with respect; it may work miracles in the hands of those who know how to use it! (Turgenev 2001: 204)

In *Salvage*, it is especially the formation and definition of one's national identity for which language is one of the major factors. The process of constituting this identity, however, can only be achieved through delimitation against an other. Stoppard shows that language can only become a constituting factor for identity when the conscious choice of one language goes hand in hand with the rejection of other possible languages. Only then is a national identity truly constituted by language.

h.   *Salvage* and *Shipwreck:* Intertextuality and intermediality as metafictional and metabiographical means – *Fathers and Sons* and *Le Déjeuner sur l'herbe*

It has been argued before that, from a macroscopic perspective, the intertextual allusion to Turgenev's *Fathers and Sons* in *Salvage* does not necessarily disturb the presented historical unity of the trilogy. The allusion to the novel highlights the divide between the superfluous men and the nihilists and is presented as biographically valid. However, the intertextual allusion also functions as a metafictional and metabiographical means on the microscopic level. It questions the biographical validity because the conversation between Turgenev and the Doctor borrows form, content and even characters from *Fathers and Sons*. When Turgenev strikes up a conversation with the Doctor on a bench in Ventnor, the Doctor makes it clear that he only reads "books of practical utility" and criticises Turgenev's reading matter: "Pushkin! Not a damn bit of use to anyone! Give it up. You're past the age for this nonsense. A good plumber is worth twenty poets". As a useful book he names "Mackenzie's *No More Haemorrhoids*" (*Salvage* 85). The Doctor believes in nothing but practical utility. He does not believe in principles, progress or art, because he rejects abstractions. Turgenev calls him "the nihilist [...] a dark towering figure, strong, with no subtlety or mutability in him, with no history, as though he'd grown from the earth, his ill-intention complete [...,] the future arrived before his time, [...] doomed" (87). While Turgenev also believes in practical utility, his is of another kind: "I found that reading Dr Mackenzie made me very aware of mine [his Haemorrhoids] ...whereas, reading Pushkin, I quite forgot them. Practical utility. I believe in it" (86). He agrees with the Doctor about practical utility, but his is transported through art, which the Doctor does not recognise.

Just as the Doctor reproaches Turgenev for reading Pushkin in Stoppard's play, Bazarov in *Fathers and Sons* tells his protégé Arkady that he saw his father reading Pushkin, that he thinks him too old for this nonsense and that he ought rather to read Büchner's *Stoff und Kraft* (cf. Turgenev 1998: 54). Bazarov also mentions that a "good chemist's twenty times more useful than a poet" and he only recognises the "art of making money, or no more haemorrhoids!" (31).[176] With regard to the intertextual congruency between *Fathers and Sons* and the conversation in *Salvage*, Stoppard's Turgenev resembles Pavel Petrovich, Arkady's dandy uncle, who constantly cross-examines Bazarov throughout the novel and dislikes his nihilist attitude: "Previously there used to be Hegelians, now there are nihilists. Let's wait and see how you get on in a vacuum, in airless space" (27). While Petrovich opposes Bazarov to such an extent that he challenges him to a duel, Turgenev in *The Coast of Utopia* detaches himself from all sides, without, however, abandoning the perspective of the dandy artist. As much as he agrees with other standpoints, he does not take to Hegelianism or nihilism as this, similar-

---

[176] In his explanatory notes, Richard Freeborn links Bazarov's remark to "*No More Haemorrhoids* by a Dr Mackenzie, translated from the German (St Petersburg, 1846)" (Turgenev 1998: 256*n*31).

ly to Herzen and Belinsky, would leave man in airless space, without a personal history.

The intertextual allusion to *Fathers and Sons* presents the biographical reconstruction with the help of the biographee's art in an artificial way. It echoes Wilde's *bon mot* that life imitates art far more than art imitates life – or here rather that life-writing imitates art far more than art imitates life-writing. Accordingly, "The Decay of Lying" draws on the Nihilist as an example of life imitating art: "The Nihilist, that strange martyr who has no faith, who goes to the stake without enthusiasm, and dies for what he does not believe in, is a purely literary product. He was invented by Tourguenieff, and completed by Dostoevski" (Wilde 1976: 983). In the case of *Salvage*, then, a life episode is reconstructed in *verbatim* accordance with a novel, i.e. fiction. This conscious rendering of fiction exposes the narrative principles of biography. The metafictional reference to literature and especially *Fathers and Sons* in and through the conversation also emphasises the position of biography between fact and fiction. Thus, with the conversation between Turgenev and his most famous fictional character Bazarov, Stoppard reflects on the practical utility of art in general and the conflicting composition of biography through scientific facts and fictional means in particular.

Similarly to *Fathers and Sons*, Manet's *Le Déjeuner sur l'herbe* receives a different meaning on the microscopic level. When we consider the hypomedium more closely, we find in Manet's painting an ambiguity which we can also discover in Stoppard's trilogy and which thus works as a metafictional means in his drama.

Despite its many possible interpretations, *Le Déjeuner sur l'herbe* is usually considered a realist painting, realism here meaning the convention-free, detailed imitation of the physical world. The resemblance/imitation theory of realism has it that "a picture is realistic to the extent that it closely resembles the model depicted" (Stalnaker 1999: 246). However, this becomes problematic when considering certain aspects of *Le Déjeuner sur l'herbe*. Firstly, it is in itself an intramedial allusion to various paintings, particularly to *The Judgement of Paris* (*c*1488-1530), a Marcantonio Raimondi etching after Raphael.¹⁷⁷ Especially the pose of the undressed woman in the foreground connects the picture "to an authentic tradition that traces back to classical sources – and exposes the false classicism of the nudes of Manet's day" (259). Secondly, perspective and colouring do not comply with the rules of realism, as can be seen on page 324. For example, the woman bathing in the brook in the background is of the size of a giant compared to the boat on her right and the trees, and the overall colouring consists of contrasting colours and not of harmonising halftones. Perspective and colouring cause a sense of isolation. The seated group and the stooping woman are isolated from the landscape and the still life, making for an arrangement of the figures without coherence (cf. Körner 1996: 70).

Manet breaks the rules of realism for a reason. He violates the rules of perspective to show the recipients that they are looking at a mere picture, an "artificial" depiction, and that studio perspective actually undermines realism rather than creating it, because "the rules of perspective have the power to create a realism that is mere style, which can be added, in a mechanical way, to any substance, imaginary or real" (Stalnaker 1999: 256). The violation of the rules of perspective at the same time increases the response to the colour and surface texture of the painting and, thus, again to its artificiality. All this considered, Manet's realism – which Stalnaker calls "causal realism" – makes for a different way of looking at the picture:

> On this view, what I experience in the painting is not the actual object but the painter's act of representing the object in paint, which conjures up the presence of the object enhanced by the formal metaphor. The result is not an illusion, but an experience of the depicted object made vivid and concrete by the awareness of the painted surface.¹⁷⁸ It is this duality – of an image of the world experienced

---

¹⁷⁷ On the various other hypomedia of *Le Déjeuner sur l'herbe*, cf. Tucker 1998: 12ff.

¹⁷⁸ Elizabeth Prettejohn makes the same observation for Pre-Raphaelite art, which features prominently in *Indian Ink* (cf. VII.4): "the human figures in the pictures convey the same sense that a model must have 'been there', before the artist's eyes. The viewer does not need to know that F.G. Stephens sat for the figure of Ferdinand, in Millais's picture of *Ferdinand Lured by Ariel* […], to experience a strong sense that the figure is modelled on a specific individual" (Prettejohn 2000: 189).

> within the experience of the strokes of paint on the surface – that Impressionists like Monet so dramatically exploit, following Manet's lead. Mallarmé, serving as Manet's spokesman, explains that in one's awareness of what is pictured, the recognition of the painting remains: 'the spectator ... whilst recognizing that he is before a painting half believes he sees the mirage of some natural scene.' So just as the artist is causally acted on by the physical presence of the model as he paints, the viewer is acted on by the presence of the painting as a physical object that conveys the artist's encounter. (Stalnaker 1999: 252f.)

But why does Stoppard refer to *Le Déjeuner sur l'herbe* in *Shipwreck*? The audience is aware that they are witnessing a stage enactment of Manet's painting, *"a tableau which anticipates – by fourteen years – the painting by Manet"* (*Shipwreck* 73). Stoppard thus breaks up the unity of time by presenting Manet *before* Manet *after* Manet, i.e. *Le Déjeuner sur l'herbe* is integrated into the plot *before* the time of its drawing while *Shipwreck* was of course written *after* its creation. The intermedial allusion to Manet's painting makes the recipients aware of the dramatic construction of the historical plot, which does not need to succumb to the laws of chronicity. And the allusion goes even deeper, taking into account the peculiarities of Manet's painting and his causal realism, when the stage directions continue:

> *The broader composition includes Turgenev, who is at first glance sketching Natalie but in fact sketching Emma. The tableau, however, is an overlapping of two locations, Natalie and George being in one, while Herzen, Emma and Turgenev are together elsewhere.* (74)

Stoppard does justice to the incoherent arrangement of the figures in Manet's painting. While in Manet's *Le Déjeuner sur l'herbe*, the figures are isolated from the scenery and the still life, in Stoppard's *Le Déjeuner sur l'herbe* Natalie and George are isolated from the rest of the group. Like Manet, Stoppard breaks the laws of realism by violating perspective, i.e. by presenting two different locations in one and the same place. He even goes a step further by integrating the alleged artist of the composition. It is Turgenev who takes the role of the painter and who debunks, literally, the artificiality of his painting.

To gain insight into the significance of this intermedial allusion in the context of *The Coast of Utopia*, we need to transfer Manet's causal realism to Stoppard's trilogy by modifying Stalnaker's conclusions.

Then, what the recipients experience in the trilogy is not an authentic biographical depiction but the dramatist's act of representing the biographees on stage, which conjures up the presence of the subjects enhanced by the formal dramatisation. The result is not an illusion, but an experience of the depicted subjects made vivid and concrete by the awareness of the staging. The main duality in the trilogy is the revisioning of historical personalities experienced within the experience of the dramatisation of the lives of the biographical subjects on stage. While the recipients are constantly made aware, through intermedial and intertextual allusions – through language and the apposition of ideas and arguments – that they are watching an innovative biography play, i.e. a fictional representation of the lives of historical personalities, the historical illusion is not permanently destroyed. It is rather partly upheld – through costume, language and the smooth integration of intermedial and intertextual elements – as in traditional biographical drama. Just as Stoppard is causally acted on by engaging with his subject matter through research and reflecting on the sources as he writes, the recipients are acted on by the performance and the text as the representation of biographical subjects that convey the artist's encounter.

3. The dialectics of *The Coast of Utopia*

It has been shown in detail that, on a macroscopic level, *The Coast of Utopia* follows the Aristotelian plot with introduction, climax and catastrophe. The three plays *Voyage*, *Shipwreck* and *Salvage* comply to this arrangement, i.e. *Voyage* becomes the introduction, *Shipwreck* the climax and *Salvage* the catastrophe of the trilogy. We have also seen that the structure of *Voyage* is dialectical, with the antitheses of idealism/illusion and realism/truth being presented. If we now consider Hegel's drama theory more closely, we will realise that the titles of the individual plays are also fashioned dialectically. In his *Aesthetics: Lectures on Fine Art* (*Vorlesungen über die Ästhetik*, 1835), Hegel says:

> Because drama has been developed into the most perfect totality of content and form, it must be regarded as the highest stage of poetry and of art generally. For in contrast to the other perceptible materials, stone, wood, colour, and notes,

speech is alone the element worthy of the expression of spirit; and of the particular kinds of the art of speech dramatic poetry is the one which unites the objectivity of epic with the subjective character of lyric. It displays a complete action as actually taking place before our eyes; the action originates in the minds of the characters who bring it about, but at the same time its outcome is decided by the really substantive nature of the aims, individuals, and collisions involved.[179]

(Hegel 1998: 1158)

Drama is the synthesis of the stylistic antithesis of the epic and the lyric poetic, the sublation of the spiritual powers and individual characters into an art form:

> For in a mythological epic the spiritual powers are simply different, and their significance becomes vaguer owing to the many ways in which they are individualized in fact; but in a drama they enter in their simple and fundamental character and they *oppose* one another as 'pathos' in individuals. And the drama is the dissolution of the one-sidedness of these powers which are making themselves independent in the dramatic characters, whether, as in tragedy, their attitude to one another is hostile, or whether, as in comedy, they are revealed directly as inwardly self-dissolving.[180] (1163)

This dialectic is, according to Hegel, also immanent in dramatic action, which needs to progress teleologically to resolve its conflict:

---

[179] "Das Drama muß, weil es seinem Inhalte wie seiner Form nach sich zur vollendetesten Totalität ausbildet, als die höchste Stufe der Poesie und der Kunst überhaupt angesehen werden. Denn den sonstigen sinnlichen Stoffen, dem Stein, Holz, der Farbe, dem Ton gegenüber, ist die Rede allein das der Exposition des Geistes würdige Element und unter den besonderen Gattungen der redenden Kunst wiederum die dramatische Poesie diejenige, welche die Objektivität des Epos mit dem subjektiven Prinzip der Lyrik in sich vereinigt, indem sie eine in sich abgeschlossene Handlung als wirkliche, ebensosehr aus dem Inneren des sich durchführenden Charakters entspringende als in ihrem Resultat aus der substantiellen Natur der Zwecke, Individuen und Kollisionen entschiedene Handlung in unmittelbarer Gegenwärtigkeit darstellt" (Hegel 1970e: 474).

[180] "Denn die in dem mythologischen Epos nur verschiedenen und durch die vielseitige *reale* Individualisierung in ihrer *Bedeutung* unbestimmter werdenden geistigen Mächte treten im Dramatischen ihrem einfachen substantiellen Inhalte nach als Pathos von Individuen *gegeneinander* auf, und das Drama ist die Auflösung der Einseitigkeit dieser Mächte, welche in den Individuen sich verselbständigen; sei es nun, daß sie sich, wie in der Tragödie, feindselig gegenüberstehen oder, wie in der Komödie, sich als sich an ihnen selbst unmittelbar auflösend zeigen" (Hegel 1970e: 481).

The Coast of Utopia: The 'Causal-Realistic' Presentation of Biography

> The dramatic action therefore rests essentially on an action producing collisions, and the true unity can only be grounded in the total movement, i.e., given the determinate nature of the particular circumstances, the characters, and their ends, the collision is displayed as conforming with the characters and their ends, and finally their contradiction is annulled and unity is restored.[181] (1166)

As in Hegel's Absolute Idealism and his concept of world history, drama progresses teleologically through an antithetical conflict, the *collision*: "The progress of drama is strictly a steady movement forward to the final catastrophe. This is clear from the simple fact that *collision* is the prominent point on which the whole turns" (1168).[182]

What does this imply for Stoppard's trilogy? When, on the macroscopic level, *The Coast of Utopia* follows the presentation of the Aristotelian plot with a conflict at its centre which has to be resolved, it also means that it progresses in a dialectical manner. Thus, *Voyage* becomes the thesis, *Shipwreck* the antithesis and *Salvage* the synthesis. This also becomes clear when we consider the threefold meaning of the Hegelian synthesis in which thesis and antithesis are not restricted but sublated (*aufgehoben*), i.e. 1) annulled; 2) preserved in a higher unity; and 3) lifted onto a higher level, in which both cease to appear as excluding opposites (cf. Störig 1999: 521). If we apply this threefold definition of Hegelian dialectics to the trilogy's individual titles, sublation in *The Coast of Utopia* implies firstly that the voyage of the protagonists towards a distant shore and the shipwreck they suffer during the progress of the journey annul their endeavour. However, in a second meaning, the voyage as well as the shipwreck are preserved in a higher unity, the salvage of the ship and its (intellectual) cargo. And thirdly, voyage and shipwreck are, through this salvage, lifted onto a higher level, where they do not appear as excluding opposites, but as the trilogy itself. The

---

[181] "Die dramatische Handlung beruht deshalb wesentlich auf einem *kollidierenden* Handeln, und die wahrhafte Einheit kann nur in der totalen Bewegung ihren Grund haben, daß nach der Bestimmtheit der besonderen Umstände, Charaktere und Zwecke die Kollision sich ebensosehr den Zwecken und Charakteren gemäß herausstelle, als ihren Widerspruch aufhebe" (Hegel 1970e: 485).

[182] "Der eigentlich dramatische Verlauf ist die stete *Fortbewegung* zur Endkatastrophe. Dies erklärt sich einfach daraus, daß den hervorstechenden Angelpunkt die *Kollision* ausmacht" (Hegel 1970e: 488).

315

dialectical structure of *The Coast of Utopia* implies the dramatic progress from the self-contained plays towards the sequential trilogy, because causal-chronologically, a *Salvage* presupposes a *Shipwreck*, which requires a *Voyage*.

While Hegel's dialectic dominates the structure of the trilogy, a gigantic Ginger Cat becomes its hypostasis throughout the plays. Stoppard's Cat has many sources. It is for one an allusion to Mikhail Bulgakov's cat Behemoth in his *Master and Margarita* (*Master i Margarita*, 1966; cf. Duncan-Jones 2002: 27). Like Stoppard's cat, which Herzen remembers first to have encountered at a fancy-dress ball (cf. *Voyage* 104), where Belinsky also meets it again some years later, the (albeit black) cat Behemoth opens Woland's "Spring Ball of the Full Moon, or the Ball of a Hundred Kings" (Bulgakov 1996: 215 and cf. 224). It is also Behemoth who softly replies when confronted with the allegation that he is telling lies: "History will be the judge" (237). Ruth Rischin, on the other hand, finds Stoppard's sources in texts from E.T.A. Hoffmann's *Kater Murr* (*Lebensansichten des Katers Murr*, 1819/21) to T.S. Eliot's "Macavity: The Mystery Cat" from his *Old Possum's Book of Practical Cats* (1939; cf. Rischin 2003). It is especially the latter feline literary representation that Stoppard alludes to. In the stage directions, the Ginger Cat is described as a *"huge, upright disreputable cat"* concealing its identity (*Voyage* 106). Eliot's Macavity is also a "very tall and thin" ginger cat whose "footprints are not found in any file of Scotland Yard's". He is "a monster of depravity" and all the other cats "Are nothing more than agents for the Cat who all the time / Just controls their operations: the Napoleon of Crime!" (Eliot 1984: 37f.). Stoppard's Cat personifies the World-Spirit, and the other characters are merely its agents to carry out History's purpose; just like Napoleon, whom Hegel names (besides Alexander the Great and Julius Caesar) as an example of a World-Historical individual (cf. Hegel 1952: 167). The French emperor had made a great impression on the German philosopher when he saw him in Jena in 1806. To him, Napoleon was 'the World-Spirit on horseback': "I saw the Emperor – this world-soul – riding out of the city on reconnaissance. It is indeed a wonderful sensation to see such an individual, who, concentrated here at a single point, astride a horse, reaches out over the world and masters it" (Hegel 1984:

114).¹⁸³ Herzen also identifies his nihilistic main antagonist with such an agent when, after bloody riots due to the failed Emancipation in Russia, he says: "Chernyshevsky must be laughing into his whiskers" (*Salvage* 90). Stoppard's trilogy, thus, is dominated by Hegelian dialectic *structurally*, with the trilogy *The Coast of Utopia* progressing dialectically through the three sequential plays *Voyage*, *Shipwreck* and *Salvage*; and *thematically*: extrinsically, in the form of the Ginger Cat as the embodiment of the World-Spirit, as well as intrinsically, with its intertextual allusion to Eliot's Macavity as the Napoleon of Crime, i.e. to one of Hegel's World-Historical individuals.

4. Recapitulation: *History itself is the main character of the drama and also its author*

To embrace the full meaning of Stoppard's *The Coast of Utopia*, it must be regarded from two perspectives: the macro- and the micro-perspective. On the macroscopic level, with all three plays taken as a sequential unit, biography is presented in a conventional and realistic manner. Stoppard refers to, and quotes from, primary as well as secondary sources and thus explicitly positions his trilogy in the discourse on Russian history, giving a historical and scenic portrait of the lives and times of his protagonists. He only seems to stray from his sources for reasons of theatricality and thematic complexity. This faithful reproduction of the historical subject matter is substantiated through historical stage realism. Although *The Coast of Utopia* does not present the full life of its subjects but merely life episodes, it is arranged teleologically and chronologically in an Aristotelian manner, dating from Summer 1833 to August 1868. By and large, Stoppard follows the archetypical biographical plot by first depicting the adolescent years of his protagonists, followed by their development to mature personalities and their displacement by the next generation of nihilists. Different languages are pres-

---

¹⁸³ "[D]en Kaiser – diese Weltseele – sah ich durch die Stadt zum Rekognoszieren hinausreiten; – es ist in der Tat eine wunderbare Empfindung, ein solches Individuum zu sehen, das hier auf einen Punkt konzentriert, auf einem Pferde sitzend, über die Welt übergreift und sie beherrscht" (Hegel 1961: 120).

ented on stage to give an authentic picture of aristocratic Russian life and of a journey through mid-nineteenth century Europe. Stoppard utilises Chekhovian and Brechtian epic drama to mediate the recipients' transition into the historical world presented. Intertextual and intermedial allusions help to place the main characters in their cultural epoch and intellectual patterns of thought. The titles of the plays *Voyage*, *Shipwreck* and *Salvage* which make up the trilogy follow the dialectical pattern of thesis, antithesis and synthesis, emphasising the teleological progress of history. On the macroscopic level, the Hegelian World-Spirit, and thus, History, becomes the main character and the author of *The Coast of Utopia*.

On the microscopic level, i.e. seeing all three plays as self-contained, the picture is a different one. In *Voyage*, the Aristotelian cause-and-effect chain is reversed. The question of narrative and ideological structure is reflected upon thematically in the antithesis of idealism and realism, and structurally in the Chekhovian antithesis of illusion and truth. In *Shipwreck*, reprise and continuation arch back over the plot and give the play the form of a semi-swirl. *Salvage* again follows the conventions of Aristotelian tragedy and the conventional biography play. In their contrast, all three plays break up the trilogy's suprastructure innovatively and make for a different reading of history, which, however, in their sequence, lead to the conventional structure of the trilogy again. This is illustrated in figure 3 on page 327.

The Coast of Utopia apposes and opposes different historical concepts on the structural, thematic and character level, rather than accentuating one particular concept (such as circular time, as Barker and Campbell argue; cf. Barker 2005: *passim* and Campbell 2007: 212f.). On the structural level, the Aristotelian and dialectical macrostructure of the trilogy stands in contrast to the three individual microstructures of each play: "Hegel's theory of the dialectical movement of history (so influential to Marxist thought) is one of the dominant ideas of the trilogy, providing Stoppard with both an intellectual thesis to refute and a structural principle to guide the drama" (Mullin 2002: 4). The three plays lead from the reversal of Aristotelian causality in *Voyage* via the recurrent change in *Shipwreck* back to the Aristotelian plot of *Salvage*. Each play features a particular metaphor which allegorises each structure: in *Voy-*

age it is the farce of Belinsky's penknife, in *Shipwreck* it is Kolya's spinning top and the sound of distant thunder and in *Salvage* it is the loss and recovery of a glove. These objects, which are an integral part of each plot, connect the structural and the thematic levels.

The thematic level is also suffused with antagonisms such as idealism and realism. *Voyage* depicts the development from the Schellingian conviction that the material world is a mere illusion to Hegel's dictum that what is rational is real and what is real is rational. However, in the reversal of the cause-and-effect chain, Stoppard countermands German Idealism as well. He rather follows Kant's idea of the *a priori* category of causality, which does not affect the things-in-themselves but their appearances. The stage becomes the world of appearances, and the recipients constantly engage in constructing causal relationships between Act I and Act II and back to Act I. Through the simple reversal of cause and effect, the process of historical and biographical reconstruction is deconstructed, because the alleged logic of causality appears to the audience as an unconscious but merely subjective construct, which is proven either correct or false, depending on the recipients' conclusions. Although causal relations do exist between the two acts, the reversal leaves the recipients temporarily in uncertainty and debunks the alleged logic of historical causality as artificial.

The recurring generation conflict between Russian aristocrats like Alexander Bakunin and the superfluous men like Alexander Herzen, and the superfluous men and the nihilists like Nicholas Chernyshevsky, contradicts the teleology of the trilogy. As Barker observes, *Voyage* and *Salvage* both end with Alexander Bakunin and Alexander Herzen and their daughters Tatiana and Liza, respectively, answering 'yes', Tatiana even doing so thrice (cf. Barker 2005: 715). By the end of the trilogy, Herzen has taken Alexander Bakunin's position, namely "that of the eloquent but moribund *père de famille*, whose politics, philosophy, and passions belong to an earlier age and who watches the sun set over his world with his daughter beside him" (717). The dialectical progress of history turns into the cyclical repetition of history, although it appears that *Salvage* ends on a more positive note than *Voyage*, namely with summer lightning rather than with a sunset.

The apposition of historical concepts is continued through the protagonists. Although many different characters stand for different historical convictions throughout the trilogy, it is the four main characters who best represent the major concepts in *The Coast of Utopia*: Bakunin and his Left Hegelianism, Herzen and personal liberty and non-determinism, Belinsky's concept of art and recurrent change and Turgenev's ambiguity of history. Stoppard affords Herzen most room and sympathy to state his opinions. His idea of non-determinism and personal liberty, and his criticism of Hegelianism and Marxism, are what Stoppard already addressed in *Rosencrantz and Guildenstern are Dead*, *Arcadia* and *Travesties*. And it is Herzen who has the last lines in the trilogy, which are affirmed by his youngest daughter Liza. However, even this last affirmation of Herzen defending his convictions after personal and political blows leaves a bitter taste, if one keeps in mind that the historical Liza Herzen committed suicide, provoked by unrequited love (cf. Paperno 1997: 178).[184] Hence, the character who epitomises the trilogy in all its facets most is the character of Turgenev. That is why he is integrated by Herzen in his dream about Marx as his interlocutor. Turgenev's metacharacter expresses what the trilogy, in its complexity

---

[184] In 1876, Dostoevsky wrote about Liza Herzen's suicide in his column *The Diary of a Writer* (*Dnevnik pisatelja*, 1873-1881), published in the conservative journal *The Citizen* (*Grazhdanin*). In his reflection, called "Two Suicides" ("Dva samoubiistva", 1876), he quotes her suicide note which read: "'Je m'en vais entreprendre un long voyage. Si cela ne réussit pas qu'on se rassamble pour fêter ma réssurection avec du Cliqout. *Si cela réussit*, je prie qu'on ne me laisse enterrer que tout à fait morte, puisqu'il est très desegréable de se réveiller dans un cercueil sous terre. *Ce n'est pas chic!*' Which means: 'I am undertaking a long journey. If I should not succeed, let people gather to celebrate my resurrection with a bottle of Cliquot. *If I should succeed*, I ask that I be interred only after I am altogether dead, since it is very disagreeable to awake in a coffin in the earth. It is not *chic!*'" (Dostoevsky 1954: 469). This note is interesting in the context of Stoppard's trilogy, since it has the theme of the voyage, albeit to another shore, and as it is written in French, i.e. even the historical Liza, at the time of her death, did not obey her father's wish with respect to his Russian mother tongue as expressed in *Salvage*. Dostoevsky, accordingly, describes Liza to be "of Russian parents, but almost not a Russian at all by upbringing" (469). On this incident, cf. also "On Suicide and Haughtiness" (545-547); on the generation gap between the historical Herzen and his daughter Liza, cf. Paperno 1997: 179f.

of opposing and complementing the macro- and microscopic levels stands for, namely the ambiguity of history with an emphasis on the importance of the individual in history and life. As Stoppard himself wrote in the programme to the New York production of his trilogy:

> But it is Turgenev who brings us closest to the world of the nineteenth century Russian intelligentsia, and, moreover, his *A Sportsman's Sketches* was plausibly said to have done more than anything else to turn the "Reforming Tsar" Alexander II toward abolishing serfdom. Perhaps it is the artist, after all, rather than the three publicists of genius [Belinsky, Bakunin and Herzen], who is the true hero of *The Coast of Utopia*.[185] (Stoppard 2006a: 7)

In his 'group biography plays', Stoppard concentrates on the interwoven lives of his main characters and of the role of the individual in history. With the apposition of macro- and microstructure, the trilogy sublates the alleged distinction in history of the behaviour of men as individuals from their behaviour as members of groups. As in *The Invention of Love*, but on a larger scale, Stoppard apposes sociological and psychological factors in the depiction of his biographees. He confronts the individual lives of members of the Russian intelligentsia and their loves with historical forces, which appear beyond their control. The macrostructure of the trilogy emphasises historical social forces, and the characters appear to be at their mercy. However, at the same time, *The Coast of Utopia*, in order to function as a trilogy, must *per definitionem* consist of three individual plays. They in turn stress the individual and emphasise different characters, respectively: Bakunin becomes the centre in *Voyage*, Belinsky and Herzen in *Shipwreck*, and Herzen in *Salvage*. Personal concerns such as the love interests of the Bakunin sisters, Natalie Herzen's adultery or Herzen's affair with his best friend's wife come into focus and make the social concerns appear secondary. This appositional view of history is similar to the one represented by the historian

---

[185] By comparing Turgenev the artist with Belinsky, Bakunin and Herzen the publicists, Stoppard seems to finally have settled his inner conflict about the possible impotence of political art. He enunciated this argument for the first time during an interview in 1973 when he quoted W.H. Auden saying that "his poetry didn't save one Jew from the gas chamber" (Watts 1994: 50). He rephrased it a year later when he attributed a short-term importance to journalism and only a long-term importance to art (cf. Hudson/Itzin/Trussler 1974: 14).

Carr,[186] mentioned earlier as the author of two invaluable sources for *The Coast of Utopia*. He sees the distinction between the behaviour of men as individuals and men as members of a group as misleading and writes in the chapter "Society and the Individual" of his influential book *What is History?*:

> History, then, in both senses of the word – meaning both the enquiry conducted by the historian and the facts of the past into which he enquires – is a social process, in which individuals are engaged as social beings; and the imaginary antithesis between society and the individual is no more than a red herring drawn across our path to confuse our thinking. (Carr 1961: 49)

The Coast of Utopia, then, presents history as an apposition of the individual and of society, the one determined by the other and *vice versa*. Social progress and personal happiness become an interdependent unity that "makes" history and "writes" biography.

By apposing different characters, Stoppard contrasts different historical concepts and biographical arrangements: Left Hegelianism, non-determinism and personal liberty, recurrent change and the ambiguity of history. The topic of historical ambiguity is also taken up by language, which is shown, albeit through language, to be ambiguous, but at the same time necessary to the creation of and demarcation from national identities. Intertextual allusions to, for example, Chekhov, Turgenev, Eliot and Dostoevsky parade the artificiality and designed character of the biography play and of biography. The intermedial allusion to Manet explains Stoppard's macroscopic realism in terms of microscopic causal realism. The plays become the experience of the depicted subjects made vivid and concrete by the awareness of the staging, situating the trilogy between the realistic and innovative biography play, and between biographical fact and fiction. *The Coast of Utopia* reflects on the biographical genre. It broaches the issue of what we have referred to above as the aporia of biography, i.e. the necessity of life-writing to consist of scientific fact and artistic fiction, to situate itself between, in Woolf's terms, granite and rainbow. It uses and discloses grand narrative structures such as Hegelian dialectic and causal-chronological teleology. It incorporates language as a tool for representing history and a life while

---

[186] On Carr's view of history, cf. Peacock 1991: 9f. and Jenkins 1995: 43-63.

reflecting at the same time on its ambiguity and its importance for identity formation on the part of the biographer. It discloses the concept of causality while making it a part of its macrostructure. It makes the recipients become aware of an objective reality, the representation of which, however, is merely subjective. Stoppard succeeds in functionalising the biographical conflict between granite and rainbow by making us aware of the fictional artificiality and the factional elements which form the trilogy's basis. Historical and biographical facts become the things-in-themselves which exist but cannot be perceived. It is only their subjective appearance which is accessible to the author and biographer as well as to the recipient.

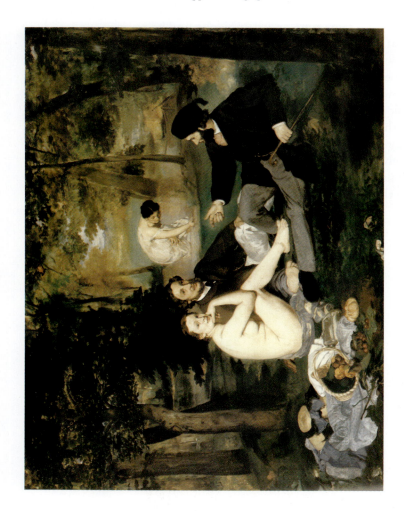

Edouard Manet, *Le Déjeuner sur l'herbe* (*Luncheon on the Grass*, 1863)

The Coast of Utopia: The 'Causal-Realistic' Presentation of Biography

Shipwreck, National Theatre London, July 2002 (photo by Ivan Kyncl/ArenaPAL)

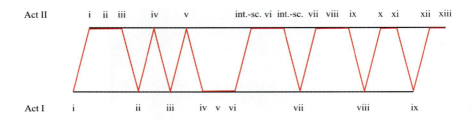

Figure 1:
Voyage: The reversal of the Aristotelian cause-and-effect chain

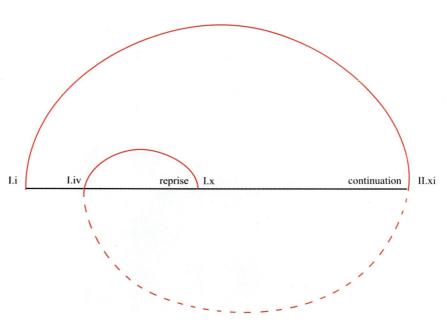

Figure 2:
Shipwreck: The swirl of history

The Coast of Utopia: The 'Causal-Realistic' Presentation of Biography

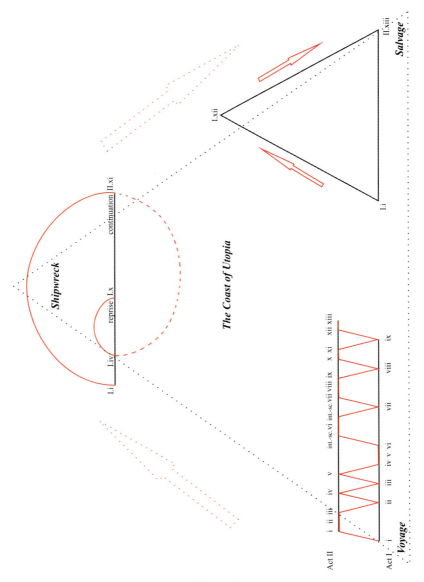

Figure 3:
Macro- and microscopic perspectives

X. Conclusion

Any study about a contemporary playwright who has inspired entire shelves full of secondary literature must justify its own contribution. Borrowing from Woolf's afore-mentioned remark on biography, a study on Stoppard might claim to enlarge the scope of his dramatic work "by hanging up looking glasses at odd corners" so that "from all this diversity it will bring out, not a riot of confusion, but a richer unity". The "odd corner" at which the study at hand aims to hang up its looking glass in the context of Stoppard's drama is biography, and I hope to have succeeded in bringing out a "richer unity" of his biography plays from *Rosencrantz and Guildenstern are Dead*, *Travesties*, *Arcadia*, *Indian Ink* and *The Invention of Love*, to *The Coast of Utopia*: *Voyage*, *Shipwreck* and *Salvage*.

The first biography play considered above is *Rosencrantz and Guildenstern are Dead*. As we have seen, it takes the mythopoeic quality of *Hamlet* and its myth as a reference matrix for the deconstruction of the audience's stereotypes about Shakespeare's play, its characters and tragedy in general. The protagonists Ros and Guil are taken from the margins of dramatic history, and with regard to the focus of characters in comparison to *Hamlet*, Stoppard exchanges periphery and centre. The hypotext functions as a basis for the dramatic communication between playwright, actors and recipients, and the references to *Hamlet* take on the function of a 'primary source', from which the biographer reconstructs the dark areas of his subjects Ros and Guil. Stoppard's biography play questions what for conventional biography are constituent factors of its subject, namely a unique character, a history and a *telos* in life. The central question in *Rosencrantz and Guildenstern are Dead* is whether life progresses through the individual's free will, whether it is determined by supernatural causes or by a succession of accidents. By depicting Ros and Guil as anti-heroes, Stoppard presents the end of a world view that saw history as a drama directed by great men, a view similar to Lord Malquist's in Stoppard's only novel *Lord Malquist and Mr Moon*.

The biographical quintessence of the play, however, is that the representation of a life with artistic devices such as in life-writing is dependent on authorial design and artistic conventions. As a postbiography play, *Rosencrantz and Guildenstern are Dead* emphasises the blurred transition from myth to biography. The play has as its centre two undefined or unfixed character identities, incorporates anachronisms with regard to Elizabethan drama, and puts dramatic before temporal and naturalistic logic. The play questions the status of objective truth, and hence, of biography as a truthful depiction of the life of a historical subject. Biography is exposed as a narration by a dominant author dependent on intertextual allusions, her or his *Weltanschauung* and artistic conventions.

While with Joyce, Lenin, Tzara and even the historical nonentity Carr the number of authentic historical figures in *Travesties* is diametrically opposed to that of *Rosencrantz and Guildenstern are Dead*, Stoppard adapts the latter's dramatic structure by parallelising the former's "historical" events with another dramatic fiction, namely *The Importance of Being Earnest*. Again, it shows that biography is saturated by fiction, and the play points out how close the ranks between literature and historiography are. Nonetheless, Stoppard advances his mode of biographical presentation by introducing a second time level, on which Old Carr depicts the events from his memory, thus making *Travesties* a *memory* or rather *memoir play* and a metabiographical drama. Thereby, it reflects upon subjectivity, incoherence and the construction processes of life-writing. Old Carr's self-stylisation caused by vested interest and the subjectively distorted perception of the past manifests itself in the stereotypes which influence his historical view and his depiction of the biographees. In a similar way to the effect Woolf describes in her essay "The New Biography", through his biographical account, the audience learns more about Old Carr's attitude towards the subjects of his reminiscences than about the historical personalities or events themselves. Stoppard's biographical drama becomes an arena of dispute for opposing views on history and art, but ultimately resists taking sides. As in *Rosencrantz and Guildenstern are Dead*, the inner plot of *Travesties* does not follow the conventional Aristotelian criteria of relevance of a conclusive story in which the ending refers to the beginning. This is only given in the external plots with regard to the hypotexts *Hamlet* and *The Importance of Being Earnest*: *Rosencrantz and Guildenstern are Dead* ends with the tableau of court and corpses of *Hamlet*, and *Travesties* travesties the denouement of Wilde's comedy.

In *Arcadia*, Stoppard continues his presentation of biography in so far as the only authentic historical figure, Lord Byron, is moved to the (stage) margins of the play. A dominant hypotextual allusion is this time exchanged for scientific and mathematical references. Modern mathematics and physics are employed to question requirements of conventional drama and biography such as causality, rationality and mimesis. *Arcadia* breaches neither historical authenticity nor scientific principles, while at the same time self-reflexively emphasising its own artificiality. Like *Travesties*, *Arcadia* incorporates two time levels and thus breaks up the unity of time but stays faithful to the unity of place. The Aristotelian idea of the logical progress of the action through cause and effect is questioned in the play by bifurcations and strange attractors. Both disturb the linear progress *and* lead to order at the same time. Therefore, it can be said that *Arcadia* still features a plot as regards the (futile) reconstruction attempts concerning Byron and the Sidley hermit in the present and the relationship between Thomasina and Septimus in the past. The 'Byrongraphic' intertext acts as metanarrative and metabiography. Byron, his biography and myth, reveal the principle of indeterminableness or the relativity of truth in life-writing. The metabiographical discourse questions objective historical authenticity and alleged facts in the same way as the metascientific discourse questions the notion of absolute truth and understanding of nature. Both levels of discourse exemplify the subjectivity of explanatory models and historical concepts. *Arcadia*, however, also emphasises the importance of the epistemological process and the conscious considerations of its bifurcations and indeterminacies.

In *Indian Ink*, as in *Arcadia*, all onstage characters are purely fictitious. It is a biography play which concentrates on individual life sketches of fictitious characters in a fictitious native state in India, contextualised by authentic historical figures and events. The play presents historical truth as relative and dependent on the cultural and personal standpoint. Like *Travesties* and *Arcadia*, it is a metabiographical play, as the plot incorporates two time levels and addresses the process of biographical reconstruction. It depicts its subjects as constructed and deconstructed through continual relations of participation and opposition. Stoppard does not present identity as a clear-cut, integral and unified whole, but as complex and in flux like the change of time and place in *Indian Ink*. In the play, the unities of time and place are dissolved, and through the fluent shuttling between time periods and geographical locations, the plot of the play does not obey the Aristotelian chronological, causal progression. However, it can still be said that *Indian Ink* features a plot as regards the (artistic) relationship between Flora and Das in the past and its reconstruction attempts by Pike and Dilip and Mrs Swan and Anish in the present. The play questions the relationship between art and life facts, which proves ambiguous. Art is shown to carry subjective truth which makes it manifold in its interpretation. Neither art nor life is to be interpreted via an either/or model, but only via a both/and paradigm. Through Pike's relentless biographical research, the deviating views on colonial history and the different interpretations of Das's paintings, *Indian Ink* continues the notion expressed in *Arcadia* about the relevance of the epistemological process. Contrary to *Arcadia*, however, *Indian Ink* itself becomes an ambiguous dramatic fiction that is both realistic and symbolic, giving no final answer to the question of a romance between Flora and Das.

The Invention of Love takes in the dichotomy of the classicist and romantic world views from *Arcadia*, which Stoppard this time obtains from his biographical subject. A.E. Housman's life is presented as a *dream-memory play*, which underlines the unreliability of his reminiscences. As Old Carr does in *Travesties* with fictional hypotexts such as *The Importance of Being Earnest*, AEH continuously refers to poetic expressions of desire coming from classical authors such as Sappho, Catullus, Horace and Vergil, which deconstruct biography's claim to objectivity. These references, however, at the same time depict AEH's inmost truth. The unities of plot, time and place are dissolved in the play. The repetition of certain scenes and dialogue, the surreal presentation of the plot and the dichotomous structure of the play negate an Aristotelian chronological, causal progression. It presents a curvilinear time in which past and present co-exist, refractorily mirroring each other, rendering *The Invention of Love* a metabiography play. This goes hand in hand with a fluent change of place between the River Styx/Isis/Thames, Oxford, Worcestershire, London and France. In the biographical presentation of his subject, Stoppard apposes socio- and psychobiographical factors, rejecting the myth of personal coherence. He questions the depiction of the subject as an integral whole according to an either/or model. By considering the difference between biographical fact and artistic truth, *The Invention of Love* is also a postbiography play. It visualises AEH's varying conceptions of himself by presenting the biographical subject as literally a divided self. The Wilde character takes on a metabiographical function and becomes, in Nietzschean terms, a work of art. With Wilde, Stoppard underlines that, while conventional biography may be a compilation of facts, it holds no deeper truth about its biographee. This, in turn, is only accomplished in and through art. By taking historical facts and subordinating them to his own art, Stoppard in *The Invention of Love* dramatically realises the notion of art addressed in *Indian Ink* and expressed by Wilde in his own play. At the same time, the character of AEH and his principle of knowledge-for-knowledge's sake continues Stoppard's emphasis of the epistemological process begun in *Arcadia*, although he acknowledges that the retrieval of an authentic original, be it in classical philology or in biography, is impossible.

The last play, or rather plays, that have been considered in the study at hand are *Voyage*, *Shipwreck* and *Salvage*, which constitute the trilogy *The Coast of Utopia*. On the macroscopic level of the trilogy, i.e. taking all three plays as a sequential unit, biography is presented in a conventional and realistic manner which follows the Aristotelian plot conventions. Conversely, on the microscopic level, i.e. seeing all three plays as self-contained, biography is presented differently. *Voyage* reverses the Aristotelian cause-and-effect chain. The question of narrative and ideological structure is reflected upon thematically by the antithesis of idealism and realism and structurally by the Chekhovian antithesis of illusion and truth. *Shipwreck* takes on the form of a semi-swirl, because reprise and continuation arch back over the plot. *Salvage* follows the Aristotelian plot again. In their contrasting structures, all three plays innovatively break up the trilogy's macrostructure and make for discrepant readings of history which, however, in their sequence lead again to the conventional structure of the trilogy. Stoppard's macroscopic realism changes to a microscopic causal realism, and the plays become the experience of the depicted subjects made vivid and concrete by the awareness of the staging. This situates the trilogy between the realistic and innovative biography play and, hence, between biographical fact and fiction. Like *Travesties*, *The Coast of Utopia* apposes and opposes different historical concepts on the levels of structure, theme and character. It is Turgenev's metacharacter that expresses best what the trilogy in its complexity of opposing and complementing macro- and microscopic levels stands for: the ambiguity of history with an emphasis on the individual in history. In the trilogy, Stoppard functionalises the biographical conflict of fact and fiction. He maintains the topic and method of *The Invention of Love* by subjecting historical and biographical facts to his own art, which holds subjective truth. Hence, in the logic of structural and artistic development of Stoppard's drama, in *The Coast of Utopia* he can abandon the structural principle of a second time level in his drama.

Rosencrantz and Guildenstern are Dead as Stoppard's first biography play introduces elements which have become defining features of his biographical drama. It takes its protagonists from the margins of (dramatic) history, it presupposes myth as the basis of communication between playwright, actors and recipients, it debunks its heroes, it imaginatively reconstructs the dark areas of its main characters, it is preoccupied with the process of identity formation and construction of its subjects and it questions objective truth. All these factors can also be found in *Travesties*, with the exception that *dramatic* myth is now exchanged for *life* myth, i.e. historical biography, and that with Old Carr as the mnemonic mediator, the play introduces a second time level. In their metadramatic and metabiographical composition, both plays together can be seen as Stoppard's most artistic, self-reflexive and stylistically refined engagement with the topic of biography in drama. They have become points of reference and development for the playwright himself. Compared with these two plays, *Arcadia*, *Indian Ink* and *The Invention of Love* constitute a new phase in Stoppard's engagement with biography. In these three plays, the unities of time, place and plot are consecutively dissolved, while the metabiographical focus shifts from the question of the relativity of truth to the emphasis of the epistemological process itself. The quest for biographical and historical facts is understood to be a defining feature of human nature, but while the facts are identified as existential, it is art which is presented as essential in that it alone transports subjective truth. This artistic development in Stoppard's biographical drama in the nineties is exactly the reason why in *The Coast of Utopia*, he abandons the structural device of a second time level. Stoppard incorporates into the trilogy the paradigm developed over the three antecedent plays which have defined art, and hence, Stoppard's own plays, as subjective truth. This engagement renders a second time level irrelevant, which explicitly and self-reflexively emphasises the artificiality of biographical and dramatic construction. Starting with the trilogy, it is the notion of causal realism which begins to dominate Stoppard's biographical presentation, explicitly exemplified in *Shipwreck* with its intermedial allusion to Manet's *Le Déjeuner sur l'herbe*. And it is also Kant's dualism of a phenomenal and a noumenal world which reflects Stoppard's biographical approach in his drama and which features thematically in *Voyage*, as well. Facts, i.e. the things-in-themselves, which exist in the noumenal world, are constituted as objects of knowledge in the process of perception inside the limits of the phenomenal world. They only become truth through our subjective interpretation via categories such as cause and effect and in and through art.

This causal-realistic approach to biography in drama is continued in Stoppard's latest play, *Rock 'n' Roll*. It could more aptly be called a fictional auto/biography play since it is in part, as Stoppard explains in the introduction, the realisation of a play he often thought about writing, "an autobiography in a parallel world where I returned 'home' after the war" (Stoppard 2006: ix). Historically, it depicts the political and cultural situation in Czechoslovakia from the Prague Spring of 1968 until a year after the Velvet Revolution of 1989 from the perspective of the Czech student Jan in Prague and the Communist Professor of Philosophy Max Morrow in Cambridge. Hence, *Rock 'n' Roll* shuttles between two places, and, like the trilogy, it progresses chronologically without a second time level. It incorporates many of the trilogy's devices such as the projection of the respective historical date at the beginning of each scene and the differentiation between "Czech characters speaking

'Czech' to each other [...] without accents" and "Czech characters speaking English [...] with a 'Czech accent'" (xxii). Thus, *Rock 'n' Roll* is again a play which appears to be committed to historical realism. However, in his introduction, Stoppard also makes it clear that fictional works such as Milan Kundera's novel *The Unbearable Lightness of Being* (*Nesnesitelná lehkost bytí*, 1982/84) or Václav Havel's plays and essays had a large influence on the play, as the music of *Pink Floyd* and others unmistakeably did, too. By incorporating Havel's political essays, Stoppard on the one hand describes the genesis of Charter 77, which was in part motivated by the arrest of the psychedelic Czech band *The Plastic People of the Universe*. The band's history was also an inspiration for the play, and it features prominently offstage. On the other hand, rock music from three decades and the biography of Syd Barrett, one of the founding members of *Pink Floyd*, hold the play together. And this despite the fact that the musician actually appears on stage only briefly, at the very beginning, as Pan, or rather *The Piper at the Gates of Dawn* (1967), alluding to the *Pink Floyd* debut album of the same title. By pointing out the relevance of rock-and-roll music as a symbol of freedom in a politically oppressed country and as a means of communication in a personal relationship, Stoppard focuses again on the individual in history. The play becomes another debate with an emphasis on historical materialism, namely whether it is men's social existence that determines their consciousness or *vice versa*. This is most strongly debated between Max and his cancer-afflicted wife Eleanor in the context of her decaying body and Sappho's love poetry. *Rock 'n' Roll*, then, might be described as an innovative fictional auto/biography play with strong inclinations towards realistic historical drama.[187] This is best summarised by Stoppard himself:

> Even if *Rock 'n' Roll* were entirely about the Czech experience between the Prague Spring and the Velvet Revolution, it could only hope to be a diagram. Yet, a diagram can pick out lines of force which may be faint or dotted on the intricate map of history that takes in all accounts. (xvi)

---

[187] On *Rock 'n' Roll* as an example of a recent (re)turn to documentary theatre, cf. Innes 2007.

Conclusion

The play continues Stoppard's engagement with the topic of biography and history after *The Coast of Utopia*, and it will be interesting to see what historical personalities Stoppard will summon next onto the stage, and whether he will continue this turn towards autobiography in his forthcoming works of drama.

The genre of biography, its conventions and contradictions, appear to be a "natural" genre for Stoppard to reflect his most important concerns in drama. For one thing, this is due to the various possible functions of the genre. As we have seen, biography can be seen as the possibility to gather knowledge about the life of other people in different times and cultures and under different conditions than our own, and it can be understood as the reflection or reinforcement of the cultural values under which the biography was written. It can become a tool for constructing collective identities and national images, a way of understanding the biographee's or the biographer's personality alike, and it can be seen as a literary challenge to put all these miscellaneous functions into a narrative and an imaginative (re)construction of someone's life.

For the cultural historian Stoppard, it is the life of historical personalities and the debate with different cultures and different times that often trigger an idea for a play, be it, for example, the fact that Joyce, Lenin and Tzara all spent some time in Zurich during the First World War, or that Belinsky preferred to live and work under Tsarist suppression rather than in France, where he would have been able to publish unhindered by censorship. The biographical preoccupation in his plays shows Stoppard's concern with, and emphasis on, the individual in history while at the same time exploring contemporary issues such as the ambiguity of history and the relativity of truth. His biographical drama becomes an emblem of his ethical postmodernism. He metabiographically deals with the processes of identity formation and construction of the biographical subject, as well as metadramatically with the constructed nature of life-writing. A further central topic in Stoppard's biographical drama is the relationship between fact and fiction. This relationship also constitutes the aporia of biography, the irreconcilability of fact with fiction already inherent in the conventional understanding of biography. Paradoxically, however, a biography must consist of both elements. Life-writing, then, becomes for Stoppard an ideal arena of dispute in that he apposes diametrically opposed views and *Weltanschauungen* on art, history and life. Biography becomes a perfect platform for the playwright to broach contemporary issues such as the question of identity, the sublation of boundaries, the processing of history and the turn towards self-reflexivity. It represents Stoppard's notion that life is complex, a mixture of fact and fiction, of social existence and individual consciousness. His biographical drama itself enlarges the scope of the genre by hanging up looking glasses at odd corners, reflecting historical subject, biographical drama and even the mirror of life-writing alike.

Works Cited

(A date in square brackets after a title indicates the year of its first publication; a date in square brackets after the name of the publishing house indicates the year of the first publication of this edition.)

Abbotson, Susan C.W. (1998), "Stoppard's (Re)Vision of Rosencrantz and Guildenstern: A Lesson in Moral Responsibility", *English Studies: A Journal of English Language and Literature* 79.2: 171-183

Abrams, M.H. (2005), *A Glossary of Literary Terms*, 8th, int. student ed., with contributions by Geoffrey Galt Harpham, Boston et al.: Thomson Wadsworth

Adams, Douglas (1996), *The Hitch Hiker's Guide to the Galaxy: A Trilogy in Five Parts*, London: Heinemann [1995]

Ahrens, Rüdiger; Volkmann, Laurenz (eds.) (1996), *Why Literature Matters: Theories and Functions of Literature* [= Anglistische Forschung, Vol. 241], Heidelberg: Universitätsverlag Winter

Alexander, Peter F. (1996), "Biography: A Case for the Defence", in: McCalman; Parvey; Cook (eds.): 75-93

Allen, Paul (1994), "Third Ear", BBC Radio Three, 16 April 1991, reprinted in: Delaney (ed.): 239-247

Alwes, Derek B. (2000), "'Oh, Phooey to Death!': Boethian Consolation in Tom Stoppard's *Arcadia*", *Papers on Language and Literature: A Journal for Scholars and Critics of Language and Literature* 36.4: 392-404

Amossy, Ruth (2002), "Die Idee des Stereotyps in der zeitgenössischen Diskussion", in: Freund, Wolfgang; Guinan, Cédric; Seidel, Ralph S. (eds.), *Begegnungen: Perspektiven Interkultureller Kommunikation*, Frankfurt a.M.; London: IKO: 222-255

Andretta, Richard A. (1994), "'The Importance of Being Flora Crewe': The Artist's Way of Apprehending and Expressing Reality as Compared with the Critic's and the Scholar's in Tom Stoppard's *In The Native State*", *Journal of King Saud University* 6, *Arts* 2: 33-52

Antor, Heinz (1998), "The Arts, the Sciences, and the Making of Meaning: Tom Stoppard's *Arcadia* as a Post-Structuralist Play", *Anglia: Zeitschrift für Englische Philologie* 116: 326-354

Aristotle (1977), "On the Art of Poetry", in: *Classical Literary Criticism: Aristotle, Horace, Longinus*, trans. T.S. Dorsch, Harmondsworth; New York; Ringwood *et al.*: Penguin Books [1965]: 29-75

Arnold, Matthew (1945), *The Poetical Works*, reprint, Oxford: Oxford University Press [1903]

Averintsev, Sergei S. (2002), "From Biography to Hagiography: Some Stable Patterns in the Greek and Latin Tradition of Lives, including Lives of the Saints", in: France; St Clair (eds.): 19-36

Backscheider, Paula R. (2002), *Reflections on Biography*, reprint, Oxford: Oxford University Press [1999]

Barker, Roberta (2005), "The Circle Game: Gender, Time, and 'Revolution' in Tom Stoppard's *The Coast of Utopia*", *Modern Drama* 48.4: 706-725

Barthes, Roland (1995), "The Death of the Author", reprinted in: Burke (ed.): 125-130

Barthes, Roland (2002), "La mort de l'auteur", *Manteia* 5 (1968): 12-17; reprinted in: Marty, Éric (ed.), *Roland Barthes: Œuvres complètes. Tome III: 1968-1971*, Paris: Éditions du Seuil: 40-45

Batchelor, John (ed.) (1995), *The Art of Literary Biography*, Oxford: Clarendon Press

Beach, Milo Cleveland (1992), *Mughal and Rajput Painting* [= The New Cambridge History of India, Vol. 1.3], Cambridge: Cambridge University Press

Berlin, Isaiah (1978), *Russian Thinkers*, ed. Henry Hardy and Aileen Kelly [= Selected Writings], London: The Hogarth Press

Berninger, Mark (2001), "The Absence of the Intercultural? – The History of Anglo-Indian Relations in Ayub Khan-Din's *Last Dance at Dum Dum* and Tom Stoppard's *Indian Ink*", in: Reitz, Bernhard; von Rothkirch, Alyce (eds.), *Crossing Borders: Intercultural Drama and Theatre at the Turn of the Millennium* [CDE: Contemporary Drama in English, Vol. 8], Trier: WVT: 39-48

Berninger, Mark (2002), "Variations of a Genre: The British History Play in the Nineties", in: Reitz; Berninger (eds.): 37-64

Berninger, Mark (2006), *Neue Formen des Geschichtsdramas in Großbritannien und Irland seit 1970* [= CDE Studies, Vol. 13], Trier: WVT

Beye, Charles Rowan (2002), "Sailing to Utopia", *greekworks.com* 2.14, <http://www.greekworks.com/content/index.php/weblog/extended/sailing_to_utopia> (26 March 2007)

Bigsby, Christopher W.E. (1976), *Tom Stoppard* [= Writers and their Work, Vol. 250], Harlow: Longman House

Billman, Carol (1980), "The Art of History in Tom Stoppard's *Travesties*", *Kansas Quarterly* 12.4: 47-52

Boireau, Nicole (1995), "Marginalizing the Centre: The Case of Tom Stoppard", in: Reitz, Bernhard (ed.), *Centres and Margins* [= CDE: Contemporary Drama in English, Vol. 2], Trier: WVT: 99-107

Böker, Uwe; Corballis, Richard; Hibbard, Julie (eds.) (2002), *The Importance of Reinventing Oscar: Versions of Wilde during the Last 100 Years* [= Internationale Forschungen zur Allgemeinen und Vergleichenden Literaturwissenschaft, Vol. 61], Amsterdam; New York: Rodopi

Borel, Émile (1972), "La Mécanique Statistique et l'Irréversibilité", *J. Phys.* 5.3 (1913): 189-196; reprinted in: *id., Œuvres de Emile Borel*, Vol. 3, Paris: Centre National de la Recherche Scientifique: 1697-1704

Borgmeier, Raimund (2002), "'Convergences of Different Threads': Tom Stoppard's *The Invention of Love* (1997)", in: Reitz; Berninger (eds.): 149-163

Boswell, James (1952), *Life of Samuel Johnson LL.D.* [1791] [= Great Books of the Western World, Vol. 44: Boswell], Chicago; London; Toronto *et al.*: Encyclopaedia Britannica

Boswell, James (1962), [From his journal, 19 October 1775], in: Scott, Geoffrey (ed.), *The Private Papers of James Boswell from Malahide Castle*, Vol. 6, 1929; partly reprinted in: Clifford (ed.): 50-53

Boswell, James (1973), "The Hypochondriack [On Diaries]", *London Magazine* 66 (March 1783); reprinted in: Bailey, Margery (ed.), *The Hypochondriack: Being the Seventy Essays by the celebrated biographer, James Boswell, appearing in the London Magazine,* from *November, 1777,* to *August, 1783, and here first Reprinted* [= The Hypochondriack, Vol. 2], New York: AMS Press [1928]: 256-266

Bowie, Malcolm (2002), "Freud and the Art of Biography", in: France; St Clair (eds.): 177-192

Brandejská, Zdenka (2002), "Devising Consolation: The Mental Landscapes of Stoppard's *Arcadia*", *Brno Studies in English: Sborník Prací Filozofické Fakulty Brnensk Univerzity, S: Rada Anglistická/Series Anglica* 28.8: 103-118

Brassel, Tim (1987), *Tom Stoppard: An Assessment*, Hong Kong: Macmillan [1985]

Brater, Enoch (2005), "Playing for Time (and Playing with Time) in Tom Stoppard's *Arcadia*", *Comparative Drama* 39.2: 157-168

Broich, Ulrich (1987), "Symposium – Das Europäische Geschichtsdrama nach 1945: Einleitung", *Literaturwissenschaftliches Jahrbuch* 28: 153-165

Broich, Ulrich (1993), "Geschichte und Intertextualität im englischen Drama der Gegenwart", in: Müller, Klaus Peter (ed.), *Englisches Theater der Gegenwart: Geschichte(n) und Strukturen* [= Forum Modernes Theater, Vol. 10], Tübingen: Gunter Narr: 413-431

Brunkhorst, Martin (1980), "Der Erzähler im Drama: Versionen des *memory play* bei Fry, Shaffer, Stoppard und Beckett", *AAA: Arbeiten aus Anglistik und Amerikanistik* 5: 225-240

Buckridge, Patrick (1998), "Private Scandals and Public Actions: The Politics of Reputation in the Career of Brian Penton", in: Gould; Staley (eds.): 313-319

Bulgakov, Mikhail (1996), *The Master and Margarita* [1966], trans. Diana Burgin and Katherine Tiernan O'Connor, New York: Vintage International

Bull, John (2001), "Tom Stoppard and Politics", in: Kelly (ed.): 136-153

Bull, John (2003), "From Illyria to Arcadia: Uses of Pastoral in Modern English Theater", *Triquarterly* 116: 57-72

Burke, Seán (1992), *The Death and Return of the Author: Criticism and Subjectivity in Barthes, Foucault and Derrida*, Edinburgh: Edinburgh University Press

Burke, Seán (ed.) (1995), *Authorship: From Plato to the Postmodern. A Reader*, Edinburgh: Edinburgh University Press

Burton, Antoinette (2001), "India, Inc.? Nostalgia, Memory and the Empire of Things", in: Ward, Stuart (ed.), *British Culture and the End of Empire*, Manchester: Manchester University Press: 217-232

Buse, Peter (2001), *Drama + Theory: Critical Approaches to Modern British Drama*, Manchester: Manchester University Press

Cahn, Victor L. (1979), *Beyond Absurdity: The Plays of Tom Stoppard*, Cranbury, NJ; London: Associated University Press

Callen, Anthony (1969), "Stoppard's Godot: Some French influences on Post-War English Drama", *New Theatre Magazine* 10: 22-30

Campbell, Thomas Harlan (2007), "Restaging the Gercen 'Family Drama': Tom Stoppard's *Shipwreck* and the Discourse of English 'Herzenism'", *Russian Literature* 61.1-2: 207-243

Caponigri, A. Robert (1963), *Philosophy from the Renaissance to the Romantic Age* [= A History of Western Philosophy, Vol. 3], Notre Dame; London: University of Notre Dame Press

Carle, Melissa J.A.; Steen, Carla (2000), "*The Invention of Love:* Studyguide", <http://www.guthrietheater.org/Portals/0/StudyGuide/invention.pdf> (26 March 2007)

Carlyle, Thomas (1962), [From a review of Croker's edition of James Boswell's *Life of Johnson*] *Fraser's Magazine* (April 1832): 253-259; partly reprinted in: Clifford (ed.): 78-86

Carr, Edward Hallett (1940), *The Twenty Years' Crisis 1919-1939: An Introduction to the Study of International Relations*, reprint, London: Macmillan [1939]

Carr, Edward Hallett (1961), *What is History? The George Macaulay Trevelyan Lectures delivered in the University of Cambridge, January-March 1961*, London: Macmillan

Cavendish, Dominic (2002), "The long voyage of Sir Tom", *Daily Telegraph*, 29 June, <http://www.telegraph.co.uk/arts/main.jhtml?xml=/arts/2002/06/29/btstop29.xml> (26 March 2007)

Chekhov, Anton Pavlovich (2001), *The Major Plays:* Ivanov, The Sea Gull, Uncle Vanya, The Three Sisters, The Cherry Orchard, trans. Ann Dunnigan, New York: Signet Classic [1964]

Chetta, Peter N. (1992), "Multiplicities of Illusion in Tom Stoppard's Plays", in: Murphy, Patrick D. (ed.), *Staging the Impossible: The Fantastic Mode in Modern Drama* [= Contributions to the Study of Science Fiction and Fantasy, Vol. 54], Westport, Conn. *et al*.: Greenwood Press: 127-136

Chung, Moonyoung (2005), "Stage as Hyperspace: Theatricality of Stoppard", *Modern Drama* 48.4: 689-705

Churchwell, Sarah (2006), "Radiant, glorious queen", *Times Literary Supplement* 5411 (15 December): 7

Clayton, Jay (2003), *Charles Dickens in Cyberspace: The Afterlife of the Nineteenth Century in Postmodern Culture*, Oxford: Oxford University Press

Clifford, James L. (1970), *From Puzzles to Portraits: Problems of a Literary Biographer*, Chapel Hill; London: University of North Carolina Press

Clifford, James L. (1978), "'Hanging Up Looking Glasses at Odd Corners': Ethnobiographical Prospects", in: Aaron, Daniel (ed.), *Studies in Biography* [= Harvard English Studies, Vol. 8], Cambridge, MA: Harvard University Press: 41-56

Clifford, James L. (ed.) (1962), *Biography as an Art: Selected Criticism 1560-1960*, Oxford: Oxford University Press

Clyman, Toby W. (ed.) (1985), *A Chekhov Companion*, Westport, CT; London: Greenwood Press

Conrad, Peter (1998), "Thomas the think engine", *Observer*, 1 November, <http://observer.guardian.co.uk/review/story/0,,726582,00.html> (26 March 2007)

Cooke, John William (1981), "The Optical Allusion: Perception and Form in Stoppard's *Travesties*", *Modern Drama* 24.4: 523-539

Cott, Thomas (2001), *A Conversation with Tom Stoppard*, Lincoln Center Theater, 28 February, <http://www.lct.org/calendar/platform_detail.cfm?id_event=32593717> (26 March 2007)

Coupe, Laurence (1997), *Myth* [= The New Critical Idiom], London; New York: Routledge

Coursen, H.R. (1999), "Stoppard's *Rosencrantz and Guildenstern Are Dead*: The Film", in: Potter, Lois; Kinney, Arthur F. (eds.), *Shakespeare: Text and Theater. Essays in Honor of Jay L. Halio*, Newark, DE; London: University of Delaware Press; Associated University Press: 183-193

Crane, Ralph J. (2002), *Inventing India: A History of India in English-Language Fiction*, Basingstoke; New York: Palgrave Macmillan [1992]

Crewe, Jonathan (1988), "The Wolsey Paradigm?", *Criticism: A Quarterly for Literature and the Arts* 30.2: 153-169

Curnutt, Kirk (1999/2000), "Inside and Outside: Gertrude Stein on Identity, Celebrity, and Authenticity", *Journal of Modern Literature* 23.2: 291-308

De Vos, Laurens (2007), "Stoppard's Dallying with Spectres: Rosencrantz and Guildenstern Live On and On", in: Henke, Christoph; Middeke, Martin (eds.), *Drama and/after Postmodernism* [= CDE: Contemporary Drama in English, Vol. 14], Trier: WVT: 105-125

Delaney, Paul (2001), "Exit Tomáš Straüssler, Enter Sir Tom Stoppard", in: Kelly (ed.): 25-37

Delaney, Paul (ed.) (1994), *Tom Stoppard in Conversation*, Ann Arbor: The University of Michigan Press

Demastes, William W. (1998), *Theatre of Chaos: Beyond Absurdism, into Orderly Disorder*, Cambridge: Cambridge University Press

Dentith, Simon (2000), *Parody* [= The New Critical Idiom], London; New York: Routledge

Derrida, Jacques (1967), *De la Grammatologie* [= Collection "Critique"], Paris: Les Éditions de Minuit

Derrida, Jacques (1995), "The Exorbitant: Question of Method", reprinted in: Burke (ed.): 117-124

Donaldson, Christine Frances (1986), *Russian Nihilism of the 1860's: A Science-Based Social Movement* [1979], Ann Arbor; London: University Microfilms International

Dorschel, Andreas (2000), *Rethinking Prejudice* [= Ashgate New Critical Thinking in Philosophy], Aldershot; Burlington USA; Singapore *et al.*: Ashgate

Dostoevsky, Fyodor Mikhailovich (1952), *The Brothers Karamazov* [1879-80], trans. Constance Garnett [= Great Books of the Western World, Vol. 52: Dostoevsky], Chicago; London; Toronto *et al.*: Encyclopaedia Britannica

Dostoevsky, Fyodor Mikhailovich (1954), *The Diary of a Writer* [1873-1881], trans. and an. Boris Brasol, New York: George Braziller

Draudt, Manfred (1985), "The Paradoxical Concept of Reality in Modern European Drama: A Systems Approach", *Maske und Kothurn* 31: 33-55

Duncan-Jones, Katherine (2002), "Continental drift: Katherine Duncan-Jones on how Tom Stoppard's study of philosophy and revolution slips its moorings", *New Statesman* 15.721: 26-27

Duncan, Andy (2003), "Alternate History", in: James, Edward; Mendlesohn, Farah (eds.), *The Cambridge Companion to Science Fiction* [= Cambridge Companions to Literature], Cambridge: Cambridge University Press: 209-218

Dürrenmatt, Friedrich (1980), "Theaterprobleme" [1954], in: *id.*, *Theater: Essays, Gedichte und Reden* [= Werkausgabe, Vol. 24], Zürich: Verlag der Arche: 31-72

Dürrenmatt, Friedrich (2006), "Theater Problems", in: *id.*, *Selected Writings, Volume 3: Essays*, trans. Joel Agee, ed. Kenneth J. Northcott, Chicago; London: The University of Chicago Press: 137-161

Durst, Uwe (2004), "Zur Poetik der parahistorischen Literatur", *Neohelicon: Acta Comparationis Litterarum Universarum* 31.2: 201-220

Eddington, Arthur Stanley (1929), *The Nature of the Physical World: Gifford Lectures. 1927*, 4th impr., Cambridge: Cambridge University Press [1928]

Edel, Leon (1981), "Biography and the Science of Man", in: Friedson (ed.): 1-11

Edel, Leon (1984), *Writing Lives: Principia Biographica*, New York, London: W.W. Norton & Company [1959]

Edwards, Paul (2001), "Science in *Hapgood* and *Arcadia*", in: Kelly (ed.): 171-184

Eliot, T.S. (1984), *Old Possum's Book of Practical Cats* [1939], with drawings by Edward Gorey, reprint, London: Faber and Faber [1982]

Ellmann, Richard (1974), "The Zealots of Zurich", *Times Literary Supplement* 3775 (12 July): 744

Elms, Alan C. (1994), *Uncovering Lives: The Uneasy Alliance of Biography and Psychology*, Oxford: Oxford University Press

Emilsson, Wilhelm (2003), "Living at the Turning Point of the World: Stoppard and Wilde", *English Studies in Canada* 29.1-2: 131-48

Epstein, William H. (1991), "Introduction: Contesting the Subject", in: Epstein (ed.): 1-7

Epstein, William H. (ed.) (1991), *Contesting the Subject: Essays in the Postmodern Theory and Practice of Biography and Biographical Criticism* [= The Theory and Practice of Biography and Biographical Criticism, Vol. 1], West Lafayette: Purdue University Press

Er, Zekiye (2005), "Tom Stoppard, New Historicism, and Estrangement in *Travesties*", *New Theatre Quarterly* 21.3: 230-240

Fedderson, Kim; Richardson, J.M. (2001), "'Love Like There Has Never Been in a Play': *Shakespeare in Love* as Bardspawn", *West Virginia University Philological Papers* 47: 145-149

Fejérvári, Boldizsár (2003), "Rosencrantz and Guildenstern Meet Edward II: A Study in Intertextuality", *The AnaChronisT*: 173-196

Fetz, Bernhard (2006), "Schreiben wie die Götter: Über Wahrheit und Lüge im Biographischen", in: *id.*; Schweiger, Hannes (eds.), *Spiegel und Maske: Konstruktionen biographischer Wahrheit* [= Profile: Magazin des Österreichischen Literaturarchivs der Österreichischen Nationalbibliothek, Vol. 13], Wien: Paul Zsolnay: 7-20

Fichte, Johann Gottlieb (1845/46), *Erste Einleitung in die Wissenschaftslehre* [1797] [= Sämmtliche Werke, Vol. 1], Berlin: Veit & Comp.

Fichte, Johann Gottlieb (1982), *Science of Knowledge with the First and Second Introductions*, ed. and trans. Peter Heath and John Lachs [= Texts in German Philosophy], London et al.: Cambridge University Press

Fischer-Seidel, Therese (1986), *Mythenparodie im modernen englischen und amerikanischen Drama: Tradition und Kommunikation bei Tennessee Williams, Edward Albee, Samuel Beckett und Harold Pinter* [= Anglistische Forschungen, Vol. 174], Heidelberg: Universitätsverlag Winter

Fischer-Seidel, Therese (1996), "Biography in Drama: Genre and Gender in Tom Stoppard's *Travesties* and Liz Lochhead's *Blood and Ice*", in: Ahrens; Volkmann (eds.): 197-210

Fischer-Seidel, Therese (1997), "Chaos Theory, Landscape Gardening, and Tom Stoppard's Dramatology of Coincidence in *Arcadia*", in: Keller, Rudi; Menges, Karl (eds.), *Emerging Structures in Interdisciplinary Perspective* [= Kultur und Erkenntnis: Schriften der Philosophischen Fakultät der Heinrich-Heine-Universität Düsseldorf, Vol. 15], Tübingen; Basel: Francke: 93-114

Fish, Stanley (1991), "Biography and Intention", in: Epstein (ed.): 9-16

Fleming, John (2001), *Stoppard's Theatre: Finding Order amid Chaos* [= Literary Modernism Series], Austin: University of Texas Press

Forster, E.M. (1978), *A Passage to India* [1924] [= The Abinger Edition to E.M. Forster, Vol. 6], London: Edward Arnold

Fort, Alice B.; Kates, Herbert S. (1935), *Minute History of the Drama: From Its Earliest Beginnings to the Present Day*, New York: Grosset & Dunlap

Foucault, Michel (1994), "Qu'est-ce qu'un auteur?", in: *id.*, *Dits et Écrits: 1954-1969* [= Dits et Écrits: 1954-1988, Vol. 1], Paris: Gallimard: 789-821

Foucault, Michel (1995), "What Is an Author?", partly reprinted in: Burke (ed.): 233-246

France, Peter (2002), "From Eulogy to Biography: The French Academic *Eloge*", in: France; St Clair (eds.): 83-101

France, Peter; St Clair, William (eds.) (2002), *Mapping Lives: The Uses of Biography*, Oxford: Oxford University Press

Freeborn, Richard (1998), "Introduction", in: Turgenev: vii-xxxiii

Freud, Sigmund (1989), *Leonardo da Vinci and a Memory of His Childhood* [= The Standard Edition] [1910], ed. James Strachey, trans. Alan Tyson, New York; London: W.W. Norton

Freud, Sigmund (1995), *Eine Kindheitserinnerung des Leonardo da Vinci* [1910], Frankfurt a.M.: Fischer Taschenbuch Verlag

Freytag, Gustav (1896), *Technique of the Drama: An Exposition of Dramatic Composition and Art*, trans. Elias J. MacEwan, 2nd ed., Chicago: Griggs [1894]

Freytag, Gustav (1975), *Die Technik des Dramas* [1863], unaltered reprographic reprint of the 13th ed., Leipzig 1922, Darmstadt: Wissenschaftliche Buchgesellschaft

Friedson, Anthony M. (ed.) (1981), *New Directions in Biography: Essays by Phyllis Auty, Leon Edel, Michael Holroyd, Noel C. Manganyi, Gabriel Merle, Margot Peters and Shoichi Saeki* [= A Biography Monograph], Honolulu: Hawaii University Press

Gadamer, Hans-Georg (1975), *Wahrheit und Methode: Grundzüge einer philosophischen Hermeneutik*, 4th ed., Tübingen: J.C.B. Mohr (Paul Siebeck)

Gamm, Gerhard (1997), *Der Deutsche Idealismus: Eine Einführung in die Philosophie von Fichte, Hegel und Schelling*, Stuttgart: Reclam

Gautier, Théophile (1966), *Mademoiselle de Maupin*, texte complet (1835), édition augmenteé d'un sommaire biographique, texte établi avec introduction et notes par Adolphe Boschot, Paris: Garnier

Geraths, Armin (1979), "Geschichte und Geschichtskritik in Tom Stoppards 'Ideen-Komödie' *Travesties*", in: Diller, Hans-Jürgen (ed.), *Modernes englisches Drama* [= anglistik & englischunterricht, Vol. 7], Heidelberg: Universitätsverlag Winter: 89-101

Gleick, James (1987), *Chaos: Making a new science*, New York *et al.*: Viking

Goer, Charis (2003), "Gertrice/Altrude oder: Ich ist eine andere. (Auto-)Biographik in Gertrude Steins *Autobiography of Alice B. Toklas*", *Orbis Litterarum: International Review of Literary Studies* 58.2: 101-115

Goetsch, Paul (1973), "Das Englische Drama seit Shaw", in: Nünning, Josefa (ed.), *Das Englische Drama* [= Grundriss der Literaturgeschichte nach Gattungen], Darmstadt: Wissenschaftliche Buchgesellschaft: 403-507

Goetsch, Paul (1992), *Bauformen des modernen englischen und amerikanischen Dramas* [1977], 2nd ed., Darmstadt: Wissenschaftliche Buchgesellschaft

Gordon, Robert (1991), Rosencrantz and Guildenstern are Dead, Jumpers *and* The Real Thing [= Text and Performance], Basingstoke: Macmillan

Gosse, Edmund (1910), "Biography", in: *The Encyclopaedia Britannica: A Dictionary of Arts, Sciences, Literature and General Information*, 11th ed. [=

The Encyclopaedia Britannica, Vol. 3: Austria Lower to Bisectrix], New York: Encyclopaedia Britannica: 952-954

Gould, Warwick; Staley, Thomas F. (eds.) (1998), *Writing the Lives of Writers*, London: Macmillan

Grace, Sherrill (2006), "Theatre and the AutoBiographical Pact: An Introduction", in: *id.*; Wassermann, Jerry (eds.), *Theatre and AutoBiography: Writing and Performing Lives in Theory and Practice*, Vancouver: Talonbooks: 13-29

Graham, Peter W. (1995), "Et in *Arcadia* Nos", *Nineteenth Century Contexts* 18: 311-319

Graves, Richard Perceval (1981), *A.E. Housman: The Scholar-Poet* [1979], Oxford: Oxford University Press

Gruber, William E. (1988), "'Wheels within wheels, etcetera': Artistic Design in *Rosencrantz and Guildenstern Are Dead*" [1981-1982], in: Harty (ed.): 21-46

Grundy, Isobel (1998), "'Acquainted with all the Modes of Life': The Difficulty of Biography", in: Gould; Staley (eds.): 107-124

Gruteser, Michael; Klein, Thomas; Rauscher, Andreas (2002), "Die gelben Seiten von Springfield: Eine Einführung", in: *id.* (eds.), *Subversion zur Primetime: Die Simpsons und die Mythen der Gesellschaft*, Marburg: Schüren: 11-17

Guaspari, David (1996), "Stoppard's *Arcadia*", *Antioch Review* 54.2: 222-238

Guralnick, Elissa S. (2001), "Stoppard's Radio and Television Plays", in: Kelly (ed.): 68-81

Gustafsson, Lars (1970), "Über die Räumlichkeit der Literatur", in: *id.*, *Utopien: Essays*, trans. Hanns Grössel *et al.* [= Reihe Hanser, Vol. 53], München: Carl Hanser: 26-33

Guthke, Karl S. (1976), "A Stage for the Anti-Hero: Metaphysical Farce in the Modern Theatre", in: Furst, Lilian R.; Wilson, James D. (eds.), *The Anti-Hero: His Emergence and Transformations* [= Studies in the Literary Imagination, Vol. 9.1], Atlanta: Georgia State University, Department of English: 119-137

Hamilton, Nigel (2007), *Biography: A Brief History*, Cambridge, MA; London: Harvard University Press

Hammerschmidt, Hildegard (1972), *Das historische Drama in England (1956-1971): Erscheinungsformen und Entwicklungstendenzen* [= Studien zur Anglistik], Wiesbaden; Frankfurt a.M.: Humanitas

Harben, Niloufer (1988), *Twentieth-Century English History Plays: From Shaw to Bond*, Houndmills; Basingstoke; Hampshire et al.: Macmillan

Harty, John (ed.) (1988), *Tom Stoppard: A Casebook* [= Casebooks on Modern Dramatists, Vol. 1], New York; London: Garland

Hayman, Ronald (1982), *Tom Stoppard*, 4th ed. [= Contemporary Playwrights], Heinemann: London [1977]

Hegel, Georg Wilhelm Friedrich (1952), *The Philosophy of Right, The Philosophy of History*, trans. T.M. Knox and J. Sibree [= Great Books of the Western World, Vol. 46: Hegel], Chicago; London; Toronto et al.: Encyclopaedia Britannica

Hegel, Georg Wilhelm Friedrich (1961), *Briefe von und an Hegel. Band I: 1785-1812*, ed. Johannes Hoffmeister, 2nd ed. [= Philosophische Bibliothek, Vol. 235], Hamburg: Meiner [1952]

Hegel, Georg Wilhelm Friedrich (1966), *Science of Logic: Vol. 1*, trans. W.H. Johnston and L.G. Struthers, 4th impr. [= The Muirhead Library of Philosophy], London: Unwin [1929]

Hegel, Georg Wilhelm Friedrich (1970), *Die Wissenschaft der Logik. Erster Teil: Die objektive Logik* [1812] [= Werke in 20 Bänden, Vol. 5], Frankfurt a.M.: Suhrkamp

Hegel, Georg Wilhelm Friedrich (1970a), *Grundlinien der Philosophie des Rechts* [1821] [= Werke in 20 Bänden, Vol. 7], Frankfurt a.M.: Suhrkamp

Hegel, Georg Wilhelm Friedrich (1970b), *Enzyklopädie der philosophischen Wissenschaften im Grundriss. Erster Teil: Die Wissenschaft der Logik* [1830] [= Werke in 20 Bänden, Vol. 8], Frankfurt a.M.: Suhrkamp

Hegel, Georg Wilhelm Friedrich (1970c), *Enzyklopädie der philosophischen Wissenschaften im Grundriss. Dritter Teil: Die Philosophie des Geistes* [1830] [= Werke in 20 Bänden, Vol. 10], Frankfurt a.M.: Suhrkamp

Hegel, Georg Wilhelm Friedrich (1970d), *Vorlesungen über die Philosophie der Geschichte* [1837] [= Werke in 20 Bänden, Vol. 12], Frankfurt a.M.: Suhrkamp

Hegel, Georg Wilhelm Friedrich (1970e), *Vorlesungen über die Ästhetik. Dritter Teil: Das System der einzelnen Künste* [Fortsetzung] [1835] [= Werke in 20 Bänden, Vol. 15], Frankfurt a.M.: Suhrkamp

Hegel, Georg Wilhelm Friedrich (1975), *Hegel's Logic: Being Part One of the Encyclopaedia of the Philosophical Sciences (1830)*, trans. William Wallace, 3rd ed., Oxford: Clarendon [1873]

Hegel, Georg Wilhelm Friedrich (1984), *Hegel: The Letters*, trans. Clark Butler and Christiane Seiler, Bloomington: Indiana University Press

Hegel, Georg Wilhelm Friedrich (1998), *Aesthetics: Lectures on Fine Art, Vol. 2*, trans. T.M. Knox, Oxford: Oxford University Press [1975]

Hegel, Georg Wilhelm Friedrich (2003), *Hegel's Philosophy of Mind: Being Part Three of the* Encyclopaedia of the Philosophical Sciences *(1830) together with the* Zusätze *in Boumann's Text (1845)*, trans. William Wallace and A.V. Miller, reprint, Oxford: Clarendon [1894]

Herzen, Alexander (1969), *Vom anderen Ufer* [1850], ed. Axel Matthes, trans. Alfred Kurella, München: Rogner & Bernhard

Herzen, Alexander (1982), *My Past and Thoughts: The Memoirs of Alexander Herzen* [1861–67], abr. Dwight Macdonald, trans. Constance Garnett, Berkeley; Los Angeles; London: University of California Press

Hesse, Beatrix (2002), "Stoppard's Oscar Wilde: Travesty and Invention", in: Böker; Corballis; Hibbard (eds.): 189-195

Hoberman, Ruth (2001), "Biography: General Survey", in: Jolly (ed.): 109-112

Hodgson, Terry (ed.) (2001), *The Plays of Tom Stoppard for Stage, Radio, TV and Film: A Reader's Guide to Essential Criticism* [= Icon Reader's Guides], Cambridge: Icon Books

Höfele, Andreas (1990), "The Writer on Stage: Some Contemporary British Plays about Authors", in: Reitz, Bernhard (ed.), *British Drama in the 1980s. New Perspectives* [= anglistik & englischunterricht, Vol. 41], Heidelberg: Universitätsverlag Winter: 79-91

Hoffmann, Monika (1992), *Gertrude Steins Autobiographien:* The Autobiography of Alice B. Toklas *und* Everybody's Autobiography [= Mainzer Studien zur Amerikanistik, Vol. 25], Lang: Frankfurt a.M. *et al.*

Holubetz, Margarete (1982), "A Mocking of Theatrical Conventions: The Fake Death Scenes in *The White Devil* and *Rosencrantz and Guildenstern Are Dead*", *English Studies: A Journal of English Language and Literature* 63.5: 426-429

Honan, Park (1995), "Jane Austen, Matthew Arnold, Shakespeare: The Problem of the *Opus*", in: Batchelor (ed.): 187-199

Hoskins, W.G. (1977), *The Making of the English Landcape* [1955], 2nd impr., London *et al.*: Hodder and Stoughton

Hotchkiss, Lia M. (2000), "The Cinematic Appropriation of Theater: Introjection and Incorporation in *Rosencrantz and Guildenstern Are Dead*", *Quarterly Review of Film and Video* 17.2: 161-186

Housman, A.E. (1997), *The Poems of A.E. Housman*, ed. Archie Burnett, Oxford: Clarendon

Houswitschka, Christoph; Knappe, Gabriele; Müller, Anja (eds.) (2006), *Anglistentag 2005 Bamberg: Proceedings* [= Proceedings of the Conference of the German Association of University Teachers of English, Vol. 27], Trier: WVT

Huber, Werner (1999), "Tom Stoppard and the English Disease", in: Neumann, Fritz Wilhelm; Schülting, Sabine (eds.), *Anglistentag 1998 Erfurt: Proceedings* [= Proceedings of the Conference of the German Association of University Teachers of English, Vol. 20], Trier: WVT: 457-466

Huber, Werner; Middeke, Martin (1996), "Biography in Contemporary Drama", in: Reitz (ed.): 133-143

Hudson, Roger; Itzin, Catherine; Trussler, Simon (1974), "Ambushes for the Audience: Towards a High Comedy of Ideas" [Interview], *Theatre Quarterly* 4.14: 3-17

Hunt, John Dixon (1996), "'A breakthrough in dahlia studies': on *Arcadia* by Tom Stoppard", *Landscape Journal* 15.1: 58-64

Hunter, Jim (2000), *Tom Stoppard:* Rosencrantz and Guildenstern Are Dead, Jumpers, Travesties, Arcadia [= Faber Critical Guides], London; New York: Faber and Faber

Hunter, Jim (2005), *About Stoppard: The Playwright and the Work*, London: Faber and Faber

Huston, J. Dennis (1988), "'Misreading' *Hamlet*: Problems of Perspective in *Rosencrantz & Guildenstern Are Dead*", in: Harty (ed.): 47-66

Hutcheon, Linda (1987), *A Poetics of Postmodernism: History, Theory, Fiction*, New York; London: Routledge

Hyde, H. Montgomery (ed.) (1960), *The Trials of Oscar Wilde*, 5th ed. [= Notable British Trials], London; Edinburgh; Glasgow: William Hodge [1948]

Hynes, Samuel L. (1964), "The Complete Literary Rascal", *Times Literary Supplement* 3272 (12 November): 1018

Innes, Christopher (2004), "Cross-Cultural Connections – Indian Signs/English Conventions", in: Mohr, Hans-Ulrich; Mächler, Kerstin (eds.), *Extending the Code: New Forms of Dramatic and Theatrical Expression* [= CDE: Contemporary Drama in English, Vol. 11], Trier: WVT: 183-196

Innes, Christopher (2006), "Allegories from the Past: Stoppard's Uses of History", *Modern Drama* 49.2: 223-237

Innes, Christopher (2006a), "The Past is the Present: Stoppard's Historiographic Eye", in: Rieuwerts, Sigrid (ed.), *History and Drama: Essays in Honour of Bernhard Reitz* [= MUSE: Mainz University Studies, Vol. 9], Trier: WVT: 175-188

Innes, Christopher (2007), "Towards a Post-millennial Mainstream? Documents of the Times", *Modern Drama* 50.3: 435-452

Ives, David (1995), "Words, Words, Words", in: *id.*, *All in the Timing: Fourteen Plays*, New York: Vintage: 19-30

Jenkins, Keith (1995), *On "What is History?" From Carr and Elton to Rorty and White*, London; New York: Routledge

Jernigan, Daniel (2003), "Tom Stoppard and 'Postmodern Science': Normalizing Radical Epistemologies in *Hapgood* and *Arcadia*", *Comparative Drama* 37.1: 3-35

Johnson, Samuel (1962), *The Rambler* 60 (Saturday, 13 October 1750); reprinted in: Clifford (ed.): 40-43

Johnson, Samuel (1962a), *Idler* 84 (24 November 1759); reprinted in: Clifford (ed.): 43-45

Jolly, Margaretta (ed.) (2001), *Encyclopedia of Life Writing: Autobiographical and Biographical Forms*, Vol. 1: A-K, London: Fitzroy Dearborn

Joyce, James (1998), *Ulysses* [= Oxford World's Classics], ed. Jeri Johnson, Oxford: Oxford University Press

Kant, Immanuel (1952), *The Critique of Pure Reason, The Critique of Practical Reason and other Ethical Treatises, The Critique of Judgement*, trans. Thomas Kingsmill Abbott, J.M.D. Meiklejohn *et al.* [= Great Books of the Western World, Vol. 42: Kant], Chicago; London; Toronto *et al.*: Encyclopaedia Britannica

Kant, Immanuel (1977), "Prolegomena zu einer jeden künftigen Metaphysik, die als Wissenschaft wird auftreten können" [1783], in: *id.*, *Schriften zur Metaphysik und Logik 1*, ed. Wilhelm Weischedel [= Werkausgabe, Vol. 5], Frankfurt a.M.: Suhrkamp: 109-264

Kant, Immanuel (1977a), "Grundlegung zur Metaphysik der Sitten" [1785], in: *id.*, *Kritik der praktischen Vernunft, Grundlegung zur Metaphysik der Sitten*, ed. Wilhelm Weischedel [= Werkausgabe, Vol. 7], Frankfurt a.M.: Suhrkamp: 7-102

Kant, Immanuel (1987), *Prolegomena to Any Future Metaphysics That Will Be Able to Come Forward as Science*, trans. Paul Carus and James W. Ellington, 6th printing, Indianapolis: Hackett [1977]

Kaplan, Laurie (1998), "*In the Native State/Indian Ink*: Footnoting the Footnotes on Empire", *Modern Drama* 41.3: 337-346

Kaufman, Myron (2002), *Principles of Thermodynamics* [= Undergraduate Chemistry, Vol. 15], New York; Basel: Dekker

Kelly, Aidan A. (2001), "Neopaganism", in: Lewis, James R. (ed.), *Odd Gods: New Religions and the Cult Controversy*, Amherst, NY: Prometheus Books: 310-324

Kelly, Katherine E. (ed.) (2001), *The Cambridge Companion to Tom Stoppard* [= Cambridge Companions to Literature], Cambridge: Cambridge University Press

Kermode, Frank (1968), *The Sense of an Ending: Studies in the Theory of Fiction*, London; Oxford; New York: Oxford University Press [1967]

King, Ross (2006), *The Judgement of Paris: Manet, Meissonier and an Artistic Revolution*, London: Chatto & Windus

Kinkead-Weekes, Mark (2002), "Writing Lives Forward: A Case for Strictly Chronological Biography", in: France; St Clair (eds.): 235-252

Klein, Alfons (1998), "Ein Dandy als Historiker: Kulturgeschichte als Komödieninszenierung in Tom Stoppards *Travesties*", in: Ahrens, Rüdiger; Neumann, Fritz-Wilhelm (eds.), *Fiktion und Geschichte in der angloamerikanischen Literatur: Festschrift für Heinz-Joachim Müllenbrock zum 60. Geburtstag* [= Anglistische Forschungen, Vol. 256], Heidelberg: Universitätsverlag Winter: 377-94

Körner, Hans (1996), *Edouard Manet: Dandy, Flaneur, Maler*, München: Wilhelm Fink Verlag

Kramer, Jeffrey and Prapassaree (1997), "Stoppard's *Arcadia*: Research, Time, Loss", *Modern Drama* 40.1: 1-10

Kramer, Stephanie (2000), *Fiktionale Biographien: (Re-)Visionen und (Re-)Konstruktionen weiblicher Lebensentwürfe in Dramen britischer Autorinnen seit 1970. Ein Beitrag zur Typologie und Entwicklung des historischen Dramas* [= CDE Studies, Vol. 6], Trier: WVT

Krämer, Lucia (2000), "Der Dichter als tragischer Held und Ideenträger: Eine Analyse jüngster Oscar Wilde-Darstellungen in Drama und Film", in: Zimmermann (ed.): 285-300

Krämer, Lucia (2003), *Oscar Wilde in Roman, Drama und Film: Eine medienkomparatistische Analyse fiktionaler Biographien* [= Regensburger Arbeiten zur Anglistik und Amerikanistik, Vol. 46], Frankfurt a.M.: Lang

Kreis-Schinck, Annette (1998), "Sprache als Abbild, Sprache als Spiel: Zur Instanz des sprechenden Subjektes bei Beckett und Stoppard", *Forum Modernes Theater* 13.2: 195-206

Krieger, Gottfried (1996), "Das englische Drama seit 1956 aus gattungstheoretischer Perspektive", in: Nünning, Ansgar (ed.), *Eine andere Geschichte der englischen Literatur: Epochen, Gattungen und Teilgebiete im Überblick* [= WVT-Handbücher zum Literaturwissenschaftlichen Studium, Vol. 2], Trier: WVT: 267-296.

Krieger, Gottfried (1998), *Das englische Drama des 20. Jahrhunderts* [= Uni-Wissen: Anglistik, Amerikanistik], Stuttgart et al.: Klett

Laplace, Pierre-Simon (1814), *Essai Philosophique sur les Probabilités*, 2nd ed., revue et augmentée, Paris: Courcier

Lee, Josephine (2001), "*In the Native State* and *Indian Ink*", in: Kelly (ed.): 38-52

Lemon, Brendan (2006/07), "The Ginger Cat", in: *id., The Coast of Utopia: Backstage Blog*, <http://www.lct.org/coast/event_detail_explore.cfm?section=blog#8> (26 March 2007)

Lenoff, Leslee (1982), "Life Within Limits: Stoppard on the HMS *Hamlet*", *Arizona Quarterly: A Journal of American Literature, Culture, and Theory* 38.1: 45-61

Levenson, Jill L. (2001), "Stoppard's Shakespeare: Textual Re-Visions", in: Kelly (ed.): 154-170

Lindheim, Ralph (1985), "Chekhov's Major Themes", in: Clyman (ed.): 55-69

Lippmann, Walter (1998), *Public Opinion* [1922], 2nd ed., New Brunswick; London: Transaction

Lodge, David (1993), *Changing Places: A Tale of Two Campuses* [1975], in: *id., A David Lodge Trilogy:* Changing Places, Small World, Nice Work, London et al.: Penguin: 1-218

Londré, Felicia Hardison (1981), *Tom Stoppard* [= Modern Literature Series], New York: Frederick Ungar

Lyotard, Jean-François (1979), *La Condition Postmoderne: Rapport sur le Savoir* [= Collection "Critique"], Paris: Les Editions de Minuit

Lyotard, Jean-François (1994), *The Postmodern Condition: A Report on Knowledge*, trans. Geoff Bennington and Brian Massumi [= Theory and History of Literature, Vol. 10], Manchester: Manchester University Press

Mader, Doris (2000), *Wirklichkeitsillusion und Wirklichkeitserkenntnis: Eine themen- und strukturanalytische Untersuchung ausgewählter großer Bühnendramen Tom Stoppards*, Heidelberg: Universitätsverlag Winter

Mader, Doris (2003), "Inversion (in) der Zeit: Sterben als Kaleidoskop des Lebens in Tom Stoppards *The Invention of Love*", *Anglia: Zeitschrift für Englische Philologie* 121.1: 58-86

Makowski, Ilse (1980), *Stoppards "Rosencrantz and Guildenstern are Dead" und sein Bezug zu Shakespeare's "Hamlet": Eine Untersuchung der Bedeutungsschichten, insbesondere der Ebene von Fiktionserzeugung und -durchbrechung*, Hannover: Univ. Diss.

Marcus, Laura (1998), "'Looking Glasses at Odd Corners': Biography and Psychoanalysis in the Early Twentieth Century", *New Comparison* 25: 52-70

Marcus, Laura (2002), "The Newness of the 'New Biography': Biographical Theory and Practice in the Early Twentieth Century", in: France; St Clair (eds.): 193-218

Marsh, Jan (1995), *Pre-Raphaelite Women: Images of Femininity in Pre-Raphaelite Art*, London: Weidenfeld and Nicolson [1987]

Marx, Karl; Engels, Friedrich (1952), "Manifesto of the Communist Party", ed. Friedrich Engels, trans. Samuel Moore, in: Marx, Karl, *Capital*, ed. Friedrich Engels [= Great Books of the Western World, Vol. 50: Marx], Chicago; London; Toronto et al.: Encyclopaedia Britannica: 413-434

Marx, Karl; Engels, Friedrich (1959), *Manifest der kommunistischen Partei* [1848] [= Werke, Vol. 4], Berlin/DDR: Dietz-Verlag

McCalman, Iain; Parvey, Jodi; Cook, Misty (eds.) (1996), *National Biographies & National Identity: A Critical Approach to Theory and Editorial Practice* [= The Humanities Research Centre Monograph Series, Vol. 11], Canberra: Goanna Press

McCauley, Anne (1998), "Sex and the Salon: Defining Art and Immorality in 1863", in: Tucker (ed.): 38-74

McKinney, Ronald H. (2003), "Comedy, Chaos, and Casuistry: Tom Stoppard's *Arcadia*", *Philosophy Today* 47.4: 392-403

McLaughlin, Martin (2002), "Biography and Autobiography in the Italian Renaissance", in: France; St Clair (eds.): 37-65

Melbourne, Lucy (1998), "'Plotting the Apple of Knowledge': Tom Stoppard's *Arcadia* as Iterated Theatrical Algorithm", *Modern Drama* 41.4: 557-572

Merkin, Daphne (2006), "Playing with Ideas: Tom Stoppard has made an art of cleverness, in the theater and in life", *New York Times Magazine*, 26 November: 38-43

Meyer, Kinereth (1989), "'It Is Written': Tom Stoppard and the Drama of the Intertext", *Comparative Drama* 23.2: 105-122

Middeke, Martin (1999), "Introduction", in: Middeke; Huber (eds.): 1-25

Middeke, Martin; Huber, Werner (eds.) (1999), *Biofictions: The Rewriting of Romantic Lives in Contemporary Fiction and Drama* [= Studies in English and American Literature, Linguistics, and Culture], Rochester; Woodbridge: Camden House

Morris, John (1987), *Doubtful Designs: A Study of the Works of Tom Stoppard*, Exeter: Univ. Diss.

Müller-Muth, Anja (2001), *Repräsentationen: Eine Studie des intertextuellen und intermedialen Spiels von Tom Stoppards* Arcadia [= CDE Studies, Vol. 7], Trier: WVT

Müller-Muth, Anja (2002), "Writing 'Wilde': The Importance of Re-Presenting Oscar Wilde in Fin-de-Millénaire Drama in English (Stoppard, Hare, Ravenhill)", in: Böker; Corballis; Hibbard (eds.): 219-227

Müller-Muth, Anja (2002/03), "'It's wanting to know that makes us matter': Scepticism or Affirmation in Tom Stoppard's *Arcadia*. A Response to Burkhard Niederhoff", *Connotations: A Journal for Critical Debate* 12.2-3: 281-291

Mullin, Brian (2002), "Radical comedy: Stoppard's new *Utopia* trilogy", *The Oxonian Review of Books* 2.1: 1-6, <http://www.oxonianreview.org/Assets/r/issue-2-1.pdf> (26 March 2007)

Muza, Anna (2003), "The Sound of Distant Thunder: The Chekhovian Subtext in *The Coast of Utopia*", paper given at the AATSEEL (American Association of Teachers of Slavic and Eastern European Languages) conference in San Diego, 27-30 December [unpublished]

Nadel, Ira Bruce (1984), *Biography: Fiction, Fact and Form*, London; Basingstoke: Macmillan

Nadel, Ira Bruce (2001), "Stoppard and Film", in: Kelly (ed.): 84-103

Nadel, Ira Bruce (2004), *Double Act: A Life of Tom Stoppard*, London: Methuen [2002]

Nadel, Ira Bruce (2004a), "Tom Stoppard: In the Russian Court", *Modern Drama* 47.3: 500-524

Nadj, Julijana (2006), *Die fiktionale Metabiographie – Gattungsgedächtnis und Gattungskritik in einem neuen Genre der englischsprachigen Erzählliteratur* [= ELCH: Studies in English Literary and Cultural History, Vol. 18], Trier: WVT

Nadj, Julijana (2006a), "Towards a Theory and Typology of Fictional Metabiographies: Forms and Functions of a New Genre", in: Houswitschka; Knappe; Müller (eds.): 411-423

Naiditch, Paul (1995), *Problems in the Life and Writings of A.E. Housman*, Beverly Hills: Krown & Spellman

Nathan, David (1993), "In a country garden (if it is a garden)", *Sunday Telegraph*, 28 March

Nestle, Eberhard (ed.) (1963), *Novum Testamentum: Graece et Latine*, 22nd ed., Stuttgart: Württembergische Bibelanstalt [1906]

Neumeier, Beate (1986), *Spiel und Politik: Aspekte der Komik bei Tom Stoppard*, München: Fink

Niederhoff, Burkhard (2001/02), "'Fortuitous Wit': Dialogue and Epistemology in Tom Stoppard's *Arcadia*", *Connotations: A Journal for Critical Debate* 11.1: 42-59

Niederhoff, Burkhard (2003/04), "Who Shot the Hare in Stoppard's *Arcadia*? A Reply to Anja Müller-Muth", *Connotations: A Journal for Critical Debate* 13.1-2: 170-178

Nietzsche, Friedrich (1972), *Die Geburt der Tragödie, Unzeitgemäße Betrachtungen I-III (1872-1874)* [= Werke: Kritische Gesamtausgabe, Vol. 3.1], Berlin; New York: de Gruyter

Nietzsche, Friedrich (1995), *The Birth of Tragedy*, trans. Clifton P. Fadiman [= Dover Thrift Editions], New York: Dover

Nünning, Ansgar (2000), "Von der fiktionalen Biographie zur biographischen Metafiktion: Prolegomena zu einer Theorie, Typologie und Funktionsgeschichte eines hybriden Genres", in: Zimmermann (ed.): 15-36

Oberholzner, Werner (1989), *Strukturen des Vorurteils im modernen britischen Drama* [= Horizonte: Studien zu Texten und Ideen der europäischen Moderne, Vol. 1], Trier: WVT

Ogden, Charles Kay; Richards, Ivor Armstrong (1969), *The Meaning of Meaning: A Study of the Influence of Language upon Thought and of the Science of Symbolism*, 10th ed., London: Routledge & Kegan Paul [1923]

Orlich, Ileana Alexandra (2004), "Tom Stoppard's *Travesties* and the Politics of Earnestness", *East European Quarterly* 38.3: 371-382

Oxford English Dictionary (1989), 2nd ed., *OED Online*, Oxford University Press, <http://dictionary.oed.com>

Page, Malcolm (comp.) (1986), *File on Stoppard* [= Writer Files], London; New York: Methuen

Palmer, Richard H. (1998), *The Contemporary British History Play* [= Contribution in Drama and Theatre Studies, Vol. 81], Westport, CN; London: Greenwood

Pankratz, Annette (2005), *"Death is ... not": Repräsentationen von Tod und Sterben im zeitgenössischen britischen Drama* [= CDE Studies, Vol. 11], Trier: WVT

Paperno, Irina (1997), *Suicide as a Cultural Institution in Dostoevsky's Russia*, Ithaca: Cornell University Press

Parke, Catherine N. (2002), *Biography: Writing Lives* [= Genres in Context], New York; London: Routledge

Pater, Walter (1980), *The Renaissance: Studies in Art and Poetry. The 1893 Text* [1873], ed. Donald L. Hill, Berkeley; Los Angeles; London: California University Press

Peacock, D. Keith (1991), *Radical Stages: Alternative History in Modern British Drama* [= Contributions in Drama and Theatre Studies, Vol. 43], New York; Westport; London: Greenwood

Peter, John (2002), "Stoppard gives theatre longest day in Utopia", *Sunday Times*, 4 August, <http://www.cdi.org/russia/johnson/6385.txt> (26 March 2007)

Peters, Catherine (1995), "Secondary Lives: Biography in Context", in: Batchelor (ed.): 43-56

Peters, Margot (1981), "Group Biography: Challenges and Methods", in: Friedson (ed.): 41-51

Peters, Susanne (2003), *Briefe im Theater: Erscheinungsformen und Funktionswandel schriftlicher Kommunikation im englischen Drama von der Shakespeare-Zeit bis zur Gegenwart*, [= Anglistische Forschungen, Vol. 334], Heidelberg: Universitätsverlag Winter

Phiddian, Robert (1995), *Swift's Parody*, Cambridge: Cambridge University Press

Phillips, Adams (2000), *Promises, Promises: Essays on Literature and Psychoanalysis*, London: Faber and Faber

Piroschkow, Vera (1961), *Alexander Herzen: Der Zusammenbruch einer Utopie*, München: Anton Pustet

Pite, Ralph (2003), "Writing Biography that is not Romantic", in: Bradley, Arthur; Rawes, Alan (eds.), *Romantic Biography*, Aldershot: Ashgate: 168-185

Poljakow, M.J. (1952), "Kommentar zu 'Hamlet, ein Trauerspiel von Shakespeare: Motschalow in der Rolle Hamlets 1837'", in: Belinskij, Vissarion G., *Hamlet: Deutung und Darstellung*, trans. Albert Kloeckner, Berlin: Henschel: 168-174

Popper, Karl R. (1979), *Das Elend des Historizismus* [1957], trans. Leonhard Walentik, 5th ed. [= Die Einheit der Gesellschaftswissenschaften: Studien in den Grenzbereichen der Wirtschafts- und Sozialwissenschaften, Vol. 3], Tübingen: Mohr [1965]

Prettejohn, Elizabeth (2000), *The Art of the Pre-Raphaelites*, London: Tate Publishing

Puschmann-Nalenz, Barbara (2001), "Nachwort", in: Norman, Marc; Stoppard, Tom, *Shakespeare in Love: A Screenplay* [= Fremdsprachentexte], ed. Barbara Puschmann-Nalenz, Stuttgart: Reclam: 175-181

Rajewsky, Irina O. (2002), *Intermedialität*, Tübingen; Basel: Francke

Reitz, Bernhard (1996), "Beyond Newton's Universe – Science and Art in Tom Stoppard's *Arcadia*", in: *id.* (ed.): 165-177

Reitz, Bernhard (ed.) (1996), *Drama and Reality* [= CDE: Contemporary Drama in English, Vol. 3], Trier: WVT

Reitz, Bernhard; Berninger, Mark (eds.) (2002), *British Drama of the 1990s* [= anglistik & englischunterricht, Vol. 64], Heidelberg: Universitätsverlag Winter

Richardson, Brian (1997), *Unlikely Stories: Causality and the Nature of Modern Narrative*, Cranbury, NJ; London; Mississauga, CAN: Associated University Press

Ricks, Christopher (1989), "Introduction", in: Housman, A.E., *Collected Poems and Selected Prose*, ed. Christopher Ricks, London: Penguin: 7-18

Rischin, Ruth (2003), "'The Absolute Whole Perpetually Renewing Itself': Tom Stoppard's Cat", abstract for the AATSEEL (American Association of Teachers of Slavic and Eastern European Languages) conference in San Diego, 27-30 December, <http://aatseel.org/program/aatseel/2003/abstracts/Rischin.htm> (26 March 2006)

Robson, Mark (1998), "Writing Contexts in William Roper's *Life of Thomas More*", in: Gould; Staley (eds.): 79-89

Rod, David K. (1983), "Carr's Views on Art and Politics in Tom Stoppard's *Travesties*", *Modern Drama* 26.4: 536-542

Rollyson, Carl (2001), "Biography and Fiction", in: Jolly (ed.): 112-114

Ronnick, Michele Valerie (1996), "Tom Stoppard's *Arcadia*, Hermes' Tortoise and Apollo's Lyre", *Classical and Modern Literature* 16.2: 177-182

Rose, Margaret A. (1995), *Parody: Ancient, Modern, and Post-Modern*, Cambridge: Cambridge University Press [1993]

Rose, Phyllis (1985), *Writing of Women: Essays in a Renaissance*, Middletown: Wesleyan University Press

Rusinko, Susan (1986), *Tom Stoppard* [= Twayne's English Authors Series], Boston: Twayne

Ruskin, John (1903), *Lectures on Art: Delivered Before the University of Oxford in Hilary Term, 1870*, London: Allen

Russell, Richard Rankin (2004), "'It Will Make Us Friends': Cultural Reconciliation in Tom Stoppard's *Indian Ink*", *Journal of Modern Literature* 27.3: 1-18

Rzhevsky, Nicholas (2003), "Dostoevsky and the Coast of Utopia", paper given at the AATSEEL (American Association of Teachers of Slavic and Eastern European Languages) conference in San Diego, 27-30 December [unpublished]

Sales, Roger (1988), *Rosencrantz and Guildenstern are Dead* [= Penguin Critical Studies], London: Penguin

Sammells, Neil (1986), "Earning Liberties: *Travesties* and *The Importance of Being Earnest*", *Modern Drama* 29.3: 376-387

Sandkühler, Hans Jörg (ed.) (2005), *Handbuch Deutscher Idealismus*, Stuttgart; Weimar: J.B. Metzler

Schabert, Ina (1990), *In Quest of the Other Person: Fiction as Biography*, Tübingen: Francke

Schaff, Barbara (1992), *Das zeitgenössische britische Künstlerdrama* [= Passauer Schriften zu Sprache und Literatur, Vol. 7], Passau: Karl Stutz

Schelling, Friedrich Wilhelm Joseph (von) (1907), *System des transzendentalen Idealismus* [1800] [= Werke. Auswahl in drei Bänden, Vol. 2], Leipzig: Fritz Eckardt

Schelling, Friedrich Wilhelm Joseph (von) (1993), *System of Transcendental Idealism (1800)*, trans. Peter Heath, 3rd printing, Charlottesville: University Press of Virginia [1978]

Schiavi, Michael R. (2004), "Wildean War: Politics of *Fins-de-siècle* Spectatorship", *Modern Drama* 47.3: 399-422

Schlaeger, Jürgen (1995), "Biography: Cult as Culture", in: Batchelor (ed.): 57-71

Schlaeger, Jürgen (2006), "Selves for the Twenty-First Century", in: Houswitschka; Knappe; Müller (eds.): 425-436

Schmid, Susanne (2002), "Byron and Wilde: The Dandy and the Public Sphere", in: Böker; Corballis; Hibbard (eds.): 81-89

Schnabl, Gerlinde (1982), *Historische Stoffe im neueren politischen Drama Großbritanniens* [= Reihe Siegen: Beiträge zur Literatur- und Sprachwissenschaft, Vol. 43], Heidelberg: Universitätsverlag Winter

Schnierer, Peter Paul (1999), "*In Arcadia Nemo*: The Pastoral of Romanticism", in: Middeke; Huber (eds.): 152-161

Scolnicov, Hanna (2004), "'Before' and 'After' in Stoppard's *Arcadia*", *Modern Drama* 47.3: 480-499

Seeber, Hans Ulrich (1999), "*The Invention of Love*: Stoppard's Dramatic Elegy for A.E. Housman", in: Kamm, Jürgen (ed.), *Twentieth-Century Theatre and Drama in English: Festschrift for Heins Kosok on the Occasion of his 65th Birthday*, Trier: WVT: 363-379

Seymour, Miranda (2002), "Shaping the Truth", in: France; St Clair (eds.): 253-266

Shaffer, Elinor S. (2002), "Shaping Victorian Biography: From Anecdote to *Bildungsroman*", in: France; St Clair (eds.): 115-133

Shakespeare, William (1974), *The Riverside Shakespeare*, ed. Gwynne Blakemore Evans, Boston *et al.*: Houghton Mifflin

Sheidley, William E. (1994), "The Play(s) within the Film: Tom Stoppard's *Rosencrantz & Guildenstern Are Dead*", in: Skovmand, Michael; Caudery, Tim (eds.), *Screen Shakespeare*, Cambridge: Aarhus University Press: 99-112

Shultz, Shirley (1984), *"Jumpers" and "Travesties": The Quixotic Symposium Comedies of Tom Stoppard*, Atlanta: Emory Univ. Diss.

Silva, N. Takei da (1990), *Modernism and Virginia Woolf*, Windsor: Windsor Publications

Simard, Rodney (1988), "Seriousness Compromised by Frivolity: Structure and Meaning in Tom Stoppard's *Travesties*", in: Harty (ed.): 173-194

Skeat, Walter W. (ed.) (1972), *Shakespeare's Plutarch: Being a Selection from the Lives in North's Plutarch which Illustrate Shakespeare's Plays* [1875], New York: AMS

Spencer, Charles (1999), "What Tom thinks of Oscar", *Daily Telegraph*, 27 February: A1+6

Stalnaker, Nan (1999), "Manet's Realism in *Déjeuner sur l'herbe*", *Word & Image* 15.3: 243-261

Stanfield, James Field (1962), *An Essay on the Study and Composition of Biography*, Sunderland 1813; partly reprinted in: Clifford (ed.): 60-71

Stannard, Martin (1996), "The Necrophiliac Art?", in: Salwak, Dale (ed.), *The Literary Biography: Problems and Solutions*, London: Macmillan: 32-40

Stannard, Martin (1998), "A Matter of Life and Death", in: Gould; Staley (eds.): 1-18

Steel, Ronald (1983), "Responses", in: Veninga (ed.): 26-29

Stein, Gertrude (1990), *The Autobiography of Alice B. Toklas* [1933], New York: Vintage

Stern, Guy (1996), "Romantic *vs.* Postmodern Reality: An Examination of Tom Stoppard's *Arcadia*", in: Reitz (ed.): 155-164

Sternlieb, Lisa; Selleck, Nancy (2003), "'What Is Carnal Embrace?': Learning to Converse in Stoppard's *Arcadia*", *Modern Drama* 46.3: 482-502

Stoppard, Tom (1969), *Rosencrantz and Guildenstern are Dead* [1967] [*RaGaD*], reprint, London: Faber and Faber [1968]

Stoppard, Tom (1975), *Travesties*, London: Faber and Faber

Stoppard, Tom (1984), *Squaring the Circle* with *Every Good Boy Deserves Favour* and *Professional Foul* [both 1978], London; Boston: Faber and Faber

Stoppard, Tom (1990), *Artist Descending a Staircase* [1973], in: *id.*, *The Plays for Radio: 1964-1983*, London: Faber and Faber: 109-156

Stoppard, Tom (1991), *In the Native State* [*ItNS*], London: Faber and Faber

Stoppard, Tom (1993), *Another Moon Called Earth* [1967], in: *id.*, *The Television Plays: 1965-1984*, London: Faber and Faber: 45-67

Stoppard, Tom (1993), *Arcadia*, reprinted with corrections, London: Faber and Faber

Stoppard, Tom (1993), *Travesties*, rev. ed., London: Faber and Faber

Stoppard, Tom (1995), *Indian Ink*, reprinted with corrections, London: Faber and Faber

Stoppard, Tom (1997), *Dialogue* [Discussion on *The Invention of Love*], Lyttelton Theatre, 10 October, Chair: Michael Bywater, National Theatre Archive London, RNT/PL/3/418

Stoppard, Tom (1998), *The Invention of Love* [*TIoL*], 2nd ed., London: Faber and Faber [1997]

Stoppard, Tom (2002), *Voyage: The Coast of Utopia part I*, London: Faber and Faber

Stoppard, Tom (2002), *Shipwreck: The Coast of Utopia part II*, London: Faber and Faber

Stoppard, Tom (2002), *Salvage: The Coast of Utopia part III*, London: Faber and Faber

Stoppard, Tom (2002), *The Coast of Utopia – Voyage* [Prompt Script], National Theatre Archive London, RNT/SM/1/481B

Stoppard, Tom (2002), *The Coast of Utopia – Salvage* [Prompt Script], National Theatre Archive London, RNT/SM/1/483

Stoppard, Tom (2005), *Lord Malquist and Mr Moon* [1966] [*LMaMM*], London: Faber and Faber

Stoppard, Tom (2006), *Rock 'n' Roll*, London: Faber and Faber

Stoppard, Tom (2006a), "I'm writing three plays called Bakunin, Belinsky and Herzen… I think", *Lincoln Center Theater Review* 43: 6-7

Stoppard, Tom (2007), *The Coast of Utopia: Voyage, Shipwreck, Salvage*, rev. ed., New York: Grove Press

Störig, Hans Joachim (1999), *Kleine Weltgeschichte der Philosophie*, 17th ed., Stuttgart; Berlin; Köln: W. Kohlhammer

Strachey, Lytton (2002), *Eminent Victorians – The Definitive Edition: Cardinal Manning ~ Florence Nightingale ~ Dr Arnold ~ General Gordon* [1918], London; New York: Continuum

Stroebe, Wolfgang; Insko, Chester A. (1989), "Stereotype, Prejudice, and Discrimination: Changing Conceptions in Theory and Research", in: Bar-Tal, Daniel; Graumann, Carl F.; Kruglanski, Arie W.; Stroebe, Wolfgang (eds.), *Stereotyping and Prejudice: Changing Conceptions* [= Springer Series in Social Psychology], New York; Berlin; Heidelberg et al.: Springer: 3-34

Sturken, Marita (1996), "Personal Stories and National Meanings: Memory, Re-enactment and the Image", in: Rhiel, Mary; Suchoff, David (eds.), *The Se-

ductions of Biography [= Culture Work], New York; London: Routledge: 31-41

Styan, J.L. (1985), "Chekhov's Dramatic Technique", in: Clyman (ed.): 107-122

Tan, Peter K.W. (1993), "A Stylistics of Drama: With Special Focus on Stoppard's *Travesties*", Singapore: Singapore University Press

Tandello, Emmanuela (1993), "Characters With(out) a Text: Script as Destiny in Stoppard and Pirandello", *YSPS: The Yearbook of the Society for Pirandello Studies* 13: 35-45

Tetzeli von Rosador, Kurt (1976), *Das englische Geschichtsdrama seit Shaw* [= Anglistische Forschungen, Vol. 112], Heidelberg: Universitätsverlag Winter

Tomasch, Sylvia (2004), "Editing as Palinode: *The Invention of Love* and the Text of the Canterbury Tales", *Exemplaria: A Journal of Theory in Medieval and Renaissance Studies* 16.2: 457-76

Treglown, Jeremy (1997), "Those who can, teach also. Art, biography, Housman and history: the instructive quirks of Tom Stoppard", *Times Literary Supplement* 4932 (10 October): 20

Tucker, Herbert F. (2005), "History Played Back: In Defense of Stoppard's *Coast of Utopia*", *Raritan* 24.4: 149-169

Tucker, Paul Hayes (1998), "Making Sense of Edouard Manet's *Le Déjeuner sur l'herbe*", in: *id.* (ed.): 1-37

Tucker, Paul Hayes (ed.) (1998), *Manet's* Le Déjeuner sur l'herbe [= Masterpieces of Western Paintings], Cambridge: Cambridge University Press

Turgenev, Ivan (1998), *Fathers and Sons* [1862], trans. and ed. Richard Freeborn [= Oxford World's Classics], Oxford: Oxford University Press

Turgenev, Ivan (2001), "Apropos of *Fathers and Sons*", in: *id.*, *Literary Reminiscences and Autobiographical Fragments* [1874/80], trans. David Magarshack, Chicago: Ivan R. Dee [1958]: 193-204

Ulanowicz, Robert E. (1986), *Growth and Development*, New York; Berlin; Heidelberg *et al.*: Springer

Vees-Gulani, Susanne (1999), "Hidden Order in the 'Stoppard Set': Chaos Theory in the Content and Structure of Tom Stoppard's *Arcadia*", *Modern Drama* 42.3: 411-426

Veeser, H. Aram (1989), "Introduction", in: *id.* (ed.): ix-xvi

Veeser, H. Aram (ed.) (1989), *The New Historicism*, New York; London: Routledge

Veninga, James Frank (1983), "Biography: The Self and the Sacred Canopy", in: *id.* (ed.): 59-79

Veninga, James Frank (ed.) (1983), *The Biographer's Gift: Life Histories and Humanism*, College Station: Texas A&M University Press

Volkmann, Laurenz (1996), "Reconstructing a Useable Past: The New Historicism and History", in: Ahrens; Volkmann (eds.): 325-344

Volkmer, Jon (2001), "A.E. and Me", *Parnassus: Poetry in Review* 26.1: 82-96

Walter, James (1996), "Seven Questions About National Biography", in: McCalman; Parvey; Cook (eds.): 19-34

Walter, James (2002), "'The Solace of Doubt'? Biographical Methodology after the Short Twentieth Century", in: France; St Clair (eds.): 321-335

Watts, Janet (1994), "Tom Stoppard", *The Guardian*, 21 March 1973, reprinted in: Delaney (ed.): 46-50

Wells, H.G. (1927), "History is One", in: *id.*, *The History of the World* [= The Works of H.G. Wells: Atlantic Edition, Vol. 27], London: T. Fisher Unwin: 1-16

Welsch, Norbert; Liebmann, Claus Chr. (2003), *Farben: Natur, Technik, Kunst*, Heidelberg; Berlin: Spektrum Akademischer Verlag

Weltman, Sharon Aronofsky (2002), "Victorians on Broadway at the Present Time: John Ruskin's Life on Stage", in: Krueger, Christine L. (ed.), *Functions of Victorian Culture at the Present Time*, Athens, OH: Ohio University Press: 79-94

Wheatley, Alison E. (2004), "Aesthetic Consolation and the Genius of the Place in Stoppard's *Arcadia*", *Mosaic: A Journal for the Interdisciplinary Study of Literature* 37.3: 171-184

Wheeler, Elizabeth (1991), "Light It Up and Move It Around: *Rosencrantz and Guildenstern Are Dead*", *Shakespeare on Film Newsletter* 16.1: 5

Whitaker, Thomas (1999), "The Music of Serious Farce: Wilde, Shaw, Orton and Stoppard", in: *id.*, *Mirrors of Our Playing: Paradigms and Presences in Modern Drama* [= Theater: Theory/Text/Performance, Vol. 24], Ann Arbor: University of Michigan Press: 41-64

White, Hayden (1989), "New Historicism: A Comment", in: Veeser (ed.): 293-302

Wilde, Oscar (1976), *Complete Works of Oscar Wilde*, Collins: London; Glasgow [1948]

Wimsatt, W.K.; Beardsley, Monroe C. (1967), "The Intentional Fallacy", *Sewanee Review* LIV (1946); reprinted in: Wimsatt, W.K., *The Verbal Icon* [= Kentucky Paperbacks, Vol. 111], Lexington: University of Kentucky Press: 1-18

Wittgenstein, Ludwig (1962), *Tractatus Logico-Philosophicus*, 9th impression [= International Library of Psychology, Philosophy and Scientific Method], London: Routledge [1922]

Wolf, Werner (1986), "Geschichtsfiktion im Kontext dekonstruktivistischer Tendenzen in neuerer Historik und literarischer Postmoderne: Tom Stoppards *Travesties*", *Poetica: Zeitschrift für Sprach- und Literaturwissenschaft* 18.3-4: 305-357

Womack, Kenneth; Davis, Todd F. (2004), "Reading (and Writing) the Ethics of Authorship: *Shakespeare in Love* as Postmodern Metanarrative", *Literature Film Quarterly* 32.2: 153-162

Woolf, Virginia (1958), "The New Biography", *New York Herald Tribune*, 30 October 1927; reprinted in: *id.*, *Granite and Rainbow: Essays by Virginia Woolf*, London: Hogarth: 149-155

Woolf, Virginia (1981), "The Art of Biography", *Atlantic Monthly*, April 1939: 506-510; reprinted in: *id.*, *The Death of the Moth and Other Essays*, 6th ed., London: Hogarth: 119-126

Wren, Celia (2002), "Housman à la Mode", *American Theatre* 19.9: 42

Yacowar, Maurice (2003), "Just a Moment in Stoppard's *Utopia*", *Journal of Dramatic Theory and Criticism* 18.1: 77-84

Zeifman, Hersh (2001), "The Comedy of Eros: Stoppard in Love", in: Kelly (ed.): 185-200

Zima, Peter V. (2000), *Theorie des Subjekts: Subjektivität und Identität zwischen Moderne und Postmoderne* [= UTB für Wissenschaft, Vol. 2176], Tübingen; Basel: Francke

Zimmermann, Christian von (ed.) (2000), *Fakten und Fiktionen: Strategien fiktionalbiographischer Dichterdarstellungen in Roman, Drama und Film seit 1970. Beiträge des Bad Homburger Kolloquiums, 21.-23. Juni 1999* [= Mannheimer Beiträge zur Sprach- und Literaturwissenschaft, Vol. 48], Tübingen: Gunter Narr

CDE · Contemporary Drama in English

General Editor: Martin Middeke

Vol. 15 **Non-Standard Forms of Contemporary Drama and Theatre**
Edited by Ellen Redling and Peter Paul Schnierer
ISBN 978-3-86821-040-8, 260 S., kt., EUR 26,50 (2008)

Vol. 14 **Drama and/after Postmodernism.** Edited by Christoph Henke, Martin Middeke
ISBN 978-3-88476-936-2, 396 S., kt., EUR 35,00 (2007)

Vol. 13 **Mapping Uncertain Territories: Space and Place in Contemporary Theatre and Drama.** Edited by Thomas Rommel, Mark Schreiber
ISBN 3-88476-826-3, 216 S., kt., EUR 23,00 (2006)

Vol. 12 **Staging Displacement, Exile and Diaspora**
Edited by Christoph Houswitschka, Anja Müller
ISBN 3-88476-751-8, 256 S., kt., EUR 24,00 (2005)

Vol. 11 **Extending the Code: New Forms of Dramatic and Theatrical Expression**
Edited by Hans-Ulrich Mohr, Kerstin Mächler
ISBN 3-88476-681-3, 264 S., 10 Abb., kt., EUR 24,00 (2004)

Vol. 10 **Global Challenges and Regional Responses in Contemporary Drama in English**
Edited by Jochen Achilles, Ina Bergmann, Birgit Däwes
ISBN 3-88476-590-6, 280 S., kt., EUR 24,50 (2003)

Vol. 9 **(Dis)Continuities. Trends and Traditions in Contemporary Theatre and Drama in English.** Edited by Margarete Rubik, Elke Mettinger-Schartmann
ISBN 3-88476-520-5, 246 S., kt., EUR 23,00 (2002)

Vol. 8 **Crossing Borders: Intercultural Drama and Theatre at the Turn of the Millennium**
Edited by Bernhard Reitz, Alyce von Rothkirch
ISBN 3-88476-464-0, 204 S., kt., EUR 20,50 (2001)

Vol. 7 **Mediated Drama / Dramatized Media.** Edited by Eckart Voigts-Virchow
ISBN 3-88476-441-1, 232 S., 13 Abb., kt., EUR 20,50 (2000)

Vol. 6 **Race and Religion in Contemporary Theatre and Drama in English**
Edited by Bernhard Reitz (1999, vergriffen)

Vol. 5 **Anthropological Perspectives.** Edited by Werner Huber, Martin Middeke
ISBN 3-88476-298-2, 212 S., kt., EUR 20,00 (1998)

Vol. 4 **Beyond the Mainstream.** Edited by Peter Paul Schnierer
ISBN 3-88476-266-4, 156 S., kt., EUR 18,00 (1997)

Vol. 3 **Drama and Reality.** Edited by Bernhard Reitz
ISBN 3-88476-201-X, 222 S., kt., EUR 20,50 (1996)

Vol. 2 **Centres and Margins.** Edited by Bernhard Reitz
ISBN 3-88476-146-3, 196 S., kt., EUR19,00 (1995)

Vol. 1 **New Forms of Comedy.** Edited by Bernhard Reitz
ISBN 3-88476-118-8, 168 S., kt., EUR 18,00 (1994)

Ausführliche Beschreibungen sämtlicher Bände der Reihe unter *www.wvttrier.de*

CDE · Studies

Edited by Martin Middeke

Vol. 16　Christine Quay: **Mythopoiesis vor dem Ende? Formen des Mythischen im zeitgenössischen britischen und irischen Drama.** ISBN 978-3-88476-899-0, 372 S., kt., EUR 34,50 (2007)

Vol. 15　Ricarda Klüßendorf: *The Great Work Begins* – Tony Kushner's Theatre for Change in America. ISBN 978-3-88476-978-2, 312 S., kt., EUR 30,00 (2007)

Vol. 14　Günter U. Beck: *Defending Dreamer's Rock* – Geschichte, Geschichtsbewusstsein und Geschichtskultur im *Native Drama* der USA und Kanadas ISBN 978-3-88476-954-6, 460 S., kt., EUR 42,50 (2007)

Vol. 13　Mark Berninger: **Neue Formen des Geschichtsdramas in Großbritannien und Irland seit 1970.** ISBN 978-3-88476-810-5, 424 S., kt., EUR 38,50 (2006)

Vol. 12　Kathleen Starck: **"I Believe in the Power of Theatre". British Women's Drama of the 1980s and 1990s.** ISBN 3-88476-753-4, 272 S., kt., EUR 28,- (2005)

Vol. 11　Annette Pankratz: **"Death is … not". Repräsentationen von Tod und Sterben im zeitgenössischen britischen Drama.** ISBN 3-88476-752-6, 400 S., kt., EUR 34,50 (2005)

Vol. 10　Christiane Schlote, Peter Zenzinger (Eds.): **New Beginnings in Twentieth-Century Theatre and Drama. Essays in Honour of Armin Geraths** ISBN 3-88476-639-2, 496 S., kt., EUR 32,50 (2003)

Vol. 9　Rudolf Weiss: **Der Januskopf der traditionellen Moderne. Die Dramenästhetik St. John Hankins und John Galsworthys.** ISBN 3-88476-514-0, 368 S., kt., EUR 32,50 (2002)

Vol. 8　Bernhard Reitz, Heiko Stahl (Eds.): **What Revels are in Hand? Assessments of Contemporary Drama in English in Honour of Wolfgang Lippke** ISBN 3-88476-462-4, 372 S., kt., EUR 33,- (2001)

Vol. 7　Anja Müller-Muth: **Repräsentationen. Eine Studie des intertextuellen und intermedialen Spiels von Tom Stoppards *Arcadia*.** ISBN 3-88476-420-9, 344 S., kt., EUR 33,- (2001)

Vol. 6　Stephanie Kramer: **Fiktionale Biographien: (Re-)Visionen und (Re-) Konstruktionen weiblicher Lebensentwürfe in Dramen britischer Autorinnen seit 1970. Ein Beitrag zur Typologie und Entwicklung des historischen Dramas** ISBN 3-88476-419-5, 336 S., kt., EUR 29,- (2000)

Vol. 5　Klaus Peter Müller: **Wertstrukturen und Wertewandel im englischen Drama der Gegenwart.** ISBN 3-88476-395-4, 372 S., kt., EUR 32,50 (2000)

Vol. 4　Michael Raab: **Erfahrungsräume. Das englische Drama der neunziger Jahre** ISBN 3-88476-355-5, 152 S., kt., EUR 18,- (1999)

Vol. 3　Jale Abdollahzadeh: **Das zeitgenössische englische Frauendrama zwischen politischem Engagement und ästhetischer Reflexion. Eine Studie ausgewählter Dramentexte.** ISBN 3-88476-250-8, 164 S., kt., EUR 22,- (1997)

Vol. 2　Ute Berns: **Mikropolitik im englischen Gegenwartsdrama. Studien zur Dramatisierung gesellschaftlicher Macht- und Ausschließungsmechanismen bei Pinter, Keeffe und Churchill.** ISBN 3-88476-236-2, 348 S., kt., EUR 28,50 (1997)

Vol. 1　Eberhard Bort (Ed.): **The State of Play: Irish Theatre in the 'Nineties** ISBN 3-88476-232-X, 208 S., kt., EUR 19,50 (1996)

Ausführliche Beschreibungen sämtlicher Bände der Reihe unter *www.wvttrier.de*